The **Rough Guide** to

Prague

written and researched by

Rob Humphreys

www.roughguides.com

Contents

Art Nouveau Prague
colour section
following p.56

Czech Beer
colour section
following p.184

Pražský hrad
(Prague Castle) **Colour maps** following
p.288

◀◀ Týn church and the astronomical clock ◀ Staroměstské náměstí

Introduction to
Prague

First things first: Prague is a very beautiful city. With some six hundred years of architecture virtually untouched by natural disaster or war, few other cities, anywhere in Europe, look as good. Straddling the winding River Vltava, with a steep wooded hill to one side, the city retains much of its medieval layout and the street facades remain smothered in a rich mantle of Baroque, Rococo and Art Nouveau, all of which successfully escaped the vanities and excesses of twentieth-century redevelopment. For forty years the city lay hidden behind the Iron Curtain, seldom visited by Westerners. All that changed in the 1990s, and now Prague is one of the most popular city-break destinations in Europe, with a highly developed tourist industry and a large expat population who, if nothing else, help to boost the city's nightlife.

 Prague's emergence as one of Europe's leading cities has come as a surprise to many people – but not the Czechs. After all, Prague was at the forefront of the European avant-garde for much of the last century, boasting a Cubist movement second only to Paris, and, between the wars, a modernist architectural flowering to rival Bauhaus. With a playwright and human rights activist as their president, the Czechs easily grabbed the headlines in the 1990s. Even today, the country's athletes and models enjoy a very high profile, and its writers, artists and film directors continue to exert an influence on European culture out of all proportion to their number.

Prague is back at the heart of Europe where it has always felt it belonged – no longer an Eastern Bloc city but a cultured metropolis in central Europe.

After all, it's more than twenty years since the fall of Communism, and a whole generation has grown up feeling very much part of a wider, united Europe. Prague has changed – and mostly for the better – but with the Czech crown riding high and the country hoping to adopt the Euro in the not-too-distant future, the city is no longer quite the budget destination it once was. However, one thing you can be sure of is that the beer is still better and cheaper than anywhere else in the EU.

What to see

With a population of just one and a quarter million, Prague (Praha to the Czechs) is relatively small as capital cities go. It originally developed as four separate self-governing towns and a Jewish ghetto, whose individual identities and medieval street plans have been preserved, to a greater or lesser extent, to this day. Almost everything of any historical interest lies within these compact central districts, the majority of which are easy to master quickly on foot. Only in the last hundred years has Prague spread beyond its ancient perimeter, and its suburbs now stretch across the hills for miles on every side. There's a cheap and efficient transport system on which to explore them – a decent map is all you need to find your way around.

Prague is divided into two unequal halves by the **River Vltava**. The steeply inclined left bank is dominated by the castle district of **Hradčany** (Chapter 1), which contains the city's most obvious sight: Pražský hrad or **Prague Castle** (known simply as the Hrad in Czech), home to the city's cathedral, and the old royal palace and gardens, as well as a host of museums and galleries. Squeezed between the castle hill and the river are the picturesque Baroque

▼ The River Vltava at night

palaces and houses of the "Little Quarter", or **Malá Strana** (Chapter 2) – a neighbourhood of twisting cobbled streets and secret walled gardens – home to the Czech parliament and most of the city's embassies, and dominated by the green dome and tower of the church of **sv Mikuláš**. At the southern end of Malá Strana, a funicular railway carries you out of the cramped streets to the top of **Petřín** hill, the city's most central leafy escape, with a wonderful view across the river.

The city's twisting matrix of streets is at its most confusing in the original medieval hub of the city, **Staré Město** (Chapter 3) – literally, the "Old Town" – on the right bank of the Vltava. The Karlův most, or **Charles Bridge**, its main link with the opposite bank, is easily the city's most popular historical monument, and the best place from which to view Prague Castle. Staré Město's other great showpiece is its main square, **Staroměstské náměstí**, where you can view Prague's famous astronomical clock. Enclosed within the boundaries of Staré Město is the former Jewish quarter, or **Josefov** (Chapter 4). The ghetto walls have long since gone and the whole area was remodelled at the turn of the century, but six synagogues, a medieval cemetery and a town hall survive as powerful reminders of a community that has existed here for over a millennium.

South and east of the Old Town is the large sprawling district of **Nové Město** (Chapter 5), whose main arteries make up the city's commercial and business centre. The nexus of Nové Město is **Wenceslas Square** (Václavské náměstí), focus of the political upheavals of the modern-day republic. Further afield lie various **suburbs**, most of which were developed only in the last hundred years or so. The single exception is **Vyšehrad**, one of the original fortress settlements of the newly arrived Slavs in the last millennium, now the final resting-place of leading Czech artists of the modern age, including the composers Smetana and Dvořák. To the east is the eminently desirable residential suburb of **Vinohrady**, peppered with parks and squares; and neighbouring **Žižkov**, whose two landmarks – the Žižkov monument and the futuristic TV tower – are visible for miles around. All of these areas are covered in Chapter 6.

Nineteenth-century suburbs also sprang up to the north of the city centre in **Holešovice**, now home to the city's chief modern art museum, **Veletržní palác**. The area also boasts two huge swathes of greenery: the Letná plain, overlooking the city; and the Stromovka park, beyond which lie the chateau of **Troja** and the zoo. Further west, leafy interwar suburbs like **Dejvice** and **Střešovice**, dotted with modernist family villas, give an entirely different angle on Prague. All these places are covered in Chapter 7.

Prague's outer suburbs, where most of the population lives, are more typical of the old Eastern Bloc: bleak high-rise housing estates, known locally as *paneláky*. However, once you're clear of the city limits, the traditional, provincial feel of **Bohemia** (Čechy) immediately makes itself felt. Many Praguers

Sightseeing by public transport

If there's one thing every visitor would like to take home with them from Prague, it's the public transport system. The **metro** – one of the few legacies of the Soviet period that the locals are truly grateful for – is clean and constantly expanding, while the much-loved cream and red Tatra trams negotiate the city's cobbles and bridges with remarkable dexterity. You can have a lot of fun with your 24-hour travel pass. If you take **tram #22** from Národní třída, you can get a free tour of the city, crossing the river, ploughing through picturesque Malá Strana and taking on a couple of impressive hairpin bends, before ending up outside the gates of Prague Castle. Alternatively, for an extra 35Kč, you can catch **tram #91**, an old 1930s tramcar with a conductor, which takes a circuitous route through the city centre en route to or from Prague Castle. Your travel pass also covers the city's **funicular**, which will whisk you to the top of Petřín hill, home to the mirror maze and miniature Eiffel Tower. Even more quirky are the city transport's summer-only **motor boat services** between the islands in the Vltava, which allow you to zig-zag up the river at leisure. For details and prices see p.25.

Historic house signs

One of the most appealing features of the old houses in Prague is that they often retain their ancient **house signs**, which you'll see carved into the gables, on hanging wooden signs or inscribed on the facade. The system originated in medieval times and still survives today, especially by pubs, restaurants and hotels.

Some signs were deliberately chosen to draw custom to the business of the house, like **U zeleného hroznu** (The Green Bunch of Grapes), a wine shop in the Malá Strana; others, like **U železných dveří** (The Iron Door), simply referred to some distinguishing feature of the house, often long since disappeared. The pervasive use of *zlatý* (gold) derives from the city's popular epithet, Zlatá Praha (Golden Prague), which could either refer to the halcyon days of Charles IV, when the new Gothic copper roofing shone like gold, or to the period of alchemy under Rudolf II.

In the 1770s, the Habsburgs introduced a numerical system, with each house in the city entered onto a register according to a strict chronology. Later, however, the conventional system of progressive street numbering was introduced, so don't be surprised if seventeenth-century pubs like **U medvídků** (The Little Bears) have two numbers in addition to a house sign, in this case 7 and 345. The former, Habsburg number, is written on a red background; the latter, modern number, on blue.

own a *chata*, or country cottage, somewhere in these rural backwaters, and every weekend the roads are jammed with folk heading for the hills. For visitors, few places are more than an hour from the city by public transport, making day-trips relatively easy.

▶ The Charles Bridge in the snow

The most popular destinations for day-trippers are the castles of **Karlštejn** and **Konopiště**, both surrounded by beautiful wooded countryside. Alternatively you can head north, away from the hills and the crowds, to the wine town of **Mělník**, perched high above the confluence of the Vltava and Labe (Elbe) rivers. Further north is **Terezín**, the wartime Jewish ghetto that is a living testament to the Holocaust. One of the most popular day-trips is to the medieval silver-mining town of **Kutná Hora**, 60km to the east, which boasts a glorious Gothic cathedral and a macabre ossuary. Day-trips are covered in Chapter 8.

When to go

Lying at the heart of central Europe, Prague has a continental climate: winters can be pretty cold, summers correspondingly scorching. The best times to visit, in terms of weather, are late spring and early autumn. Summer in the city can be pretty stifling, but the real reason for avoiding the peak season is that it can get uncomfortably crowded in the centre – finding a place to eat in the evening, let alone securing a room, can become fraught with difficulties. If you're looking for good weather, April is the earliest you can guarantee

▲ Loreto church

at least some sunny days, and October is the last warm month. If you don't mind the cold, the city looks beautiful in the snowy winter months, though it can also fall prey to "inversions", which blanket the city in a grey smog for a week or more.

Average temperatures (°C), hours of sunshine and monthly rainfall

	Jan	Feb	Mar	Apr	May	Jun	Jul	Aug	Sep	Oct	Nov	Dec
Temperature												
min °C	-4	-3	-0	2	8	11	12	13	9	3	0	-2
max °C	1	2	8	12	18	21	22	23	18	12	5	1
Sunshine												
Hours	2	3	4	6	7	7	7	7	5	4	2	2
Rainfall												
mm	18	17	25	35	58	68	66	64	40	30	28	22

21

things not to miss

*It's not possible to see everything Prague has to offer on a short trip –
and we don't suggest you try. What follows is a subjective selection of
the city's highlights, from Art Nouveau masterpieces and medieval
backstreets to tranquil Baroque terraced gardens and great day-trip
destinations around the city – all arranged in colour-coded categories
to help you find the very best things to see, do and experience. All
entries have a page reference to take you straight into the Guide,
where you can find out more.*

01 **Karlův most (Charles Bridge)** Page **78** • Prague's wonderful medieval stone bridge, peppered with Baroque statuary, has been the main link between the two banks of the river for over five hundred years.

02 **Pražský hrad (Prague Castle)** Page **41** • The city's most spectacular landmark, and home to the cathedral, royal palace and a host of museums and galleries.

03 **Veletržní palác (Trade Fair Palace)** Page **148** • The city's chief gallery of modern art is housed in a functionalist masterpiece.

04 **Staroměstské naměstí (Old Town Square)** Page **88** • Prague's busy showpiece square, dominated by the Art Nouveau Hus Monument, and best known for its astronomical clock.

05 **Bílkova vila** Page **57** • House and studio (now museum) of the maverick Czech artist, František Bílek.

06 **Nightlife** Page **203** • From DJs to Dvořák, Prague boasts a surprisingly varied nightlife.

07 **Prague pubs** Page **197** • With the best beer in the world on tap, Prague's pubs are not to be missed.

08 **Prague trams** Page **27** • Cute and efficient, no visit to the city is complete without a ride on one of its red-and-cream trams.

09 UPM Page **108** • Prague's stylish applied art museum contains artistic gems from the country's cultural heyday in the first half of the twentieth century.

10 Church of sv Mikuláš

Page **68** • Experience the theatre of the High Baroque in this landmark of Malá Strana.

11 The view from the Astronomická věž Page **86** • The central tower of the Klementinum to a frescoed Baroque library and the best viewing gallery in the Staré Město.

12 Vyšehrad Page **133** • Leafy, riverside fortress which houses the country's most exclusive cemetery, resting place of composers Dvořák and Smetana.

13 Prague's Habsburg-era cafés Page **186** • Prague retains a handful of grandiose cafés from the days of the Habsburgs at the beginning of the twentieth century.

14 Petřín Page **76** • Take the funicular up the wooded hill of Petřín, home to a mirror maze, an observatory and a miniature Eiffel Tower, as well as spectacular views across Prague.

15 **Terezín** Page **162** • Habsburg fortress outside Prague, turned into a "model Jewish ghetto" by the Nazis and now a chilling memorial to the Holocaust.

16 **Josefov** Page **99** • Six synagogues, a town hall and a medieval cemetery survive from the city's fascinating former Jewish ghetto.

17 **Backstreets of Staré Město** Page **96** • Lose the crowds (and yourself) in the twisted matrix of Staré Město's backstreets.

18 **Stavovské divadlo** Page **94** • Venue for the premiere of Mozart's *Don Giovanni*, Prague's oldest theatre is worth visiting for its architecture alone.

19 **Obecní dům** Page **119** • The largest and most impressive Art Nouveau building in the city houses a café, a bar, two restaurants, exhibition space and a concert hall.

20 **Shopping in Prague's pasáže** Page **115** • The covered shopping malls, or *pasáže*, on and around Wenceslas Square, are just the place to do a bit of window-shopping.

21 **Malá Strana's palace gardens** Page **71** • Hidden behind the palaces of Malá Strana, these terraced gardens are the perfect inner-city escape.

Basics

Basics

Getting there

Unless you're coming from a neighbouring European country, the quickest and easiest way to get to Prague is by plane. There are direct flights from just about every European capital city, with flight times from London just under two hours. There are also one or two non-stop flights from North America, though you'll get a much wider choice – and often lower fares – if you fly via London or another European gateway.

With most airlines, how much you pay depends on how far in advance you book and how much demand there is during that period – the earlier you book, the cheaper the prices.

Another option, if you're travelling from Britain or elsewhere in Europe, is to go by **train**, **bus** or **car**, though these usually take considerably longer than a plane and may not work out that much cheaper, but it's undoubtedly better for the environment.

Flights from Britain and Ireland

You can fly **direct to Prague** from all over Britain and Ireland, including from Bristol and Belfast, or from the likes of Dublin, Liverpool or Leeds. The most competitive airfares from Britain are with the **budget airlines**, though the national airlines, British Airways and Czech Airlines (ČSA), have to stay competitive. If you book far enough in advance or can be flexible about your dates, you can get return fares from London to Prague for as little as £50 (taxes included). From Ireland, return airfares start at around €130 return from Dublin. Of course, if you don't book early, prices can skyrocket.

Flights from the US and Canada

Czech Airlines (ČSA) is the only airline to offer **non-stop flights** from North America to Prague. You'll get a much wider choice of flights and ticket prices, though, if you opt for an **indirect flight** with one or two changes of plane, allowing you to depart from any number of North American cities and travel via one of the major European gateways.

Flying time from New York direct to Prague is about eight hours. **Fares** depend very much on the flexibility of the ticket and on availability, with a New York–Prague direct return costing $1000–1500, and a Toronto–Prague non-direct return costing Can$1000–1500.

Flights from Australia and New Zealand

Flight times from **Australia and New Zealand** to Prague are twenty hours or more, depending on routes and transfer times. There's a wide variety of routes, with those touching down in southeast Asia the quickest and cheapest on average. Given the length of the journey involved, you might be better off including a night's stopover in your itinerary, and indeed some airlines include one in the price of the flight.

The cheapest direct scheduled flights to London are usually to be found on one of the Asian airlines. Average **return fares** (including taxes) from eastern gateways to London are Aus$1500–2000 in low season, Aus$2000–2500 in high season. Fares from Perth or Darwin cost around Aus$200 less. You'll then need to add Aus$100–200 onto all these for the connecting flight to Prague. Return fares from Auckland to London range between NZ$2000 and NZ$3000 depending on the season, route and carrier.

Airlines

Aer Lingus ⓦ www.aerlingus.com
Air Canada ⓦ www.aircanada.com
Air New Zealand ⓦ www.airnewzealand.com
Air Transat ⓦ www.airtransat.com
American Airlines ⓦ www.aa.com
Asiana Airlines ⓦ www.flyasiana.com

bmi ⓦ www.flybmi.com
bmibaby ⓦ www.bmibaby.com
British Airways ⓦ www.ba.com
Cathay Pacific ⓦ www.cathaypacific.com
Continental Airlines ⓦ www.continental.com
Czech Airlines (ČSA) ⓦ www.czechairlines.com
Delta ⓦ www.delta.com
easyJet ⓦ www.easyjet.com
Gulf Air ⓦ www.gulfair.com
Jet2 ⓦ www.jet2.com
KLM ⓦ www.klm.com
Lufthansa ⓦ www.lufthansa.com
Malaysia Airlines ⓦ www.malaysiaairlines.com
Qantas ⓦ www.qantas.com
Royal Brunei ⓦ www.bruneiair.com
Ryanair ⓦ www.ryanair.com
Singapore Airlines ⓦ www.singaporeair.com
Thai Airways ⓦ www.thaiair.com
United Airlines ⓦ www.united.com
Virgin Atlantic ⓦ www.virgin-atlantic.com

Agents and operators

ČEDOK ⓦ www.cedok.com. Former state-owned tourist board offering flights, accommodation and package deals.

Czech Travel ⓦ www.czechtravel.co.uk. Package deals, plus hotel rooms and apartments in Prague.

ebookers ⓦ www.ebookers.com. Low fares on an extensive selection of scheduled flights and package deals.

Martin Randall Travel ⓦ www.martinrandall.com. Small-group cultural tours to European destinations, including Prague, led by experts on art, archaeology or music.

North South Travel ⓦ www.northsouthtravel.co.uk. Friendly, competitive travel agency, offering discounted fares worldwide. Profits are used to support projects in the developing world, especially the promotion of sustainable tourism.

STA Travel ⓦ www.statravel.com. Worldwide specialists in independent travel; also student IDs, travel insurance, car rental, rail passes, and more. Good discounts for students and under-26s.

Trailfinders ⓦ www.trailfinders.com. One of the best-informed and most efficient agents for independent travellers.

Travel CUTS ⓦ www.travelcuts.com. Canadian youth and student travel firm.

USIT ⓦ www.usit.ie. Ireland's main student and youth travel specialists.

By train

You can travel **by train** from London to Prague overnight in around twenty hours. Fares start at around £125 return but depend on the route you take and how far in advance you book your ticket.

To reach Prague by train you first have to take the **Eurostar** from London St Pancras to **Brussels**. From there, the most direct, and

Six steps to a better kind of travel

At Rough Guides we are passionately committed to travel. We feel strongly that only through travelling do we truly come to understand the world we live in and the people we share it with. But the extraordinary growth in tourism has also damaged some places irreparably, and of course **climate change** is exacerbated by most forms of transport, especially flying. This means that now more than ever it's important to travel thoughtfully and responsibly. At Rough Guides we feel there are six main areas in which you can make a difference:

• Consider what you're contributing to the **local economy**, and how much the services you use do the same.

• Consider the **environment** on holiday as well as at home. Try to patronize businesses that take account of this.

• Travel with a purpose, not just to tick off experiences. Consider **spending longer** in a place, and getting to know it.

• Give thought to how often you **fly**. Try to avoid short hops by air and more harmful night flights.

• Consider **alternatives to flying**, travelling instead by bus, train, boat and even by bike or on foot where possible.

• Make your trips "**climate neutral**" via a reputable carbon offset scheme. All Rough Guide flights are offset, and every year we donate money to a variety of charities devoted to combating the effects of climate change.

usually cheapest, route is **via Cologne**, from which there's an overnight service to Prague, arriving around 9am the following morning.

Although you can crash out on the seats, it makes sense to book a **couchette**, which costs an extra £15 one way in a six-berth compartment, rising to £25 in a three-berth compartment. Couchettes are mixed-sex and allow little privacy; for a bit more comfort, you can book a bed in a single-sex two-berth **sleeper** for around £50.

Fares for continental rail travel are much more flexible than they used to be, so it's worth shopping around for the best deal, rather than taking the first offer you get. Tickets are usually valid for two months and allow as many stopovers as you want on the specified route. If you're travelling with one or more companions, you may be eligible for a further discount.

The cheapest way to book tickets is usually **online**, but you may have to use several websites to get the best deals. For more details, visit the superb website ⓦ www.seat61.com.

Train information

Deutsche Bahn ☎ 0871 880 8066 (phone lines open Mon–Fri 9am–5pm), ⓦ www.bahn.com. Competitive discounted fares for any journey from London across Europe, with very reasonable prices for journeys passing through Germany. Phone for prices from London.

European Rail ☎ 020/7619 1083 (phone lines open Mon–Fri 9am–5pm), ⓦ www.europeanrail .com. Rail specialist that consistently offers competitive prices on international rail tickets from anywhere in the UK.

Eurostar ☎ 08705 186 186 (phone lines open Mon–Fri 8am–7pm, Sat & Sun 9am–5pm), ⓦ www .eurostar.com. Latest fares and youth discounts (plus online booking) on the Eurostar service, plus competitive add-on fares from the rest of the UK.

Man in Seat 61 ⓦ www.seat61.com. The world's finest train website, full of incredibly useful tips and links for rail travel anywhere in the world.

National Rail ☎ 0845 748 4950 (phone lines open 24hr), ⓦ www.nationalrail.co.uk. First stop for details of all train travel within the UK – fares, passes, train times and delays due to engineering works.

Rail Europe ☎ 08705 848 848 (phone lines open Mon–Fri 9am–7pm, Sat 9am–6pm), ⓦ www .raileurope.co.uk. SNCF-owned information and ticket agent for all European passes and journeys from

London. They also have an office at 1 Regent St, London SW1 (Mon–Fri 10am–6pm, Sat 10am–4pm).
Trainseurope ☎ 0871 700 7722 (phone lines Mon–Fri 9am–5.30pm), ⓦ www.trainseurope.co.uk. Agent specializing in discounted international rail travel.

By bus

One of the cheapest ways to get to Prague is by **bus**. There are direct services from London's Victoria Station more or less daily throughout the year. Coaches tend to depart in the evening, arriving eighteen hours later in Prague's main bus terminal, Florenc, in the early afternoon. The journey is bearable (just about), with short breaks every three to four hours, but only really worth it if you've left it too late to find a budget flight. Prices between companies vary only slightly; a return ticket starts at around £80, less if you're under 26 or over 60.

Bus contacts

Eurolines UK ☎ 08717 818181 (phone lines open daily 8am–8pm), ⓦ www.eurolines.co.uk. Tickets can also be purchased from any National Express agent.

Student Agency ☎ 020/7828 1001, ⓦ www .studentagency.cz. Despite the name, anyone can travel with this Czech-based company, which runs a regular bus service from London to Prague.

By car

With two or more passengers, **driving to Prague** can work out relatively inexpensive. However, it is not the most relaxing option, unless you enjoy pounding along the motorway systems of Europe for the best part of a day and a night.

Eurotunnel operates a 24-hour train service carrying vehicles and their passengers from Folkestone to Calais. At peak times, services run every ten minutes, with the journey lasting 35 minutes. Off-peak fares in the high season start at £150 return per vehicle (passengers included). The alternative is to catch one of the **ferries** between Dover and Calais, Boulogne or Dunkirk, or between Ramsgate and Ostend. Prices vary enormously but if you book in advance, summer fares can be as little as £70 return per carload. Journey times are usually around ninety minutes. If you're travelling from north of London, however, it might be worth taking one of the longer ferry journeys from Rosyth, Newcastle, Hull or Harwich.

Once you've made it onto the Continent, you have some **1000km of driving** ahead of you. Theoretically, you could make it in twelve hours solid, but realistically it will take you longer. The most direct route from Calais is via Brussels, Liège (Luik), Cologne (Köln), Frankfurt, Würzburg and Nuremberg (Nürnberg), entering the Czech Republic at the **Waidhaus–Rozvadov** border crossing. **Motorways** in Belgium and Germany are free, but within the Czech Republic you need to buy the relevant tax disc (dálniční známka), available from all border crossings: a ten-day sticker costs 250Kč, a month-long one costs 350Kč. If you're travelling by car, you'll need proof of ownership, or a letter from the owner giving you permission to drive the car, and international proof of insurance, otherwise known as a Green Card. You also need a red warning triangle in case you break down and a first-aid kit, both of which are compulsory in the Czech Republic.

Cross-Channel contacts

To find out the cheapest fares across the Channel, check out ⓦ www.ferrysmart.co.uk.
DFDS Seaways ☎ 0871 522 9955, ⓦ www .dfdsseaways.co.uk. Newcastle to Amsterdam.
Eurotunnel ☎ 0844 335 3535, ⓦ www.eurotunnel .com. Folkstone to Calais through the tunnel.
LD Lines Network UK ☎ 0800 917 1201, ⓦ www .ldlines.co.uk. Dover to Boulogne and Ramsgate to Ostend.
Norfolkline ☎ 020/8127 8303, ⓦ www .norfolkline-ferries.co.uk. Dover to Dunkirk and Rosyth (near Edinburgh) to Zeebrugge.
P&O Stena Line ☎ 0871 664 5645, ⓦ www .poferries.com. Dover to Calais and Hull to Rotterdam and Zeebrugge.
SeaFrance ☎ 0871 423 7119, ⓦ www.seafrance .com. Dover to Calais.
Stena Line ☎ 0844 770 7070, ⓦ www.stenaline .co.uk. Harwich to the Hook of Holland.

Arrival

Prague is one of Europe's smaller capital cities, with a population of around one and a quarter million. The airport lies just over 10km northwest of the city centre with only a bus link or taxi to get you into town. Both international train stations and the main bus terminal are linked to the centre by the fast and efficient metro system.

By air

Prague's **Ruzyně airport** (☎ 220 113 314, ⓦ www.pragueairport.co.uk) is connected to the city by minibus, bus and taxi. The Cedaz (ⓦ www.cedaz.cz) shared **minibus service** will take you (and several others) to your hotel for around 480Kč. The minibus also runs a scheduled service (daily 7.30am–7pm; every 30min), which stops first at Dejvická metro station, at the end of metro line A (journey time 20min) and ends up at V celnici, off náměstí Republiky (journey time 30min); the full journey costs 120Kč. Another option is the **Prague Airport Shuttle** minibus/taxi service (ⓦ www.prague-airport-shuttle.com), which will take up to four passengers into town for 550Kč.

The cheapest way to get into town is on **local bus #119** (daily 5am–midnight; every 15–20min; journey time 25min), which stops frequently and also ends its journey outside Dejvická metro station. You can buy your ticket from the public transport (DP) information desk in arrivals (daily 7am–10pm), or from the nearby machines or newsagents. If you're going to use public transport whilst in Prague, you might as well buy a pass straightaway (see p.25). If you arrive between midnight and 5am, you can catch the hourly

night bus **#510** to Divoká Šárka, the terminus for night tram #51, which will take you on to Národní in the centre of town. Another cheap alternative is **Linka AE** (Airport Express), a non-stop bus link with Dejvická metro (30Kč) and Praha hlavní nádraží (daily 7am–9pm; every 30min; 50Kč).

If you're thinking of taking a **taxi** from the airport into the centre, make sure you choose the reliable AAA Taxi (☎14014, ⓦwww.aaataxi.cz), as Prague taxi drivers have a reputation for overcharging. AAA have a rank outside arrivals and the journey to the city centre should cost around 400–500Kč.

By train and bus

International trains arrive either at the old Art Nouveau **Praha hlavní nádraží**, on the edge of Nové Město and Vinohrady, or at the unprepossessing **Nádraží Holešovice** (Praha-Holešovice), which lies in an industrial suburb north of the city centre. At both stations you'll find exchange outlets, accommodation agencies (see p.177), and at Hlavní nádraží a branch of the PIS tourist office (see p.38). Both stations are on metro lines, and Hlavní nádraží is only a five-minute walk from Václavské náměstí (Wenceslas Square). If you arrive late at night, there's even a hostel in Hlavní nádraží itself (see p.185).

Domestic trains usually wind up at **Praha hlavní nádraží** or the central **Masarykovo nádraží** on Hybernská, a couple of blocks east of náměstí Republiky. Slower trains and various provincial services arrive at a variety of obscure suburban stations: trains from the southwest pull into Praha-Smíchov (metro Smichovské nádraží); trains from the east arrive at Praha-Vysočany (metro Českomoravská); trains from the west at Praha-Dejvice (metro Hradčanská); and trains from the south very occasionally rumble into Praha-Vršovice (tram #6 or #24 to Václavské náměstí).

If you're catching a **train out of Prague**, don't leave buying your ticket until the last minute, as the queues can be long and slow, and make sure you check which station your train is departing from. You can buy **international train tickets** (*mezinárodní jizdenky*) at either Praha hlavní nádraží or Praha-Holešovice.

Prague's main **bus terminal** is Florenc or Praha-Florenc (metro Florenc), on the eastern edge of Nové Město, where virtually all long-distance international and domestic services terminate. It's a confusing (and ugly) place to end up, but it has a left-luggage office upstairs (daily 5am–11pm) and you can make a quick exit to the adjacent metro station.

City transport

The centre of Prague, where most of the city's sights are concentrated, is reasonably small and best explored on foot. At some point, however, in order to cross the city quickly or reach some of the more widely dispersed attractions, you'll need to use the city's cheap and efficient public transport system, known as dopravní podnik or DP (☎296 191 817, ⓦwww.dpp.cz), comprising the metro and a network of trams and buses. To get a clearer picture, it's good to invest in a city map, which marks all the tram, bus and metro lines.

Tickets and passes

Most Praguers buy monthly passes, and to avoid having to understand the complexities of the single ticket system, you too are best

off buying a **travel pass** (*časová jízdenka*) for either 24 hours (*1 den*; 100Kč), 3 days (*3 dny*; 330Kč), or 5 days (*na 5 dny*; 500Kč); no photos or ID are needed, though you

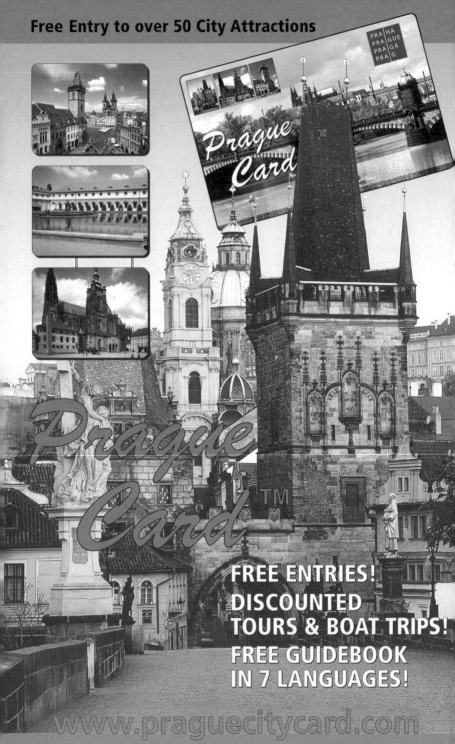

must write your name and date of birth on the reverse of the ticket, and punch it to validate it when you first use it. For a monthly (*měsíční*; 550Kč), quarterly (*čtvrtletní*; 1480Kč) or yearly (*roční*; 4750Kč) pass you need ID and a passport-sized photo. All the passes are available from travel information office (also known as DP outlets – see below), and the 24-hour pass is also available from ticket machines in metro stations.

To buy a single ticket, you'll need to master the ridiculously complicated **ticket machines**, found inside all metro stations and at some bus and tram stops. Despite the multitude of buttons on the machines, for a **single ticket** (*lístek* or *jízdenka*) in the two central zones (*2 pásma*), there are just two basic choices. The 18Kč version (*limitovaná*) allows you to travel for up to twenty minutes on the trams or buses, or up to five stops on the metro; it's known as a *nepřestupní jízdenka*, or "no change ticket", although you can in fact change metro lines (but not buses or trams). The 26Kč version (*plnocenná*) is valid for 75 minutes during which you may change trams, buses or metro lines as many times as you like, hence its name, *přestupní jízdenka*, or "changing ticket". A full-price ticket is called *plnocenná*; discounted tickets, or *zvýhodněna*, are available for children aged 6–15; under-6s travel free. To buy a ticket you must press the appropriate button – press it once for one ticket, twice for two and so on – followed by the *výdej*/enter button, after which you put your money in. The machines do give change, but if you don't have enough coins, you may find the person on duty in the metro office by the barriers can give you change or sell you a ticket.

Tickets can also be bought, en masse, and rather more easily, from a tobacconist (*tabák*), street kiosk, newsagent, PIS office or any place that displays the yellow DP sticker. When you enter the metro, or board a tram or bus, you must validate your ticket by placing it in one of the electronic machines to hand.

There are no barriers, but plain-clothes inspectors (*revizoři*) make random checks and will issue an **on-the-spot fine** of 700Kč to anyone caught without a valid ticket or pass; controllers should show you their ID (a small metal disc) and give you a receipt (*paragon*).

Metro

Prague's futuristic, Soviet-built **metro** is fast, smooth and ultra-clean, running daily from 5am to midnight with trains every two minutes during peak hours, slowing down to every four to ten minutes by late in the evening. Its three lines intersect at various points in the city centre and the route plans are easy to follow (see the colour map at the back of the book).

The **stations** are fairly discreetly marked above ground with the metro logo, in green (line A), yellow (line B) or red (line C). The constant bleeping at metro entrances is to enable blind people to locate the escalators, which are a free-for-all, with no fast lane. Once inside the metro, it's worth knowing that *výstup* means exit and *přestup* will lead you to one of the connecting lines at an interchange. The digital clock at the end of the platform tells you what time it is and how long it was since the last train.

Trams

The electric **tram** (*tramvaj*) system, in operation since 1891, negotiates Prague's hills and cobbles with remarkable dexterity. Modern Škoda low-floor trams are being introduced, but much of the fleet (traditionally decked out in red and cream) dates back to the Communist era. After the metro, trams are the fastest and most efficient way

BASICS | City transport

Travel information offices

To get free maps (as well as to buy tickets and passes), head for the **DP information offices** of the public transport system at both airport terminals (daily 7am–10pm), Nádraží Holešovice (daily 7am–6pm), Muzeum (daily 7am–9pm) and Anděl (daily 7am–9pm) metro stations.

trams pass along Lazarská in Nové Město. For more tram routes, see the colour map at the back of the book.

Buses

You'll rarely need to get on a **bus** (*autobus*) within Prague itself, since most of them keep well out of the centre of town. If you're intent on visiting the zoo or staying in some of the city's more obscure suburbs, though, you may need to use them: their hours of operation are similar to those of the trams (though services are generally less frequent); route numbers are given in the text where appropriate. **Night buses** (*noční autobusy*) run just once an hour between midnight and 5am from náměstí Republiky.

Out of Prague, you're more likely to find yourself using buses, though timetables are designed around the needs of commuters, and tend to fizzle out at the weekend. Most services depart from Prague's main bus terminal, Praha-Florenc (metro Florenc), which is run with train-like efficiency, though finding the right departure stand (*stání*) can be a daunting task. Some services, however, depart from Prague's suburban bus terminals; for example buses to Lidice (see p.173) depart from metro Dejvická. For most minor routes, simply buy your ticket from the driver; for popular long-distance routes, and for travel at peak times, it's best to try and book your seat in advance.

Bus **timetables** (ⓦ www.idos.cz) are more difficult to figure out than train ones, as there are no maps to help you out. In the detailed timetables displayed at the main bus station, each service is listed separately, so you may have to scour several timetables before you discover when the next bus is. A better bet is to look at the departures and arrivals board. Make sure you check on which day the service runs, since many run only on certain days (see the section below on trains for the key phrases). Minor bus stops are marked with a rusty metal sign saying *zastávka*. If you want to get off, ask *já chci vystoupit?*; "the next stop" is *příští zastávka*.

Trains

The most relaxing way to take a day-trip from Prague is by **train** (*vlak*), run, for the most part, by Czech Railways, **České**

of getting around, running every six to eight minutes at peak times, and every five to fifteen minutes at other times – check the timetables posted at every stop (*zastávka*), which list the departure times from that specific stop. Note that stops are often named after the sidestreets and not the main street along which they run. Note, too, that it is the custom for younger folk (and men of all ages) to vacate their seat when an older woman enters the carriage.

Tram #22, which runs from Vinohrady to Hradčany via the centre of town and Malá Strana, is a good way to get to grips with the lie of the land, and a cheap way of sightseeing, though you should beware of pickpockets. From March to November, interwar **nostalgic tram #91** runs from the Transport Museum to Výstaviště, via Prague Castle, Malá Strana, Wenceslas Square and náměstí Republiky and back again (Sat & Sun hourly noon–5.30pm; 40min; 35Kč, passes not valid). **Night trams** (*noční tramvaje*; #51–58) run roughly every thirty to forty minutes from around midnight to 4.30am; the routes are different from the daytime ones, though at some point all night

dráhy or **ČD** (☎840 112 113, ⊛www .cd.cz). Trains marked "Os" (*osobní* or *zastavkový*) are local trains that stop at just about every station, while those marked "R" (*rychlík* or *spěšný*) are faster, stopping only at major towns. Fast trains are further divided, in descending order of speed, into "SC" (SuperCity) – for which you must pay a supplement – "EC" (EuroCity) or "IC" (InterCity) and "Ex" (Expres).

To buy a **ticket**, simply state your destination – return fares (*zpáteční*) are slightly less than double and two or more people travelling together get a discount (*sleva pro skupiny*). Note that up to two **children** aged 5 and under travel for free, any extra kids and those aged 6 to 15 travel half-price.

Large train stations have a simple airport-style arrivals and departures board, which includes information on delays under the heading *zpoždění*. Many stations have poster-style displays of arrivals (*příjezd*) and departures (*odjezd*), the former on white paper, the latter on yellow, with fast trains printed in red. All but the smallest stations also have a comprehensive display of **timetables and route information** on rollers. First find the route you need to take on the diagrammatic map and make a note of the number printed beside it, then follow the timetable rollers through until you come to the appropriate number. Some of the more common Czech notes at the side of the timetable are *jezdí jen v…* (only running on…), or *nejezdí v* or *nechodí v…* (not running on…), followed by a date or a symbol: a cross or an "N" for a Sunday, a big "S" for a Saturday, two crossed hammers for a weekday, "A" for a Friday and so on. Small stations may simply have a board with a list of departures under the title *směr* (direction) followed by a town. Note that a platform, or *nástupiště*, is usually divided into two *kolej* on either side.

Ferries and boats

The public transport system runs a handful of small summer **ferry services** (*přívoz*) on the Vltava between the islands and the riverbanks (April–Oct daily 6am–10pm; every 30min). In the summer months there are also regular **boat trips** on the River Vltava run by the PPS (*Pražská paroplavební společnost*;

☎224 930 017, ⊛www.paroplavba.cz) from just south of Jiráskův most on Rašínovo nábřeží (see map on p.112). Three or four boats a day in summer run to Troja (see p.153) in the northern suburbs (May to mid-Sept daily; April & mid-Sept to Oct Sat & Sun only; 220Kč return).

The PPS also offers boat trips around Prague (April to mid-Sept daily 1–2hr; 220–290Kč) on board a 1930s paddle-steamer. Another option is to hop aboard the much smaller boats run by Pražské Benátky/Prague-Venice (☎776 776 779, ⊛www.prazskebenatky.cz), which depart year round for a half-hour meander over to the Čertovka by Kampa island (300Kč). The boats leave from the north side of the Charles Bridge on the Staré Město bank.

Taxis

Taxis come in all shapes and sizes, and, theoretically at least, are relatively cheap. However, many Prague taxi drivers will attempt to overcharge; the worst offenders hang out at the taxi ranks closest to the tourist sights. Officially, the initial fare on the meter should be around 40Kč plus 28Kč/km within Prague and 6Kč/min waiting time. The best advice is to have your hotel or pension call you one – you then qualify for a cheaper rate – rather than hail one or pick one up at the taxi ranks. The cab company with the best reputation is AAA Taxi (☎14014, ⊛www.aaataxi.cz), which has metered taxis all over Prague.

Driving

Negotiating cobbles, trams and traffic jams, along with trying to find somewhere to park, makes **driving** by far the worst option available for getting around the city. If you have to drive, bear in mind the **rules of the road** (even if no one else does). The basic rules are: drive on the right (introduced by the Nazis in 1939); stick to the speed limit (50kph/30mph) in built-up areas; compulsory wearing of seat belts; headlights on at all times from November to March; and no under-12s in the front seat. Watch out for restricted streets (signalled by a blank circular sign with a red border), and give way to pedestrians crossing the road when turning left or right, even when you've been given a green light; drivers are also supposed to give way to pedestrians at zebra crossings, though they usually take some persuading. You must also give way to trams, and, if there's no safety island at a tram stop, must stop immediately and allow passengers to get on and off.

The other big nightmare is **parking**. There are three colour-coded parking zones, with pay-and-display meters: the orange zone allows you to park for up to two hours; the green zone allows you up to six hours; the blue zone is for locals only. Illegally parked cars will either be clamped or towed away – if this happens, phone ☎158 to find out the worst. If you're staying outside the centre, you'll have no problems; if you're at a hotel in the centre, they'll probably have a few parking spaces reserved for guests, though whether you'll find one vacant is another matter.

Cycling

Cycling is seen as more of a leisure activity in the Czech Republic than a means of transport. Prague has a handful of brave cycle couriers but the combination of hills, cobbled streets, tram lines and sulphurous air is enough to put most people off. Facilities for **bike rental** are still not that widespread, but if you're determined to cycle, head for City Bike, Královodská 5, Staré Město (☎776 180 284 ⊛www.citybike-prague.com; metro Náměstí Republiky) or Praha Bike, Dlouhá 24, Staré Město (☎732 388 880, ⊛www.prahabike.cz; metro Náměstí Republiky); both outfits also organize group rides through Prague. A bike (*kolo*) needs a half-price ticket to travel on the metro or the train (they're not allowed on trams and buses); they travel in the guard's van on trains, and in the last carriage of the metro.

The media

You'll find the full range of foreign newspapers for sale at kiosks on Wenceslas Square and elsewhere. They're generally a day old, though one that you can buy on the day of issue is the European edition of The Guardian, printed in Frankfurt (it arrives on the streets of Prague around mid-morning). Similarly, the International Herald Tribune is widely available the same day, and contains a useful distilled English version of the Frankfurter Allgemeine Zeitung.

The Prague Post (⊛www.praguepost.com) is an **English-language weekly** aimed at the expat community, but good for visitors, too; it's a quality paper with strong business coverage and a useful pull-out listings section (for more on listings, see p.203). In the **magazine** market, you'll find the best coverage of contemporary Czech politics in English in *The New Presence/Přítomnost* (⊛www.new-presence.cz), a bilingual current affairs magazine, directly inspired by the Masaryk-funded *Přítomnost*, which was one of the leading periodicals of the First Republic. Various arty magazines run by expats have come and gone over the years;

it's worth calling in at one of Prague's English-language bookstores (see p.217) for the latest titles.

It's a sign of the times that the majority of **Czech newspapers** are German-owned. The only Czech-owned paper is the left-wing *Právo*, formerly the official mouthpiece of the Communist Party (when it was known as *Rudé právo* or "Red Justice"). Its chief competitor is *Mladá fronta Dnes*, former mouthpiece of the Communist youth movement, now a very popular right-wing daily. *Lidové noviny* (the best-known *samizdat* or underground publication under the Communists and the equivalent of *The Times* under the First Republic) is now a populist centre-right daily, while the orange-coloured *Hospodářské noviny* is the Czech equivalent of the *Financial Times* or *Wall Street Journal*. The country's most popular newspaper is *Blesk* (*Lightning*), a sensationalist tabloid with lurid colour pictures, naked women and reactionary politics. If all you want, however, is yesterday's (or, more often than not, the day before yesterday's) international sports results, pick up a copy of the daily *Sport*.

TV and radio

Česká televize's two state-owned **TV channels**, ČT1 and ČT2, have both been eclipsed as far as ratings go by the runaway success of the commercial channel Nova, best known for its short-lived striptease weather programme, and to a lesser extent, Prima, which exists on a diet of dubbed American imports. ČT2 is your best bet for interesting music programmes and foreign films with subtitles.

On the **radio**, the **BBC World Service** (ⓦ www.bbc.co.uk/worldservice) broadcasts loud and clear on 101.1FM, mostly in English, with occasional bits of Czech programming. The state-run Český rozhlas broadcasts numerous stations including ČR1 (94.6FM), mainly made up of current affairs programmes, ČR2 (91.3FM), which features more magazine-style programming, and ČR3 Vltava (105FM), a culture and arts station that plays a fair amount of classical music. The three top commercial channels are the French-owned Evropa 2 (88.2FM), Rádio Bonton (99.7FM) and Kiss 98 FM (98FM), which dish out bland Euro-pop. More interesting is Radio 1 (91.9FM), which plays a wide range of alternative music.

Festivals

Prague's **annual festive calendar** is light compared to most European capitals, with just a handful of arts events, in addition to the usual religious festivities. For public holidays see p.37.

Epiphany (Den tří králů)

On **January 6**, the letters K + M + B (for Kašpar, Melichar and Baltazar) followed by the date of the new year are chalked on doorways across the capital to celebrate the "Day of the Three Kings" when the Magi came to worship Christ.

Masopust or Carnavale (Shrove Tuesday)

The approach of Masopust (the Czech version of **Mardi Gras**) is celebrated locally in the Žižkov district of Prague, where there's a five-day programme of parties, concerts and parades; a more mainstream series of events takes place under the umbrella of

Carnevale, in the city centre. ⓦ www .carnevale.cz

Easter (Velikonoce)

The age-old sexist ritual of whipping girls' calves with braided birch twigs tied together with ribbons (*pomlázky*) is still practised outside Prague. To prevent such a fate, the girls are supposed to offer the boys a coloured Easter egg and pour a bucket of cold water over them. You'll see *pomlázky* and Easter eggs on sale, but precious little whipping.

Days of European Film (Dny evropského filmu)

Held over two weeks in **April**, this is the nearest Prague comes to a film festival: a fortnight of arty European films shown at various screens across the capital. ⓦ www .eurofilmfest.cz.

"Burning of the Witches" (pálení čarodějnic)

Halloween comes early to the Czech Republic when bonfires are lit across the country, and old brooms thrown out and burnt on **April 30,** as everyone celebrates the end of the long winter.

International Book Fair and Literary Festival

The fair usually takes place in **mid-May** at the Výstaviště fairgrounds (see p.151), and attracts an impressive array of international literary talent; the language of the discussions and readings is often English. @www .bookworld.cz.

Prague Spring Festival (Pražské jaro)

The biggest annual arts event and the country's most prestigious international music festival. Established in 1946, Traditionally begins on **May 12**, the anniversary of Smetana's death, with a procession from his grave in Vyšehrad to the Obecní dům where the composer's *Má vlast* (*My Country*) is performed in the presence of the president, finishing on June 2 with a rendition of Beethoven's Ninth Symphony. Tickets for the festival sell out fast – try your luck by writing, a month before the festival begins, to the Prague Spring Festival box office at Hellichova 18, Malá Strana; ☎257 312 547, @www.festival.cz.

Prague International Marathon

Runners from over fifty countries come to run through the cobbled streets and over the Charles Bridge in **late May.** @www .praguemarathon.com.

World Roma Festival (Khamoro)

Held in **late May**, Khamoro is an international Roma festival of music, dance and film, plus seminars and workshops. @www .khamoro.cz.

Czech Beer Festival

The Czechs think they produce the best beer in the world, and this two-week event

in **late May**, held in Výstaviště Letňany, at the end of metro line C, is the place in which to test that theory out. Admission is free. @www.ceskypivnifestival.cz.

World Festival of Puppet Art

Week-long international puppet festival in **late May/early June** organized by Prague's chief puppetry institute. @www.puppetart .com.

Respect Festival

World music weekend held at various venues across the city in **June**, including Akropolis and the Štvanice island (☎296 330 988, @www.respectmusic.cz).

Dance Prague (Tanec Praha)

An established highlight of Prague's cultural calendar, this international festival of modern dance takes place over three weeks in **June** throughout the city. @www.tanecpha.cz.

Burčák

At the **end of September** for a couple of weeks, temporary stalls sell the year's partially fermented new wine, known as *burčák*, a misty heady brew.

Christmas markets

Christmas markets selling gifts, food and mulled wine (*svařák*) are set up at several places around the city in **December**: the biggest ones are on Wenceslas Square and the Old Town Square. Temporary ice rinks are also constructed at various locations.

Barbara's Day

On the saint's feast day of **December 4**, cherry tree branches are bought as decorations, the aim being to get them to blossom before Christmas.

Eve of St Nicholas

On the evening of **December 5**, numerous trios, dressed up as St Nicholas (*svatý Mikuláš*), an angel and a devil, tour the streets, the angel handing out sweets and fruit to children who've been good, while the devil rattles his chains and dishes out coal and potatoes to those who've been naughty. The Czech St Nicholas has white hair and a beard, and dresses not in red but in a white priest's outfit, with a bishop's mitre.

Bohuslav Martinů Festival

Annual festival of music in **early December** celebrating the least well known of the big four Czech composers. ⓦ www.martinu.cz.

Christmas Eve (Štědrý večer)

December 24 is traditionally a day of fasting, broken only when the evening star appears, signalling the beginning of the Christmas feast of carp, potato salad, schnitzel and sweetbreads. Only after the meal are the children allowed to open their presents, which miraculously appear beneath the tree, thanks not to Santa Claus, but to Baby Jesus (*Ježíšek*).

Travel essentials

Addresses

The street name is always written before the number in Prague **addresses**. The word for street (*ulice*) is either abbreviated to *ul.* or missed out altogether – Celetná ulice, for instance, is commonly known as Celetná. Other terms often abbreviated are *náměstí* (square), *třída* (avenue) and *nábřeži* (embankment), which become *nám.*, *tř.* and *nábř.* respectively. Prague is divided into numbered **postal districts** (see map, p.179) – these are too large to be very much help in orientation, so in this guide, we have generally opted for the names of the smaller historic districts as they appear on street signs, for example Hradčany, Nové Město, Smíchov etc.

Children

Despite a friendly attitude to kids and babies in general, you'll see very few **children** in museums and galleries, or in pubs, restaurants or cafés. Apart from the mirror maze, the aquarium in Výstaviště and the zoo, there aren't very many attractions specifically aimed at kids. The castle and the Petřín funicular usually go down well, as does a ride on a tram.

Costs

Accommodation is expensive in Prague and many cafés and restaurants now charge prices that are above the EU average. That said, beer is still very cheap, and museums, galleries and clubs are reasonable, too. At the bottom end of the scale, if you stay in a hostel and stick to pubs and takeaways, you could get by on a minimum of £20/$30 a day. If you stay in a cheapish hotels and eat in lower-price restaurants, you could manage on £40/$60 a day. For more details on the costs of accommodation and eating, see chapters 9 and 10.

Crime

The Czech papers are full of the latest robbery, mafia shooting or terrorist intrigue, but the **crime rate** is still very low compared with most European or North American cities. Pickpockets are the biggest hassle, especially in summer around the most popular tourist sights and on the trams and metro.

There are two main types of **police**: the *Policie* are the national force with white shirts, navy blue jackets and grey trousers, while the *Městská policie*, run by the Prague city authorities, are distinguishable by their all-black uniforms. The main central police station is at Bartolomějská 6, Staré Město (metro Národní třída); they should, in theory, be able to provide an English-speaker here.

In addition, there are various private **security guards**, who also dress in black – hence their nickname, *Černé šerii* (Black Sheriffs) – employed mostly by hotels and banks. They are allowed to carry guns, but have no powers of arrest, and you are not legally obliged to show them your ID.

For **emergency telephone numbers**, see opposite.

Discounts

Most sights and some cinemas and theatres in Prague offer **concessions** for senior citizens, the unemployed, full-time students and children under 16, with under-5s being admitted free almost everywhere – proof of eligibility will be required in most cases. **Youth/student ID cards** soon pay for themselves in savings. Full-time students are eligible for the International Student Identity Card or **ISIC** (ⓦwww.isic.org), which entitles the bearer to special air, rail and bus fares, and discounts at museums, theatres and other attractions. The card costs around £9/$22. If you're not a student, but you are 25 or younger, you can get an International Youth Travel Card, or **IYTC**, which costs the same as the ISIC and carries the same benefits.

Electricity

The standard continental 220 volts AC. Most European appliances should work as long as you have an adaptor for continental-style two-pin round plugs. North Americans will need this plus a transformer.

Embassies and consulates

Australia Klimentská 10, Nové Město ☎251 018 350; metro Náměstí Republiky.
Belarus Sádky 626, Troja ☎233 540 899, ⓦwww.belarus.by; bus #112 from metro Nádraží Holešovice.
Canada Muchova 6, Dejvice ☎272 101 890, ⓦwww.canada.cz; metro Hradčanská.
Ireland Tržiště 13 ☎257 530 061, ⓦwww.embassyofireland.cz; metro Malostranská.

New Zealand Dykova 19, Vinohrady ☎222 514 672; metro Jiřího z Poděbrad.
Poland Valdštejnská 8, Malá Strana ☎257 099 500, ⓦwww.ambpol.cz; metro Malostranská.
Russia Pod kaštany 1, Bubeneč ☎233 374 100, ⓦwww.russianembassy.net; metro Dejvická.
Slovakia Pelléova 12, Bubeneč ☎233 113 051, ⓦwww.slovakemb.cz; metro Hradčanská.
South Africa Ruská 65, Vršovice ☎267 311 114, ⓦwww.saprague.cz; metro Flora.
UK Thunovská 14, Malá Strana ☎257 402 111, ⓦukinczechrepublic.fco.gov.uk; metro Malostranská.
Ukraine Charlese de Gaulla 29, Bubeneč ☎233 342 000, ⓦwww.ukraine.cz; metro Dejvická.
US Tržiště 15, Malá Strana ☎257 530 663, ⓦwww.usembassy.cz; metro Malostranská.

Emergency numbers

Emergencies ☎112
Ambulance ☎155
Police ☎158
Fire ☎150

Entry requirements

Citizens of the EU, US, Canada, Australia and New Zealand need only a full **passport** to enter the Czech Republic, though the passport itself must be valid for at least six months beyond your return date. UK citizens can stay up to 180 days; all other EU and US citizens, Australians and New Zealanders can stay up to ninety days. Citizens of most other countries require a **visa**, obtainable from a Czech embassy or consulate in the country of application (see ⓦwww.mvcr.cz for a list). All visitors must register with the police within three days of arrival (if you're staying in a campsite, hostel, pension or hotel, this will be done for you). Visa requirements do change, however, and it is always advisable to check the current situation before leaving home.

If your visa only allows you to stay thirty days and you wish to **extend your stay** to ninety days, you need to get a *výjezdní vízum* from the Cizinecká policie (Foreigners' Police), Olšanská 2 (tram #9 or #26). If you want to stay longer than ninety days, you'll need either a really good excuse for a **residence permit** (*občanský průkaz*), which is difficult to obtain unless you're studying in the country or have a job (and, therefore, a work permit).

Health

EU health-care privileges apply in the Czech Republic, so EU citizens are entitled to free emergency **hospital** treatment on production of a European Health Insurance Card or **EHIC**. The main hospital is Nemocnice na Homolce, Roentgenova 2, Motol (bus #167 from metro Anděl), which runs a 24-hour emergency service and has English-speaking doctors. Nevertheless, all visitors would do well to take out insurance (see below) to cover themselves against medical emergencies. Many medicines are available over the counter at a **pharmacy** (*lékárna*). Most pharmacies are open Monday to Friday 7.30am to 6pm, but some open 24 hours (all pharmacies should have directions to the nearest 24-hour pharmacy posted in the window) – try Palackého 5 (☏224 946 982) or Bekgická 37 (☏222 513 396). For an emergency **dentist**, head for Palackého 5, Nové Město (☏224 946 981; metro Můstek).

Insurance

EU health-care privileges apply in the Czech Republic, but you should get **travel insurance** against theft, loss and illness or injury. For non-EU citizens, it's worth checking whether you are already covered before you buy a new policy. If you need to take out insurance, you might want to consider the travel insurance offered by Rough Guides (see below).

Internet access

With any luck the hotel or hostel you're staying at will have **internet access**. Plenty of Prague's cafés and bars have **free wi-fi** – if you don't have a laptop, head for the Globe (see p.194).

Laundry

Most hotels offer a **laundry service** and most hostels have washing machines. Prague's expats tend to head for one of the following laundries, which all have internet access, TV, service washes and self-service machines.
Laundry Kings Dejvická 16, Dejvice ☏233 343 743, ⓦwww.laundry.czweb.org; metro Hradčanská. Mon–Fri 6am–10pm, Sat & Sun 8am–10pm.
Laundryland Na příkopě 12, Nové Město and several other branches ☏221 014 632, ⓦwww.laundryland.cz; metro Můstek. Mon–Fri 9am–8pm, Sat 9am–7pm & Sun 11am–7pm.
Prague Andy's Laundromat Korunní 14, Vinohrady ☏222 510 180, ⓦwww.praguelaundromat.cz; metro Náměstí Míru. Daily 8am–8pm.

Left luggage

Prague's main bus and train stations have lockers and/or a 24-hour **left-luggage** office (*úschovna zavazadel*), with instructions in English.

Lost property

The main train stations have **lost property** offices – look for the sign *ztráty a nálezy* – and there's a central municipal one at Karoliny Světlé 5 (Mon–Fri only). If you've lost your passport, then get in touch with your embassy (see opposite).

Mail

Outbound **post** is reasonably reliable, with letters or cards taking around five working

---

Rough Guides travel insurance

Rough Guides has teamed up with WorldNomads.com to offer great **travel insurance** deals. Policies are available to residents of over 150 countries, with cover for a wide range of adventure sports, 24-hour emergency assistance, high levels of medical and evacuation cover and a stream of travel safety information. Roughguides.com users can take advantage of their policies online 24/7, from anywhere in the world – even if you're already travelling. And since plans often change when you're on the road, you can extend your policy and even claim online. Roughguides.com users who buy travel insurance with WorldNomads.com can also leave a positive footprint and donate to a community development project. For more information go to ⓦwww.roughguides.com/shop.

days to Britain and Ireland, and one week to ten days to North America or Australasia. You can buy **stamps** from newsagents, tobacconists and some kiosks, as well as at post offices. Postal charges at the time of going to print were 11Kč for postcards within Europe and 12Kč to North America (check ⓦwww.cpost.cz for the latest).

The **main post office** (*hlavní pošta*) is at Jindřišská 14, Nové Město (☎840 111 244; open 24hr), just off Wenceslas Square; take a ticket and wait for your number to come up. A more tourist-friendly branch exists in the third courtyard of Prague Castle. **Poste restante** (pronounced as five syllables in Czech) letters to Prague will automatically arrive at the main post office (the postcode is 110 00 PRAHA 1), though you may use any post office as long as you use the correct postcode.

To send a **parcel over 2kg** (but below 15kg) you must go to the Celní Pošta (customs parcel office) at the junction of Plzeňská and Vrchlického in Prague 5 (tram #6, #9, #10 or #16 to Klamovka). After filling in two separate forms for shipping and customs, you then have a choice of sending your parcel by ship, air or express. Alternatively, you can send it by EMS (Express Mail System) or via a courier company such as DHL (☎840 103 000, ⓦwww.dhl.cz).

Maps

The **maps** in this book should be adequate for holiday purposes, but you might also want to buy the *Rough Guide Prague Map*, a comprehensive full-colour, waterproof and non-tearable map detailing restaurants, bars, shops and visitor attractions. If you're staying out in the suburbs, however, you may wish to buy something even more comprehensive. The best maps of Prague are produced by Kartografie Praha, whose 1:20,000 booklet (*plán města*) covers the whole city and includes the tram and bus routes, too. It's easy enough to get hold of maps once you've arrived in Prague, from the tourist office, bookstores or your hotel.

Money

The currency is the **Czech crown** or koruna česká (abbreviated to Kč or CZK). At the time of going to press there were roughly 30Kč to the pound sterling, 25Kč to the euro and around 20Kč to the US dollar. For up-to-date exchange rates, consult ⓦwww .oanda.com or ⓦwww.xe.com.

Notes come in 20Kč, 50Kč, 100Kč, 200Kč, 500Kč, 1000Kč and 2000Kč (and less frequently 5000Kč) denominations; **coins** as 1Kč, 2Kč, 5Kč, 10Kč, 20Kč and 50Kč. Notes of 2000Kč and 5000Kč are rarely used for transactions of less than 200Kč. Banking hours are Monday to Friday from 8am to 5pm, often with a break at lunchtime. ATMs can be found across the city, from which you should be able to take out money using either a debit or credit card.

Opening hours

Shops in Prague are generally open Monday to Friday from 9am to 5pm, though most supermarkets and tourist shops stay open until 6pm or later. Some shops close by noon or 1pm on Saturday and close all day Sunday, but there's no law against opening on Sundays and many shops in the centre do (including main supermarkets and department stores). Traditional **pubs** tend to close by 11pm and rarely serve food after 9pm; **restaurants** stay open until at least 11pm or midnight; and there are plenty of late-night **bars** where you can continue drinking until the early hours.

Opening hours for **museums and galleries** are generally 10am to 6pm every day except Monday (when they are closed) all year round. Full opening hours are detailed in the text. Getting into churches can present more of a problem. Some of the more central ones operate in much the same way as museums and occasionally even have an entry charge. Most **churches**, however, are kept locked, with perhaps just the vestibule open, allowing you at least a glimpse of the interior, opening fully only for worship in the early morning (around 7am or 8am on weekdays, more like 10am on Sundays) and/or the evening (around 6pm or 7pm).

Phones

Most **public phones** take only phone cards (*telefonní karty*), available from post offices, tobacconists and some shops (prices vary).

Useful telephone numbers

Phoning Prague from abroad
From the UK and Ireland ☏00 + 420 (Czech Republic) + number.
From the US and Canada ☏011 + 420 (Czech Republic) + number.
From Australia and New Zealand ☏0011 + 420 (Czech Republic) + number.

Phoning abroad from Prague
To the UK ☏0044 + area code minus zero + number.
To Ireland ☏00353 + area code minus zero + number.
To the US & Canada ☏001 + area code minus zero + number.
To Australia ☏0061 + area code minus zero + number.
To New Zealand ☏0064 + area code minus zero + number.

The best-value ones are **pre-paid phone cards** that give you a phone number and a code to enter. There are instructions in English, and if you press the appropriate button the language on the digital read-out will change to English.

Nearly all Prague **phone numbers** are nine digit. There are no separate city/area codes in the Czech Republic.

The **dialling tone** is a short pulse followed by a long one; the **ringing tone** is long and regular; **engaged** is short and rapid (not to be confused with the connecting tone, which is very short and rapid). The standard Czech response is *prosím*; the word for "extension" is *linka*. If you have any problems, ring ☏1181 to get through to international information.

If you're taking your **mobile/cell phone** with you, check with your service provider whether your phone will work abroad and what the call charges will be. Mobiles bought for use in Europe, Australia and New Zealand should work fine, though a mobile bought for use in the US is unlikely to work unless it's a tri-band phone.

Public holidays

National **holidays** (*Státní svátek*) have always been a potential source of contention for the Czechs. May Day, a nationwide compulsory march under the Communists, remains a public holiday, though only the skinheads, anarchists and die-hard Stalinists take to the streets nowadays. Of the other *slavné májové dny* (Glorious May Days), as they used to be known, May 5, the beginning of the 1945 Prague Uprising,

has been binned, and VE Day is now celebrated along with the Western Allies on May 8, and not on May 9, as it was under the Communists, and still is in Russia. September 28, the feast day of the country's patron saint, St Wenceslas, is now Czech State Day. Strangely, however, October 28, the day on which the First Republic was founded in 1918, is still celebrated, despite being a "Czechoslovak" holiday (and, for a while, under the Communists, Nationalization Day).

January 1 New Year's Day (Nový rok)
Easter Monday (Velikonoční pondělí)
May 1 May Day (Svátek práce)
May 8 VE Day (Den osvobození)
July 5 Introduction of Christianity (Den slovanských věrozvěstů Cyrila a Metoděje)
July 6 Death of Jan Hus (Den upálení mistra Jana Husa)
September 28 Czech State Day (Den české státnosti)
October 28 Foundation of the Republic (Den vzniku samostatného československého státu)
November 17 Battle for Freedom and Democracy Day (Den boje za svobodu a demokracii)
December 24 Christmas Eve (Štědrý den)
December 25 Christmas Day (Vánoce)
December 26 St Stephen's Day (Den sv Štěpana)

Time

The Czech Republic is in **Central European Time** (CET), one hour ahead of Britain (UTC+01) and six hours ahead of EST, with the clocks going forward in spring for summer time and back again some time in autumn – the exact date changes from year to year. Generally speaking, Czechs use the **24-hour clock**.

Tipping

Tipping is normal practice in cafés, bars, restaurants and taxis, though it is usually done simply by rounding up the total. For example, if the waiter tots up the bill and asks you for 74Kč, you should hand him a 100Kč note and say "take 80Kč".

Tourist information

In Prague, the main **tourist office** is the **Prague Information Service**, or **PIS** (Pražská informační služba), whose main branch is within the Staroměstská radnice on Staroměstské náměstí (April–Oct Mon–Fri 9am–7pm, Sat & Sun 9am–6pm; Nov–March Mon–Fri 9am–6pm, Sat & Sun 9am–5pm; ®www.prague-info.cz). There are also PIS offices at Rytířská 31, Staré Město (metro Můstek), in the main train station, Praha hlavní nádraží, plus an (April–Oct only) office in the Malá Strana bridge tower on the Charles Bridge. PIS staff speak English, but their helpfulness varies enormously; however, they can usually answer most enquiries, organize accommodation, and sell maps, guides and theatre tickets.

PIS also distributes and sells some useful **listings** publications, including *Culture in Prague/Česká kultura* (®www.ceskakultura.cz), a monthly English-language booklet listing the major events, concerts and exhibitions; *Přehled*, a more comprehensive monthly listings magazine (in Czech only); and the weekly English-language paper, *Prague Post* (®www.praguepost.com), which carries selective listings.

Useful websites

Bohemica ®www.bohemica.com. Lots of articles and information on Czech traditions, culture and language, plus links to Czech sites.
Expats ®www.expats.cz. Fantastic online resource for anyone staying in Prague: visitor information, news, listings and message boards galore.
Fleet Sheet ®www.fsfinalword.cz. Daily one-page digest of the day's Czech news sent as a free email.

Language ®www.locallingo.com. Great resource for learning the language online.
Living Prague ®www.livingprague.com. Very personal online guide to the city by an English expat who's been living in the capital for over fifteen years.
Maps ®www.mapy.cz. This site will provide you with a thumbnail map to help you find any hotel, restaurant, pub, shop or street in Prague (and elsewhere in the Czech Republic).
Prague Daily ®praguedaily.com. Daily online news from Prague.
Prague Post ®www.praguepost.com. A very useful site for the latest news and for general tourist information.
Prague TV ®prague.tv. Not in fact a TV station at all, but a great online source for listings and news about Prague, updated daily.
Radio Prague ®www.radio.cz. Czech Radio's informative English-language site, with updated news and weather as audio or text.
Welcome to the Czech Republic ®www.czech.cz. Basic information on the country in English, and on the worldwide network of Czech Centres run by the Czech Foreign Ministry.

Travellers with disabilities

Disabled access in the Czech Republic still has a long way to go, although attitudes are slowly changing and some legislation has been put in place. Transport is a major problem. Buses and old trams are inaccessible for wheelchairs, though the new metro stations have facilities for people with disabilities, and the two train stations (Hlavní nádraží and nádraží Holešovice) actually have self-operating lifts. Prague's cobbles and general lack of ramps also make life hard on the streets.

For a list of wheelchair-friendly hotels, restaurants, metro stations and so forth, order the **guidebook** *Accessible Prague/Přístupná Praha* from the Prague Wheelchair Association (Pražská organizace vozíčkářů), Benediktská 6, Staré Město (☎224 827 210, ®www.pov.cz). The association can organize an airport pick-up if you contact them well in advance, and can help with transporting wheelchairs.

The City

The City

Hradčany

Prague is wholly dominated by the omnipresent landmark of **Pražský hrad** (**Prague Castle**), the vast hilltop complex that looks out over the city centre from the west bank of the River Vltava. Site of a Slav settlement in the seventh or eighth century AD, there's been a castle here since at least the late ninth century, and since then whoever has had control of the Hrad has exercised authority over the Czech Lands. It continues to serve as the seat of the president, though the public are free to wander round from the early hours until late at night, since the castle is also home to several museums and galleries.

The rest of **HRADČANY**, the castle district, has always been a mere appendage, its inhabitants serving and working for their masters in the Hrad. Even now, despite the odd restaurant or *pivnice* (pub) in among the palaces (and even in the Hrad itself), there's very little real life here beyond the stream of tourists who trek through the castle and the civil servants who work either for the president or the government, whose departmental tentacles spread right across Hradčany and down into neighbouring Malá Strana. All of which makes it a very peaceful and attractive area in which to take a stroll, and lose the crowds who crawl all over the Hrad.

Stretched out along a high spur above the River Vltava, Hradčany shows a suitable disdain for the public transport system. There's a choice of **approaches** from Malá Strana, all of which involve at least some walking. From Malostranská metro station, most people take the steep short cut up the Staré zámecké schody, which brings you into the castle from its rear end. A better approach is further west, up the stately Zámecké schody, where you can stop and admire the view, before entering the castle via the main gates. From April to October, you might also consider coming up through Malá Strana's wonderful terraced gardens (see p.71), which are connected to the castle gardens. The alternative to all this climbing is to take **tram #22** from Malostranská metro, which tackles the hairpin bends of Chotkova with ease, and deposits you either at the Pražský hrad stop outside the Královská zahrada (Royal Gardens) to the north of the castle, or, if you prefer, at the Pohořelec stop outside the gates of the Strahovský klášter (monastery), at the far western edge of Hradčany.

Pražský hrad (Prague Castle)

Viewed from the Charles Bridge, **PRAŽSKÝ HRAD** (known to the Czechs simply as the Hrad) stands aloof from the rest of the city, protected not by bastions and castellated towers, but by a rather austere palatial facade – an "immense unbroken sheer blank wall", as Hilaire Belloc described it – above which rises the

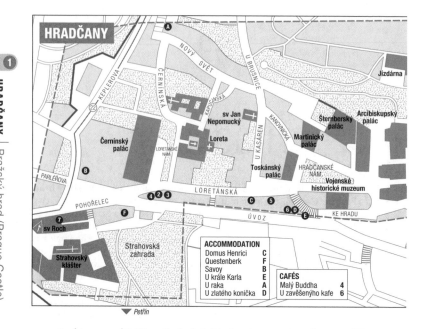

▼ Petřín

great Gothic mass of St Vitus Cathedral. It's the picture-postcard image of Prague, and is spectacularly lit up at night, though for the Czechs the castle has been an object of disdain as much as admiration, its alternating fortunes mirroring the

Visiting the castle

The castle (☎224 373 368, ⊛www.hrad.cz) is open daily April to October from 5am to midnight, and November to March from 6am to 11pm; sights within the castle (unless otherwise stated) are open daily April to October from 9am to 6pm, and November to March from 9am to 4pm.

You can wander freely through most of the streets, courtyards and gardens of the castle and watch the changing of the guard without a ticket. For the sights within the castle (excluding the cathedral) there are two main types of **multi-entry ticket** available: the velký okruh or **long tour** (350Kč), which gives you entry to most sights, including the Old Royal Palace, the Basilica and Convent of sv Jiří, the Prague Castle Picture Gallery and the Zlatá ulička; and the malý okruh or **short tour** (250Kč), which only covers the Old Royal Palace, the Basilica of sv Jiří and the Zlatá ulička. Tickets are valid for two days and available from several places, including the main **information centre** in the third courtyard, opposite the cathedral, where you can also rent an English-language **audioguide** (200Kč for 2hr). The Muzeum hraček, Lobkovický palác and any **temporary exhibitions** such as those held in Císařská konírna and Jízdárna, all have different opening hours and separate admission charges (see the relevant entries for details). The **state rooms** used by the president are open to the public two days a year: currently the Saturday after May 8 and the Saturday after October 28.

Within the castle precincts there are several cafés and restaurants, none of which is anything to get excited about. If you simply want a quick cup of coffee, the best one to head for is the **Café Poet**, which has outside tables and is hidden away in the peaceful and little-visited Zahrada na baště at the western end of the castle.

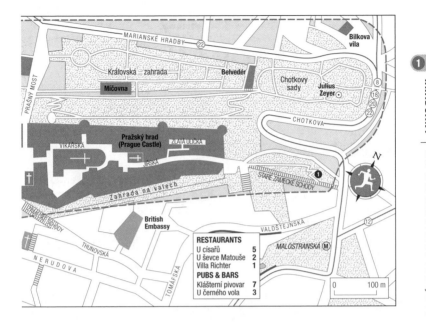

shifts in the nation's history. The golden age of Charles IV and Rudolf II and the dark ages of the later Habsburgs, interwar democracy and Stalinist terror – all have emanated from the Hrad. When the first posters appeared in December 1989 demanding "HAVEL NA HRAD" (Václav Havel to the Castle), they weren't asking for his re-incarceration. Havel's occupancy of the Hrad was the sign that the reins of government had finally been wrested from the Communist regime.

The site has been successively built on since the Přemyslid princes erected the first castle here in the ninth century, but two **architects** in particular bear responsibility for the present outward appearance of the Hrad. The first is **Nicolò Pacassi**, court architect to Empress Maria Theresa, whose austere restorations went hand in hand with the deliberate running down of the Hrad until it was little more than an administrative barracks. For the Czechs, his grey-green eighteenth-century cover-up, which hides a variety of much older buildings, is unforgivable. Less apparent, though no less controversial, is the hand of **Josip Plečnik** (see box, p.46), the Slovene architect who was commissioned by T.G. Masaryk, president of the newly founded Czechoslovak Republic, to restore and modernize the castle in his highly distinctive style in the 1920s.

The first and second courtyards

The **first courtyard** (první nádvoří), which opens onto Hradčanské náměstí, is guarded by Ignaz Platzer's blood-curdling *Battling Titans* – two gargantuan figures, one on each of the gate piers, wielding club and dagger and about to inflict fatal blows on their respective victims. Below them stand a couple of impassive presidential sentries, sporting slightly camp sky-blue and grey uniforms that deliberately recall those of the First Republic. They were designed by the Oscar-winning costume designer for Miloš Forman's film *Amadeus*, and chosen by Havel himself. The hourly **Changing of the Guard** (Střídaní stráží) is a fairly subdued affair, but

43

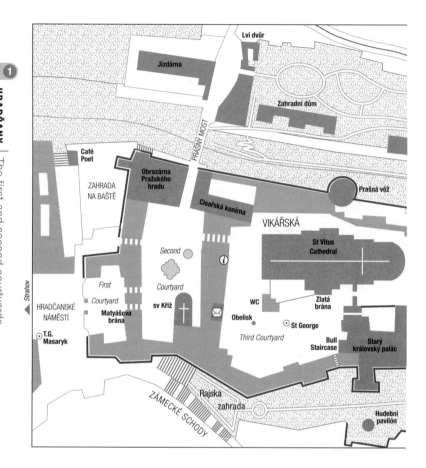

every day at noon there's a much more elaborate parade, accompanied by a brass ensemble which appears at the first-floor windows to play local rock star Michal Kocáb's specially commissioned, gentle, modern fanfare.

To reach the **second courtyard** (druhé nádvoří), you must pass through the early Baroque Matyášova brána (Matthias Gate), originally a freestanding triumphal arch in the middle of the long-since defunct moat, now set into one of Pacassi's featureless wings. A grand stairway leads to the presidential apartments in the south wing, while to the north you can peek in at the beautiful Neoclassical lines of Plečnik's Hall of Columns, which leads to the two grandest reception rooms in the entire complex: the **Španělský sál** (Spanish Hall) and the **Rudolfova galerie** (Rudolf Gallery) in the north wing. Sadly, both are generally out of bounds, though concerts are occasionally held in the Španělský sál. Both rooms were redecorated in the 1860s with lots of gilded chandeliers and mirrors for Emperor Franz-Joseph I's coronation as King of Bohemia, though in the end he decided not to turn up. Under the Communists, the Rudolfova galerie was the incongruous setting for Politburo meetings.

Surrounded by monotonous Pacassi plasterwork, the courtyard itself is really just a through-route to the cathedral, with an early Baroque stone fountain, the **Kohlova kašna**, and a wrought-iron well grille the only obvious distractions. The

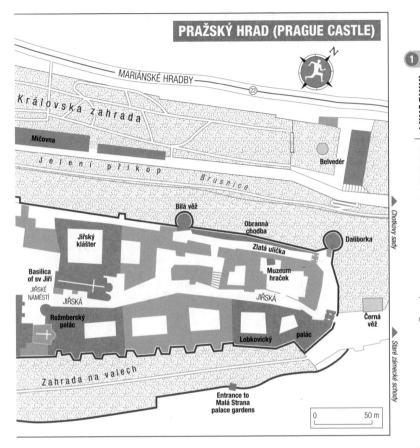

PRAŽSKÝ HRAD (PRAGUE CASTLE)

MARIÁNSKÉ HRADBY

Královská zahrada

Míčovna

Jelení příkop

Brusnice

Belvedér

Bílá věž

Obranná chodba

Zlatá ulička

Daliborka

Jiřský klášter

Muzeum hraček

Basilica of sv Jiří

JIŘSKÉ NÁMĚSTÍ

JIŘSKÁ

JIŘSKÁ

Černá věž

Rožmberský palác

Lobkovický   palác

Zahrada na valech

Entrance to Malá Strana palace gardens

0   50 m

Chotkovy sady

Staré zámecké schody

striking gilded sculpture of a winged leopard by Bořek Šípek, at the entrance to the east wing, is a postmodern homage to Plečnik. Occupying the southeast corner of the courtyard is Anselmo Lurago's **Chapel of sv Kříž**, whose richly painted interior, dating mostly from the mid-nineteenth century, can be entered via the information office in the vestibule. On the opposite side of the courtyard are the former **Císařská konírna** (Imperial Stables), which still boast their original, magnificent Renaissance vaulting dating from the reign of Rudolf II, and are now used to house temporary exhibitions (Tues–Sun 10am–6pm).

Obrazárna Pražského hradu (Prague Castle Picture Gallery)

Remnants of the imperial collection, begun by the Habsburg Emperor Rudolf II (see box, p.54), are housed in the five rooms of the **Obrazárna Pražského hradu** (Prague Castle Picture Gallery; daily: April–Oct 10am–6pm; Nov–March 9am–4pm; 150Kč; ⓦwww.obrazarna-hradu.cz), on the north side of the second courtyard. However, the best of what Rudolf amassed was either taken as booty by the marauding Saxons and Swedes, or sold off by his successors. Of the many

Plečnik: a postmodernist before his day

Born in Ljubljana, **Josip Plečnik** (1872–1957) graduated in carpentry and furniture design from his secondary school in Graz before studying under the great Viennese architect Otto Wagner at the Viennese Academy of Fine Arts. He moved to Prague in 1911 and was appointed chief architect to Prague Castle shortly after the foundation of the First Republic. Despite having the backing of the leading Czech architect Jan Kotěra, and of President Masaryk himself, controversy surrounded him as soon as the appointment was announced; his non-Czech background and, moreover, his quirky, eclectic style placed him at odds with the architectural establishment of the day. In fact, it wasn't until thirty years after his death, following a major retrospective exhibition at the Pompidou in Paris in 1986, that his work was brought to a wider audience. In the 1990s, Plečnik's style, which happily borrows elements from any number of genres from classical to Assyrian architecture, proved an inspiration to a new generation of postmodern architects.

Plečnik's most conspicuous contributions to the castle are the **fir-tree flag poles** in the first courtyard and the **granite obelisk** in the third courtyard, but his light-hearted touch can be seen throughout the castle and its gardens: check out the jokey palm tree with roped-on copper leaves outside the Jízdárna; the **Bull Staircase**, which leads down to the Zahrada na valech; or the impressive **Sloupová síň** (Hall of Columns), which contains the stairs going up to the **Španělský sál**, and can be peeked at through the glass doors between the first and second courtyards. Sadly, much of Plečnik's work – in particular the president's private apartments – remains hidden from public view, though thanks partly to Havel (a keen Plečnik fan), public access has been greatly increased.

surrealist portraits by **Giuseppe Arcimboldo** that Rudolf once owned, only one now remains in Prague: *Vertumnus*, a portrait of Rudolf himself as a collage of fruit, with his eyes as cherries, cheeks as apples and hair as grapes. The rest of the collection is definitely patchy, but it does contain one or two other masterpieces that are well worth seeing, and visiting the gallery is a great way to escape the castle crowds.

In the first room, Heintz the Elder, one of Rudolf's many court painters, provides an unusually upbeat take on the Last Judgement, with a party atmosphere prevailing. The illusionist triple portrait of Rudolf (when viewed from the left), and his Habsburg predecessors (when viewed from the right), by Paulus Roy, is representative of the sort of tricksy work that appealed to the emperor. There are other good royal portraits here, and in the adjacent room, including several by **Cranach the Elder** and one by **Holbein** of Lady Vaux, wife of a poet from the court of Henry VIII.

Immediately down the stairs is one of the collection's finest paintings, **Rubens'** richly coloured *Assembly of the Gods at Olympus*, featuring a typically voluptuous Venus and a slightly fazed Zeus. Elsewhere, there's an early, very beautiful *Young Woman at her Toilet* by **Titian**, and a superbly observed *Portrait of a Musician* by one of his pupils, Bordone. **Veronese's** best offering is his portrait of Jakob König, a German art dealer in Venice who worked for Rudolf II among others, and who was also a personal friend of the artist. Look out, too, for **Tintoretto's** *Flagellation of Christ*, a late work in which the artist makes very effective and dramatic use of light.

St Vitus Cathedral

St Vitus Cathedral (March–Oct Mon–Sat 9am–5pm, Sun noon–5pm; Nov–Feb closes 4pm; free; Ⓦwww.mekapha.cz) is squeezed so tightly into the third courtyard that it's difficult to get an overall impression of this chaotic Gothic edifice. Its asymmetrical appearance is the product of a long and chequered history, for although the foundation stone was laid in 1344, the cathedral was not completed until 1929 – exactly 1000 years after the death of Bohemia's most famous patron saint, Wenceslas.

The site of the present cathedral was originally a sacrificial altar to the heathen fertility god **Svantovit**, which partly explains why the first church, founded in 929 by Prince Václav, was dedicated to St Vitus (svatý Vít in Czech). Vitus allegedly exorcized the Emperor Diocletian's son and was thereafter known as the patron saint of epileptics and of sufferers from the convulsive disorder Sydenham's chorea (hence its popular name, St Vitus' Dance). The inspiration for the medieval cathedral came from **Emperor Charles IV** (1346–78), who, while still only heir to the throne, not only wangled an independent archbishopric for Prague, but also managed to gather together the relics of St Vitus.

Inspired by the cathedral at Narbonne in France, Charles commissioned the Frenchman **Matthias of Arras** to start work on a similar structure. Matthias died eight years into the job in 1352, with the cathedral barely started, so Charles summoned **Peter Parler**, a precocious 23-year-old from a family of great German masons, to continue the work. For the next 46 years, Parler imprinted his slightly flashier, more inventive *SonderGotik* ("Unusual Gothic") style on the city, but the cathedral advanced no further than the construction of the choir and the south transept before his death in 1399.

Little significant work was carried out during the next four centuries and the half-built cathedral became a symbol of the Czechs' frustrated aspirations to nationhood. Not until the Czech national revival, or *národní obrození*, of the nineteenth century did building begin again in earnest, with the foundation, in 1859, of the **Union for the Completion of the Cathedral**. A succession of architects, including Josef Mocker and Kamil Hilbert, oversaw the completion of the entire west end, and, with the help of countless other Czech artists and sculptors, the building was transformed into a treasure-house of Czech art. The

▲ St Vitus Cathedral

cathedral was finally given an official opening ceremony in 1929, though work, in fact, continued right up to and beyond World War II.

The exterior

The sooty Prague air has made it hard now to differentiate between the two building periods. Close inspection, however, reveals that the **western facade**, including the twin spires, sports the rigorous if unimaginative work of the neo-Gothic restorers (their besuited portraits can be found below the rose window), while the **eastern section** – best viewed from the Belvedere – shows the building's authentic Gothic roots. The south door, known as the Zlatá brána (see p.50), is also pure Parler. Oddly then, it's above the south door that the cathedral's tallest steeple reveals the most conspicuous stylistic join: Pacassi's Baroque topping resting absurdly on a Renaissance parapet of light stone, which is itself glued onto the blackened body of the original Gothic tower.

The nave

The cathedral is the country's largest and, once inside, it's difficult not to be impressed by the sheer height of the **nave**. This is the newest part of the building, and, consequently, is decorated mostly with twentieth-century furnishings. The most arresting of these are the cathedral's modern **stained-glass windows**, which on sunny days send shafts of rainbow light into the nave. The effect is stunning, though entirely out of keeping with Parler's original concept, which was to have almost exclusively clear-glass windows. The most unusual windows are those by František Kysela, which look as though they have been shattered into hundreds of tiny pieces, a mosaic-like technique used to brilliant effect in the kaleidoscopic rose window over the west door with its *Creation of the World* (1921).

Another great window is Max Švabinský's *Day of Judgement* from 1939, which stars the Archangel Michael in green, jewel-encrusted armour brandishing a blood-red sword. Portraits of various Czech rulers feature among the chosen ones; the damned, meanwhile, are being thrown headlong into Hell's lava flow.

In keeping with its secular nature, two of the works from the time of the First Republic were paid for by financial institutions. The *Cyril and Methodius* window, in the third chapel in the north wall, was commissioned from Art Nouveau artist **Alfons Mucha** by the Banka Slavie, while on the opposite side of the nave, the window *Those Who Sow in Tears Shall Reap in Joy* was sponsored by a Prague insurance company.

One of the most striking later additions to the church is František Bílek's **wooden altar**, in the north aisle, whose anguished portrait of Christ on the cross breaks free of the neo-Gothic strictures that hamper other contemporary works inside.

Chapel of sv Václav

Of the cathedral's 22 side chapels, the grand **Chapel of sv Václav**, by the south door, is easily the main attraction. Although officially dedicated to St Vitus, spiritually the cathedral belongs as much to the Přemysl prince, Václav (Wenceslas, of "Good King" fame; see box opposite), the country's patron saint, who was killed by his pagan brother, Boleslav the Cruel. Ten years later, in 939, Boleslav repented, converted and apparently transferred his brother's remains to this very spot. Charles, who was keen to promote the cult of Wenceslas in order to cement his own Luxembourgeois dynasty's rather tenuous claim to the Bohemian throne, had Peter Parler build the present chapel on top of the original grave; the lion's head **door-ring** set into the north door is said to be the one to which Václav clung before being killed. The chapel's rich, almost Byzantine

Good King Wenceslas

There's very little substance to the story related in the nineteenth-century English Christmas carol, "Good King Wenceslas looked out", by J.M. Neale, itself a reworking of the medieval spring song "Tempus adest floridum". For a start, **Václav** was only a duke and never a king (though he did become a saint); he wasn't even that "good", except in comparison with the rest of his family; Prague's St Agnes fountain, by which "yonder peasant dwelt", wasn't built until the thirteenth century; and he was killed a good three months before the Feast of Stephen (Boxing Day) – the traditional day for giving to the poor, hence the narrative of the carol.

Born in 907, Václav inherited his title at the tender age of 13. His Christian grandmother, **Ludmila**, was appointed regent in preference to Drahomíra, his pagan mother, who subsequently had Ludmila murdered in a fit of jealousy in 921. On coming of age in 925, Václav became duke in his own right and took a vow of celibacy, intent on promoting Christianity throughout the dukedom. Even so, the local Christians didn't take to him, and when he began making conciliatory overtures to the neighbouring Germans, they persuaded his pagan younger brother, **Boleslav the Cruel**, to do away with him. On September 20, 929, Václav was stabbed to death by Boleslav at the entrance to a church just outside Prague.

decoration is like the inside of a jewel casket: the gilded walls are inlaid with approximately 1372 semiprecious Bohemian stones (corresponding to the year of its creation and symbolizing the New Jerusalem from the Book of Revelation), set around ethereal fourteenth-century frescoes of the Passion; meanwhile, the tragedy of Wenceslas unfolds above the cornice in the later paintings of the Litoměřice school, dating from 1509.

Though a dazzling testament to the golden age of Charles IV's reign, it's not just the chapel's artistic merit that draws visitors. A door in the south wall gives access to a staircase leading to the coronation chamber (only very rarely open to the public), which houses the **Bohemian crown jewels**, including the gold crown of St Wenceslas, studded with some of the largest sapphires in the world. Closed to the public since 1867, the door is secured by seven different locks, the keys kept by seven different people, starting with the president himself – like the seven seals of the holy scroll from Revelation. The tight security is partly to prevent any pretenders to the throne trying on the headgear, an allegedly fatal act: the Nazi *Reichsprotektor* Reinhard Heydrich tried it, only to suffer the inevitable consequences (see box, p.128). Replicas of the crown jewels are on display in the Story of Prague Castle exhibition (see p.52).

The chancel

There's a one-way system in the **chancel**, so head off to the north choir aisle. Following the ambulatory round, make sure you check out the high-relief seventeenth-century wooden panelling between the arcading on the right, which glories in the flight of the "Winter King", Frederick of the Palatinate (he's depicted crossing the Charles Bridge), following the disastrous Battle of Bílá hora in 1620. The remains of various early Czech rulers are scattered throughout the side chapels, most notably those of Přemysl Otakar I and II, in the Saxon Chapel (the fifth one along), whose limestone tombs are the work of Peter Parler and his workshop; you can also pay your respects to Rudolf II's internal organs, buried in the chapel vault.

Slap bang in the middle of the ambulatory, close to the Saxon Chapel, is the perfect Baroque answer to the medieval chapel of sv Václav, the **Tomb of sv Jan of Nepomuk**, plonked here in 1736. It's a work of grotesque excess, designed by

Johann Bernhard Fischer von Erlach's son, Johann Michael, and sculpted in solid silver with free-flying angels holding up the heavy drapery of the baldachin. On the lid of the tomb, back-to-back with Jan of Nepomuk himself, a cherub points to the martyr's severed tongue (see p.84).

Between the tomb of sv Jan of Nepomuk and the chapel of sv Václav, Bohemia's one and only Polish ruler, Vladislav Jagiello, built a **Royal Oratory**, connected to his bedroom in the royal palace by a covered bridge. The balustrade sports heraldic shields from Bohemia's (at the time) quite considerable lands, while the hanging vault is smothered in an unusual branch-like decoration, courtesy of Benedikt Ried. To the left, the statue of a miner is a reminder of just how important Kutná Hora's silver mines were in funding such artistic ventures.

Imperial Mausoleum, Royal Crypt and Hlavná věž

Before you leave the chancel, check out the sixteenth-century marble **Imperial Mausoleum**, situated in the centre of the choir, and surrounded by a fine Renaissance grille on which numerous cherubs are irreverently larking about. It was commissioned by Rudolf II and contains the remains of his grandfather Ferdinand I, his Polish grandmother and his father Maximilian II, the first Habsburgs to wear the Bohemian crown.

Rudolf himself rests beneath them, in one of the two pewter coffins in the somewhat cramped **Royal Crypt** (Královská hrobka), whose entrance is beside the Royal Oratory. Rudolf's coffin (at the back, in the centre) features yet more cherubs, brandishing quills, while the one to the right contains the remains of Maria Amelia, daughter of the Empress Maria Theresa. A good number of other Czech kings and queens are buried here, too, reinterred this century in incongruously modern 1930s sarcophagi, among them the Hussite King George of Poděbrady, Charles IV and, sharing a single sarcophagus, all four of his wives. The exit from the crypt brings you out in the centre of the nave.

From noon, you can get a great view over the castle and the city from the cathedral's **Hlavná věž** (Great Tower; daily: March–Oct noon–4.15pm; Nov–Feb noon–3.15pm), the entrance to which is in the south aisle – but be warned, there are around three hundred steps before you reach the top.

The third courtyard

The **third courtyard** (třetí nádvoří) reveals yet more of Pacassi's monotonous plasterwork. Plečnik's deliberately priapic granite **monolith** is, in fact, a stunted and unfinished obelisk, originally designed to complement the granite bowl in the Jižní zahrady (South Gardens). Close by is a replica fourteenth-century **bronze statue** and fountain, executed by a couple of Transylvanian Saxon sculptors, and depicting a rather diminutive St George astride a disturbingly large horse (actually two hundred years younger than the rest of the ensemble), slaying an extremely puny dragon – the original is in Old Royal Palace (see opposite).

The other reason for hanging about in the third courtyard is to clock Parler's **Zlatá brána** (Golden Gate), decorated with a remarkable fourteenth-century mosaic of the Last Judgement, which has been restored to something like its original, rich colouring – it remains to be seen how it fares in Prague's polluted atmosphere. For the moment, you can clearly see the angels helping the dead out of their tombs, and the devils dragging off the wicked by a golden rope towards the red flames of Hell. On the opposite side of the courtyard is Plečnik's **Bull Staircase**, which leads down to the Jižní zahrady or South Gardens (see p.55).

Starý královský palác (Old Royal Palace)

The **Starý královský palác** (Old Royal Palace), on the east side of the third courtyard, was home to the princes and kings of Bohemia from the eleventh to the sixteenth century. It's a sandwich of royal apartments, built one on top of the other by successive generations, but left largely unfurnished and unused for the past three hundred years. The original Romanesque palace of Soběslav I now forms the cellars of the present building, above which Charles IV built his own Gothic chambers; these days you enter at the third and top floor, built at the end of the fifteenth century.

Immediately past the antechamber is the bare expanse of the massive **Vladislavský sál** (Vladislav Hall), the work of Benedikt Ried, the German mason appointed by Vladislav Jagiello as his court architect. It displays some remarkable, sweeping rib-vaulting which forms floral patterns on the ceiling, the petals reaching almost to the floor. It was here that the early Bohemian kings were elected, and since 1918 every president from Masaryk onwards has been sworn into office in the hall. In medieval times, the hall was also used for banquets and jousting tournaments, which explains the ramp-like **Riders' Staircase** in the north wing (now the exit). At the far end of the hall, to the right, there's an outdoor **viewing platform**, from which you can enjoy a magnificent view of Prague (at its best in the late afternoon). You can also look down onto the chapel of **Všech svatých**, which Parler added to Charles IV's palace, but which had to be rebuilt after the 1541 fire, and has since been Baroquified. Its only point of interest is the remains of the Czech saint, Prokop (Procopius), which are contained within an eighteenth-century wooden tomb along the north wall.

In the southwest corner of the hall, you can gain access to the **Bohemian Chancellery** (Česká kancelář), scene of Prague's **second defenestration** (see box below). There's some controversy about the exact window from which the victims were ejected, although it's agreed that they survived to tell the tale, landing in a medieval dung heap below, and – so the story goes – precipitating the Thirty Years' War. On the other side of the Vladislavský sál, to the right of the Riders' Staircase, a door leads into the vaulted room of the **Diet**, whose (purely decorative) ribs imitate those of the Vladislavský sál. The room is laid out as if for a seventeenth-century session of the Diet: the king on his throne, the archbishop to his right, the judiciary to his left, the nobility facing him, and representatives from towns across Bohemia (with just one collective vote) confined to the gallery by the window. A staircase to the left of the Riders' Staircase takes you up to the sparsely

The second defenestration

After almost two centuries of uneasy coexistence between Catholics and Protestants, matters came to a head over the succession to the throne of the Habsburg archduke Ferdinand, a notoriously intolerant Catholic. On **May 23, 1618**, a posse of more than one hundred Protestant nobles, led by Count Thurn, marched to the chancellery for a showdown with **Jaroslav Bořita z Martinic** and **Vilém Slavata**, the two Catholic governors appointed by Ferdinand I. After a "stormy discussion", the two councillors (and their personal secretary, Filip Fabricius) were thrown out of the window. As a contemporary historian recounted: "No mercy was granted them and they were both thrown dressed in their cloaks with their rapiers and decoration head first out of the western window into a moat beneath the palace. They loudly screamed ach, ach, oweh! and attempted to hold onto the narrow window-ledge, but Thurn beat their knuckles with the hilt of his sword until they were both obliged to let go."

furnished rooms of the New Land Rolls, whose walls are tattooed with coats of arms. There's a forty-minute film on the history of the castle by the Riders' Staircase.

The Story of Prague Castle

A state-of-the-art, if slightly overlong, exhibition is housed in the palace's subterranean Gothic and Romanesque chambers, called **The Story of Prague Castle** (Příběh Pražského hradu). On display are one or two exceptional works of art, like the Vyšehrad Codex, an illuminated manuscript made for the coronation of Vratislav II, first king of Bohemia, in 1086. There are also several historically charged items, such as the chain mail and helmet which may have belonged to sv Václav. Also featured are the grave robes of several Přemyslids and the very impressive grave jewels of the Habsburgs. Don't miss the Communist dinner service from the 1970s, which rivals the Habsburgs for gilded kitsch, nor the small room containing replicas of the Bohemian crown jewels.

The Basilica of sv Jiří

Don't be fooled by the russet-red Baroque facade of the **Basilica of sv Jiří** (St George; daily 9am–5pm; 100Kč) which dominates Jiřské náměstí; inside is Prague's most beautiful Romanesque building, meticulously scrubbed clean and restored to re-create something like the honey-coloured stone basilica that replaced the original tenth-century church in 1173. The double staircase to the chancel is a remarkably harmonious late Baroque addition and now provides a perfect stage for chamber music concerts. The choir vault contains a rare early thirteenth-century painting of the New Jerusalem from Revelation – not to be confused with the very patchy sixteenth-century painting on the apse – while to the right of the chancel, only partially visible, are sixteenth-century frescoes of the **burial chapel of sv Ludmila**, grandmother of St Wenceslas, who was murdered by her own daughter-in-law in 921 (see box, p.49), thus becoming Bohemia's first Christian martyr and saint. There's a replica of the recumbent Ludmila, which you can inspect at close quarters, in the south aisle. Also worth a quick peek is the Romanesque crypt, situated beneath the choir, which contains a macabre sixteenth-century green wax statue of Vanity, whose shrouded, skeletal body is crawling with snakes and lizards.

Jiřský klášter – Czech nineteenth-century art

Bohemia's first monastery, the **Jiřský klášter** (St George's Convent; daily 10am–6pm; 150Kč; Ⓦwww.ngprague.cz) is next door to the Basilica of sv Jiří. Founded in 973 by Mlada, sister of the Přemyslid prince Boleslav the Pious, who became its first abbess, it was closed down and turned into a barracks by Joseph II in 1782, and now houses the Národní galerie's **Czech nineteenth-century art collection**. It's a strange choice for such a prime location as the majority of stuff displayed here is pretty unexceptional, though it's always blissfully peaceful and crowd-free compared with the rest of the castle. Before heading upstairs, you can visit the chapel off the cloisters containing Mlada's sepulchre, set into the wall behind a seventeenth-century gilded grille.

The collection kicks off on the first floor with Antonín Machek's eye-catching series of 32 naive scenes depicting Bohemian rulers from Krok to Ferdinand IV. There are numerous works by members of the influential **Mánes family**. Antonín Mánes succeeded in getting the Czech countryside to look like Italy, and thus gave birth to Romantic Czech landscape painting. Three of his offspring took up the brush: Quido specialized in idealized peasant genre pictures; Amálie obeyed her father's wishes and restricted herself to a little gentle landscape painting; Josef was the most successful of the trio, much in demand as a portrait artist, and one of the leading exponents of patriotically uplifting depictions of national events (he himself took part in the 1848 disturbances in Prague).

Whatever you do, make sure you check out the eye-catching paintings of Yugoslavia by **Jaroslav Čermák**, a man who lived life to the full, was decorated for his bravery by the Montenegrin prince Nicholas I and died of a heart attack at the age of just 48. František Ženíšek's depiction of the Přemyslid prince Oldřich eyeing up his future peasant princess, Božena, is typical of the sort of dramatic patriotic painting that proved very popular with the late nineteenth-century Czech audience. Prize for most striking portrait, however, goes to Václav Brožík's *Lady with a Greyhound*, possibly a portrayal of his wife, the daughter of a wealthy Parisian art dealer.

Mikuláš Aleš, whose sgraffito designs can be seen on many of the city's nineteenth-century buildings, is under represented, though you can admire his wonderfully decorative depiction of the historical meeting between George of Poděbrady and Matthias Corvinus. Close by are the four saints that appear on the city's Wenceslas Monument by **Josef Václav Myslbek**, the father of Czech sculpture. Beyond hang several misty, moody streetscapes by **Jakub Schikaneder** (one of whose ancestors was Mozart's librettist).

Zlatá ulička (Golden Lane)

Around the corner from the convent is the **Zlatá ulička** (Golden Lane), a seemingly blind alley of miniature cottages in dolly-mixture colours, built in the sixteenth century for the 24 members of Rudolf II's castle guard. The contrast in scale with the rest of the Hrad makes this by far the most popular sight in the entire complex, and during the day, at least, the whole street is mobbed, so if you want to try and recapture some of the original atmosphere, you really need to get here early. The lane takes its name from the goldsmiths who followed (and modified the buildings) a century later. By the nineteenth century, it had become a kind of palace slum, attracting artists and craftsmen, its two most famous inhabitants being Jaroslav Seifert, the Czech Nobel prize-winning poet, and Franz Kafka. Kafka's youngest sister, Ottla, rented no. 22, and during the winter of 1916 he came here in the evenings to write short stories. Finally, in 1951, the Communists kicked out the remaining residents and turned most of the houses into souvenir shops for tourists.

At no. 24, you can climb a flight of stairs to the **Obranná chodba** (defence corridor), which is lined with wooden shields, suits of armour and period costumes. The **Bílá věž** (White Tower), at the western end of the corridor, was the city's main prison from Rudolf's reign onwards – there's a reconstructed torture chamber to underline the fact. Edward Kelley, the English alchemist, was locked up here by Rudolf for failing to turn base metal into gold, while the emperor's treasurer hanged himself by his gold cord on the treasury keys, after being accused of embezzlement.

In the opposite direction, the corridor leads to a shooting range, where for a small fee you can have a few shots with a crossbow. The tower that lies beyond is the **Daliborka**, a miserable place of imprisonment, now filled with various torture instruments. The tower is named for its first prisoner, the young Czech noble, Dalibor z Kozojed, accused of supporting a peasants' revolt at the beginning of the fifteenth century. According to Prague legend, he learnt to play the violin while imprisoned here, and his playing could be heard all over the castle until his execution in 1498 – a tale that provided material for Smetana's opera *Dalibor*.

Prašná věž (Powder Tower)

The **Prašná věž** (Powder Tower) or Mihulka, on Vikářská, the street which runs along the north side of the cathedral, once served as the workshop of gunsmith and bell-founder Tomáš Jaroš. The tower's original name comes from the lamprey (*mihule*), an eel-like fish supposedly bred here for royal consumption, though it's actually more noteworthy as the place where Rudolf's team of alchemists (including Kelly) were put to work trying to discover the secret of the philosopher's stone (see box below). The tower now houses an exhibition on the **Hradní stráž** (Castle Guard), which was established in 1918. Due the vicissitudes of Czech history, the guards' uniforms have changed numerous times since they first went on duty in the disparate uniforms of the Czechoslovak Legion in 1918.

Muzeum hraček (Toy Museum)

The former Purkrabství (Burgrave's House), on Jiřská, now houses a toy museum or **Muzeum hraček** (daily 9.30am–5.30pm; 100Kč; ⓦ www.muzeumhracek.cz), the private toy collection of Ivan Steiger. The succession of glass cabinets contains everything from toy cars and motorbikes to tin robots and even Barbie dolls, but there are only a few buttons for younger kids to press, so unless you have a specialist interest in toys, you could happily skip the whole enterprise.

Rudolf II – alchemy, astrology and art

In 1583 **Emperor Rudolf II** (1576–1612) switched the imperial court from Vienna to Prague. This was to be the first and last occasion in which Prague would hold centre-stage in the Habsburg Empire, and as such is seen as something of a second golden age for the city (the first being under Emperor Charles IV; see p.85). Bad-tempered, paranoid and probably insane, Rudolf had little interest in the affairs of state – instead, he holed up in the Hrad and indulged his own personal passions of alchemy, astrology and art. Thus, Rudolfine Prague played host to an impressive array of international artists, including the idiosyncratic **Giuseppe Arcimboldo**, whose surrealist portrait heads were composed entirely of objects. The astronomers **Johannes Kepler** and **Tycho Brahe** were summoned to Rudolf's court to chart the planetary movements and assuage Rudolf's superstitions, and the English alchemists **Edward Kelley** and **John Dee** were employed in order to discover the secret of the philosopher's stone, the mythical substance that would transmute base metal into gold.

Accompanied by his **pet African lion**, Otakar, Rudolf spent less and less time in public, hiding out in the Hrad, where he "loved to paint, weave and dabble in inlaying and watchmaking", according to modern novelist Angelo Maria Ripellino. With the Turks rapidly approaching the gates of Vienna, Rudolf spent his days amassing exotic curios for his strange and vast **Kunst- und Wunderkammer**, which contained such items as "two nails from Noah's Ark…a lump of clay out of which God formed Adam…and large mandrake roots in the shape of little men reclining on soft velvet cushions in small cases resembling doll beds". He refused to marry, though he sired numerous bastards, since he had been warned in a horoscope that a legitimate heir would rob him of the throne. He was also especially wary of the numerous religious orders which inhabited Prague at the time, having been warned in another horoscope that he would be killed by a monk. In the end, he was relieved of his throne by his younger brother, **Matthias**, in 1611, and died the following year, the day after the death of his beloved pet lion.

Rožmberský palác (Rosenberg Palace)

For the first time in its history, the **Rožmberský palác** on Jiřská, is now open to the public, having been in the hands of the Ministry of the Interior since 1918. It was built by the powerful Rožmberk family in the sixteenth century. Rudolf II gained possession in 1600, in exchange for what is now the Schwarzenberský palác on Hradčanské náměstí (see p.58). The Rožmberský sál (Rosenberg Hall), with its wonderful *trompe l'oeil* frescoes, survives from those days, but the rest of the rooms have been decked out with period furniture to evoke a later period, from 1753, when the palace became the Institute of Noblewomen (Ústav šlechtičen), a sort of retirement home for aristocratic ladies. There's a very nice café on the ground floor, with tables in the courtyard.

Lobkovický palác (Lobkowicz Palace)

The **Lobkovický palác** (daily 10.30am–6pm; 275Kč; ⓦ www.lobkowiczevents .cz), on Jiřská, was appropriated from the aristocratic family in 1939 and again in 1948 and has only recently been handed back. It now displays an impressive selection of the Lobkowicz family's prize possessions (with audioguide accompaniment by US-born William Lobkowicz himself), including an armoury and a vast art collection. Among them are a portrait of the 4-year old Infanta Margarita Teresa (possibly by Velázquez), niece and first wife of Emperor Leopold I. The family has a long history of musical patronage (most notably Beethoven, who dedicated two of his symphonies to the seventh prince), and the original working manuscripts by Mozart and Beethoven on show are pretty impressive. Other highlights include Pieter Brueghel the Elder's sublime *Haymaking* from the artist's famous cycle of seasons, and two views of London by Canaletto. There's a decent **café** in the courtyard and **concerts** of classical music are held daily at 1pm in the palace's Baroque concert hall (tickets are available from the desk near the palace café).

The Castle Gardens

The Hrad boasts some of the city's loveliest **gardens** (daily: April & Oct 10am–6pm; May & Sept 10am–7pm; June & July 10am–9pm; Aug 10am–8pm), particularly in terms of views. The Jižní zahrady (South Gardens) enjoy wonderful vistas over the city and link up the terraced gardens of Malá Strana (see p.71), while the Královská zahrada (Royal Gardens) allow a better view of the cathedral and the Vltava's many bridges.

Jižní zahrady (South Gardens)

For recuperation and a superlative view over the rest of Prague – not to mention a chance to inspect some of Plečnik's quirky additions to the castle – head for the **Jižní zahrady**, accessible via Plečnik's copper-canopied Bull Staircase on the south side of the third courtyard. Originally laid out in the sixteenth century, but thoroughly remodelled in the 1920s by Josip Plečnik, the first garden you come to from the Bull Staircase, the **Zahrada na valech** (Garden on the Ramparts), features an observation terrace and colonnaded pavilion, below which is an earlier eighteenth-century **Hudební pavilón** (Music Pavilion). Two sandstone obelisks under the windows of the Old Royal Palace record the arrival of Slavata and Martinic following their defenestration (see box opposite). In the opposite direction, beyond the Baroque fountain lies the smaller **Rajská zahrada** (Paradise Garden), on whose lawn Plečnik plonked an ornamental forty-ton granite basin suspended on two small blocks. From here, a quick slog up the monumental staircase will bring you out onto Hradčanské náměstí.

Královská zahrada (Royal Gardens)

Before exploring the rest of Hradčany, it's worth taking a stroll through the north gate of the second courtyard and across the **Prašný most** (Powder Bridge), erected in the sixteenth century to connect the newly established royal gardens with the Hrad (the original wooden structure has long since been replaced). Below lies the steep wooded **Jelení příkop** (Stag Ditch), once used by the Habsburgs for growing figs and lemons, and storing game for the royal hunts, but now accessible to the public. Above the ditch, the castle's falconers stage regular **falconry displays** (May–Oct daily 10am–6pm).

Beyond the bridge is the entrance to the most verdant of all the castle's gardens, the **Královská zahrada**, founded by Emperor Ferdinand I in the 1530s on the site of a former vineyard. Burned down by the Saxons and Swedes during the Thirty Years' War, and blown up by the Prussians, the gardens were only saved from French attack in 1741 by the payment of thirty pineapples. Today, these are some of the best-kept gardens in the capital, with fully functioning fountains and immaculately cropped lawns. Consequently, it's a very popular spot, though more a place for admiring the azaleas and almond trees than lounging around on the grass. It was here that tulips brought from Turkey were first acclimatized to Europe, before being exported to the Netherlands, and every spring there's an impressive, disciplined crop.

At the main entrance to the gardens is the **Lví dvůr** (Lion's Court), now a restaurant but originally built by Rudolf II to house his private zoo, which included leopards, lynxes, bears, wolves and lions, all of whom lived in heated cages to protect them from the Prague winter. Rudolf was also responsible for the Renaissance ball-game court, known as the **Míčovna** (occasionally open to the public for concerts and exhibitions), built into the south terrace and tattooed with sgraffito by his court architect Bonifaz Wolmut. If you look carefully at the top row of allegorical figures on either side of the sandstone half-columns, you can see that the figure of Industry, between Justice (Justicia) and Loyalty (Fides), is holding a hammer and sickle and a copy of the Five-Year Plan, thoughtfully added by Communist restorers in the 1950s. Incidentally, the guarded ochre building to the right of the Míčovna, the **Zahradní dům**, was built as a summer-house by Kilian Ignaz Dientzenhofer only to be destroyed during the Prussian bombardment of 1757. It was later restored by Pavel Janák, who added the building's two modern wings on a postwar whim of the ill-fated President Beneš; it now serves as a presidential hideaway.

The Belvéder

At the end of the Royal Gardens is Prague's most celebrated Renaissance legacy, **Letohrádek královny Anny** (Queen Anne's Summer Palace), popularly known as the **Belvéder** (Tues–Sun 10am–6pm), a delicately arcaded summerhouse topped by an inverted copper ship's hull, built by Ferdinand I for his wife, Anne – though she didn't live long enough to see it completed. It was designed by the Genoese architect Paolo della Stella, one of a number of Italian masons who settled in Prague in the sixteenth century, and is decorated with a series of lovely figural reliefs depicting scenes from mythology. The Belvéder is mainly used for exhibitions by contemporary artists and, unlike the gardens, is open for most of the year, depending on what exhibitions are on; if the gardens are closed you'll have to head down Mariánské hradby to reach the Belvéder. At the centre of the palace's

Art Nouveau Prague

The emergence of Art Nouveau in the late 1890s, with its
curvaceous sculptural decoration and floral motifs, had an
enormous impact on the art and architecture of Prague.
Although the movement originated in Paris, Czech artists
and designers drew their primary inspiration from the more
restrained, rectilinear Secession style of the Viennese
school. Thanks to the lack of war damage and postwar
redevelopment, Prague has retained an impressive variety of

Obecní dům ▲
Hlahol on Masarykovo nábřeží ▼

The Czech Secession

Many of the Czech artists and designers of the period studied in the imperial capital of Vienna, where Art Nouveau was dominated by the **Secession movement** – a group of young artists who wanted to leave behind the current vogue of simply rehashing the styles of the past from Classicism to the Baroque. The Czechs, too, wanted to break with the official imperial style, and took their term for Art Nouveau – *secesní* – from the Viennese. The Czech national revival movement – *národní obrození* – embraced the new style with enthusiasm, culminating in the completion of the Czech cultural centre of the **Obecní dům** in 1912, an Art Nouveau paean to the Czech nation inside and out.

In 1915, the city's other great Art Nouveau monument was unveiled, the gargantuan sculpture of the Czech religious reformer, Jan Hus, that dominates Old Town Square. By this point, Art Nouveau was no longer cutting-edge, but it persisted as a popular style in the newly founded Czechoslovakia, partly thanks to artists like Alfons Mucha, who helped design the new republic's stamps, banknotes and posters. By the end of the decade, the style had been usurped by the modernist movement, which more radically articulated the interwar republic's break with its imperialist past.

Alfons Mucha

The artist **Alfons Mucha** (1860–1939) is the best-known Czech exponent of Art Nouveau, partly as he achieved fame and fortune abroad. Mucha moved to Paris in 1887 and shot to fame with the posters he produced for the actress Sarah Bernhardt in 1894 in a sumptuous style that came to epitomize the Belle Époque

– although Mucha himself came to despise his commercial period. He was one of the many artists involved in the decoration of the Obecní dům, designing the lavish Primátorský sál. When Czechoslovakia achieved independence in 1918, Mucha threw himself into designing state publications, banknotes and stamps, examples of which can be seen in the Postal Museum (see p.122). Mucha also created two strikingly colourful windows for St Vitus Cathedral (see p.46), though the largest selection of his works is in the Mucha Museum (see p.118).

František Bílek

A religious visionary in the William Blake mould, **František Bílek** (1872–1941) was one of the most original Czech Art Nouveau artists. Bílek never achieved the commercial success or fame of Mucha, partly because he spent much of his life in relative isolation in his home town of Chýnov, in southern Bohemia. Having been diagnosed with colour-blindness, Bílek concentrated on sculpture and drawing, rather than painting, developing a style that tapped into the symbolism and melodrama of Art Nouveau, which was perfectly suited to the anguished biblical themes he often chose. His most complete work is the Bílkova vila (see p.57), the studio-house he designed and built for himself in 1911. The studio is filled with Bílek's works, in wood, bronze and stone, and even some of the furniture Bílek designed and carved. One of his finest works is his relief of *Christ Crucified* in St Vitus Cathedral (see p.46), wrought in his preferred medium of wood, which was for him a symbol of life, with its roots in the earth and its crown reaching to the heavens.

▲ Grand Hotel Evropa

▼ Bílek's Christ Crucified

Praha hlavní nádraží ▲

Primátorský sál in Obecní dům ▼

Top ten: Art Nouveau

▶▶ **Obecní dům** Just about every leading Czech artist of the time worked on the Obecní dům. The ornate wrought-iron entrance canopy, the mosaic in the arched gable and the gilded copper dome above, give a foretaste of the kind of ornamental detail that lies within, including a sumptuously decorated café and restaurant, and the Smetanova síň concert hall. **See p.119**

▶▶ **Jan Hus Monument** 1915 monument to Jan Hus – the centrepiece of Staroměstské náměstí. **See p.90**

▶▶ **Grand Hotel Evropa** Once Wenceslas Square's finest café, the *Evropa* retains its original 1905 decor. **See p.115**

▶▶ **Praha hlavní nádraží** Fight your way through the subterranean modern station section and head upstairs to admire the fading splendour of Josef Fanta's glorious 1909 creation. **See p.117**

▶▶ **Pojišťovna Praha** If only all insurance company offices were this beautiful, with five lozenge-shaped windows forming the word PRAHA, surrounded by floral mosaics. Designed by Osvald Polívka, as was neighbouring Topičův dům. **See p.124**

▶▶ **U Nováků** Former department store featuring exquisitely delicate ironwork and a mosaic facade by Jan Preisler. **See p.125**

▶▶ **Josefov** The old Jewish ghetto was demolished in the 1890s and replaced with luxurious five-storey blocks, giving Josefov the highest density of Art Nouveau buildings in the city. **See p.99**

▶▶ **Masarykovo nábřeží** From the most Legií, with its curlicue lampposts, the embankment of Masarykovo nábřeží is a non-stop parade of neo-Gothic and Art Nouveau mansions, with Hlahol (at no. 16) the best of the lot. **See p.129**

▶▶ **Palacký Monument** Less well known than the Jan Hus Monument but even more striking. **See p.130**

▶▶ **Průmyslový palác** A flamboyant steel and glass exhibition hall built for the 1891 Prague Exhibition, centrepiece of the trade-fair grounds. **See p.151** miniature formal garden is the **Zpívající fontána** (Singing Fountain), built shortly after the palace and named for the musical sound the drops of water used to make when falling in the metal bowls below. From the garden terrace, you also have an unrivalled view of the castle's finest treasure – the cathedral.

Chotkovy sady

Adjacent to the Belvedér is the **Chotkovy sady**, Prague's first public park, founded in 1833 by the ecologically minded city governor, Count Chotek. The atmosphere here is a lot more relaxed than in the nearby Královská zahrada, and you can happily stretch out on the grass and soak up the sun, or head for the south wall, which enjoys an unrivalled view of the bridges and islands of the Vltava. At the centre of the park there's a bizarre, melodramatic grotto-like memorial to the Romantic poet **Julius Zeyer** (1841–1901), an elaborate monument from which life-sized characters from Zeyer's works, carved in white marble, emerge from the blackened rocks amid much drapery.

Bílkova vila

Hidden behind its overgrown garden at Mieckiewiczova 1, the **Bílkova vila** (Sat & Sun 10am–5pm; 50Kč; ⓦ www.ghmp.cz) honours one of the most original of all Czech sculptors, **František Bílek** (1872–1941). Born in a part of South Bohemia steeped in the Hussite tradition, Bílek lived a monkish life, spending years in spiritual contemplation, reading the works of Hus and other Czech reformers. The Bílkova vila was built in 1911 to the artist's own design, intended as both a "cathedral of art" and the family home. At first sight, it appears a strangely mute red-brick building, out of keeping with the extravagant Symbolist style of Bílek's sculptures. It's meant to symbolize a cornfield, with the front porch supported by giant sheaves of corn; only a sculptural group, depicting the fleeing Comenius and his followers, in the garden, gives a clue as to what lies within.

Inside, the brickwork gives way to bare stone walls lined with Bílek's religious sculptures, giving the impression that you've walked into a chapel rather than an artist's studio: "a workshop and temple", in Bílek's own words. In addition to his sculptural and relief work in wood and stone, often wildly expressive and spiritually tortured, there are also ceramics, graphics and a few mementoes of Bílek's life. His work is little known outside his native country, but his contemporary admirers included Franz Kafka, Julius Zeyer and Otakar Březina, whose poems and novels provided the inspiration for much of Bílek's art. Bílek's living quarters have also been restored and opened to the public, with much of the original wooden furniture, designed and carved by Bílek himself, still in place. Check out the dressing table for his wife, shaped like some giant church lectern, and the wardrobe decorated with a border of hearts, a penis, a nose, an ear, an eye plus the sun, stars and moon.

The rest of Hradčany

The monumental scale and appearance of the rest of Hradčany, outside the castle, is a direct result of the **great fire of 1541**, which swept up from Malá Strana and wiped out most of the old dwelling places belonging to the serfs, tradesmen, clergy and masons who had settled here in the Middle Ages. With the Turks at the gates of Vienna, the Habsburg nobility were more inclined to pursue their major building projects in Prague instead, and, following the Battle of Bílá hora in 1620, the palaces of the exiled (or executed) Protestant nobility were up for grabs too. The newly ensconced Catholic aristocrats were keen to spend some of their expropriated wealth, and over the next two centuries they turned Hradčany into a grand architectural showpiece. As the Turkish threat subsided, the political focus of the empire gradually shifted back to Vienna and the building spree stopped. For the last two hundred years, Hradčany has been frozen in time, and, two world wars on, its buildings have survived better than those of any other central European capital.

Hradčanské náměstí

Hradčanské náměstí fans out from the castle gates, surrounded by the oversized palaces of the old Catholic nobility. For the most part it's a tranquil space that's overlooked by the tour groups marching through, intent on the Hrad. The one spot everyone heads for is the ramparts in the southeastern corner, by the top of the Zámecké schody, which allow an unrivalled view over the red rooftops of Malá Strana, past the famous green dome and tower of the church of sv Mikuláš and beyond, to the Charles Bridge and the spires of Staré Město. Few people make use of the square's central green patch, which is heralded by a giant green wrought-iron lamppost decked with eight separate lamps from the 1860s, and, behind it, a Baroque plague column, with saintly statues by Ferdinand Maximilian Brokof.

Until the great fire of 1541, the square was the hub of Hradčany, lined with medieval shops and stalls but with no real market as such. After the fire, the developers moved in; the showiest palace on the square is the **Schwarzenberský palác** (see below). At no. 1 was another Schwarzenberg pile, the **Salmovský palác**, which served as the Swedish embassy until the 1970s when the dissident writer Pavel Kohout took refuge there. Frustrated in their attempts to force him out, the Communists closed the embassy down and it's now a hotel. Beside the Salmovský palác stands a statue of the country's founder, **T.G. Masaryk**, unveiled in 2000. On the opposite side of the square, just outside the castle gates, stands the sumptuous vanilla-coloured **Arcibiskupský palác** (Archbishop's Palace), seat of the archbishop of Prague since the beginning of the Roman Catholic church's suzerainty over the Czechs, following the Battle of Bílá hora. The Rococo exterior only hints at the even more extravagant furnishings inside, though the interior is open to the public only on Maundy Thursday (the Thursday before Easter).

Schwarzenberský palác – Czech Baroque art

The powerful Lobkowicz family replaced seven houses on the south side of the square with the over-the-top sgraffitoed pile at no. 2, known as the **Schwarzenberský palác** after its last aristocratic owners. For a brief period, it belonged to the Rožmberk family, whose last in line, Petr Vok, held the infamous banquet that proved fatal to the Danish astronomer Tycho Brahe. So as not to offend his host, Tycho refrained from leaving the table before Vok, only to burst his bladder, after which he staggered off to his house in Nový Svět, where he died five days later. The palace now houses the Národní galerie's **Czech Baroque art collection** (Tues–Sun 10am–6pm; 150Kč; ⓦwww.ngprague.cz), a vast collection of only limited interest to the non-specialist. Chronologically, the collection begins on the second floor, where you can get a brief glimpse of the overtly sensual and erotic taste of Rudolf II, who enjoyed works such as Hans von Aachen's sexually charged *Suicide of Lucretia* and Josef Heintz's riotous orgy in his *Last Judgement*. The paltry remains of Rudolf's *Kunstkammer* are pretty disappointing, but the adjacent room contains some superb woodcuts by Dürer, Holbein and Altdorfer, among othewr including some wonderfully imaginative depictions of Satan and the Whore of Babylon. The rest of the gallery, which is spread over three floors, is given over to the likes of Karel Škréta and Petr Brandl, whose paintings and sculptures spearheaded the Counter-Reformation and fill chapels and churches across the Czech Lands. Perhaps the most compelling reason to wade through the gallery is to admire the vigorous, gesticulating sculptures of Matthias Bernhard Braun and Ferdinand Maximilian Brokof.

Šternberský palác – European art from the Classical to the Baroque

A passage down the side of the archbishop's palace from Hradčanské náměstí leads to the early eighteenth-century **Šternberský palác** (Tues–Sun 10am–6pm; 150Kč; Ⓦ www.ngprague.cz), which houses the Národní galerie's vast **European art collection**, mostly ranging from the fourteenth to the eighteenth century, but excluding works by Czech artists of the period (which you'll find in the Schwarzenberský palác, see opposite, and in the Anežský klášter, see p.94). The gallery's handful of masterpieces makes a visit here worthwhile, and there's an elegant café in the courtyard. To see the Národní galerie's more impressive nineteenth- and twentieth-century European art collection, you need to pay a visit to the Veletržní palác (see p.148).

The collection begins on the **first floor** with Tuscan religious art, most notably a series of exquisite miniature triptychs by Bernardo Daddi, plus several striking triangular-framed portraits of holy figures by Pietro Lorenzetti, including a very fine *St Anthony the Abbot*, with long curly hair and beard. Before you move on, take a detour to the side room 11, which contains Orthodox icons from Venice, the Balkans and Russia. Moving swiftly into the gallery's large Flemish collection, it's worth checking out Dieric Bouts's *Lamentation*, a complex composition crowded with figures in medieval garb. Other works worth picking out are Caroto's effeminate *St John the Evangelist on Patmos*, in room 10, lazily dreaming of the apocalypse, and the two richly coloured Bronzino portraits in room 12. One of the most eye-catching works is Jan Gossaert's *St Luke Drawing the Virgin*, in room 13, an exercise in architectural geometry and perspective which used to hang in the cathedral.

The **second floor** is huge and best taken at a canter. Outstanding works here include Tintoretto's *St Jerome* (room 17), a searching portrait of old age; a wonderfully rugged portrait of a Spanish guerilla leader from the Peninsular War by Goya (room 22); and a mesmerizing *Praying Christ* by El Greco (room 23). Be sure, too, to have a look at the Čínský kabinet (room 35), a small oval chamber smothered in gaudy Baroque chinoiserie, and one of the palace's few surviving slices of original decor. Elsewhere, there are a series of canvases by the Brueghel family (room 26), Rembrandt's *Scholar in his Study* (room 29) and Rubens' colossal *Murder of St Thomas* (room 30), with its pink-buttocked cherubs hovering over the bloody scene. Nearby, in the vast (and uneven) Dutch section, there's a wonderful portrait of an arrogant "young gun" named Jasper by Frans Hals (room 31).

The **ground floor** galleries contain one of the most prized paintings in the whole collection: the *Feast of the Rosary* by Albrecht Dürer, in room 1, depicting, among others, the Virgin Mary, the Pope, the Holy Roman Emperor, and even a self-portrait of Dürer himself (top right). This was one of Rudolf II's most prized acquisitions (he was an avid Dürer fan), and was transported on foot across the Alps to Prague (he didn't trust wheeled transport with such a precious object). Also in this room are several superb canvases by Lucas Cranach the Elder. The only other ground floor room worth bothering with is room 3, harbouring Hans Raphons's multi-panelled *Passion Altar* – look out for *Christ in Purgatory* featuring some wicked devils, especially the green she-devil with cudgel.

Martinický palác – Museum of Mechanical Musical Instruments

Compared to the other palaces on the square, the **Martinický palác** (daily 10am–6pm; 150Kč; Ⓦwww.martinickypalac.cz), at no. 8, is a fairly modest pile, built in 1620 by one of the councillors who survived the second defenestration (see box, p.51). Its rich sgraffito decoration, which continues in the inner courtyard, was only discovered during restoration work in the 1970s. On the facade, you can easily make out Potiphar's wife making a grab at a naked and unwilling Joseph. Guided tours of the interior are available, which along with a series of fine Renaissance ceilings, holds the **Museum of Mechanical Musical Instruments** (Muzeum hudebních strojů). It's an impressive collection ranging from café orchestrions and fairground barrel organs to early wax phonographs and portable gramophones. Best of all, though, is the fact that almost every exhibit is in working order – as the curators will demonstrate. The museum has a particularly fine array of music boxes, as well as several much rarer polyphones such as manopans, aristons and mignons, not to mention an original Edison Dictaphone from 1877.

Nový Svět

Nestling in a shallow dip in the northwest corner of Hradčany, **Nový Svět** (meaning "New World", though nothing to do with Dvořák) provides a glimpse of life on a totally different scale from Hradčanské náměstí. Similar in many ways to the Golden Lane in the Hrad, this cluster of brightly coloured cottages, which curls around the corner into Černínská, is all that's left of Hradčany's medieval slums, painted up and sanitized in the eighteenth and nineteenth centuries. Despite having all the same ingredients for mass tourist appeal as Golden Lane, it remains remarkably undisturbed, save for a few swish wine bars, and **Gambra**, a surrealist art gallery at Černínská 5 (March–Oct Wed–Sun noon–6pm; Nov–Feb Sat & Sun noon–5.30pm; free), which sells original works by, among others, the renowned Czech animator, **Jan Švankmajer**, and his late wife Eva.

Černínský palác

Up the hill from Nový Svět, Loretánské náměstí is dominated by the phenomenal 135-metre-long facade of the **Černínský palác** (not open to the public), decorated with thirty Palladian half-columns and supported by a swathe of diamond-pointed rustication. For all its grandeur – it's the largest palace in Prague, for the sake of which two whole streets were demolished – it's a pretty brutal building, commissioned in the 1660s by Count Humprecht Jan Černín, one-time imperial ambassador to Venice and a man of monumental self-importance. After quarrelling with the master of Italian Baroque, Giovanni Bernini, and disagreeing with Prague's own Carlo Lurago, Count Černín settled on Francesco Caratti as his architect, only to have the finished building panned by critics as a tasteless mass of stone. The grandiose plans, which were nowhere near completion when the count died, nearly bankrupted future generations of Černíns, who were eventually forced to sell the palace in 1851 to the Austrian state, which converted it into military barracks.

Since the First Republic, the palace has housed the **Ministry of Foreign Affairs**, and during the war it was, for a while, the Nazi *Reichsprotektor*'s residence.

On March 10, 1948, it was the scene of Prague's third defenestration. Only a week or so after the Communist coup, **Jan Masaryk**, the only son of the founder of the Republic, and the last non-Communist in Gottwald's cabinet, plunged fifteen metres to his death from the top-floor bathroom window of the palace. Whether it was suicide (he had been suffering from bouts of depression, partly induced by the country's political path) or murder will probably never be satisfactorily resolved, but for most people Masaryk's death cast a dark shadow over the newly established regime.

Loreta

The facade of the **Loreta** (Tues–Sun 9am–12.15pm & 1–4.30pm; 110Kč; ⓦwww.loreta.cz), an elaborate Baroque pilgrimage complex immediately opposite the Černínský palác on Loretánské náměstí, was built by the Dientzen-hofers, a Bavarian family of architects, in the early part of the eighteenth century, and is the perfect antidote to Caratti's humourless monster. It's all hot flourishes and twirls, topped by a tower which lights up like a Chinese lantern at night, and by day clanks out the hymn "We Greet Thee a Thousand Times" on its 27 Dutch bells (it also does special performances of other tunes from time to time).

The facade and the cloisters, which were provided a century earlier to shelter pilgrims from the elements, are, in fact, just the outer casing for the focus of the complex, the **Santa Casa**, the oldest part of the Loreta, founded by Kateřina Lobkowicz in 1626 and smothered in a rich mantle of stucco depicting the build-ing's miraculous transportation from the Holy Land. Legend has it that the Santa Casa (Mary's home in Nazareth), under threat from the heathen Turks, was trans-ported by a host of angels to a small village in Dalmatia and from there, via a number of brief stop-offs, to a small laurel grove (*lauretum* in Latin, hence Loreta) in northern Italy. News of the miracle spread across the Catholic lands, prompting a spate of copycat shrines, and during the Counter-Reformation the cult was actively encouraged in an attempt to broaden the popular appeal of Catholicism. The Prague Loreta was one of fifty to be built in the Czech Lands, each of the shrines following an identical design, with pride of place given to a lime-wood statue, the *Black Madonna and Child*, encased in silver.

Behind the Santa Casa, the Dientzenhofers built the much larger **Church of Narození Páně** (Church of the Nativity), which is like a mini version of sv Mikuláš, down in Malá Strana. There's a high cherub count, plenty of gilding and a lovely organ replete with music-making angels and putti. On either side of the main altar are glass cabinets containing the fully clothed and wax-headed standing skeletons of Spanish saints Felicissimus and Marcia and, next to them, paintings of St Apollonia – who had her teeth smashed in during her martyrdom and is now invoked for toothache – and St Agatha, carrying her severed breasts on a dish. As in the church, most of the saints honoured in the **cloisters** are women. Without doubt, the weirdest of the lot is St Wilgefortis (Starosta in Czech), whose statue stands in the final chapel of the cloisters. Daughter of the king of Portugal, she was due to marry the king of Sicily, despite having taken a vow of virginity. God intervened and she grew a beard, whereupon the king of Sicily broke off the marriage and her father had her crucified. Wilgefortis thus became the patron saint of unhappily married women, and is depicted bearded on the cross (and easily mistaken for Christ in drag).

You can get some idea of the Loreta's serious financial backing in the **treasury** (situated on the first floor of the west wing), much ransacked over the years but still stuffed full of gold. The light fittings are a Communist period piece, but most folk come here to gawp at the master exhibit, an outrageous Viennese silver monstrance designed by Fischer von Erlach in 1699, and studded with diamonds taken from the wedding dress of Countess Kolovrat, who made the Loreta sole heir to her fortune.

Strahovský klášter

The arcaded street-cum-square of Pohořelec, west of Loretánské náměstí, leads to the chunky remnants of the zigzag eighteenth-century fortifications that mark the edge of the old city, as defined by Charles IV back in the fourteenth century. On the south side of Pohořelec is the **Strahovský klášter** (Strahov Monastery; ⓦ www.strahovmonastery.cz), founded in 1140 by the Premonstratensian order. Strahov was one of the lucky few to escape Joseph II's 1783 dissolution of the monasteries, a feat it managed by declaring itself a scholarly institution – the monks had, in fact, amassed one of the finest libraries in Bohemia. It continued to function until shortly after the Communists took power, when, along with all other religious establishments, it was closed down and most of its inmates thrown into prison; following the happy events of 1989, the white-robed monks have returned.

The Baroque entrance to the monastery is topped by a statue of **sv Norbert**, twelfth-century founder of the Premonstratensian order of clerical monks, whose relics were brought here in 1627. Just inside the cobbled outer courtyard is a tiny deconsecrated church built by Rudolf II and dedicated to **sv Roch**, protector against plagues, one of which had very nearly rampaged through Prague in 1599; it's now an art gallery. The other church in this peaceful little courtyard is the still functioning twelfth-century monastery church of **Nanebezvetí Panny Marie**, which was given its last remodelling in Baroque times by Anselmo Lurago – it's well worth a peek for its colourful frescoes relating to St Norbert's life.

Leaving the monastery through the narrow doorway in the eastern wall, you enter the gardens and orchards of the **Strahovská zahrada**, from where you can see the whole city in perspective. The gardens form part of a wooded hill known as Petřín, and the path to the right contours round to the Stations of the Cross that lead up to the miniature Eiffel Tower known as the Rozhledna (see p.76). Alternatively, you can catch tram #22 from outside Strahov's main entrance to Malostranská metro or the centre of town.

The monastery libraries and art gallery

The real reason most visitors come to Strahov is to see the monastery's two ornate **libraries** (daily 9am–noon & 1–5pm; 80Kč); the entrance for both is to the right as you enter the outer courtyard. The first library you come to is the later and larger of the two, the **Filosofický sál** (Philosophical Hall), built in some haste in the 1780s, in order to accommodate the books and bookcases from Louka monastery in Moravia that failed to escape Joseph's decree. The walnut bookcases are so tall they touch the library's lofty ceiling, which is busily decorated with frescoes by the Viennese painter Franz Maulbertsch on the theme of the search for truth. Don't, whatever you do, miss the collection of curios exhibited in the glass cabinets outside the library, which features shells, turtles, crabs, lobsters, dried-up sea monsters, butterflies, beetles, plastic fruit and moths. There's even a pair of whales' penises displayed alongside a narwhal horn, several harpoons and a model ship. The other main room is the low-ceilinged **Teologický sál** (Theological Hall), studded with ancient globes, its wedding-cake stucco framing frescoes on a similar theme, executed by one of the monks seventy years earlier. Outside the hall the library's oldest book, the ninth-century gem-studded Strahov Gospel, is displayed. Look out, too, for the cabinet of books documenting Czech trees, each of which has the bark of the tree on its spine.

An archway on the far side of the church contains the ticket office for the monastery's art gallery, the **Strahovská obrazárna** (Tues–Sun 9am–noon & 12.30–5pm; 60Kč), situated above the cloisters and accessible from the door on the right, beyond the ticket office. The gallery's collection of religious art, church plate and reliquaries – a mere fraction of the monastery's total – may not be to everyone's taste, but it does contain the odd gem from Rudolf II's collection, including a portrait of the emperor himself by Hans von Aachen, plus a superb portrait of Rembrandt's elderly mother by Gerrit Dou. Also housed in this section of the monastery are exhibitions put on by the **Památník národního písemnictví** (National Literary Monument; Tues–Sun 9am–noon & 1–5pm; 30Kč; ⓦwww .pamatniknarodnihopisemnictvi.cz), only of interest to those with some Czech, though the book covers on display are often works of art in themselves.

Muzeum miniatur

The monastery also houses the **Muzeum miniatur** (Museum of Miniatures; daily 9am–5pm; 50Kč; ⓦwww.muzeumminiatur.com), in the northeastern corner of the main courtyard. Displayed in this small museum are forty or so works by **Anatoly Konyenko**, a Russian who holds the record for constructing the smallest book in the world, a thirty-page edition of Chekhov's *Chameleon*. Among the other miracles of miniature manufacture are a (real, though dead) flea bearing golden horseshoes, scissors and a key and lock, the Lord's Prayer written on a human hair and a caravan of camels passing through the eye of a needle.

Malá Strana

MALÁ STRANA, Prague's picturesque "Little Quarter", sits below the Castle and is, in many ways, the city's most entrancing area. Its peaceful, often hilly, eighteenth-century backstreets have changed very little since Mozart walked them during his frequent visits to Prague between 1787 and 1791. Despite the quarter's minuscule size – it takes up a mere 600 square metres of land squeezed in between the river and Hradčany – it's easy enough to lose the crowds, many of whom never stray from the well-trodden route that links the Charles Bridge with the castle. Its streets conceal a whole host of quiet terraced gardens, as well as the wooded hill of **Petřín**, which together provide the perfect inner-city escape in the summer months. The **Church of sv Mikuláš**, by far the finest Baroque church in Prague, and the **Museum Kampa**, with its unrivalled collection of works by František Kupka, are the two major sights.

Long before the Přemyslid king Otakar II decided to establish a German community here in 1257, a mixture of Jews, merchants and monks had settled on the slopes below the castle. But, as with Hradčany, it was the fire of 1541 – which devastated the entire left bank of the Vltava – and the expulsion of the Protestants after 1620 that together had the greatest impact on the visual and social make-up of the quarter. In place of the old Gothic town, the newly ascendant Catholic

Mozart in Prague

Mozart made the first of several visits to Prague with his wife Constanze in 1787, staying with his friend and patron Count Thun in what is now the British embassy (Thunovská 14). A year earlier, his opera *The Marriage of Figaro*, which had failed to please the critics in Vienna, had been given a rapturous reception at Prague's Nostitz Theatre (now the Stavovské divadlo; see p.94), and on his arrival in 1787 Mozart was already flavour of the month. As he wrote in his diary: "Here they talk about nothing but *Figaro*. Nothing is played, sung or whistled but *Figaro*. Nothing, nothing but *Figaro*. Certainly a great honour for me!" Encouraged by this, he chose to premiere his next opera, *Don Giovanni*, later that year, in Prague rather than Vienna. He arrived with an incomplete score in hand, and wrote the overture at the Dušeks' Bertramka villa in Smíchov, dedicating it to the "good people of Prague". Apart from a brief sojourn whilst on a concert tour, Mozart's fourth and final visit to Prague took place in 1791, the year of his death. The climax of the stay was the premiere of his final opera, *La Clemenza di Tito*, commissioned for the coronation of Leopold II as king of Bohemia (and completed whilst on the coach from Vienna to Prague). The opera didn't go down quite as well as previous ones – the empress is alleged to have shouted "German hogwash" from her box. Nevertheless, four thousand people turned out for the composer's memorial service, held in Malá Strana's church of sv Mikuláš to the strains of his *Requiem Mass*.

nobility built numerous palaces here, though generally without quite the same destructive glee as up in Hradčany.

In 1918, the majority of these buildings became home to the chief foreign embassies in Czechoslovakia, and after 1948 the rest of the district's real estate was turned into flats to alleviate the postwar housing shortage. The cycle has come full circle again with property in Malá Strana now among the most sought-after in Prague. Yet despite all the changes, the new hotels and the souvenir shops, much of Malá Strana remains relatively undisturbed and, in parts, remarkably tranquil. The island of Kampa, in particular, makes up one of the most peaceful stretches of riverfront in Prague.

Malostranské náměstí

The main focus of Malá Strana has always been the sloping, cobbled **Malostranské náměstí**, which is dominated and divided into two by the church of sv Mikuláš (see p.68). Trams and cars hurtle across it, regularly dodged by a procession of people – some heading up the hill to the Hrad, others pausing for coffee and cakes at the numerous bars and restaurants hidden in the square's arcades and Gothic vaults. The most famous (and the most central) of the cafés was the **Malostranská kavárna**, established in 1874, an occasional haunt of Kafka, Brod, Werfel and friends in the 1920s, and now, inevitably, a *Starbucks*.

On every side, Neoclassical facades line the square, imitating the colour and grandeur of those of Hradčanské and Staroměstské náměstí. The largest Baroque redevelopment, the **Lichtenštejnský palác**, takes up the square's entire west side and is home to the university music faculty, as well as being a concert venue, art gallery and café. Its pleasing frontage hides a history linked to repression: first as the home of Karl von Liechtenstein, the man who pronounced the death sentence on the 27 Protestant leaders in 1621; then as headquarters for the Swedes during the 1648 siege; and later as the base of the Austrian General Windischgrätz, scourge of the 1848 revolution.

▲ Tram on Malostranské náměstí

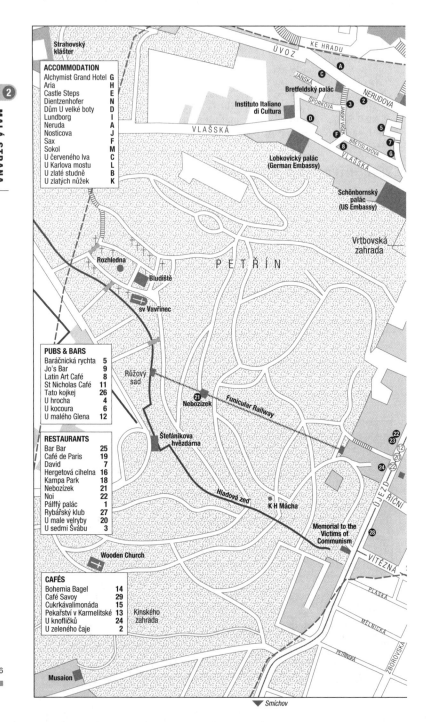

Strahovský
klášter

ACCOMMODATION
Alchymist Grand Hotel	G
Aria	H
Castle Steps	E
Dientzenhofer	N
Dům U velké boty	D
Lundborg	I
Neruda	A
Nosticova	J
Sax	F
Sokol	M
U červeného lva	C
U Karlova mostu	L
U zlaté studně	B
U zlatých nůžek	K

ÚVOZ

KE HRADU

JANSKÁ

Bretfeldský palác

NERUDOVA

ŠPORKOVÁ

Instituto Italiano
di Cultura

VLAŠSKÁ

BŘETISLAVOVA

VLAŠSKÁ

Lobkovický palác
(German Embassy)

Schönbornský
palác
(US Embassy)

Vrtbovská
zahrada

Rozhledna

P E T Ř Í N

Bludiště

sv Vavřinec

PUBS & BARS
Baráčnická rychta	5
Jo's Bar	9
Latin Art Café	8
St Nicholas Café	11
Tato kojkej	26
U hrocha	4
U kocoura	6
U malého Glena	12

Růžový
sád

Nebozízek

Funicular Railway

Štefánikova
hvězdárna

RESTAURANTS
Bar Bar	25
Café de Paris	19
David	7
Hergetová cihelna	16
Kampa Park	18
Nebozízek	21
Noi	22
Pálffý palác	1
Rybářský klub	27
U male velryby	20
U sedmi Švábu	3

ÚJEZD

ŘÍČNÍ

Hladová zeď

K H Mácha

Memorial to the
Victims of
Communism

VÍTĚZNÁ

Wooden Church

CAFÉS
Bohemia Bagel	14
Café Savoy	29
Cukrkávalimonáda	15
Pekařství v Karmelitské	13
U knoflíčků	24
U zeleného čaje	2

Kinského
zahrada

PLASKÁ

MĚLNICKÁ

PETŘINSKÁ

Musaion

TBOROVSKÁ

Smíchov

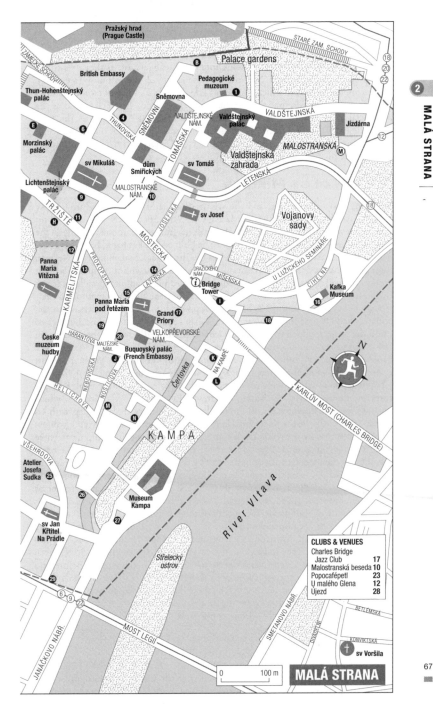

Pražský hrad
(Prague Castle)

STARÉ ZÁM. SCHODY

Palace gardens

B

British Embassy

Pedagogické
muzeum **1**

Thun-Hohenštejnský
palác

Sněmovna

VALDŠTEJNSKÁ

E

4

THUNOVSKÁ

SNĚMOVNÍ

VALDŠTEJNSKÉ
NÁM.

Valdštejnský
palác

Jízdárna

6

Morzinský
palác

TOMÁŠSKÁ

Valdštejnská
zahrada

MALOSTRANSKÁ

M

sv Mikuláš

dům
Smiřických

sv Tomáš

Lichtenštejnský
palác

9

MALOSTRANSKÉ
NÁM. **10**

LETENSKÁ

TRŽIŠTĚ

11

JOSEFSKÁ

sv Josef

Vojanovy
sady

H

12

MOSTECKÁ

18

Panna
Maria
Vítězná

13

PROKOPSKÁ

14

DRAŽICKÉHO
NÁM.

MÍŠENSKÁ

U LUŽICKÉHO SEMINÁŘE

KARMELITSKÁ

LÁZEŇSKÁ

15

Bridge
Tower

CIHELNÁ

Kafka
Museum

Panna Maria
pod řetězem

Grand
Priory **17**

i

I

16

19

HARANTOVA

20

VELKOPŘEVORSKÉ
NÁM.

18

České
muzeum
hudby

MALTÉZSKÉ
NÁM.

Buquoyský palác
(French Embassy)

K

NEBOVIDSKÁ

NOSTICOVA

J

Čertovka

NA KAMPĚ

L

HELLICHOVA

M

N

KAMPA

KARLŮV MOST (CHARLES BRIDGE)

VŠEHRDOVA

Atelier
Josefa
Sudka **25**

N

26

Museum
Kampa

sv Jan
Křtitel
Na Prádle

27

River Vltava

Střelecký
ostrov

29

6 9

22

JANÁČKOVO NÁBŘ.

MOST LEGIÍ

SMETANOVO NÁBŘ.

DIVADELNÍ

BETLÉMSKÁ

KONVIKTSKÁ

sv Voršila

CLUBS & VENUES
Charles Bridge
  Jazz Club   **17**
Malostranská beseda **10**
Popocafépetl   **23**
U malého Glena   **12**
Újezd   **28**

0   100 m

MALÁ STRANA

On the north side, distinguished by its two little turrets and rather shocking pistachio and vanilla colour scheme, is the **dům Smiřických** (no. 18), where the Protestant posse met up in 1618 to decide how to get rid of Emperor Ferdinand's Catholic governors: whether to attack them with daggers, or, as they eventually attempted to do, kill them by chucking them out of the window (see p.51). Sněmovní, the sidestreet which runs alongside the palace's western facade, takes its name from the **Sněmovna**, the Neoclassical palace at no. 4, which served as the provincial Diet in the nineteenth century, the National Assembly of the First Republic in 1918, the Czech National Council after federalization in 1968 and, finally, since 1993, as home to the Chamber of Deputies, the (more important) lower house of the **Czech Parliament**.

Church of sv Mikuláš

Towering above the square, and the whole of Malá Strana, is the church of **sv Mikuláš** or St Nicholas (daily: March–Oct 9am–5pm; Nov–Feb 9am–4pm; 70Kč; ⓦ www.psalterium.cz), easily the most magnificent Baroque building in the city, and one of the last great structures to be built on the left bank, begun in 1702. This was the most prestigious commission of Christoph Dientzenhofer, a German immigrant from a dynasty of Bavarian architects, and is, without doubt, his finest work. For the Jesuits, who were already ensconced in the adjoining college, it was their most ambitious project yet in Bohemia, and the ultimate symbol of their stranglehold on the country. When Christoph died in 1722, it was left to his son Kilian Ignaz Dientzenhofer, along with Kilian's son-in-law, Anselmo Lurago, to finish the project, which they did with a masterful flourish, adding the giant green dome and tower – now among the most characteristic landmarks on Prague's left bank. Sadly for the Jesuits, they were able to enjoy the finished product for just twenty years, before they were banished from the Habsburg Empire in 1773.

Nothing about the relatively plain west facade prepares you for the High Baroque **interior**, dominated by the nave's vast fresco, by Johann Lukas Kracker, which portrays some of the more fanciful miraculous feats of St Nicholas. Along with his role as Santa Claus, he is also depicted here rescuing sailors in distress, saving women from prostitution by throwing them bags of gold and reprieving from death three unjustly condemned men. Even given the overwhelming proportions of the nave, the dome at the far end of the church, built by the younger Dientzenhofer, remains impressive, thanks, more than anything, to its sheer height. Leering over you as you gaze up at the dome are four terrifyingly oversized and stern Church Fathers, one of whom brandishes a gilded thunderbolt, while another garrottes a devil with his crozier, leaving no doubt as to the gravity of the Jesuit message.

Exhibitions are occasionally staged in the church's gallery, which gives you a great chance to look down on the nave and get closer to the frescoes. It's also possible to climb the **belfry** (daily: April–Oct 10am–7pm; Nov–March 10am–6pm), for fine views over Malá Strana and the Charles Bridge. Before you leave, check out the exceptional Rococo pulpit wrought in pink scagliola, busy with cherubs and a pietà, and topped by an archangel on the point of beheading some unfortunate. And don't miss the church's superb organ, its white case and gilded musical cherubs nicely offsetting the grey pipes.

Nerudova

The most important of the various cobbled streets leading up to the Hrad from Malostranské náměstí is **Nerudova**, named after the Czech journalist and writer **Jan Neruda** (1834–91), who was born at *U dvou slunců* (The Two Suns), at no. 47, an inn sporting twin Dutch gables at the top of the street; Neruda later lived for ten years at no. 44, now the swish *Hotel Neruda*. His tales of Malá Strana immortalized Bohemian life on Prague's left bank, though he's perhaps best known outside the Czech Republic via the Chilean Nobel Prize-winner, Pablo Neruda, who took his pen name from the lesser-known Czech. Historically, this was the city's main area for craftsmen, artisans and artists, though the shops and restaurants that flank Nerudova now are mostly fairly predictable and touristy.

Many of the Baroque houses that line the steep climb up to the Hrad retain their medieval barn doors, and most are adorned with their own peculiar house signs (see box, p.8). At the bottom of the street are two of Nerudova's fancier buildings: no. 5 is the **Morzinský palác**, now the Romanian embassy, its doorway designed by Giovanni Santini and supported by two Moors (a pun on the owner's name) sculpted by Brokof; diagonally opposite, no. 20 is the **Thun-Hohenštejnský palác** (also by Santini), now the Italian embassy, with two giant eagles by Braun holding up the portal. Further up the street, according to Prague tradition, Casanova and Mozart are thought to have met up at a ball given by the aristocrat owners of no. 33, the **Bretfeldský palác**, in 1791, while the latter was in town for the premiere of *La Clemenza di Tito* (see box, p.64).

Halfway up the hill, Nerudova ends at a crossroads where it meets the cobbled hairpin of Ke Hradu, which the royal coronation procession used to ascend; continuing west along **Úvoz** (The Cutting) takes you to the Strahovský klášter. On the south side of Úvoz, the houses come to an end, and a view opens up over the picturesque jumble of Malá Strana's red-tiled roofs, while to the north, narrow stairways squeeze between the towering buildings of Hradčany, emerging on the path to the Loreta.

Tržiště and Vlašská

Running (very) roughly parallel to Nerudova – and linked to it by several picturesque sidestreets and steps – is **Tržiště**, which sets off from just south of Malostranské náměstí. Halfway up on the left is the **Schönbornský palác**, now the US embassy. The entrance, and the renowned gardens, are watched over by CCTV and twitchy Czech policemen – a far cry from the dilapidated palace in which Kafka rented an apartment in March 1917, and where he suffered his first bout of the tuberculosis that was to kill him.

As Tržiště swings to the right, bear left up **Vlašská**, home to yet another **Lobkovický palác**, now the German embassy. In the summer of 1989, several thousand East Germans climbed over the garden wall and entered the embassy compound to demand West German citizenship, which had been every German's right since partition. The neighbouring streets were soon jam-packed with abandoned Trabants, as the beautiful palace gardens became a muddy home to the refugees. The Czechoslovak government gave in and organized special sealed trains to take the East Germans – cheered on their way by thousands of Praguers – over the Iron Curtain, thus prompting the exodus that eventually brought down the Berlin Wall.

The palace itself is a particularly refined building, best viewed from the rear – you'll have to approach it from Petřín (see p.76). The gardens are not open to the public, but you should be able to see David Černý's sculpture, *Quo Vadis?*, a gold Trabant on legs, erected in memory of the fleeing East Germans. Opposite the German embassy, at Vlašská 34, is the former Italian hospital, now the **Instituto Italiano di Cultura** (Italian Cultural Institute; Mon–Thurs 10am–noon & 3–6pm, Fri 10am–noon; free; Ⓦwww.iicpraga.esteri.it), worth venturing inside if there's an exhibition on, as it contains a lovely Baroque chapel on the ground floor, whose rich plasterwork frames some unusual grisaille frescoes.

Valdštejnský palác

To the north of Malostranské náměstí, up Tomášská, lies the **Valdštejnský palác**, which takes up the whole of the eastern side of Valdštejnské náměstí and Valdštejnská. As early as 1621, **Albrecht von Waldstein** started to build a palace which would reflect his status as commander of the Imperial Catholic armies of the Thirty Years' War. By buying, confiscating, and then destroying 26 houses, three gardens and a brick factory, he succeeded in ripping apart a densely populated area of Malá Strana to make way for one of the first, and largest, Baroque palaces in the city.

The Czech upper house, or **Senát**, is now housed in the palace, and at weekends you can visit several of the frescoed Baroque rooms they use (Sat & Sun: April–Sept 10am–5pm; Oct–March closes 4pm; free; Ⓦ www.senat.cz). You should also take a stroll around the palace's formal gardens, the **Valdštejnská zahrada** (April–Oct daily 10am–6pm; free) – accessible from the palace's main entrance, from the piazza outside Malostranská metro and also from a doorway in the palace walls along Letenská – are a good place to take a breather from the city streets (and have a toilet break). The focus of the gardens is the gigantic Italianate **sala terrena**, a monumental loggia decorated with frescoes of the Trojan Wars, which stands at the end of an avenue of bronze sculptures by Adriaen de Vries. The originals, which

Waldstein

Albrecht von Waldstein (known to the Czechs as Albrecht z Valdštejna, and to the English as Wallenstein – the name given to him by the German playwright Schiller in his tragic trilogy) was the most notorious warlord of the **Thirty Years' War**. If the imperial astrologer Johannes Kepler is to be believed, this is all because he was born at four in the afternoon on September 14, 1583. According to Kepler's horoscope, Waldstein was destined to be greedy, deceitful, unloved and unloving. Sure enough, at an early age he tried to kill a servant, for which he was expelled from his Lutheran school. Recuperating in Italy, he converted to Catholicism (an astute career move) and married a wealthy widow who conveniently died shortly after the marriage. Waldstein used his new fortune to cultivate a friendship with Prince Ferdinand, heir to the Habsburg Empire, who in turn thought that a rich, tame Bohemian noble could come in handy.

During the Thirty Years' War, Waldstein offered his services (and an army of thousands) to Emperor Ferdinand free of charge, but with the right to plunder as he saw fit – within five years of the **Battle of Bílá hora** in 1620 (see box, p.157), Waldstein owned a quarter of Bohemia. By 1630, Waldstein was a duke, and earned the right to keep his hat on in the imperial presence as well as the more dubious honour of handing the emperor a napkin after he had used his fingerbowl. However, at this point Ferdinand grew wary of Waldstein's ambition, and relieved him of his command.

The following year, the Saxons occupied Prague, and the emperor was forced to reinstate Waldstein. Ferdinand couldn't afford to do without the supplies from Waldstein's estates, but knew he was mortgaging large chunks of the empire to pay for his services. More alarmingly, there were persistent rumours that Waldstein was about to declare himself king of Bohemia and defect to the French enemy. In 1634, Waldstein openly rebelled against Ferdinand, who immediately hatched a plot to murder him, sending a motley posse including English, Irish and Scottish mercenaries to the border town of **Cheb** (**Eger**), where they cut the general down in his nightshirt as he tried to rise from his sickbed. Some see him as the first man to unify Germany since Charlemagne, others see him as a wily Czech hero. In reality he was probably just another ambitious, violent man, as his stars had predicted.

were intended to form a fountain, were taken off as booty by the Swedes in 1648 and now adorn the royal gardens in Drottningholm. In addition, there are a number of peacocks, a carp pond, the mother of all grottos, with mysterious doors set into it, and an old menagerie that's now home to a mini-parliament of eagle owls.

On the opposite side of the gardens, the palace's former riding school, **Valdštejnská jízdárna** (Tues–Sun 10am–6pm), has been converted into a gallery, which puts on temporary exhibitions of fine art and photography organized by the Národní galerie. The riding school is accessible only from the courtyard of the nearby Malostranská metro station.

Pedagogické muzeum

A palace on the opposite side of Valdštejnská from the Senate now houses the **Pedagogické muzeum** (Tues–Sun 10am–12.30pm & 1–5pm; 60Kč; ⓦwww .pmjak.cz), a permanent exhibition on the history of education in the Czech Lands. Despite being recently revamped, the museum is a fairly dry affair, although you do get to learn about the Czech teacher, **Jan Amos Komenský** (1592–1670) – known in English as John Comenius – who was forced to leave his homeland after the victory of Waldstein's Catholic armies, eventually settling in Protestant England. Komenský's educational methods are taken for granted now but they were revolutionary for their time: among other things, he believed in universal education, in relating education to everyday life, teaching in the vernacular and learning languages through conversation.

Letenská and sv Tomáš

Walking southwest along **Letenská** from the Valdštejnský palace gardens back towards Malostranské náměstí, takes you past **U svatého Tomáše**, the oldest *pivnice* in Prague, established in 1352 by Augustinian monks who brewed their own lethal dark beer on the premises until the Communists kicked them out. Round the corner is the priory church of **sv Tomáš** (St Thomas), rebuilt by Kilian Ignaz Dientzenhofer in the 1720s. The rich burghers of Malá Strana spared no expense, as is clear from the ornate interior, with its dinky little dome and fantastically colourful frescoes by Václav Vavřinec Reiner. They also bought a couple of Rubens for the tall main altarpiece (the originals are now in the hands of the Národní galerie) and two dead saints, St Just and St Boniface, whose gruesome clothed skeletons lie in glass coffins on either side of the nave, by the second pillar. A few traces of the church's Gothic origins can be seen in the vaulted chapel at the eastern end of the north aisle.

Malá Strana's palace gardens

One of the most elusive secrets of Malá Strana is its steeply terraced **palace gardens** (palácové zahrady; daily: April & Oct 9am–6pm; May & Sept 9am–7pm; June & July 9am–9pm, Aug 9am–8pm; 80Kč; ⓦwww.palacovezahrady.cz), hidden away behind the Baroque facades on Valdštejnská, on the slopes below the castle. There are five small, interlinking gardens in total, dotted with little pavilions and terraces hung with vines, all commanding superb views over Prague. If you're approaching from below, you can enter either via the Ledeburská zahrada on Valdštejnské náměstí, or the Kolowratská zahrada on Valdštejnská, both of which connect with the other palace gardens. You can also exit or enter via the easternmost garden, the Malá Fürstenberská zahrada, which joins up with the Zahrada na valech (see p.55) beneath the Hrad itself.

▲ Malá Strana's palace gardens

There are more gardens further south at the **Vojanovy sady** (daily: April–Sept 8am–7pm; Oct–March 8am–5pm; free), securely concealed behind a ring of high walls off U lužického semináře. Originally a monastic garden belonging to the Carmelites, it's now an informal public park, with sleeping babies, weeping willows and lots of grass on which to lounge about; outdoor art exhibitions and occasional concerts also take place here. One final Malá Strana Baroque garden worth exploring is the Vrtbovská zahrada, off Karmelitská (see below).

Kafka Museum

The Prague tourist industry is obsessed with Kafka, and, not content with the small museum on the site of his birthplace, there is now a much larger **Franz Kafka Museum** (daily 10am–6pm; 120Kč; Ⓦwww.kafkamuseum.cz) hidden away in a courtyard off Cihelná (a former medieval brickyard), with David Černý's delightful fountain of two gentlemen urinating into a pool in the shape of the Czech Republic. The exhibition has already toured Barcelona and New York, so may yet move on, but in the meantime, what you get is a fairly sophisticated rundown of Kafka's life and works (for more on which see p.106). The first section includes lots of photos of the old ghetto into which Kafka was born, an invoice from his father's shop, with the logo of a jackdaw (*kavka* in Czech), copies of his job applications, requests for sick leave, one of his reports on accident prevention in the workplace and facsimiles of his pen sketches. Upstairs, audiovisuals and theatrical trickery is employed in order to explore the torment, alienation and claustrophobia Kafka felt throughout his life and expressed through his writings.

Karmelitská and the Vrtbovská zahrada

Karmelitská is the busy cobbled street that runs south from Malostranské náměstí along the base of Petřín towards the suburb of Smíchov (see p.158), becoming Újezd at roughly its halfway point. On the corner of Karmelitská and Tržiště, at no. 25, is the entrance to one of the most elusive of Malá Strana's many Baroque

gardens, the **Vrtbovská zahrada** (April–Oct daily 10am–6pm; 55Kč; ⓦwww
.vrtbovska.cz), founded on the site of the former vineyards of the Vrtbovský palác.
Laid out on Tuscan-style terraces, dotted with ornamental urns and statues of the
gods by Matthias Bernhard Braun, the gardens twist their way up the lower slopes
of Petřín Hill to an observation terrace, from where there's a spectacular rooftop
perspective on the city.

Maltézské náměstí and around

From the trams and traffic of Karmelitská, it's a relief to cut across to the calm
restraint of **Maltézské náměstí**, one of a number of delightful little squares
between here and the river, with a plague column at the north end. The square
takes its name from the Order of the Knights of St John of Jerusalem (or Maltese
Knights), who in 1160 founded the nearby church of **Panna Maria pod řetězem**
(St Mary below-the-chain), so called because it was the Knights' job to guard the
Judith Bridge. The original Romanesque church was pulled down by the Knights
themselves in the fourteenth century, but only the chancel and towers had been
successfully rebuilt by the time of the Hussite Wars. The two bulky Gothic towers
are still standing and the apse is now thoroughly Baroque, but the nave remains
unfinished and open to the elements.

The Knights still own the church and the adjacent Grand Priory, which backs
onto **Velkopřevorské náměstí**, another pretty little square to the south, which
echoes to the sound of music from the nearby Prague conservatoire. On one side of
the square, behind a row of lime trees, is the apricot-coloured Rococo **Buquoyský
palác**, built for a French aristocratic family and appropriately enough now the
French embassy. Opposite is the **John Lennon Wall** where Prague's youth established an ad hoc graffiti shrine to the ex-Beatle after his violent death in 1980. The
running battle between police and graffiti artists continued throughout the 1990s,
with the Maltese Knights (whose wall it is) taking an equally dim view of the mural,
but a compromise has now been reached and the wall's scribblings legalized.
Another shrine has developed to the east, on the bridge over the **Čertovka**
(see below), where couples have attached **love padlocks** to the railings.

Kampa

Heading for **Kampa**, the largest of the Vltava's islands, with its cafés, old mills and
serene riverside park and playground, is the perfect way to escape the crowds on
the Charles Bridge, from which it can be accessed easily via a staircase. The island
is separated from the left bank by Prague's "Little Venice", a thin strip of water
called **Čertovka** (Devil's Stream), which used to power several mill-wheels. In
contrast to the rest of the left bank, the fire of 1541 had a positive effect on Kampa,
since the flotsam from the blaze effectively stabilized the island's shifting shoreline.
Nevertheless, Kampa was still subject to frequent flooding right up until the
Vltava was dammed in the 1950s.

For much of its history, the island was the city's main wash house, a fact
commemorated by the church of **sv Jan Křtitel Na Prádle** (St John-the-Baptist at
the Cleaners) on Říční, beyond the southernmost tip of the island. It wasn't until
the sixteenth and seventeenth centuries that the Nostitz family, who owned
Kampa, began to develop the northern half of the island; the southern half was left
untouched, and today is laid out as a public park, with riverside views across to
Staré Město. To the north, the oval main square, **Na Kampě**, once a pottery
market, is studded with slender acacia trees and cut through by the Charles Bridge,
to which it is connected by a double flight of steps.

Museum Kampa

Housed in a stylishly converted riverside watermill, the **Museum Kampa** (daily 10am–6pm; 120Kč, but free on Mon; ⓦ www.museumkampa.cz) is dedicated to the private art collection of Jan and Meda Mládek. As well as temporary exhibitions, this smart modern gallery displays the best of the Mládeks' permanent collection, including a vast series of works by the Czech artist **František Kupka** (1871–1957), in international terms the most important Czech painter of the twentieth century. Apprenticed to a saddler who initiated him into spiritualism, Kupka became a medium and took up painting, eventually moving to Paris in 1895. He secured his place in art history by being (possibly) the first artist in the Western world to exhibit abstract paintings, but though his psychedelic paintings were influential in the 1960s, abstract art was frowned upon by the Communist regime and Kupka was pretty much ignored by his native country from 1948 to 1989. The works on display here encompass early Expressionist watercolours such as the *Study for Water Bathers* (1907), transitional pastels like *Fauvist Chair* (1910) and more abstract works, such as the seminal oil paintings *Cathedral* and *Study for Fugue in Two Colours* (both around 1912).

The gallery also displays a good selection of works by the sculptor **Otto Gutfreund** (1889–1927), who started out as an enthusiastic Cubist, producing dynamic, vigorous portraits like *Viki* (1912). After World War I, during which he joined the French Foreign Legion but was interned for three years for insubordination, Gutfreund switched to depicting everyday folk in technicolour, as in *Trade* and *Lovers*, in a style that prefigures Socialist Realism. His life was cut short when he drowned while swimming in the Vltava.

Panna Maria Vítězná and the Pražské Jezulátko

On Karmelitská, on the same side of the street as Vrtbovská zahrada, is the rather plain church of **Panna Maria Vítězná** (Mon–Sat 8.30am–7pm, Sun 8.30am–8pm; free; ⓦ www.pragjesu.com), which was begun in early Baroque style by German Lutherans in 1611, and later handed over to the Carmelites after the Battle of Bílá hora. The main reason for coming here is to see the **Pražské Jezulátko** or Bambino di Praga, a high-kitsch wax effigy of the infant Jesus as a precocious 3-year-old, enthroned in a glass case, which was donated by one of the Lobkowicz family's Spanish brides in 1628. Credited with miraculous powers, the Pražské Jezulátko became an object of international pilgrimage equal in stature to the Santa Casa in Loreta (see p.61), similarly inspiring a whole series of replicas. It continues to attract visitors and boasts a vast personal wardrobe of expensive swaddling clothes – approaching a hundred separate outfits at the last count – regularly changed by the Carmelite nuns. There's a small **museum**, up the spiral staircase in the south aisle, which contains a selection of his velvet and satin overgarments sent from all over the world. There are also chalices, monstrances and a Rococo crown studded with diamonds and pearls to admire.

České muzeum hudby (Czech Music Museum)

The city's **České muzeum hudby** (Mon 1–6pm, Wed 10am–8pm, Thurs, Sat & Sun 10am–6pm, Fri 9am–6pm; 100Kč; ⓦ www.nm.cz) is housed in a former Dominican nunnery on the opposite side of Karmelitská from the Panna Maria Vítězná. Temporary exhibitions are held on the ground floor of the magnificently tall main hall (formerly the nunnery church), while the permanent collection begins upstairs. The first exhibition kicks off with a crazy cut-and-splice medley of musical film footage from the last century alongside a display of electric guitars and an early Tesla synthesizer. Next up is August Förster's pioneering quarter-tone grand piano from 1924 – you can even listen to **Alois Hába**'s microtonal *Fantazie no. 10* composed for, and performed on, its three keyboards. After this rather promising start, the museum settles down into a conventional display of old central European instruments from a precious Baumgartner clavichord and an Amati violin to Neapolitan mandolins and a vast contrabass over two metres in height. There are several violins made by the craftsmen who once lived on nearby Nerudova (once called Loutnařská, or "Lute-makers' Street") and an intriguing folk section with zithers, bagpipes, Slovak *fujara* (a shepherd's flute) and the odd barrel organ. What saves the collection from being as exhausting as it is exhaustive is the fact that you can hear many of the instruments on display being put through their paces at listening posts in each room.

Atelier Josefa Sudka

At its south end, Karmelitská becomes Újezd. Hidden behind the buildings on the east side of the street, at no. 30, is a faithful reconstruction of the **Atelier Josefa Sudka** (Wed–Sun noon–6pm; 10Kč; Wwww.sudek-atelier.cz), a cute little wooden garden studio, where **Josef Sudek** (1896–1976), the great Czech photographer, lived with his sister from 1927. Sudek moved out to Úvoz 24 (also now a photo gallery) in 1958, but he used the place as his darkroom to the end of his life. The twisted tree in the front garden will be familiar to those acquainted with the numerous photographic cycles he based around the studio. The building has a few of Sudek's personal effects and is now used for temporary exhibitions of other photographers' works.

Michnův palác

At Újezd 40 stands the **Michnův palác**, built on the site of another Dominican nunnery. The facade and gateway still incorporate elements of the Renaissance summer palace built by the Kinský family around 1580. From 1787 the building was used as an armoury and fell into disrepair until it was bought in 1921 by the Czech nationalist sports movement **Sokol**, and named after one of its founders, Miroslav Tyrš. Set up in 1862, in direct response to the German Turnverband physical education movement, Sokol (from the Czech for "falcon") played an important part in the Czech national revival (*národní obrození*). It organized mass extravaganzas of synchronized gymnastics involving thousands of participants, roughly every six years from 1882 onwards. The Communists outlawed Sokol (as the Nazis had also done) and, in its place, established a tradition of similar extravaganzas called **Spartakiáda**, held every five years in the Strahov stadium, behind Petřín. In the 1990s, the Spartakiáda, indelibly tainted by their political past, were once more replaced by events organized by the reformed Sokol.

Memorial to the Victims of Communism

In 2002, the Czechs finally erected a **Memorial to the Victims of Communism** at the foot of Petřín Hill, where Újezd meets Vítězná. The location has no particular resonance with the period, but the memorial itself has an eerie quality, especially when it's lit up at night. It consists of a series of statues, self-portraits by sculptor Olbram Zoubek, standing on steps that lead down from Petřín Hill behind, each in varying stages of disintegration. The inscription at the base of the monument reads "205,486 convicted, 248 executed, 4500 died in prison, 327 annihilated at the border, 170,938 emigrated".

Petřín

The hilly wooded slopes of **PETŘÍN**, distinguished by the Rozhledna, a scaled-down version of the Eiffel Tower, make up the largest green space in the city centre. The tower is just one of several exhibits which survive from the 1891 Prague Exhibition, whose modest legacy also includes the **funicular railway** (*lanová dráha*) which climbs up from a station just off Újezd (daily 9am–11.30pm; every 10–15min; public transport tickets and travel passes valid). The original funicular was powered by a simple but ingenious system whereby two carriages, one at either end of the steep track, were fitted with large water tanks that were alternately filled at the top and emptied at the bottom. As the carriages pass each other at the halfway station of Nebozízek, you can get out and soak in the view from the restaurant of the same name, or from the nearby *Petřínské terasy* restaurant.

At the top of the hill, it's impossible to miss the southernmost perimeter wall of the old city – popularly known as the **Hladová zeď** (Hunger Wall) – which heads northwestwards to the Strahovský klášter and eastwards back down to Újezd. Instigated in the 1460s by Charles IV, it was much lauded at the time (and later by the Communists) as a great public work which provided employment for the burgeoning ranks of the city's destitute (hence its name); in fact, much of the wall's construction was paid for by the expropriation of Jewish property.

North from the funicular to the Rozhledna

If you follow the wall northwest from the funicular, you'll come to Palliardi's twin-towered church of **sv Vavřinec** (St Lawrence), which recalls the German name for Petřín – Laurenziberg. Opposite the church are a series of buildings from the 1891 Exhibition, the most famous of which is the **Rozhledna** (daily April 10am–7pm; May–Sept 10am–10pm; Oct 10am–8pm; Nov–March 10am–6pm; 100Kč), an octagonal interpretation – though a mere fifth of the size – of the Eiffel

▲ The view from Petřín

Tower which shocked Paris in 1889, and a tribute to the city's strong cultural and political links with Paris at the time. It's 299 steps to the top, but the view from the public gallery is terrific in fine weather.

Next door is the **Bludiště** (times as above; 70Kč), a mini neo-Gothic castle complete with mock drawbridge. The first section of the interior features a **mirror maze**, a stroke of infantile genius by the exhibition organizers. This is followed by an action-packed, life-sized **diorama** of the victory of Prague's students and Jews over the Swedes on the Charles Bridge in 1648. The humour of the convex and concave mirrors that lie beyond the diorama is so simple, it has both adults and kids giggling away. From the tower and maze, the path with the **Stations of the Cross** will eventually lead you to the perimeter wall of the Strahovský klášter, giving great views over Petřín's palatial orchards and the sea of red tiles below.

South to the wooden church

If you head south from the top of the funicular, you come immediately to the aromatic **Růžový sad** (Rose Garden), whose colour-coordinated rose beds are laid out in front of Petřín's observatory, the **Štefánikova hvězdárna** (Tues–Sun, but times vary; 60Kč; Ⓦ www.observatory.cz). The small astronomical exhibition inside is hardly worth bothering with, but if it's a clear night, a quick peek through either of the observatory's two powerful telescopes is a treat.

A little further down the hill, on the other side of the wall from the observatory, stands a bust of the leading Czech nineteenth-century Romantic poet **Karel Hynek Mácha**, who penned the poem *Maj* (May), on the subject of unrequited love. In spring, and in particular on the first of May, the statue remains a popular place of pilgrimage for courting couples. Another curiosity, hidden in the trees on the southern side of the Hladová zeď, is a **wooden church** that was brought here, log by log, from an Orthodox village in Carpatho-Ruthenia (now part of Ukraine) in 1929. Churches like this are still common in eastern Slovakia, and this is a particularly ornate example from the eighteenth century, with multiple shingled domes like piles of giant acorns.

Musaion (Folk Museum)

The Kinský family's Neoclassical summer palace, built in 1827, sits on the very southern edge of Petřín hill, and now houses the **Musaion** (Tues–Sun: May–Sept 10am–6pm; Oct–April 9am–5pm; 70Kč; Ⓦ www.nm.cz), the city's ethnographic museum. For anyone interested in folk costumes and traditions, this is a wonderful museum, though the lack of English labelling will also make it slightly frustrating. The permanent collection is spread out over ten or so galleries on the *piano nobile*, with some of the best costumes in room 4, where the mannequins are decked out in their Sunday best: huge puffed sleeves, ruched ruffs and bows. Some of the most intriguing exhibits are in room 7, which displays fearsome masks and rattles from the pre-Lent Masopust festival, a terrifying Čaramura costume garlanded with eggs and snails, and garlanded *pomlázky*, with which the boys beat the girls at Easter. The Christmas section (room 9) is another highlight, with its spectacular *Betlém* (Bethlehem) scene set amidst a rocky papier-mâché townscape.

Staré Město

S TARÉ MĚSTO, literally the "Old Town", is the historic heart of the city. Its complex and utterly confusing web of narrow streets is packed full of atmospheric charm, and, in parts, thronged with tourists. Despite the crowds, however, there are still plenty of residential streets, and plenty of hidden backstreets in which to escape. The district is bounded on one side by the river, on the other by the arc of **Národní**, **Na příkopě** and **Revoluční**, and at its heart is **Staroměstské náměstí**, Prague's showpiece main square, easily the most magnificent in central Europe.

While exploring Staré Město, most visitors unknowingly retrace the **králová cesta**, the traditional route of the coronation procession from the medieval gateway, the Prašná brána (see p.119), to the Hrad. Established by the Přemyslids, the route was followed, with a few minor variations, by every king until the Emperor Ferdinand IV in 1836, the last of the Habsburgs to bother having himself crowned in Prague.

Merchants and craftsmen began settling in what is now Staré Město as early as the tenth century, and in the mid-thirteenth century it was granted town status, with jurisdiction over its own affairs. During the Counter-Reformation, the victorious Catholic nobles built fewer large palaces here than on the left bank, leaving the medieval street plan intact with the exception of the Klementinum (the Jesuits' powerhouse) and the Jewish Quarter, Josefov, which was largely reconstructed in the late nineteenth century (see p.99). Like so much of Prague, however, Staré Město is still, on the surface, overwhelmingly Baroque, built literally on top of its Gothic predecessor to guard against the floods that plagued the town.

Charles Bridge (Karlův most)

The **Charles Bridge**, or Karlův most – which for over four hundred years was the only link between the two halves of Prague – is by far the city's most familiar monument. Completed in 1402 by the court architect, Peter Parler, it's an impressive piece of medieval engineering, aligned slightly askew between two mighty Gothic gateways, but its fame is due almost entirely to the magnificent, mostly Baroque, statues (additions to the original structure) that punctuate its length. Individually, only a few of the works are outstanding, but taken collectively, set against the backdrop of the Hrad, the effect is breathtaking.

The bridge was begun by Charles IV in 1357 to replace an earlier structure, the **Judith Bridge** (Juditin most), which had been swept away by one of the Vltava's frequent floods. Given its strategic significance, it comes as no surprise that the bridge has played an important part in Prague's history: in **1648** it was the site of the last battle of the Thirty Years' War, fought between the besieging Swedes and an ad hoc army of Prague's students and Jews; in 1744 the invading Prussians were defeated at the same spot; and in **1848** it formed the front line between the revolutionaries on the Staré Město side, and the reactionary forces on the left bank.

▲ Charles Bridge

For the first four hundred years it was known simply as the Prague or Stone Bridge – only in 1870 was it officially named after its patron. Since 1950, the bridge has been closed to vehicles, and it is now one of the most popular places to hang out, day and night: the crush of sightseers never abates during the day, when the niches created by the bridge-piers are occupied by souvenir hawkers and buskers, but at night things calm down a bit, and the views are, if anything, even more spectacular.

Malostranské mostecké věže (Malá Strana bridge towers)

On the Malá Strana side two unequal bridge towers, connected by a castellated arch, form the entrance to the bridge, the **Malostranské mostecké věže**. The smaller, stumpy tower was once part of the original Judith Bridge (named after the wife of Vladislav I, who built it in the twelfth century); the taller of the two, crowned by one of the pinnacled wedge-spires more commonly associated with Prague's leading bank, contains an exhibition (April–Sept Mon–Thurs & Sun 10am–6pm, Fri & Sat 10am–7pm; Oct–March daily 10am–6pm; 70Kč) relaying the history of the bridge. You can also walk out onto the balcony that connects the two towers for a bird's-eye view of the seething masses pouring across the bridge.

The statues

A bronze **crucifix** has stood on the bridge since its construction, but the first sculpture wasn't added until 1683, when **St John of Nepomuk** appeared (see box, p.84). His statue was such a propaganda success that the Catholic church authorities ordered another 21 to be erected between 1706 and 1714. These included works by Prague's leading Baroque sculptors, led by Matthias Bernhard Braun and Ferdinand Maximilian Brokof. The sculptures, many of them crafted in sandstone, have weathered badly over the years and have mostly been replaced by copies; to see the originals, and several statues whose subjects fell out of favour and were removed, visit the Lapidárium (see p.152). For a guide to all the statuary see the box on p.82.

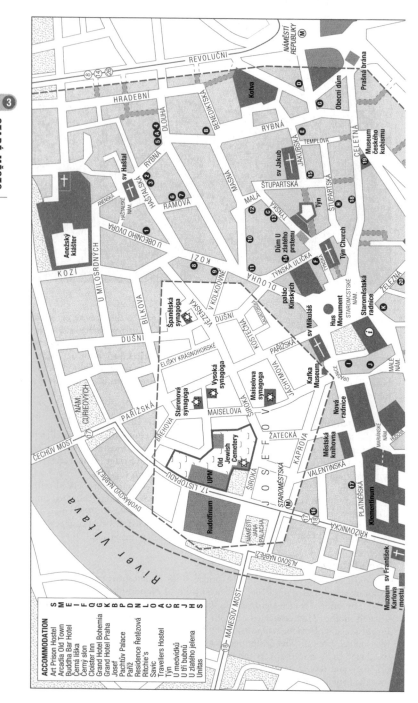

ACCOMMODATION
Art Prison Hostel — S
Arcadia Old Town — M
Buddha Bar Hotel — E
Černá liška — I
Černý slon — F
Cloister Inn — Q
Grand Hotel Bohemia — G
Grand Hotel Praha — K
Josef — B
Pachtův Palace — P
Paříž — D
Residence Řetězová — N
Ritchie's — L
Savic — O
Travellers Hostel — A
Týn — C
U medvídků — R
U tří buben — J
U zlatého jelena — H
Unitas — S

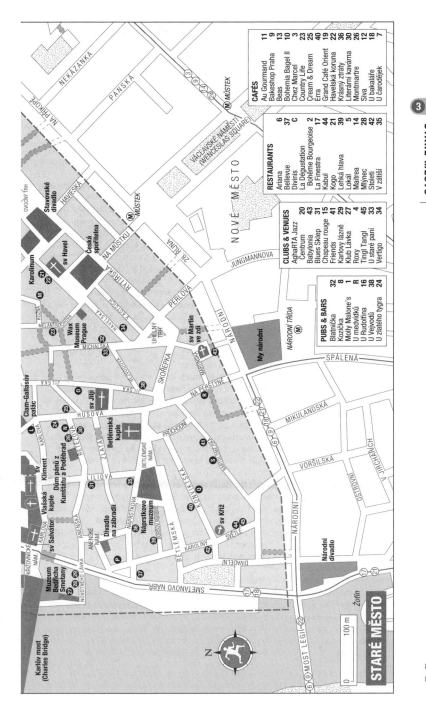

STARÉ MĚSTO

CAFÉS
Au Gourmand	11
Bakeshop Praha	9
Beas	13
Bohemia Bagel II	10
Chez Marcel	3
Country Life	23
Cream & Dream	25
Erra	40
Grand Café Orient	19
Havelská koruna	22
Krásný ztráty	36
Literární kavárna	30
Montmartre	26
Siva	12
U bakaláře	18
U čarodějek	7

RESTAURANTS
Ariana	6
Bellevue	37
Divinis	C
La Dégustation	
Bohème Bourgeoise	2
La Finestra	17
Kabul	44
Kogo	21
Lehká hlava	39
Lokal	5
Maitrea	14
Mlynec	28
Století	42
V zátiší	35

CLUBS & VENUES
AghaRTA Jazz	20
Centrum	43
Babylonia	31
Blues Sklep	15
Chapeau rouge	41
Friends	27
Karlovy lázně	29
Klub Lávka	4
Roxy	45
Tingl Tangl	14
Vertigo	34

PUBS & BARS
Blatnička	32
Kozička	8
Molly Malone´s	1
U medvídků	16
U Rudolfina	R
U Vejvodů	38
U zlatého tygra	24

The Charles Bridge statues

(1) St Cosmas and St Damian Paid for by the university medical faculty. Jesus is flanked by these twin martyrs, both dressed in medieval doctors' garb – they were renowned for offering their medical services free of charge.

(2) St Wenceslas Added by Czech nationalists in the nineteenth century.

(3) St Vitus Brokof's St Vitus is depicted as a Roman legionary, his foot being gently nibbled by one of the lions that went on to devour him in a Roman amphitheatre.

(4) The founders of the Trinitarian Order One of the most striking sculptural groups, again by Brokof: **St John of Matha**, the hermit **Felix of Valois** and his pet stag, plus, for some unknown reason, **St Ivan**, whose good works included ransoming persecuted Christians – three petrified souls can be seen through the prison bars below – from the infidels, represented by a bored Turkish jailor and his rabid dog.

(5) St Philip Benizi Amid the blackened sandstone, the lightly coloured figure of the (at the time) only recently canonized Servite friar stands out as the only marble statue. At his feet sits the papal crown, which he turned down when it was offered to him in 1268.

(6) St Adalbert Prague's second bishop, the youthful cleric who was hounded out of the city on more than one occasion by the blissfully pagan citizens of Prague.

(7) St Cajetan Another (at the time) recently canonized saint; founder of the Theatine Order, he stands in front of a column of cherubs sporting a sacred heart.

(8) St Lutgard One of the most successful statues, sculpted by Braun when he was just 26 years old. The blind Flemish Cistercian nun is depicted in the middle of her celebrated vision, in which Christ appeared so that she could kiss his wounds.

(9) St Augustine & (10) St Nicholas of Tolentino Sponsored by the Augustinians; St Nicholas of Tolentino, one of St Augustine's followers, is depicted dishing out bread to the poor. On the top-floor balcony of the house behind him is a lantern; if it goes out while you're passing by, it means you'll die within the year.

(11) St Jude Thaddaeus The apostle and patron saint of those in dire straits holds the club with which the pagans beat him to death.

(12) St Vincent Ferrer The Dominican friar stands over one of his converts to self-flagellation. The inscription below lists his miraculous achievements, including the conversion of 2500 Jews, 40 resurrections and the exorcism of 70 demons. He is joined, somewhat inexplicably, by Bohemia's best-loved hermit, **St Procopius**.

(13) Roland If you look over the side of the bridge by (12), you'll see a nineteenth-century sculpture of Roland – Bruncvík in Czech – brandishing his miraculous golden sword (the real thing is said to be embedded in the bridge, to be used in case of municipal emergency). The original, erected to protect the rights of the Staré Město over the full extent of the bridge, was destroyed in 1648.

(14) St Anthony of Padua & (15) St Francis of Assisi The Franciscan pier – St Francis is a lifeless nineteenth-century figure accompanied by two angels.

(16) St John of Nepomuk (see box, p.84). The bridge's earliest and most popular sculpture. The only bronze statue, it's now green with age, the gold-leaf halo of stars and palm branch gently blowing in the breeze. St John's appearance here in 1683 was part of the Jesuits' campaign to have him canonized; the statue inspired hundreds of copies, which adorn bridges throughout central Europe. On the base, there's a bronze relief depicting his martyrdom, the figure of John now extremely worn through years of being touched for good luck.

(17) St Ludmila A rather androgynous version of Bohemia's first martyr holds the veil with which she was strangled. Standing alongside is her grandson, St Wenceslas, depicted as a young child; his future martyrdom is recounted in the bas-relief.

(18–21) Part from Jesuit general **St Francis Borgia (19)**, these two piers are glum nineteenth-century space-fillers: a trio of Bohemian saints – **Norbert, Sigismund** and **Wenceslas (18)** – **John the Baptist (20)** and **St Christopher (21)**. Between piers 18 and 20 a small bronze cross set into the wall marks the spot where John of Nepomuk was dumped in the river; touch it and you're guaranteed to return to the city.

(22) Saints Cyril and Methodius In 1890, the two Jesuit statues on this pier were swept away by a flood: the statue of the order's founder, St Ignatius Loyola, was replaced with the most recent additions to the bridge (in 1938), these ninth-century missionaries who introduced Christianity to the Slavs.

(23) St Francis Xavier The Jesuit missionary survived the order's unpopularity and was replaced by a copy after it was swept away (see above). One of the more unusual sculptural groups: the saint, who worked in India and the Far East, is held aloft by three Moorish and two "Oriental" converts; Brokof placed himself on the saint's left side.

(24) St Anne Mary's mother with Jesus and Mary.

(25) Joseph With a slightly older Jesus at his feet, this is a nineteenth-century replacement for another Brokof, this time destroyed by gunfire during the 1848 revolution.

(26) The Crucifixion Where the original fourteenth-century crucifix stood alone on the bridge for years. The gold-leaf, Hebrew inscription, "Holy, Holy, Holy is Our Lord of the Multitude", from the Book of Isaiah, was added in 1696, paid for by a Prague Jew who was ordered to do so by the city court, having been found guilty of blasphemy before the cross. The city's Jewish community persuaded the local council to erect a plaque here, explaining that the charges were drummed up and the inscription designed to humiliate Prague's Jews. Apart from Christ himself, all the figures, and the **Pietà** opposite **(27)**, were added in the nineteenth century.

(28) The Dominicans placed their founder, **St Dominic**, and their other leading light, **St Thomas Aquinas**, beside the **Madonna**; in amongst the cherubs is a dog with a burning torch in his mouth, a reference to the vision of Dominic's mother.

(29) St Barbara The patron saint of miners, whose beautifully sculpted hands so impressed Kafka, is accompanied by **St Margaret** and **St Elizabeth**.

(30) The Madonna presides over the kneeling figure of **St Bernard**, and a bubbling mass of cherubs mucking about with the instruments of the Passion – the cock, the dice and the centurion's gauntlet.

(31) St Ivo The patron saint of lawyers, flanked by Justice and a prospective client, stands with an outstretched hand, into which Prague law students traditionally place a glass of beer after their finals.

KARLŮV MOST
(CHARLES BRIDGE)

Muzeum Karlova mostu
KŘIŽOVNICKÉ NÁM.
Staré Město bridge tower
32
30 — 31
28 — 29
26 — 27
River
Vltava
24 — 25
22 — 23
20 — 21
18 — 19
16 — 17
14 — 15
11
12 • 13
9
10
7
NA KAMPĚ
8
5
6
3
Čertovka
4
1
2
DRAŽICKÉHO NÁM.
Judith bridge tower
Malá Strana bridge tower
0   10 m
Castle

St John of Nepomuk

Where Emperor Charles IV sought to promote Václav (Wenceslas) as the nation's preferred saint, the Jesuits, with Habsburg backing, replaced him during the Counter-Reformation with another Czech martyr, **John of Nepomuk** (Jan Nepomucký). The latter had been arrested, tortured, and then thrown – bound and gagged – off the Charles Bridge in 1393 on the orders of Václav IV, allegedly for refusing to divulge the secrets of the queen's confession. A cluster of stars was said to have appeared over the spot where he drowned, hence the halo of stars on every subsequent portrayal of the saint. The Jesuits, in order to ensure his canonization, exhumed his corpse and produced what they claimed to be his tongue – alive and licking, so to speak (it was in fact his very dead brain).

The more prosaic reason for John of Nepomuk's death was simply that he was caught up in a dispute between the archbishop and the king over the appointment of the abbot of Kladruby, and backed the wrong side. John was tortured on the rack along with two other priests, who were then made to sign a document denying that they had been maltreated; John, however, died before he could sign, and his dead body was secretly dumped in the river. The Vatican finally admitted this in 1961, some 232 years after his canonization.

Staroměstská mostecká věž (Staré Město bridge tower)

The **Staroměstská mostecká věž** (daily: April–Sept 10am–10pm; Nov–March 10am–7pm; 70Kč) is arguably the finest bridge tower of the lot, built for show not for defensive purposes. The western facade was trashed in the battle of 1648 but the eastern facade is still encrusted in Gothic cake-like decorations from Peter Parler's workshop, plus a series of mini-sculptures. The central figures are St Vitus, flanked by Charles IV on the right and his son, Václav IV, on the left; above stand two of Bohemia's patron saints, Adalbert and Sigismund. The severed heads of twelve of the Protestant leaders were suspended from the tower in iron baskets following their execution on Staroměstské náměstí in 1621, and all but one remained there until the Saxons passed through the capital ten years later. The tower's permanent exhibition is dull, but, you can get a great aerial perspective on the bridge from the roof.

Křižovnické náměstí

Pass under the Staré Město bridge tower and you're in **Křižovnické náměstí**, an awkward space hemmed in by its constituent buildings, and, with traffic hurtling across the east side of the square, a dangerous spot for unwary pedestrians. Hard by the bridge tower is a nineteenth-century cast-iron statue of **Charles IV** (**32**, see map p.82), erected on the five hundredth anniversary of his founding of the university, and designed by a German, Ernst Julius Hähnel, in the days before the reawakening of Czech sculpture. To his left is an unusual plaque commemorating a Czech who was shot by mistake by the Red Army during the liberation on May 9, 1945.

The **Muzeum Karlova mostu** (daily 10am–8pm; 150Kč; Ⓦ www.muzeum karlovamostu.cz), next door, houses an exhibition on the history of the Charles Bridge. Those with an interest in stonemasonry and engineering will enjoy the exhibition; everyone else will probably get more out of the archive film footage.

The two churches facing onto the square are both quite striking and definitely worth exploring. The half-brick church of **sv František z Assisi** (St Francis of Assisi) was built in the 1680s to a design by Jean-Baptiste Mathey for the Czech Order of Knights of the Cross with a Red Star, the original gatekeepers of the old

Judith Bridge. Founded by sv Anežka (St Agnes) in the thirteenth century, the order reached the zenith of its power in the seventeenth century, during which its monks supplied most of the archbishops of Prague. The church's interior is a real period piece, dominated by its huge dome, decorated with a fresco of the Last Judgement by Václav Vavřinec Reiner, and smothered in rich marble and gilded furnishings; its design served as a blueprint for numerous subsequent Baroque churches in Prague.

Over the road is the church of **sv Salvátor** (St Saviour), its facade prickling with saintly statues which are lit up enticingly at night. Founded in 1593, but not completed until 1714, sv Salvátor marks the beginning of the Jesuits' rise to power and is part of the Klementinum complex (see p.86). Like many of their churches, its design copies that of the Gesù church in Rome; it's worth a quick look, if only for the frothy stucco plasterwork and delicate ironwork in its triple-naved interior.

Karlova

Running from Křižovnické náměstí all the way to Malé náměstí is the narrow street of **Karlova**, packed with people winding their way towards Staroměstské náměstí, their attention divided between checking out the tacky souvenir shops

Charles IV (1316–78)

There may be more legends and intrigue associated with the reign of Rudolf II (see box, p.54), but it was under **Emperor Charles IV** (Karel IV to the Czechs) that Prague enjoyed its true golden age. In just over thirty years, Charles transformed Prague into the effective capital of the Holy Roman Empire, establishing the city's archbishopric, its university, a host of monasteries and churches, an entire new town (Nové Město), plus several monuments which survive to this day, most notably St Vitus Cathedral, and, of course, the Charles Bridge (Karlův most).

Born in Prague in 1316 (and christened Václav), Charles was the only son of King John of Luxembourg and Queen Eliška, daughter of Přemyslid King Václav II. Suspecting his wife of plotting to dethrone him, King John imprisoned her and Charles, keeping his 3-year-old son in a dungeon with only "a little light coming in from a hole in the ceiling". In 1323, the young Charles was despatched to the fashionable court of his uncle Charles IV of France, to keep him out of any further trouble and complete his education – he never saw his mother again. In France he was given the name Charles and married off to Blanche de Valois, the first of his four wives.

In 1346, his father (by then totally blind) was killed at the **Battle of Crécy**, and Charles, who escaped with just a wound, inherited the Czech crown. He immediately busied himself with building up his Bohemian power base, and within two years had got himself elected **Holy Roman Emperor**. Fluent in Czech, French, German, Latin and Italian, Charles used his international contacts to gather together a whole host of foreign artists to his new capital, most famously persuading the Italian man of letters, **Petrarch**, to pay a visit.

Though later chroniclers tried to paint Charles as chaste and pure, even he admitted in his autobiography that he had strayed in his youth: "seduced by the perverted people, we were perverted by the perverts", he wrote of his Italian sojourn. And just as Rudolf II created his *Kunst- und Wunderkammer*, Charles also spent much of his spare time amassing a bizarre **collection of relics** to ensure a smooth passage into the after-life. He cajoled and blackmailed his way into obtaining part of the whip used in the Passion, two thorns from Christ's crown, a few drops of milk from the Virgin Mary and one of Mary Magdalene's breasts, all beautifully encased in reliquaries designed by Prague's finest goldsmiths.

and not losing their way. With Europop blaring from several shops, jesters' hats and puppets in abundance, and a strip club for good measure, the whole atmosphere can be oppressive in the height of summer, and is, in many ways, better savoured in the evening.

At the first wiggle in Karlova, you come to the **Vlašská kaple** (Italian Chapel), which served the community of Italian masons, sculptors and painters who settled in Prague during the Renaissance period, and is still, strictly speaking, the property of the Italian state. The present Vlašská kaple is a tiny oval Baroque chapel completed in 1600, though sadly it's rarely open except for services.

You may have more luck with the adjacent church of **sv Kliment**, accessible from the same portal. It's a minor gem of Prague Baroque by Dientzenhofer with statues by Braun, a spectacular set of frescoes depicting the life of St Clement (whose martyrdom involved being lashed to an anchor and hurled into the Black Sea), and an unusual spiky golden iconostasis added in the 1980s by its new owners, the Greek Catholic church, who observe Orthodox rites but belong to the Roman Catholic church.

On the opposite side of Karlova, at the junction with Liliová, is the former café, **U zlatého hada** (The Golden Serpent), where the Armenian Deomatus Damajan opened the city's first coffee house in 1708. According to legend, the café was always full, not least because Damajan had a red-wine fountain inside. It is now a café-restaurant, though sadly minus the fountain and original furnishings.

Klementinum

As they stroll down Karlova, few people notice the **Klementinum** (daily 6am–11pm; ⓦwww.klementinum.com), the vast former Jesuit College on the north side of the street. In 1556, Ferdinand I summoned the Jesuits to Prague to help bolster the Catholic cause in Bohemia, giving them the church of sv Kliment which Dientzenhofer later rebuilt for them. Initially, the Jesuits proceeded with caution, but once the Counter-Reformation set in, they were put in control of the entire university and provincial education system. From their secure base at sv Kliment, they began to establish space for a great Catholic seat of learning in the city by buying up the surrounding land, demolishing more than thirty old town houses and eventually occupying an area second in size only to the Hrad. In 1773, not long after the Klementinum was finally completed, the Jesuits were turfed out of the country and the building handed over to the university authorities.

The Klementinum currently houses the **Národní knihovna** (National Library) and its millions of books, including the world's largest collection of works by the early English reformer, Yorkshireman John Wycliffe, whose writings had an enormous impact on the fourteenth-century Czech religious community, inspiring preachers such as Hus to speak out against the social conditions of the time. There's a side entrance beside the church of sv Salvátor, but the **main entrance** is inconspicuously placed just past the church of sv Kliment: either lets you into a series of plain but tranquil courtyards you can stroll through in preference to Karlova. Here and there, parts of the original building have been left intact and the best bits are now open to the public.

Nearby is the visitors' entrance, where you must sign up for a thirty-minute **guided tour** (daily 10am–6pm; 220Kč) in order to see inside the Klementinum. On the ground floor is the **Zrcadlová kaple** (Mirrored Chapel), whose interior of fake marble, gilded stucco and mirror panels boasts fine acoustics and is used for concerts. Upstairs, is the **Barokní sál** (Baroque Library), a long room lined with leather tomes, whose ceiling is decorated by one continuous illusionistic fresco praising secular wisdom, and whose wrought-iron gallery balustrade is held up by wooden barley-sugar columns. At roughly the centre of the Klementinum complex, is the Jesuits' **Astronomická věž** (Astonomical Tower), from which you can enjoy a superb view over the centre of Prague. The tower is also the only place in the world that has been monitoring and recording meteorological data since 1775. Until 1928, the tower was also used to signal noon to the citizens of Prague: a man would wave a flag from the tower and a cannon would be fired from Petřín Hill.

Incidentally, Prague's most illustrious visiting scientist, **Johannes Kepler** (1571–1630), who succeeded Tycho Brahe as court astronomer to Rudolf II, lived at Karlova 4 for a number of years. A Protestant exile from his native Germany, Kepler drew up the first heliocentric laws on the movement of the planets while in Prague, though he did his planet-gazing in the Belvedér, not in the Klementinum.

Mariánské náměstí and around

Opposite the southeastern corner of the Klementinum, the Renaissance corner house **U zlaté studné** (The Golden Well) stands out like a wedge of cheese; its thick stucco reliefs of assorted saints were commissioned in 1701 by the owner in gratitude for having been spared the plague.

A short diversion here, down Seminářská, brings you out onto **Mariánské náměstí**, generally fairly deserted compared with Karlova. The rather severe **Nová radnice** (New Town Hall), on the east side of the square, is the home to the city council. It's hard to believe that it was built by Osvald Polívka, architect of the exuberant Art-Nouveau Obecní dům. The most striking features are the two gargantuan figures which stand guard at either corner, by the sculptor of the Hus Monument, Ladislav Šaloun. The one on the left, looking like Darth Vader, is the "Iron Knight", mascot of the armourers' guild; to the right is the grotesquely caricatured sixteenth-century Jewish sage and scholar, **Rabbi Löw** (see box, p.101). Löw was visited by Death on several occasions, but escaped his clutches until he reached the ripe old age of 97, when the Grim Reaper hid in a rose innocently given to him by his (in this case, naked) granddaughter.

To get back to Karlova, head down Husova, past the Baroque **Clam-Gallasův palác**, which, despite its size – it occupies the ground space of a good five or six old houses – is easy to overlook in this narrow space. It's a typically lavish affair by the Viennese architect Fischer von Erlach, with big and burly Atlantes supporting the portals. There are regular historical exhibitions (Tues–Sun 10am–6pm; 40Kč; ⓦ www.ahmp.cz) organized by the Prague City Archives, and evening concerts, which allow you to climb the grandiose staircase and have a peek at the sumptuous Baroque ceremonial rooms.

Malé náměstí

After a couple more shops, boutiques, hole-in-the-wall bars and a final twist in Karlova, you emerge onto **Malé náměstí**, originally settled by French merchants in the twelfth century. The square was also home to the first apothecary in Prague, opened by a Florentine in 1353; the pharmacy **U zlaté koruny** (The Golden Crown), at no. 13, which boasts a restored Baroque interior, with chandeliers and a few drug jars, is now a jewellers'. The square's best-known building, though, is the russet-red, neo-Renaissance **Rott Haus**, originally an ironmonger's shop founded by V.J. Rott in 1840 (and now a *Hard Rock Café*), whose facade is smothered in agricultural scenes and motifs inspired by the Czech artist Mikuláš Aleš. At the centre of the square stands a fountain, dating from 1560, which retains its beautiful, original wrought-iron canopy, though it's no longer functioning.

Staroměstské náměstí

Staroměstské náměstí (Old Town Square) is easily the most spectacular square in Prague, and the traditional heart of the city. Most of the brightly coloured houses look solidly eighteenth-century, but their Baroque facades hide considerably older buildings. From the eleventh century onwards, this was the city's main marketplace, known simply as Velké náměstí (Great Square), to which all roads in Bohemia led, and where merchants from all over Europe gathered. When the five towns that made up Prague were united in 1784, it was the **town hall** here that was made the seat of the new city council, and for the next two hundred years this square (along with Wenceslas Square) witnessed the country's most violent demonstrations and battles. Nowadays, it's busy with tourists all year round: in summer cafés spread out their tables, in winter there's a Christmas market, and every day tourists pour in to watch the town hall's astronomical clock chime, to sit on the benches in front of the **Hus Monument**, and to drink in this historic showpiece.

Staroměstská radnice

It wasn't until the reign of King John of Luxembourg (1310–46) that Staré Město was allowed to build its own town hall, the **Staroměstská radnice** (Old Town Hall). Short of funds, the citizens decided against an entirely new structure, buying a corner house on the square instead and simply adding an extra floor; later on, they added the east wing, with its graceful Gothic oriel and obligatory wedge-tower. Gradually, over the centuries, the neighbouring merchants' houses to the west were incorporated into the building, so that now it stretches all the way across to the richly sgraffitoed **Dům U minuty**, which juts out into the square.

On May 8, 1945, on the final day of the Prague Uprising, the Nazis still held on to Staroměstské náměstí, and in a last desperate act set fire to the town hall's neo-Gothic **east wing**, which stretched almost to the church of sv Mikuláš. The tower and oriel chapel were rebuilt immediately, but only a crumbling fragment remains of the east wing; the rest of it is marked by the stretch of grass to the north. Embedded in the wall of the tower is a plaque marked "Dukla", and a case

▲ View over Staroměstské náměstí to the Týn church

The astronomical clock

The town hall's most popular feature is its *orloj* or **astronomical clock** which has been here since the beginning of the fifteenth century; the working figures were added in 1490 by a **Master Hanuš** who, legend has it, was then blinded with a red-hot poker by the town councillors, to make sure he couldn't repeat the job for anyone else. In retaliation, he groped his way around the clock, succeeded in stopping it, and then promptly died of a heart attack – the clock stayed broken for over eighty years. A crowd of tourists gather every hour (9am–9pm) in front of the tower to watch a mechanical dumbshow by the clock's assorted figures: the Apostles shuffle past the top two windows, bowing to the audience, while perched on pinnacles below are the four threats to the city as perceived by the medieval mind: Death carrying his hourglass and tolling his bell, the Jew with his moneybags (since 1945 minus his stereotypical beard), Vanity admiring his reflection and a turbaned Turk shaking his head. Beneath the moving figures, four characters representing Philosophy, Religion, Astronomy and History stand motionless throughout the performance. Finally, a cockerel pops out and flaps its wings to signal that the show's over; the clock then chimes the hour.

The complex **clock face** tells three different sets of time: the golden hand points to a double set of Roman numerals from I to XII, and when the hand points to the top XII, it's noon (**Central European Time**); it also points to the outer ring of Gothic numbers from 1 to 24, which can rotate independently, and when the hand points to 24 it is sunset (**Old Bohemian Time**); finally, the numbers from 1 to 12 immediately below the Roman numerals divide the day into twelve hours, however many normal hours of daylight there are, and the golden sun tells you what time of day it is (**Babylonian Time**). The clock also charts – as the medieval astronomer saw it – the movements of the sun and planets around the earth, and the movement of the sun and moon through the signs of the zodiac; therefore, if you know how, you can determine the date. The revolving dial below the clock face is decorated with bucolic paintings of the "cycle of twelve idylls from the life of the Bohemian peasant", plus the signs of the zodiac, by **Josef Mánes**, a leading light in the Czech national revival. Around the edge, yet another pointer shows what day of the month and week it is, and, more importantly, what saint's day it is (and therefore when it's a holiday).

---

containing a handful of earth from the Slovak pass where some 80,000 Soviet and Czechoslovak soldiers lost their lives in the first (and most costly) battle to liberate the country in October 1944.

Below, set into the paving, are 27 **white crosses** commemorating the Protestant leaders who were condemned to death on the orders of the Emperor Ferdinand II, following the Battle of Bílá hora. They were publicly executed in the square on June 21, 1621, by the Prague executioner, Jan Mlydář. Twenty-four enjoyed the nobleman's privilege and had their heads lopped off; the three remaining commoners were hung, drawn and quartered. Mlydář also chopped off the right hand of three of the nobles, and hacked off the tongue of the rector of Prague University, Johannes Jessenius, which he then nailed to their respective severed heads for public display on the Charles Bridge.

The town hall is a popular place to get married, but casual visitors can also get to see the **interior**. Temporary exhibitions are held on the ground floor (40Kč), and you can climb the **tower** (Mon 11am–8pm, Tues–Sun 9am–8pm; 100Kč) for a panoramic sweep across Prague's spires; tickets are available from the third floor. If you climb the tower, you also get to see the vast **model** of contemporary Prague, on the fourth floor, made over the course of twenty years out of cardboard and plexiglass by Vlastimil Slíva and Jiří Straka.

You can also join a twenty-minute **guided tour** (Mon 11am–6pm, Tues–Sun 9am–6pm; 70–100Kč) of the rest of the building. Despite being steeped in history, there's not much of interest in the municipal chambers, apart from a few pretty decorated ceilings, striped with chunky beams, and a couple of Renaissance portals. It was in these rooms that the Bohemian kings were elected until the Habsburgs established hereditary rule, and in 1422 Jan Želivský, the fiery Hussite preacher and inspiration behind Prague's first defenestration (see p.127), was executed here. More atmospheric are the town hall's Romano-Gothic cellars, and the Gothic **chapel**, designed by Peter Parler, which has patches of medieval wall painting, and wonderful grimacing corbels at the foot of the ribbed vaulting. Visitors also get to see the clock's **Apostles** close up – and if you're there just before the clock strikes the hour, you can watch them going out on parade; the figures all had to be re-carved by a local puppeteer after the war.

The Hus Monument

The most recent arrival in the Old Town Square is the colossal **Jan Hus Monument**, a turbulent sea of blackened bodies – the oppressed to his right, the defiant to his left – out of which rises the majestic moral authority of Hus himself, gazing into the horizon (for more on Hus, see p.96). For the sculptor Ladislav Šaloun, a maverick who received no formal training, the monument was his life's work, commissioned in 1900 when the Art Nouveau-style Vienna Secession was at its peak, but strangely old-fashioned by the time it was completed in 1915. It would be difficult to claim that it blends in with its Baroque surroundings, yet this has never mattered to the Czechs, for whom its significance goes far beyond aesthetic merit.

The Austrians refused to hold an official unveiling of the statue; in protest, on July 6, 1915, the five hundredth anniversary of the death of Hus, Praguers smothered the monument in flowers. Since then it has been a powerful symbol of Czech nationalism: in March 1939 it was draped in swastikas by the invading Nazis, and in August 1968 it was shrouded in funereal black by Praguers, in protest of the Soviet invasion. The inscription along the base is a quote from the will of Comenius, one of Hus's later followers, and includes Hus's most famous dictum, *Pravda vítězí* (Truth Prevails), which has been the motto of just about every Czech revolution since then.

The church of sv Mikuláš

The destruction of the east wing of the town hall in 1945 rudely exposed Kilian Ignaz Dientzenhofer's church of **sv Mikuláš** (daily 10am–4pm; free), built in just three years between 1732 and 1735. The original church was founded by German merchants in the thirteenth century, and served as Staré Město's parish church until the Týn church (see opposite) was completed. Later, it was handed over to the Benedictines, who commissioned Dientzenhofer to replace it with the present building. His hand is obvious: the south front is decidedly luscious – Braun's blackened statuary pop up at every cornice – promising an interior to surpass even its sister church of sv Mikuláš in Malá Strana, which Dientzenhofer built with his father immediately afterwards. Inside, however, it's a much smaller space, theatrically organized into a series of interlocking curves. It's also rather plainly furnished, partly because it was closed down by Joseph II and turned into a storehouse, and partly because it's now owned by the very "low", modern, Czechoslovak Hussite Church. Instead, your eyes are drawn sharply upwards to the impressive stuccowork, the wrought-iron galleries and the *trompe l'oeil* frescoes on the dome.

Palác Kinských and the south side of the square

The largest secular building on Staroměstské náměstí is the Rococo **palác Kinských**, designed by Kilian Ignaz Dientzenhofer and built by his son-in-law Anselmo Lurago. In the nineteenth century it had a German *Gymnasium* at the rear, attended by, among others, Franz Kafka (whose father ran a haberdashery shop on the ground floor – now a Kafka bookshop). The palace is perhaps most notorious, however, as the venue for the fateful speech by the Communist prime minister, Klement Gottwald, who walked out onto the grey stone balcony one snowy February morning in 1948, flanked by his Party henchmen, to address the thousands of enthusiastic supporters who packed the square below. It was the beginning of *Vítězná února* (Victorious February), the bloodless coup which brought the Communists to power and sealed the fate of the country for the next 41 years. Gottwald's appearance forms the memorable opening to Milan Kundera's novel *The Book of Laughter and Forgetting* (see p.256). The city's Národní galerie is currently converting the top two floors in order to display its remarkably extensive **Asian art** collection.

Until the 1970s, the adjacent **Dům U kamenného zvonu** (House at the Stone Bell; Tues–Sun 10am–6pm; 120Kč; ⓦ www.ghmp.cz) was much like any other of the merchant houses that line Staroměstské náměstí – covered in a thick icing of Baroque plasterwork and topped by an undistinguished roof gable. In the process of restoration, however, it was controversially stripped down to its Gothic core, uncovering the original honey-coloured stonework and simple wedge roof, and it now serves as a central venue for cutting-edge modern art exhibitions, lectures and concerts, organized by the Galerie hlavního města Prahy (City Gallery Prague).

The south side of Staroměstské náměstí boasts a fine array of facades, mostly Baroque, with the notable exception of the neo-Renaissance **Štorchův dům**, adorned with a late nineteenth-century sgraffito painting of St Wenceslas by Mikuláš Aleš. Next door, **U bílého jednorožce** (The White Unicorn) – the sixteenth-century house sign actually depicts a one-horned ram – was Prague's most famous *salon*, run by Berta Fanta. Prague German writers Franz Kafka, Max Brod and Franz Werfel attended, as did **Albert Einstein**, who worked in Prague for a number of years before the First World War, and liked to bring his violin along to entertain the company during any breaks in the discussions.

The Týn church

Staré Město's most impressive Gothic structure, the mighty **Týn church** (Chrám Matky boží před Týnem; daily 10am–1pm & 3–5pm; free; ⓦtynska.farnost.cz), is a far more imposing building than the main square's church of sv Mikuláš. Its two irregular towers, bristling with baubles, spires and pinnacles, rise like giant antennae above the arcaded houses which otherwise obscure its facade, and are spectacularly lit up at night. Like the nearby Hus Monument, the Týn church, begun in the fourteenth century under Charles IV, is a source of Czech national pride. In an act of defiance, George of Poděbrady, the last Czech and the only Hussite king of Bohemia, adorned the high stone gable with a statue of himself and a giant gilded *kalich* (chalice), the mascot of all Hussite sects. The church remained a hotbed of Hussitism until the Protestants' crushing defeat at the Battle of Bílá hora, after which the chalice was melted down to provide the newly ensconced statue of the Virgin Mary with a golden halo, sceptre and crown.

Despite being one of the main landmarks of Staré Město, it's well-nigh impossible to appreciate the church from anything but a considerable distance, since it's boxed in by the houses around it, some of which are actually built right against the walls. To reach the entrance, take the third arch on the left, which passes under the Venetian gables of the former Týn School. The church's lofty, narrow nave is bright white, punctuated at ground level by black and gold Baroque altarpieces. One or two original Gothic furnishings survive, most notably the fifteenth-century baldachin, housing a winged altar in the north aisle, and, opposite, the pulpit, whose panels are enhanced by some sensitive nineteenth-century icons. Behind the pulpit, you'll find a superb, winged altar depicting John the Baptist, dating from 1520, and executed by the artist known as Master I.P. To view the north portal and canopy, which bears the hallmark of Peter Parler's workshop, you must go back outside and head down Týnská.

The pillar on the right of the chancel steps contains the red marble **tomb of Tycho Brahe**, the famous Danish astronomer who arrived in Prague wearing a silver and gold false nose, having lost his own in a duel over a woman in Rostock. Court astronomer to Rudolf II for just two years, Brahe laid much of the groundwork for Johannes Kepler's later discoveries – Kepler getting his chance of employment when Brahe died of a burst bladder after one of Petr Vok's notorious binges in 1601 – hence the colloquial expression *nechci umřít jako Tycho Brahe* ("I don't want to die like Tycho Brahe" – in other words, I need to go to the toilet).

Dům U zlatého prstenů

If you head down the alleyway to the north of the Týn church, known as Týnská, you'll come to the handsome Gothic town house of **Dům U zlatého prstenů** (House of the Golden Ring; Tues–Sun 10am–6pm; 150Kč; ⓦwww.ghmp.cz), now used by the City of Prague Gallery to show some of its twentieth-century Czech art. If you're not heading out to the modern art museum in the Veletržní palác (see p.148), then this is a good taster. The permanent collection is spread out over three floors, and arranged thematically rather than chronologically, while the cellar provides space for installations by up-and-coming contemporary artists; there's also a nice café across the courtyard.

On the first floor, symbolism looms large, with *Destitute Land*, Max Švabinský's none-too-subtle view of life under the Habsburg yoke, and a smattering of works by two of Bohemia's best-loved eccentrics, Josef Váchal and František Bílek. There's a decent selection of dour 1920s paintings, too, typified by *Slagheaps in the Evening II* by Jan Zrzavý, plus the usual Czech Surrealist suspects, Josef Šíma, Toyen and Jiří Štyrský. More refreshing is the sight of Eduard Stavinoha's cartoon-like *Striking Demonstrators 24.2.1948*, an ideological painting from 1948 that appears almost like Pop Art. Antonín Slavíček's easy-on-the-eye Impressionist views of Prague are displayed on the second floor, along with works by Cubist Emil Filla. Also on this floor, you'll find Zbyšek Sion's absinthe nightmare and the strange perforated metal sheets of Alena Kučerova. The selection of contemporary works on the third floor changes more frequently than the rest of the gallery.

Týn (Ungelt)

Just off Týnská, directly behind the Týn church, lies the picturesque cobbled courtyard of **Týn**, previously known by its German name, Ungelt (meaning "No Money", a pseudonym used to deter marauding invaders), which, as the trading base of German merchants, was one of the first settlements on the Vltava. A hospice, church and hostel were built for the use of the merchants, and by the fourteenth century the area had become an extremely successful international marketplace; soon afterwards the traders moved up to the Hrad, and the court was transformed into a palace. The whole complex has since been restored, and is now a great place in which to stroll; the Dominicans have moved back into one section, while the rest houses various shops, cafés, pubs, restaurants and a hotel.

Celetná

Celetná, whose name comes from the bakers who used to bake a particular type of small loaf (*calty*) here in the Middle Ages, leads east from Staroměstské náměstí direct to the Prašná brána, one of the original gateways of the old town. It's one of the oldest streets in Prague, lying along the former trade route from the old town market square, as well as on the *králová cesta*. Its buildings were smartly refaced in the Baroque period, and their pastel plasterwork is now crisply maintained. Dive down one of the covered passages to the left and into the backstreets, however, and you'll soon lose the crowds.

Muzeum českého kubismu (Museum of Czech Cubism)

Two-thirds of the way along Celetná, at the junction with Ovocný trh, is the **Dům U Černé Matky boží** (House at the Black Madonna), built as a department store in 1911–12 by Josef Gočár and one of the best examples of Czech Cubist architecture in Prague. It was a short-lived style whose most surprising attribute, in this instance, is its ability to adapt existing Baroque motifs: Gočár's house sits much more happily amongst its eighteenth-century neighbours than, for example, the functionalist shop opposite – one of Gočár's later designs from the 1930s.

Appropriately enough, the building now houses the small, but excellent, **Muzeum českého kubismu** (Museum of Czech Cubism; Tues–Sun 10am–6pm; 100Kč; Ⓦ www.ngprague.cz), with temporary exhibitions on the top floor, a permanent collection on Czech Cubism on the two floors below and a reconstruction of the original 1911 café on the first floor. In the museum itself, there's a little bit of everything – from sofas and sideboards by Gočár himself, Pavel Janák and Josef Chochol, to paintings by Emil Filla and Josef Čapek, plus some wonderful sculptures by Otto Gutfreund. If the above has only whetted your appetite, there are more Czech Cubist exhibits in the Veletržní palác, and more Cubist buildings in Vyšehrad, models of which are displayed in the museum.

The church of sv Jakub

Concealed in the backstreets north of Celetná is the Franciscan church of **sv Jakub**, or St James (daily 9.30am–noon & 2–4pm; free), with its distinctive bubbling, stucco portal on Malá Štupartská. The church's massive Gothic proportions – it has the longest nave in Prague after the cathedral – make it a favourite venue for organ recitals, Mozart masses and other concerts. After the great fire of 1689, Prague's Baroque artists remodelled the entire interior, adding huge pilasters, a series of colourful frescoes and over twenty side altars. The most famous of these is the tomb of the count of Mitrovice, in the northern aisle, designed by Fischer von Erlach and Prague's own Maximilian Brokof.

The church has close historical links with the butchers of Prague, who were given a chapel in gratitude for their defence of the city in 1611 and 1648. Hanging high up on the west wall, on the right as you enter, is a thoroughly decomposed human forearm. It has been there for over four hundred years now, ever since a thief tried to steal the jewels of the Madonna from the high altar. As the thief reached out, the Virgin supposedly grabbed his arm and refused to let go. The next day the congregation of butchers had no option but to lop it off, and it has hung there as a warning ever since.

Anežský klášter

Further north from sv Jakub through the backstreets, the **Anežský klášter** (Convent of St Agnes), Prague's oldest surviving Gothic building, stands within a stone's throw of the river as it loops around to the east. It was founded in 1233 as a Franciscan convent, and takes its name from Anežka (Agnes), youngest daughter of Přemysl Otakar I, who left her life of regal privilege to become the convent's first abbess. Anežka took her vows seriously, living on a diet of raw onions and fruit with long periods of fasting, and in 1874 she was beatified to try and combat the spread of Hussitism among the Czechs. There was much speculation about the wonders that would occur when she was officially canonized, an event which finally took place on November 12, 1989, when Czech Catholics were invited to a special Mass at St Peter's in Rome. Four days later the Velvet Revolution began: a happy coincidence, even for agnostic Czechs.

The convent itself has enjoyed a chequered history. It was used as an arsenal by the Hussites, and eventually closed down in 1782 by Joseph II, who turned it into a place where the Prague poor could live and set up their own workshops. The whole neighbourhood remained a slum area until well into the twentieth century, and its restoration only finally took place in the 1980s. The convent now provides a fittingly atmospheric setting for the National Gallery's **medieval art collection** (Tues–Sun 10am–6pm; 150Kč; Ⓦwww.ngprague.cz), in particular the art that flourished under the patronage of Charles IV.

The exhibition is arranged chronologically, starting with a remarkable silver-gilt casket from 1360 used to house the skull of sv Ludmila. The nine panels from the altarpiece of the Cistercian monastery at Vyšší Brod in South Bohemia, from around 1350, are among the finest in central Europe: the panel depicting the Annunciation is particularly rich iconographically. The real gems of the collection, however, are the six panels by **Master Theodoric**, who painted over one hundred such paintings for Charles IV's castle chapel at Karlštejn. These larger-than-life, half-length portraits of saints, Church Fathers and so on are full of intense expression and richly coloured, their depictions spilling onto the embossed frames.

The three late fourteenth-century panels by the **Master of Třeboň** show an ever greater variety of balance, delicacy and depth, and the increasing influence of Flemish paintings of the period. The quality of the works in the gallery's largest room is pretty uneven, so head straight to the end of the room where you'll find Cranach's superb *Portrait of a Young Lady Holding a Fern*. Beyond are a couple of smaller rooms, where you'll find two unusual carved wooden bust reliquaries of saints Adalbert and Wenceslas. For a glimpse of some extraordinary draughtsmanship, check out the woodcuts by Cranach the Elder, Dürer and the lesser-known Hans Burgkmair – the seven-headed beast in Dürer's *Apocalypse* cycle is particularly Harry Potter. One oil painting that stands out from the crowd is Albrecht Altdorfer's colourful, languid *Martyrdom of St Florian*. Finally, don't miss the superb sixteenth-century wood sculptures by **Master I.P.**, including an incredibly detailed *Christ the Saviour and the Last Judgement*, in which Death's entrails are in the process of being devoured by a frog.

You exit via the Gothic cloisters and the bare church that serves as a resting place for, among others, Václav I (1205–53), and Anežka herself.

Stavovské divadlo

The lime-green and white **Stavovské divadlo** (Estates Theatre) stands on **Ovocný trh**, site of the old fruit market. Built in the early 1780s for the entertainment of Prague's large and powerful German community, the theatre is one of the finest Neoclassical buildings in Prague, reflecting the enormous self-confidence of its former patrons. The Stavovské divadlo has a place in Czech history, too, for it was here that the Czech national anthem, "Kde domov můj?" (Where Is My Home?), was first performed, as part of the comedy *Fidlovačka*, by J.K. Tyl. It is also something of a place of pilgrimage for Mozart fans, since it is the only opera house left standing in which Mozart actually performed. Indeed, it was here, rather than in the hostile climate of Vienna, that the composer chose to premiere both *Don Giovanni* and *La Clemenza di Tito* – the hooded figure statue outside the theatre entrance represents Don Giovanni.

Karolinum – Charles University

On the north side of the Stavovské divadlo is the home base of the **Karolinum,** or Charles University, named after its founder Charles IV, who established it in 1348 as the first university in this part of Europe. Although it was open to all nationalities, with instruction in Latin, it wasn't long before disputes between the various "nations" came to a head. In 1408, Václav IV issued the Decree of Kutná Hora, which gave the Bohemian "nation" – both Czech- and German-speaking – a majority vote in the university. In protest, the other "nations" upped and left for Leipzig, the first of many ethnic problems which continued to bubble away throughout the university's six-hundred-year history until the forced and violent expulsion of all German-speakers after World War II.

To begin with, the university had no fixed abode; it wasn't until 1383 that Václav IV bought the present site. All that's left of the original fourteenth-century building is the Gothic oriel window which emerges from the south wall; the rest was trashed by the Nazis in 1945. The new main entrance is a modern red-brick curtain wall building by Jaroslav Fragner, set back from the street and inscribed with the original Latin name *Universitas Karolina*. Only a couple of small departments and the chancellor's office and administration are now housed here, with the rest spread over the length and breadth of the city. The heavily restored Gothic vaults, on the ground floor of the south wing, are now used as a contemporary **art gallery** (daily 10am–6pm; free).

Church of sv Havel and the market

The junction of Melantrichova and Rytířská is always teeming with people pouring out of Staroměstské náměstí and heading for Wenceslas Square. Clearly visible from Melantrichova is Santini's undulating Baroque facade of the church of **sv Havel**, sadly no relation to the playwright-president but named after the Irish monk, St Gall. It was built in the thirteenth century to serve the German-speaking community who had been invited to Prague partly to replace the Jewish traders killed in the city's 1096 pogrom. After the expulsion of the Protestants, the church was handed over to the Carmelites who redesigned the interior, now only visible through an iron grille.

Straight ahead of you as you leave sv Havel is Prague's last surviving **open-air market**, originally run by the German community, and stretching all the way from Ovocný trh to Uhelný trh. Traditionally flogging flowers and vegetables, it runs the full length of the arcaded Havelská, and sells everything from celery to CDs, with plenty of souvenirs and wooden toys in between.

Uhelný trh, sv Martin ve zdi and Bartolomějská

The market on Havelská runs west into **Uhelný trh**, which gets its name from the *uhlí* (coal) that was sold here in medieval times. South of Uhelný trh, down

Martinská, the street miraculously opens out to make room for the twelfth-century church of **sv Martin ve zdi** (St Martin-in-the-Walls). It's still essentially a Romanesque structure, adapted to suit Gothic tastes a century later. Closed down in 1784 by Joseph II and turned into a warehouse, shops and flats, the church was bought and restored by the city council in 1904; they added the creamy neo-Renaissance tower, and eventually handed the church over to the Czech Brethren. For them, it has a special significance as the place where communion "in both kinds" (bread and wine), one of the fundamental demands of the Hussites, was first administered to the whole congregation, in 1414. To be honest, there's very little to see inside, which is just as well as it's open only for concerts nowadays.

Around the corner from sv Martin ve zdi is the gloomy, lifeless street of **Bartolomějská**, dominated by a tall, grim-looking building on its south side, which served as the main interrogation centre of the **Communist secret police**, the Státní bezpečnost, or StB. As in the rest of Eastern Europe, the accusations (often unproven) and revelations of who exactly collaborated with the StB caused the downfall of leading politicians right across the political spectrum. The building is now back in the hands of the Franciscan nuns who occupied the place prior to 1948, and its former police cells now serve as rooms – you can even stay in Václav Havel's former cell (see p.184).

Betlémská kaple

The attractive little square of Betlémské náměstí is named after the **Betlémská kaple** (Tues–Sun: April–Oct 10am–6.30pm; Nov–March 10am–5.30pm; 50Kč), whose high wooden gables face onto the square. The chapel was founded in 1391 by religious reformists, who, denied the right to build a church, proceeded instead to build the largest chapel in Bohemia, with a total capacity of three thousand. Sermons were delivered not in the customary Latin, but in the language of the masses – Czech. From 1402 to 1413 **Jan Hus** (see box below) preached here, regularly pulling in more than enough commoners to fill the chapel. Hus was

Jan Hus

The legendary preacher – and Czech national hero – **Jan Hus** (often anglicized to John Huss) was born in the small village of Husinec in South Bohemia around 1372. From a childhood of poverty, he enjoyed a steady rise through the Czech education system, taking his degree at the Karolinum in the 1390s, and eventually being ordained as a deacon and priest around 1400. Although without doubt an admirer of the English religious reformer **John Wycliffe** (and the Lollards), Hus was by no means as radical as many of his colleagues who preached at the Betlémská kaple. Nor did he actually advocate many of the more famous tenets of the heretical religious movement that took his name: Hussitism. In particular, he never advocated giving communion "in both kinds" (bread and wine) to the general congregation.

In the end, it wasn't the disputes over Wycliffe, whose books were burnt on the orders of the archbishop in 1414, that proved Hus's downfall, but an argument over the sale of indulgences to fund the inter-papal wars that prompted his unofficial trial at the **Council of Constance**. Having been guaranteed safe conduct by Emperor Sigismund himself, Hus naïvely went to Constance to defend his views, and was burnt at the stake as a heretic on July 6, 1415. The Czechs were outraged, and Hus became a national hero overnight, inspiring thousands to rebel against the authorities of the day. In 1999, the pope expressed "deep regret" over his death, but refused to pardon Hus – the anniversary of Hus's death is now a **Czech national holiday**.

eventually excommunicated for his outspokenness, found guilty of heresy and burnt at the stake at the Council of Constance in 1415.

The chapel continued to attract reformists from all over Europe for another two centuries. The Anabaptist **Thomas Müntzer** preached here in the sixteenth century, having fled to Prague from Zwickau – he later became one of the leaders of the German Peasants' War. Of the original building, only the three outer walls remain, with restored patches of the biblical scenes, used to get the message across to the illiterate congregation. The rest is a scrupulous reconstruction by Jaroslav Fragner, using the original plans and a fair amount of imaginative guesswork. The initial reconstruction work was carried out after the war by the Communists, who were keen to portray Hus as a Czech nationalist and social critic as much as a religious reformer, and, of course, to dwell on the revolutionary Müntzer's later appearances here.

Náprstkovo muzeum

At the western end of Betlémské náměstí stands the **Náprstkovo muzeum** (Tues– Sun 10am–6pm; 80Kč, free first Fri of month; ⓦ www.nm.cz), whose founder, Czech nationalist Vojta Náprstek, was inspired by the great Victorian museums of London while in exile following the 1848 revolution. On his return, he turned the family brewery into a museum, initially intending it to concentrate on the virtues of industrial progress. Náprstek's interests gradually shifted towards anthropology, however, and it is his **ethnographic collections** that are now displayed in the museum; the original technological exhibits are housed in Prague's Národné technické muzeum. Despite the fact that the museum could clearly do with an injection of cash, it still manages to put on some really excellent temporary ethnographic exhibitions on the ground floor, and also does a useful job of promoting tolerance of different cultures. The permanent collection begins on the first floor, where you'll find the skeleton of a fin-whale over 20m long suspended from the ceiling. Underneath it there's a range of exhibits from the Americas, with everything from Inuit furs and Apache smoking pipes, decorated with porcupine quills and beads, to toy skeletons on bicycles from Mexico and Amazonian shrunken heads. Upstairs, there's a much smaller display of stuff from Australia and Oceania including some remarkable sculptures, but sadly the labelling is pretty minimal.

Husova

Between Betlémské náměstí and Karlova lies a confusing maze of streets, passageways and backyards, containing few sights as such, but nevertheless a joy to explore. One building that might catch your eye is the church of **sv Jiljí** (St Giles), on Husova, whose outward appearance suggests another Gothic masterpiece, but whose interior is decked out in the familiar black excess of the eighteenth century, with huge gilded acanthus-leaf capitals and barley-sugar columns galore. The **frescoes** by Václav Vavřinec Reiner (who is buried in the church) are full of praise for his patrons, the Dominicans, who took over the church after the Protestant defeat of 1620. They were expelled, in turn, after the Communists took power, only to return following the events of 1989. Reiner's paintings also depict the unhappy story of **St Giles** himself, a ninth-century hermit who is thought to have lived somewhere in Provence. Out one day with his pet deer, Giles and his companion were chased by the hounds of King Wanda of the Visigoths. The hounds were rooted to the spot by an invisible power, while the arrow from the hunters struck Giles in the foot as he defended his pet – the hermit was later looked upon as the patron saint of cripples.

Anenské náměstí and the waterfront

Heading west from Husova along Řetězová and Anenská brings you eventually to the waterfront. On **Anenské náměstí**, just before you reach the river, is the **Divadlo na zábradlí** (Theatre on the Balustrade), founded in 1958. As well as championing mime as a genre, the theatre was also at the centre of Prague's absurdist theatre scene in the 1960s, with Havel himself working first as a stagehand and later as resident playwright. Later, it became something of a refuge for film directors of the Czech New Wave who couldn't get their work shown in the cinema, and it remains one of Prague's more innovative small theatres.

The gaily decorated neo-Renaissance building at the very end of Novotného lávka, on the riverfront itself, was once the city's waterworks. It now houses, among other things, the **Muzeum Bedřicha Smetany** (daily except Tues 10am–noon & 12.30–5pm; 50Kč), situated on the first floor. Bedřich Smetana (1824–84), despite having German as his mother tongue, was without doubt the most nationalist of all the great Czech composers, taking an active part in the 1848 revolution and the later national revival movement. He enjoyed his greatest success as a composer with *Prodaná nevěsta* (*The Bartered Bride*), but he was forced to give up conducting in 1874 with the onset of deafness, and eventually died of syphilis in a mental asylum. Unfortunately, the museum fails to capture much of the spirit of the man, concentrating instead on items such as his spectacles, and the garnet jewellery of his first wife. Still, the views across to the castle are good, and you get to wave a laser baton around in order to listen to his music.

Outside, beneath the large weeping willow that droops over the embankment, the statue of the seated Smetana is rather unfortunately placed, with his back towards one of his most famous sources of inspiration, the **River Vltava** (Moldau in German). It's worth strolling south along the embankment to the little park which is centred on the **Krannerova kašna,** an enormous, elaborate and slightly lugubrious neo-Gothic memorial sheltering a bronze statue of the Emperor Franz I (1792–1835), one of the few Habsburg monuments to survive the nationalist outpouring that accompanied the foundation of Czechoslovakia in 1918. The ground plan of the monument is in the shape of an eight-pointed star and, bizarrely, the plinth also functions as a fountain with water gushing from its foundations.

Josefov

It is crowded with horses; traversed by narrow streets not remarkable for
cleanliness, and has altogether an uninviting aspect. Your sanitary reformer
would here find a strong case of overcrowding.

Walter White, "A July Holiday in Saxony, Bohemia and Silesia" (1857)

ess than half a century after Walter White's comments, all that was left of
the former Jewish ghetto of **JOSEFOV** were six synagogues, the town hall
and the medieval cemetery. At the end of the nineteenth century, a period
of great economic growth for the Habsburg Empire, it was decided that
Prague should be turned into a beautiful bourgeois city, modelled on Paris. The
key to this transformation was the *asanace* or "sanitization" of the ghetto, a
process, begun in 1893, which reduced the notoriously malodorous backstreets
and alleyways of Josefov to rubble and replaced them with block after block of
luxurious five-storey mansions. The Jews, the poor, the gypsies and the prostitutes were cleared out so that the area could become a desirable residential
quarter, rich in Art Nouveau buildings festooned with decorative murals,
doorways and sculpturing. This building frenzy marked the beginning of the end
for a community that had existed in Prague for almost a millennium.

In any other European city occupied by the Nazis in World War II, what little
was left of the old ghetto would have been demolished. But, although thousands
of Prague's Jews were transported to the new ghetto in Terezín and eventually to
Auschwitz, the Prague ghetto was preserved under the Nazis in order to provide a
record of the communities they had destroyed. By this grotesque twist of fate,
Jewish artefacts from Czechoslovakia and beyond were gathered here, and now
make up one of the richest collections of Judaica in Europe, and one of the most
fascinating sights in Prague.

Geographically, **Josefov** lies within the Staré Město, to the northwest of
Staroměstské náměstí, between the main square and the river. The warren-like
street plan of the old ghetto has long since disappeared, and through the heart of
Josefov the ultimate bourgeois avenue, **Pařížská**, now runs, a riot of turn-of-the-
twentieth-century sculpturing, spikes and turrets, its ground floor premises home
to designer boutiques and cafés. If Josefov can still be said to have a main street, it's
really the parallel street of **Maiselova**, named after the community's sixteenth-
century leader. The sheer volume of tourists – over a million a year – that visit
Josefov has brought with it the inevitable rash of souvenir stalls, flogging dubious
"Jewish" souvenirs, and, it has to be said, the whole area is now something of a
tourist trap. Yet to skip this part of the old town is to miss out on an entire slice of
the city's cultural history.

Also included in this chapter are the sights around **náměstí Jana Palacha**,
adjacent to, but strictly speaking outside, the Jewish quarter, most notably the
city's excellent **Museum of Decorative Arts** (or UPM).

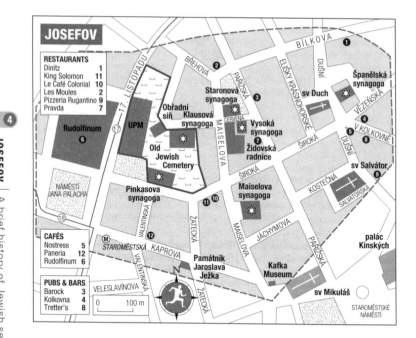

A brief history of Jewish settlement in Prague

Jews probably settled in Prague as early as the tenth century and, initially at least, are thought to have settled on both sides of the river. In 1096, at the time of the first crusade, the first recorded pogrom took place, an event which may have hastened the formation of a closely knit "Jewish town" within Staré Město during the twelfth century. It wasn't until much later that Jews were actually herded into a **walled ghetto** (and several centuries before the word "ghetto" was actually first coined in Venice), sealed off from the rest of the town and subjected to a curfew. Jews were also subject to laws restricting their choice of profession to usury and the rag trade; in addition, some form of visible identification, a cap or badge (and even, at one time, a ruff), remained a more or less constant feature of Jewish life until the Enlightenment.

In 1262, Přemysl King Otakar II issued a *Statuta Judaeorum*, which granted the Jews their own religious and civil self-administration. In effect, however, the Jews were little more than the personal property of the king, and though Otakar himself appears to have been genuine in his motives, later rulers used the *Statuta* as a form of blackmail, extorting money whenever they saw fit. In 1389, during one of the worst **pogroms**, 3000 Jews were massacred over Easter, some while sheltering in the Staronová synagoga (Old-New Synagogue) – an event commemorated every year thereafter on Yom Kippur. In 1541, a fire ripped through Hradčany and Malá Strana and a Jew was tortured into "confessing" the crime. The Bohemian Estates immediately persuaded the Emperor Ferdinand I to **expel the Jews** from Prague. In the end, however, a small number of families were allowed to remain.

By contrast, the reign of Rudolf II (1576–1612) was a time of economic and cultural prosperity for the community, which is thought to have numbered up to

10,000, making it by far the largest Jewish community in the Diaspora. The Jewish mayor, **Mordecai Maisel**, Rudolf's minister of finance, became one of the richest men in Bohemia and the success symbol of a generation; his money bought and built the Jewish quarter a town hall, a bath house, pavements and several synagogues. This was the "golden age" of the ghetto: the time of **Rabbi Löw**, the severe and conservative chief rabbi of Prague, who is now best known as the legendary creator of the Jewish Frankenstein's monster, or "golem", though, in fact, the story of Rabbi Löw and the golem first appeared only in the nineteenth century (see box below).

Amid the violence of the Thirty Years' War, the Jews enjoyed an unusual degree of protection from the emperor, who was heavily dependent on their financial acumen. In **1648**, Prague's Jews, along with the city's students, repaid their imperial bosses by repelling the marauding Swedes on the Charles Bridge, for which they won the lasting respect of Ferdinand III (1637–57). Things went into reverse again during the eighteenth century, until in 1744 Empress Maria Theresa used the community as a scapegoat for her disastrous war against the Prussians, and ordered the expulsion of all Jews from Prague. She allowed them to return in 1748, though only after much pressure from the guilds. It was the enlightened **Emperor Joseph II** (1780–90) who did most to lift the restrictions on Jews. His 1781 Edict of Tolerance ended the dress codes, opened up education to all non-Catholics, and removed the gates from the ghetto. In 1850, the community paid him homage by officially naming the ghetto Josefov, or Josefstadt.

The golem

Legends concerning the animation of unformed matter (which is what the Hebrew word **golem** means), using the mystical texts of the Kabbala, were around long before Frankenstein started playing around with corpses. Two hungry fifth-century rabbis may have made the most practical golem when they sculpted a clay calf, brought it to life and then ate it, but the most famous is undoubtedly **Rabbi Löw**'s giant servant made from the mud of the Vltava, who was brought to life when the rabbi placed a *shem* in its mouth, a tablet with a magic Hebrew inscription.

There are numerous versions of the tale, though the earliest invoking Rabbi Löw appeared only in the nineteenth century. In some, **Yossel**, the golem, is a figure of fun, flooding the rabbi's kitchen rather in the manner of Disney's *Sorcerer's Apprentice*; others portray him as the guardian of the ghetto, helping Rabbi Löw in his struggle with the anti-Semites at Rudolf II's court. In almost all versions, however, the golem finally runs amok. One particularly appealing tale is that the golem's rebellion was because Löw forgot to allow his creature to rest on the Sabbath. He was conducting the service when news of its frenzy arrived, and he immediately ran out to deal with it. The congregation, reluctant to continue without him, merely repeated the verse in the psalm the rabbi had been reciting until Löw returned. This explains the peculiarity at the **Staronová synagoga** (Old-New Synagogue) where a line in the Sabbath service is repeated even today. In all the stories, the end finally comes when Löw removes the *shem* once and for all, and carries the remains of his creature to the attic of the Staronová synagoga, where they have supposedly resided ever since (a fact disputed by the pedantic journalist Egon Erwin Kisch, who climbed in to check).

The legends are amended at each telling, and have proved an enduringly popular theme for generations of artists and writers. **Paul Wegener**'s German expressionist film versions (1914–20) and the dark psychological novel of **Gustav Meyrink** (1915) are probably two of the most powerful treatments. Meyrink's golem lives in a room which has no windows and no doors, emerging to haunt the streets of Prague every 33 years – by which reckoning, it's long overdue a reappearance.

The downside to Joseph's reforms was that he was hellbent on **Jewish assimilation**. The use of Hebrew or Yiddish in business transactions was banned, and Jews were ordered to Germanize their names (the list of permitted names comprised 109 male ones and 35 female). However, it wasn't until the social upheavals of **1848** that Jews were given equal status within the Empire and allowed officially to settle outside the confines of the ghetto – concessions that were accompanied by a number of violent anti-Semitic protests on the part of the Czechs.

From 1848 to the present day

From 1848 the ghetto went into terminal **decline**. The more prosperous Jewish families began to move to other districts of Prague, leaving behind only the poorest Jews and strictly Orthodox families, who were rapidly joined by the underprivileged ranks of Prague society: gypsies, beggars, prostitutes and alcoholics. By 1890, only twenty percent of Josefov's population were Jewish, yet it was still the most densely populated area in Prague, with a staggering 186,000 people crammed into its streets. The ghetto had become a carbuncle in the centre of bourgeois Prague, a source of disease and vice: in the words of Gustav Meyrink, a "demonic underworld, a place of anguish, a beggarly and phantasmagorical quarter whose eeriness seemed to have spread and led to paralysis".

The ending of restrictions and the **destruction of the ghetto,** which began in 1893, increased the pressure on Jews to assimilate, a process that brought with it its own set of problems. Prague's Jews were split roughly half and half between predominantly German- or Yiddish-speakers and Czech-speakers. Yet since some two-thirds of Prague's German population were Jewish, and all Jews had been forced to take German names by Joseph II, all Jews were seen by Czech nationalists as a Germanizing influence. Tensions between the country's German-speaking minority and the Czechs grew steadily worse in the run-up to World War I, and the Jewish community found itself caught in the firing line – "like powerless stowaways attempting to steer a course through the storms of embattled nationalities," as one Prague Jew put it.

Despite several anti-Semitic riots in the years before and after the war, the foundation of the new republic in 1918, and, in particular, its founder and first president, T.G. Masaryk, whose liberal credentials were impeccable, were welcomed by most Jews. For the first time in their history, Jews were given equal rights as a recognized ethnic group, though only a minority opted to be registered as Jewish. The **interwar period** was probably the nearest Prague's Jewish community came to a second "golden age", a time most clearly expressed in the now famous flowering of its *Deutsche Prager Literatur*, led by German-Jewish writers such as Franz Werfel, Franz Kafka, Max Brod and Rainer Maria Rilke.

After the **Nazis occupied Prague** on March 15, 1939, the city's Jews were subject to an increasingly harsh set of regulations, by which they were barred from most professions, placed under curfew, and compelled to wear a yellow Star of David. In November 1941, the first transport of Prague Jews set off for the new ghetto in **Terezín**, 60km northwest of Prague. Of the estimated 55,000 Jews in Prague at the time of the Nazi invasion, over 36,000 died in the camps. Many survivors emigrated to Israel and the US. Of the eight thousand who registered as Jewish in the Prague census of 1947, a significant number joined the Communist Party, only to find themselves victims of Stalinist **anti-Semitic purges** during the 1950s.

It's difficult to calculate exactly how many Jews now live in Prague – around a thousand were officially registered as such prior to 1989 – though their numbers have undoubtedly been bolstered by those Czech Jews who have rediscovered their roots, and, more significantly, by the new influx of Jewish Americans and Israelis. The controversy over Jewish property – most of which was seized by the Nazis,

Visiting Josefov

All the major sights of Josefov – five synagogues and the cemetery – (ⓦwww
.jewishmuseum.cz) are covered by an all-in-one 480Kč **ticket**, valid for one day only
and available from any of the quarter's numerous ticket offices. If you don't want to
visit the Staronová synagoga, the ticket costs just 300Kč. Your ticket also covers
entry to the Jubilejní synagoga in Nové Město (see p.121). **Opening hours** vary but
are basically daily except Saturday April to October 9am to 6pm, and November to
March 9am to 4.30pm. In order to try to regulate the flow of visitors, at peak times
a timed entry system comes into operation, giving you around twenty minutes at
each sight, though don't worry too much if you don't adhere rigidly to your timetable.

and therefore not covered by the original restitution law – has been resolved,
allowing the community to reclaim, among other things, the six synagogues, the
town hall and the cemetery of Josefov itself.

Staronová synagoga (Old-New Synagogue)

As you walk down Maiselova, it's impossible to miss the steep, sawtooth brick
gables of the **Staronová synagoga** or Altneuschul (Old-New Synagogue), so
called because when it was built it was indeed very new, though it eventually
became the oldest synagogue in Josefov. Begun in the second half of the thirteenth
century, it is, in fact, the oldest functioning synagogue in Europe, one of the
earliest Gothic buildings in Prague and still the religious centre for Prague's
Orthodox Jews. Since Jews were prevented by law from becoming architects, the
synagogue is thought to have been constructed by the builders working on the
Franciscan convent of sv Anežka. Its five-ribbed vaulting is unique for Bohemia;
the extra, purely decorative rib was added to avoid any hint of a cross.

To get to the **main hall**, you must pass through one of the two low vestibules
from which women watch the proceedings through narrow slits. Above the
entrance is an elaborate tympanum covered in the twisting branches of a vine tree,
its twelve bunches of grapes representing the tribes of Israel. The simple, plain
interior is mostly taken up with the elaborate wrought-iron cage enclosing the
bimah in the centre. In 1354, Charles IV granted Jews a red flag inscribed with a
Star of David – the first such community known to have adopted the symbol. The
red standard currently on display was a gift to the community from Emperor
Ferdinand II for helping fend off the Swedes in 1648.

Note that the synagogue closes early on Fridays, and all day during Jewish
holidays. To the north of the synagogue is one of the many statues in Prague that
were hidden from the Nazis for the duration of the war: an anguished statue of
Moses by František Bílek.

Židovská radnice and Maiselova synagoga

Just south of the Staronová synagoga stands the **Židovská radnice** (Jewish Town
Hall), one of the few such buildings in Europe to survive the Holocaust.
Founded and funded by Maisel in the sixteenth century, it was later rebuilt as the
creamy-pink Baroque building you now see, housing, among other things, a
kosher restaurant. The belfry, permission for whose construction was granted by
Ferdinand III, has a clock on each of its four sides, plus a Hebrew one stuck on the
north gable which, like the Hebrew script, goes "backwards". Adjacent to the
town hall is the **Vysoká synagoga** (High Synagogue), whose dour grey facade

belies its rich interior; it's now one of only two synagogues in Josefov which is still used for religious services and is closed to the general public.

Founded and paid for entirely by Mordecai Maisel, the neo-Gothic **Maiselova synagoga**, set back from the neighbouring houses further south down Maiselova, was, in its day, one of the most ornate synagogues in Josefov. Nowadays, its bare, whitewashed, turn-of-the-twentieth-century interior houses an exhibition on the history of the Czech-Jewish community up until the 1781 Edict of Tolerance. Along with glass cabinets filled with gold and silverwork, *hanukkah* candlesticks, *Torah* scrolls and other religious artefacts, there's also an example of the antiquated ruffs that had to be worn by all unmarried males from the age of 12, and a copy of Ferdinand I's decree enforcing the wearing of a circular yellow badge.

Pinkasova synagoga

Jutting out at an angle on the south side of the Old Jewish Cemetery (see below) with its entrance on Široká, the **Pinkasova synagoga** was built in the 1530s for the powerful Horovitz family, and has undergone countless restorations over the centuries. In 1958, the synagogue was transformed into a chilling **memorial** to the 77,297 Czech Jews killed during the Holocaust. The memorial was closed shortly after the 1967 Six Day War – due to damp, according to the Communists – and remained so, allegedly because of problems with the masonry, until it was finally painstakingly restored in the 1990s. All that remains of the synagogue's original decor today is the ornate *bimah* surrounded by a beautiful wrought-iron grille, supported by barley-sugar columns.

Of all the sights of the Jewish quarter, the Holocaust memorial is perhaps the most moving, with every bit of wall space taken up with the carved stone list of victims, stating simply their name, date of birth and date of death or transportation to the camps. It is the longest epitaph in the world, yet it represents a mere fraction of those who died in the Nazi concentration camps. Upstairs in a room beside the women's gallery, there's also a harrowing exhibition of **children's drawings** from the Jewish ghetto in Terezín, most of whom were killed in the camps.

Starý židovský hřbitov (Old Jewish Cemetery)

At the heart of Josefov is the **Starý židovský hřbitov** (Old Jewish Cemetery). Established in the fifteenth century, it was used until 1787, by which time there were an estimated 100,000 people buried here, one on top of the other, six palms apart, and as many as twelve layers deep. The enormous numbers of visitors has meant that the graves themselves have been roped off, and a one-way system introduced: you enter from the Pinkasova synagoga, on Široká, and leave by the Klausová synagoga. The oldest grave, dating from 1439, belongs to the poet Avigdor Karo, who lived to tell the tale of the 1389 pogrom. Get there before the crowds – a difficult task for much of the year – and the cemetery can be a poignant reminder of the ghetto, its inhabitants subjected to inhuman overcrowding even in death. The rest of Prague recedes beyond the tall ash trees and cramped perimeter walls, the haphazard headstones and Hebrew inscriptions casting a powerful spell.

Each headstone bears a symbol denoting the profession or tribe of the deceased: a pair of hands for the Cohens; a pitcher and basin for the Levites; scissors for a tailor; a violin for a musician. On many graves you'll see pebbles, some holding down *kvitlech* or small messages of supplication. The greatest number of these sits on the grave of Rabbi Löw (see box, p.101), who is buried by the wall directly

▲ Old Jewish Cemetery

opposite the entrance; followed closely by the rich Renaissance tomb of Mordecai Maisel, some ten metres to the southeast.

Obřadní síň and Klausová synagoga

Immediately on your left as you leave the cemetery is the **Obřadní síň**, a lugubrious neo-Renaissance house built in 1906 as a ceremonial hall by the Jewish Burial Society. Appropriately enough, it's now devoted to an exhibition on Jewish traditions of burial and death, though it would probably be more useful if you could visit it before heading off into the cemetery rather than after.

Close to the entrance to the cemetery is the **Klausová synagoga**, a late seventeenth-century building, founded in the 1690s by Mordecai Maisel on the site of several small buildings (*klausen*), in what was then a notorious red-light district of Josefov. The relatively ornate Baroque interior contains a rich display of religious objects from embroidered *kippah* to *Kiddush* cups, and explains the very basics of Jewish religious practice, and the chief festivals or High Holidays.

Španělská synagoga (Spanish Synagogue)

East of Pařížská, up Široká, stands the **Španělská synagoga** (Spanish Synagogue), built on the spot once occupied by Prague's Alt Schul or Old Synagogue. The current building, begun in 1868, is by far the most ornate synagogue in Josefov, its stunning, gilded Moorish interior deliberately imitating the Alhambra (hence its name). Every available surface is smothered with a profusion of floral motifs and geometric patterns, in vibrant reds, greens and blues, which are repeated in the synagogue's huge stained-glass windows.

The synagogue now houses an interesting exhibition on the history of Prague's Jews from the time of the 1781 Edict of Tolerance to the Holocaust. Lovely, slender, painted cast-iron columns hold up the women's gallery, where the displays include a fascinating set of photos depicting the old ghetto at the time of its demolition. There's a section on Prague's German-Jewish writers, including Kafka, and information on the Nazis' plans for a museum and on the Holocaust.

Prague never lets go of you...this little mother has claws. We ought to set fire to it at both ends, on Vyšehrad and Hradčany, and maybe then it might be possible to escape.

Franz Kafka, "Letter to Oskar Polak" (December 2, 1902)

Franz Kafka was born on July 3, 1883, above the *Batalion* Schnapps bar on the corner of Maiselova and Kaprova (only the portal remains, but a museum and a gaunt-looking modern bust commemorate the site). He lived almost his entire life within a short walk of his birthplace. His father was a small businessman from a Czech-Jewish family of kosher butchers (Kafka himself was a lifelong vegetarian), his mother from a wealthy German-Jewish family of merchants. The family owned a haberdashery shop, located at various premises on or near Staroměstské náměstí. In 1889, they moved out of Josefov and lived for the next seven years in the beautiful Renaissance Dům U minuty, next door to the Staroměstská radnice, during which time Kafka attended the *Volksschule* on Masná (now a Czech primary school), followed by a spell at an exceptionally strict German *Gymnasium*, at the back of the palác Kinských.

At 18, he began a law degree at the German half of the Karolinum, which was where he met his lifelong friend and posthumous biographer and editor, **Max Brod**. Kafka spent most of his working life in the field of **accident insurance**, until he retired through ill health in 1922. Illness and depression plagued him throughout his life and he spent many months as a patient at the innumerable spas in *Mitteleuropa*. He was engaged three times (twice to the same woman), but never married, finally leaving home at the age of 31 for bachelor digs on the corner of Dlouhá and Masná, where he wrote the bulk of his most famous work, *The Trial*. He died of **tuberculosis** at the age of 40 in a sanatorium just outside Vienna, on June 3, 1924, and is buried in the Nový židovský hřbitov in Žižkov.

As a German among Czechs, a Jew among Germans, and an agnostic among believers, Kafka had good reason to live in a constant state of alienation and fear, or *Angst*. Life was precarious for Prague's Jews, and the destruction of the Jewish quarter throughout his childhood had a profound effect on his psyche. It comes as a surprise to many Kafka readers that anyone immersed in so beautiful a city could write such claustrophobic and paranoid texts; and that, as a member of the **café society** of the time, he could write in a style so completely at odds with his verbose, artistic friends. It's also hard to understand how Kafka could find no publisher for *The Trial* during his lifetime.

After his death, Kafka's works were published in Czech and German and enjoyed brief critical acclaim, before the Nazis **banned** them. Even after the war, Kafka, along with most German-Czech authors, was deliberately overlooked in his native country. In addition, his account of the terrifying brutality and power of bureaucracy over the individual, though not in fact directed at totalitarian systems as such, was too close to the bone for the Communists. The 1962 **Writers' Union** conference at Liblice finally broke the official silence on Kafka, and, for many people, marked the beginning of the Prague Spring. In the immediate aftermath of the 1968 Soviet invasion, the Kafka bust was removed from Josefov, and his books remained unpublished in Czechoslovakia until 1990.

Having been *persona non grata* in his homeland for most of the last century, and despite the fact that most Czechs consider him a German writer, Kafka now suffers from over-exposure in Prague, due to his popularity with Western tourists. His image is plastered across T-shirts, mugs and postcards, while a tacky statue of Kafka riding on the shoulders of the golem has been erected outside the Spanish Synagogue and provides a popular photo opportunity. There's a small **Kafka exhibition** (Expozice Franze Kafky; Tues–Fri 10am–6pm, Sat 10am–5pm; 50Kč), on the site of Kafka's birthplace next door to the church of sv Mikuláš: it retells Kafka's life simply but effectively with pictures and quotes (in Czech, German and English). There's also a larger, more sophisticated **Kafka museum** (see p.72) in Malá Strana.

▲ The Spanish Synagogue

In the zimní synagoga on the first floor, there's an exhibition of silver religious artefacts, a fraction of the six thousand pieces collected here, initially for Prague's Jewish Museum, founded in 1906, and later under the Nazis. Also worth a peek are the changing Jewish art exhibitions at the **Galerie Roberta Guttmanna** (daily except Sat: April–Oct 9am–6pm; Nov–March 9am–4.30pm; 30Kč), around the back of the synagogue at U staré školy 3.

Náměstí Jana Palacha and the Rudolfinum

Kaprova and Široká emerge from Josefov at **náměstí Jana Palacha**, previously known as náměstí Krasnoarmejců (Red Army Square) and embellished with a flowerbed in the shape of a red star (now replaced by the circular vent of an underground car park), in memory of the Soviet dead who were temporarily buried here in May 1945. It was probably this, as much as the fact that the building on the east side of the square is the Faculty of Philosophy, where Jan Palach (see p.116) was a student, that prompted the new authorities to make the first of the street name changes here in 1989 (there's a bust of Palach on the corner of the building). By a happy coincidence, the road which intersects the square from the north is called **17 listopadu** (17 November), originally commemorating the day in 1939 when the Nazis closed down all Czech institutions of higher education, but now equally good for the 1989 march (see p.124).

The north side of the square is taken up by the **Rudolfinum** or Dům umělců (House of Artists), a neo-Renaissance building designed by Josef Zítek and Josef Schulz and opened in 1885. It was originally built to house an art gallery, museum and concert hall for the Czech-speaking community. In 1918, however, it became the seat of the new Czechoslovak parliament, until 1938 when it was closed down by the Nazis. According to author Jiří Weil, the Germans were keen to rid the building's balustrade of its statue of the Jewish composer Mendelssohn. However, since none of the statues was actually named, they decided to remove the one with the largest nose; unfortunately for the Nazis, this turned out to be Wagner, Hitler's favourite composer. In 1946, the building returned to its original artistic purpose and it's since been sandblasted back to its original woody-brown hue. Now one of the capital's main concert venues and exhibition spaces, home to the **Czech Philharmonic** (Tues–Sun 10am–6pm), it also boasts a café with wonderfully grand decor (see p.192), open to the general public on the first floor.

UPM (Museum of Decorative Arts)

The **UPM** or Umělecko-průmyslové muzeum on 17 listopadu (Tues 10am–7pm, Wed–Sun 10am–6pm; 120Kč, but free Tues 5–7pm; Ⓦwww.upm.cz), is installed in another of Josef Schulz's worthy late nineteenth-century creations, richly decorated in mosaics, stained glass and sculptures. Literally translated, this is a **Museum of Decorative Arts**, though the translation hardly does justice to what is one of the most fascinating museums in the capital. From its foundation in 1885 through to the end of the First Republic, the UPM received the best that the Czech modern movement had to offer – from Art Nouveau to the avant-garde – and consequently its collection is unrivalled.

The museum's consistently excellent temporary exhibitions are staged on the ground floor, with the permanent collections on the floor above. Audioguides to the collections are available for an extra 10Kč, though they're by no means essential, as there's lots of information and labelling in English. The displays start with the **Votive Hall** (Votivní sál), which is ornately decorated with *trompe l'oeil* wall hangings, lunette paintings and a bewhiskered bust of Emperor Franz-Joseph I. Next door is the **Story of the Fibre** (Příběh vlákna), which displays textile exhibits ranging from a sixteenth-century Brussels tapestry of Samson bringing down the temple to some 1930s curtains by the Surrealist artist Toyen. In the pull-out drawers you can admire numerous examples of intricate lacework through the ages. The room is dominated, however, by a double-decker costume display: above, there are richly embroidered religious vestments from the fifteenth to eighteenth century; below, fashionable attire from the eighteenth century to modern catwalk concoctions, via knock-out outfits such as a pink Charleston dress from the 1920s.

The **Arts of Fire** (Umění ohně) section is home to the museum's impressive glass, ceramic and pottery displays. The breadth of the stuff on show here means there's bound to be something to please everyone, whether you're into eighteenth-century Meissen figures, Slovak Haban folk faïence or Art Nouveau vases by Bohemian glassmakers such as Lötz. To catch the best examples of Cubist works on display, head for the room's Gočár-designed Cubist bookcase, and look out, too, for Jan Zrzavý's three-piece glass mosaic from the 1930s.

The **Print and Image** room (Tisk a obraz) is devoted mainly to Czech photography, and includes numerous prints from the art form's interwar heyday, including several of František Drtikol's remarkable 1920s geometric nudes, Jaromír Funke's superb still lifes and Josef Sudek's contemplative studio shots. In addition, there are pull-out drawers of early Czech photos from the second half of the nineteenth century, as well as examples of avant-garde graphics by Karel Teige, book designs by Josef Váchal and some of Alfons Mucha's famous turn-of-the-century Parisian advertising posters.

Finally, in the **Treasury** (Klenotnice), there's a kind of modern-day *Kunstkammer*, or cabinet of curiosities: everything from ivory objets d'art and seventeenth-century Italian *pietre dure* or hardstone mosaics, to miniature silver furniture and a goblet made from rhino horn. One or two exhibits stand out from this eclectic crowd, in particular the garnet jewellery that has long been a Bohemian speciality, and the glass cabinet stuffed full of Art Nouveau, Cubist and Rondo-Cubist metalwork.

The UPM also houses a **public library** (Mon noon–6pm, Tues 10am–8pm, Wed–Fri 10am–6pm; closed July & Aug), specializing in catalogues and material from previous exhibitions, and an excellent **café** on the ground floor (Mon–Fri 10am–7pm, Sat & Sun 10.30am–6pm).

Památník Jaroslava Ježeka

If you happen to be in the Josefov area on a Tuesday afternoon, it's worth taking the opportunity to visit the **Památník Jaroslava Ježeka** (Tues 1–6pm; 10Kč; Ⓦ www.nm.cz), which occupies one room of the first-floor flat of the avant-garde composer **Jaroslav Ježek** (1906–42), at Kaprova 10. It's a great way to escape the crowds, hear some of Ježek's music, and admire the Modrý pokoj (Blue Room), with its functionalist furniture and grand piano, in which he did his composing.

Nové Město

NOVÉ MĚSTO is the city's main commercial and business district, housing most of its big hotels, cinemas, nightclubs, fast-food outlets and department stores. Architecturally, it comes over as big, bourgeois and predominantly late nineteenth century, yet Nové Město was actually founded way back in 1348 by **Emperor Charles IV** as an entirely new town – three times as big as Staré Město – intended to link the southern fortress of Vyšehrad with Staré Město to the north. Large market squares, wide streets and a level of town planning far ahead of its time were employed to transform Prague into the new capital city of the Holy Roman Empire. Instead, however, Nové Město remained incomplete when Charles died, and quickly became the city's poorest quarter after Josefov, fertile ground for Hussites and radicals throughout the centuries.

In the second half of the nineteenth century the authorities set about a campaign of slum clearance similar to that inflicted on the Jewish quarter; only the churches and a few important historical buildings were left standing, but Charles's street layout survives pretty much intact. The leading architects of the day began to line the **wide boulevards** with ostentatious examples of their work, which were eagerly snapped up by the new class of status-conscious businessman – a process that has continued into this century, making Nové Město the most architecturally varied part of Prague.

The obvious starting point, and probably the only place in Prague most first-time visitors can put a name to, is **Wenceslas Square**, or **Václavské náměstí**, hub of the modern city, and somewhere you're bound to find yourself passing through again and again. The two principal, partially pedestrianized streets which lead off it are **Na příkopě** and 28 října, which becomes **Národní třída** – better known, and often written, as simply Národní. These streets together form the *zlatý kříž* or "golden cross", Prague's commercial axis and for over a century the most expensive slice of real estate in the capital. The *zlatý kříž* and the surrounding streets also contain some of Prague's finest late nineteenth-century, Art Nouveau and early twentieth-century architecture.

The rest of Nové Město, which spreads out northeast and southwest of Wenceslas Square, is much less explored, and for the most part still heavily residential. A few specific sights are worth singling out for attention – the museum devoted to **Dvořák** on Ke Karlovu, the **Mánes** art gallery on the waterfront and the memorial to the Czechoslovak parachutists off Karlovo náměstí, for example – but the rest is decidedly less exciting than all that's gone before. However, if your ultimate destination is Vyšehrad, you can easily take in some of the more enjoyable bits of southern Nové Město en route.

Unusually for Prague, using the metro and particularly the trams to get around here will save some unnecessary legwork. Three **tram routes** worth knowing about are: tram #24, which goes along Vodičkova from Wenceslas Square, up the side of Karlovo náměstí and past the Botanická zahrada; tram #3, which goes along Vodičkova to Karlovo náměstí and then heads off to Palackého náměstí and south along the riverfront; and tram #18, which heads south from Národní down Spálená, up the side of Karlovo náměstí and past the Botanická zahrada.

Václavské náměstí (Wenceslas Square)

The natural pivot around which modern Prague revolves, **Václavské náměstí** is more of a wide, gently sloping boulevard than a square as such. It's scarcely a conventional – or even convenient – space in which to hold mass demonstrations, yet for the last 160 years or more it has been the focus of political protest in Prague. It was here, during the November 1989 **Velvet Revolution**, that more than 250,000 people crammed into the square night after night, enduring subzero temperatures, to call for the resignation of the Communist Party leaders and to demand free elections. On November 27, the whole of Prague came to a standstill for the two-hour nationwide general strike called by Občanské fórum (Civic Forum), who led the revolution. It was this last mass mobilization that proved decisive – by noon the next day the Communist old guard had thrown in the towel.

The square's history of protest goes back to the **1848 Revolution**, whose violent denouement began here on June 12 with a peaceful open-air Mass organized by the Prague students. On the crest of the nationalist disturbances, the square – which had been known as Koňský trh (Horse Market) since its foundation as such by Charles IV – was given its present name. Naturally enough, it was one of the rallying points for the jubilant crowds on October 28, 1918, when Czechoslovakia's independence was declared. At the lowest point of the Nazi occupation, on July 3, 1942, some two weeks after the capture of Reinhard Heydrich's assassins (see box, p.128), over 200,000 Czechs gathered to swear allegiance to the Third Reich. Just six years later, in **February 1948**, the square was filled to capacity once more, this time with Communist demonstrators enthusiastically supporting the February coup. Then during the Warsaw Pact invasion of **August 1968**, it was the scene of some of the most violent confrontations between the Soviet invaders and the Czechs, during which the Národní muzeum came under fire – according to the Czechs, the Soviet officer in charge mistook it for the

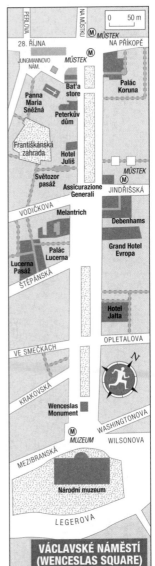

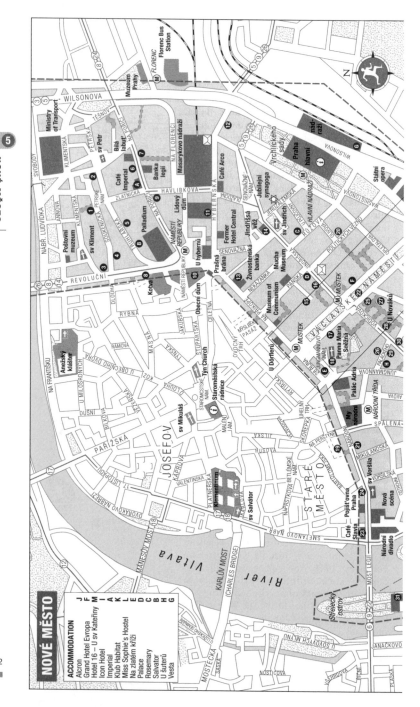

NOVÉ MĚSTO

ACCOMMODATION

Aicron	J
Grand Hotel Evropa	F
Hotel 16 – U sv Kateřiny	M
Icon Hotel	I
Imperial	A
Klub Habitat	K
Miss Sophie's Hostel	L
Na zlatém kříži	E
Palace	D
Rosemary	C
Salvator	B
U Šuterů	H
Vesta	G

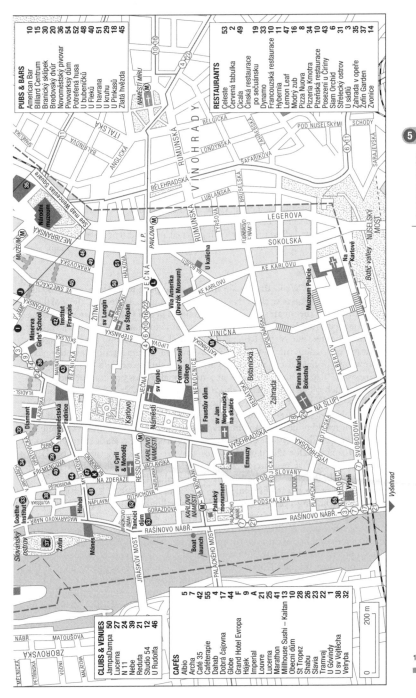

PUBS & BARS

American Bar	10
Billiard Centrum	15
Branický sklípek	30
Bredovský dvůr	20
Novoměstský pivovar	36
Pivovarský dům	54
Potrefená husa	48
U bubeníčků	40
U Fleků	51
U havrana	29
U kruhu	18
U Pinkasů	45
Zlatá hvězda	

RESTAURANTS

Celeste	53
Červená tabulka	2
Cicala	49
Čínská restaurace po sečuánsku	19
Dynamo	33
Francouzská restaurace	10
Hybernia	11
Lemon Leaf	47
Modrý zub	16
Pizza Nuova	8
Pizzeria Kmotra	34
Plzeňská restaurace	10
Posezení u Čiřiny	43
Siam Orchid	6
Střelecký ostrov	31
U sadlů	3
Zahrada v opeře	35
Žofín Garden	37
Zvonice	14

CLUBS & VENUES

JampaDampa	50
Lucerna	27
N 11	24
Nebe	39
Reduta	21
Studio 54	12
U Rudolfa	46

CAFÉS

Albio	5
Archa	7
Café 35	42
Cafétérapie	55
Dahab	4
Dobrá čajovna	17
Globe	44
Grand Hotel Evropa	9
Hájek	F
Imperial	A
Louvre	21
Lucerna	25
Marathon	41
Millhouse Sushi – Kaitan	13
Obecní dům	10
St Tropez	28
Shabu	26
Slavia	23
Tramvaj	22
U Góvindy	1
U sv Vojtěcha	38
Velryba	32

Parliament building, though they were most probably aiming for the nearby Radio Prague building, which was transmitting news of the Soviet invasion out to the West. And it was at the top of the square, on January 16, 1969, that **Jan Palach** set fire to himself in protest at the continuing occupation of the country by Russian troops.

Despite the square's medieval origins, its oldest building dates only from the eighteenth century, and the vast majority are much younger. As the city's money moved south of Staré Město during the Industrial Revolution, so the square became the **architectural showpiece** of the nation, and it is now lined with self-important six- or seven-storey buildings, representing every artistic trend of the past hundred years, from neo-Renaissance and Art Nouveau to Socialist Realism and hi-tech modernism. In addition, the square has a very good selection of period-piece arcades or **pasáže**, preserved from the commercial boom of the First Republic (see box opposite).

If you've no interest in modern architecture, there's less reason to stroll up the square since the shops and restaurants tend to reflect the familiar roll-call of multinational chains. The square has also yet to shake off entirely the seedy reputation it acquired during the 1990s: prostitution has waned and the discos have mostly closed down, but the petty criminals, dodgy cab drivers and overpriced hotels remain.

Around Můstek

The busiest part of Wenceslas Square and a popular place to meet up before hitting town is around **Můstek**, the city's most central metro station, at the northern (bottom) end of the square. The area is dominated by the **Palác Koruna**, a hulking wedge of sculptured concrete and gold, built for an insurance company in 1914 by Antonín Pfeiffer, one of Jan Kotěra's many pupils. The building is a rare mixture of heavy constructivism and gilded Secession-style ornamentation, but the pièce de résistance is the palace's pearly crown, which lights up at night.

Opposite Palác Koruna is a recent neo-functionalist glass building, accompanied by two much older functionalist shops from the late 1920s, designed by Ludvík Kysela and billed at the time as Prague's first glass curtain-wall buildings. Along with the *Hotel Juliš* (see below), they represent the perfect expression of the optimistic mood of progress and modernism that permeated the interwar republic. The second of these Kysela buildings was constructed as a **Baťa** store, one of a chain of functionalist shoeshops built for the Czech shoe magnate, Tomáš Baťa, one of the greatest patrons of avant-garde Czech architecture. Baťa fled the country in 1948, when the Communists nationalized the shoe industry, only to have several of his old stores returned to the family after 1989. Even if you've no intention of buying a pair of Baťa boots, it's worth taking the lift to the top floor for a bird's-eye view onto the square.

Twenty-five years earlier, Czech architecture was in the throes of its own version of Art Nouveau, known as *secese* (from the Viennese Secession). One of the earliest Czech practitioners was Jan Kotěra, a pupil of the great architect of the Viennese Secession, Otto Wagner. Kotěra's first work, undertaken at the age of 28, was the **Peterkův dům**, a slender, subdued essay in the new style – though he eventually moved on to a much more brutal modernism. Another supreme example of Czech functionalism, a few doors further up at no. 22, is the **Hotel Juliš**, designed by Pavel Janák, who had already made his name as one of the leading lights of the short-lived Czech Cubist (and later Rondo-Cubist) movement (see p.139). Another point of interest is the neo-Baroque building on the corner of Jindřišská, designed by Osvald Polívka and Bedřich Ohmann, and at one time the offices of the **Assicurazione Generali** – the name is still visible above the main entrance – where the young Kafka worked for a couple of years as an insurance clerk.

South of Jindřišská

One of the Communists' most miserable attempts to continue the square's tradition of grand architecture was the former **Družba** (Friendship) department store, now Debenhams, which stands like a 1970s reject on the other side of Jindřišská. Opposite is the former **Melantrich** publishing house (now a branch of Marks & Spencer), whose first floor was occupied for many years by the offices of the Socialist Party newspaper, *Svobodné slovo* (The Free Word). For forty years, the Socialist Party was a loyal puppet of the Communist government, but on the second night of the November 1989 demonstrations, the newspaper handed over its well-placed balcony to the opposition speakers of Občanské fórum (Civic Forum), and later witnessed the historic appearance of Havel and Dubček (see p.247).

Melantrich House faces probably the two most ornate buildings on the entire square, the Art Nouveau **Grand Hotel Evropa**, and its slim neighbour, the *Hotel Meran*, both with decor dating from 1903–05, designed by two of Ohmann's disciples, Bendelmayer and Dryák. The *Evropa*, in particular, has kept many of its original fittings intact, and its café retains a sumptuous interior, complete with symbolist art and elaborate brass fittings and light fixtures, all unchanged since the hotel first opened. Unfortunately, at the time of writing the whole place was at a particularly low ebb in terms of service and, consequently, popularity.

Opposite the hotel is the vast **Palác Lucerna**, one of the more appealing of the square's numerous dimly lit shopping arcades (see box below). Designed in the early part of this century in Moorish style by, among others, Havel's own grandfather, it was returned to Havel and his brother after 1989 and was subsequently the focus of much public family squabbling. Suspended from the ceiling in the centre of the arcade is David Černý's parody of the square's equestrian Wenceslas Monument, with the saint astride an upside-down charger.

Apart from a brief glance at the **Hotel Jalta**, built in the Stalinist aesthetic of the 1950s, there's nothing more to stop for, architecturally speaking, until you get to the Wenceslas Monument. However, you might, by this point, have noticed the two vintage tram cars stationed in the central reservation, reminders of the days when trams trundled down the square but now converted into the *Tramvaj* café (see p.193).

The Wenceslas Monument

A statue of St Wenceslas (see box, p.49) has stood at the top of the square since 1680, but the present **Wenceslas Monument**, by the father of Czech sculpture, Josef Václav Myslbek, was only unveiled in 1912, after thirty years on the drawing board. It's worthy and heroic but pretty unexciting, with the Czech patron saint sitting resolutely astride his mighty steed, surrounded by smaller-scale representations of

Prague's pasáže

Prague has an impressive array of old **shopping arcades**, or *pasáže* as they're known in Czech, the majority of which are located in and around Wenceslas Square and date from the first half of the twentieth century. Compared with the chic *passages* off the Champs-Élysées, Prague's *pasáže* offer more modest pleasures: a few shops, the odd café and, more often than not, a cinema. The king of the lot is the lavishly decorated **Lucerna** *pasáž* at the Palác Lucerna, which stretches all the way from Štěpánská to Vodičkova and contains an equally ornate cinema, café and concert hall. You can continue your indoor stroll on the other side of Vodičkova through the **Světozor** *pasáž*, which boasts another cinema, and a wonderful stained-glass mosaic advertising the old Communist electronics company Tesla.

▲ The Wenceslas Monument and the National Museum

four other Bohemian saints – his mother Ludmila, Procopius, Adalbert and Agnes – added in the 1920s. In 1918, 1948, 1968 and again in 1989, the monument was used as a national political notice board, festooned in posters, flags and slogans, and even now it remains the city's favourite soapbox venue. On October 28, 1939, during the demonstrations against the Nazi occupation, the medical student **Jan Opletal** was shot when troops opened fire on protesters.

Two of Prague's most famous martyrs were fatally wounded close by. On January 16, 1969, the 21-year-old philosophy student **Jan Palach** set himself alight in protest against the continuing occupation of his country by the Soviets; he died from his injuries three days later. **Jan Zajíc** followed Palach's example on February 25, the twenty-first anniversary of the Communist coup. Attempts to lay flowers on this spot on the anniversary of Palach's protest provided an annual source of confrontation with the Communist authorities; Václav Havel received the last of his many prison sentences for just such an action in January 1989. A simple memorial to *obětem komunismu* (the victims of Communism), adorned with flowers, lies close to the monument. Two mounds of cobble stones, and a cross set into the pavement outside the Národní muzeum, mark where Palach and Zajíc killed themselves.

Národní muzeum (National Museum)

At the top, southern, end of Wenceslas Square sits the broad, brooding hulk of the **Národní muzeum** (Mon–Fri 10am–6pm, Sat 10am–8pm, Sun 11am–7pm; closed first Tues of month; 150Kč; Ⓦ www.nm.cz), built by Josef Schulz in 1890. Deliberately modelled on the great European museums of Paris and Vienna, it dominates the view up the square like a giant golden eagle with outstretched wings. Along with the National Theatre, this is one of the great landmarks of the nineteenth-century Czech national revival, sporting a monumental gilt-framed glass cupola, worthy clumps of sculptural decoration and narrative frescoes from Czech history.

As a building, the museum is well worth a visit, but the displays themselves are old-fashioned and, for the most part, pretty dull. Nevertheless, it's worth taking at least a quick look at the ornate marble entrance hall and splendid monumental staircase leading to the glass-domed **Pantheon** at the top of the main staircase, which is decorated with lunette murals depicting key moments in Czech history. Meanwhile, at floor level there are 48 busts and statues of distinguished bewhiskered Czech men (plus a couple of token women and Czechophile Slovaks), including the universally adored T.G. Masaryk, the country's founding president, whose statue was removed from every other public place by the Communists.

The rest of the museum is dowdy and poorly labelled, though numismatists will enjoy the exhibition of medals and orders belonging to Václav Měřička, from the Order of the Bath to the French Légion d'Honneur. Geologists can admire rocks and minerals in tasteful mahogany cases, while non-specialists should head for the **Kabinet drahých kamenů**, at the far end, where cut and polished sapphires, rubies, emeralds and other precious stones are displayed. Those with children might like to head upstairs for the fossils and stuffed animals, where you can also view the smallest and the largest butterfly in the world, a range of lovely shells and some frighteningly large and lethal-looking beetles. The museum's temporary exhibitions, displayed on the ground floor – and over in the former Federal Assembly building (see below) – can be very good indeed, so it's always worth checking to see what's on.

Wilsonova

At the southern end of Wenceslas Square is some of the worst blight that Communist planners inflicted on Prague: above all, the six-lane highway that now separates Nové Město from the residential suburb of Vinohrady to the east and south, and effectively cuts off the Národní muzeum from Wenceslas Square. Previously known as Vítězného února (Victorious February Street) after the 1948 Communist coup, the road was renamed **Wilsonova** in honour of US President Woodrow Wilson (a personal friend of the Masaryk family), who effectively gave the country its independence from Austria-Hungary in 1918 by backing the proposal for a separate Czechoslovak state.

The former **Prague Stock Exchange** alongside the Národní muzeum, only completed in the 1930s but rendered entirely redundant by the 1948 Communist coup, was another victim of postwar "reconstruction". The architect Karel Prager was given the task of designing a new "socialist" **Federal Assembly** building on the same site, without destroying the old bourse: he opted for a supremely unappealing bronze-tinted plate-glass structure, supported by concrete stilts and sitting uncomfortably on top of its diminutive predecessor. Since the break-up of the country, the building has lost its *raison d'être* once more, and is now part of the Národní muzeum.

Next to the old Parliament building, the grandiose **Státní opera** (ⓦ www.opera .cz), built by the Viennese duo Helmer and Fellner, looks stunted and deeply affronted by the traffic which now tears past its front entrance. It was opened in 1888 as the Neues Deutsches Theater, shortly after the Czechs had built their own national theatre on the waterfront. Always second fiddle to the Stavovské divadlo, though equally ornate inside, it was one of the last great building projects of Prague's once all-powerful German-speaking minority. The velvet and gold interior is still as fresh as it was when the Bohemian-born composer Gustav Mahler brought the traffic to a standstill conducting the premiere of his *Seventh Symphony*.

The last building on this deafening freeway is **Praha hlavní nádraží**, Prague's main train station, and one of the final architectural glories of the dying Empire, designed by Josef Fanta and officially opened in 1909 as the Franz-Josefs Bahnhof. Arriving by metro, or buying tickets in the over-polished subterranean modern section, it's easy to miss the station's surviving Art Nouveau parts. The original entrance on Wilsonova still exudes imperial confidence, with its wrought-iron canopy and naked figurines clinging to the sides of the towers; on the other side of the road, two great glass protrusions signal the new entrance that opens out into the low-life green space of the Vrchlického sady. You can sit and admire the main foyer from the *Fantová kavárna* (daily 6am–11pm) and take a peek at the ceramic pillars in the former station restaurant, but the whole area has a very seedy feel.

Na příkopě

If you head northeastwards from Můstek at the bottom end of Wenceslas Square, you can join those ambling down **Na příkopě** (literally "on the moat"), which traces the course of the old Staré Město ditch, which was finally filled in in 1760. The street has been an architectural showcase for more than a century, and formed the chief venue for the weekend *passeggiata* at the end of the nineteenth century. On the south side of the street, there are grandiose buildings like the former **Haas department store** at no. 4, built in 1869–71 by Theophil Hansen, the Danish architect responsible for much of the redevelopment of the Ringstrasse in Vienna. Many of the finest turn-of-the-twentieth-century buildings like the *Café Corso* and the *Café Français*, once the favourite haunts of Prague's German-Jewish literary set – were torn down and replaced during the enthusiastic construction boom of the interwar republic. At no. 7, the Art Nouveau **U Dörflerů**, from 1905, with its gilded floral curlicues, is one of the few survivors along this stretch.

There are another couple of interesting buildings on the opposite side of the street, at **nos 18 and 20**, the latter now part of the Živnostenka banka, designed by Osvald Polívka over the course of a twenty-year period for the Zemská banka and connected by a kind of Bridge of Sighs suspended over Nekázanka. The style is 1890s neo-Renaissance, though there are Art Nouveau elements, such as Jan Preisler's gilded mosaics and Ladislav Šaloun's attic sculptures. It's worth nipping upstairs to the main banking hall of what is now the **Živnostenka banka**, at no. 20, to appreciate the financial might of the Czech capital in the last decades of the Austro-Hungarian Empire.

Yet more financial institutions, this time from the dour 1930s, line the far end of Na příkopě as it opens up into náměstí Republiky, including the palatial **Národní banka** (National Bank).

Muzeum komunismu (Museum of Communism)

It took an American expat to open Prague's first museum dedicated to the country's troubled Communist past. Situated above a branch of *McDonald's*, and in the same building as a casino, the **Muzeum komunismu** (daily 9am–9pm; 180Kč; Ⓦ www.muzeumkomunismu.cz) can be found (with some difficulty) on the first floor of the Palác Savarin, Na příkopě 10. The exhibition gives a brief and rather muddled rundown of Czech twentieth-century history, accompanied by a superb collection of Communist statues, uniforms and propaganda posters. The politics are a bit simplistic – the popular postwar support for the Party is underplayed – but it's worth tracking down for the memorabilia alone. There's a mock-up of a Communist classroom, a chilling StB (secret police) room and plenty of film footage of protests throughout the period. Wrangles with the landlord may mean the museum will move premises in the future so check the website.

Mucha Museum

The **Mucha Museum** (daily 10am–6pm; 120Kč; Ⓦ www.mucha.cz), housed in the Kaunicky palác, south off Na příkopě down Panská, is dedicated to

Alfons Mucha (1860–1939), probably the most famous (and popular) of all Czech artists, at least in the West. Mucha made his name in *fin de siècle* Paris, where he shot to fame in 1895 after designing the Art Nouveau poster *Gismonda* for the actress Sarah Bernhardt. "Le Style Mucha" became all the rage, but the artist himself came to despise this "commercial" period of his work, and in 1910, Mucha moved back to his homeland and threw himself into the national cause, designing patriotic stamps, banknotes and posters for the new republic.

The whole of Mucha's career is covered in the permanent exhibition, and there's a good selection of informal photos taken by the artist himself of his models, and of Paul Gauguin (with whom he shared a studio) playing the harmonium with his trousers down. The only work not represented here is his massive *Slav Epic*, but the excellent video (in English) covers the decade of his life he devoted to this cycle of nationalist paintings. In the end, Mucha paid for his Czech nationalism with his life; dragged in for questioning by the Gestapo after the 1939 Nazi invasion, he died shortly after being released.

Náměstí Republiky

Náměstí Republiky, at the eastern end of Na příkopě, is an amorphous space and a major tram and metro interchange. The east side is now dominated by **Palladium** (Mon–Wed & Sun 9am–9pm, Thurs–Sat 9am–10pm), Prague's premier shopping mall, built within an old army barracks and retaining the latter's salmon-pink, crenellated facade.

The oldest structure on the square is the **Prašná brána** (**Powder Gate**, April– Oct daily 10am–6pm; 70Kč), one of the eight medieval gate-towers that once guarded Staré Město. The present tower was begun by King Vladislav Jagiello in 1475, shortly after he'd moved into the royal court, which was situated next door at the time. Work stopped when he retreated to the Hrad to avoid the wrath of his subjects; later on, it was used to store gunpowder – hence the name and the reason for the damage incurred in 1757. The small historical exhibition inside traces the tower's architectural metamorphosis over the centuries, up to its present remodelling courtesy of the nineteenth-century restorer, Josef Mocker. Most people, though, ignore the displays, and climb straight up for the modest view from the top.

Obecní dům

Attached to the Powder Gate on Náměstí Republiky, and built on the ruins of the old royal court, the **Obecní dům** (Municipal House) is by far the most exciting Art Nouveau building in Prague, and one of the few places that still manages to conjure up the atmosphere of Prague's turn-of-the-twentieth-century café society. Conceived as a cultural centre for the Czech community, it's probably the finest architectural achievement of the Czech national revival, designed by **Osvald Polívka** and **Antonín Balšánek**, and extravagantly decorated inside and out with the help of almost every artist connected with the Czech Secession. From the lifts to the cloakrooms, just about all the furnishings remain as they were when the building was completed in 1911, and every square inch of the interior and exterior has been lovingly restored. Appropriately enough, it was here that Czechoslovakia's independence was declared on October 28, 1918.

The simplest way of soaking up the interior – peppered with mosaics and pendulous brass chandeliers – is to have a coffee in the cavernous café, or a full meal in the equally spacious *Francouzská restaurace* (see p.194); there's also the cheaper *Plzeňská restaurace* (see p.194) in the cellar, along with the original 1910 *American*

▲ Obecní dům

Bar (see p.200). Several rooms on the second floor are given over to temporary art exhibitions, while the building's **Smetanova síň**, Prague's largest concert hall, stages numerous concerts, including the opening salvo of the Pražské jaro (Prague Spring Festival) – traditionally a rendition of Smetana's *Má vlast* (My Country) – which takes place in the presence of the president.

For a more detailed inspection of the building's spectacular interior you can sign up for one of the regular **guided tours**, in Czech and English, at the modern information centre (daily 10am–7pm; 270Kč; Ⓦ www.obecni-dum.cz) on the ground floor, beyond the main foyer. You get to see the Smetanova síň, plus several rooms normally out of bounds to the public. Highlights include the folksy **Slovácký salónek**, which features a built-in aquarium decorated with gilded snails, the fountain in the mosaic-tiled recess in the **Salónek Boženy Němcové** and the Moorish silk walls and chandeliers of the **Orientální salónek**. The Czechoslovak declaration of independence took place in 1918 in the **Sál Grégrův**, with its mediocre murals depicting the battle between the sexes. The finest room of the lot, though, is the chapel-like **Primátorský sál**, designed by Alfons Mucha, with jewel-encrusted embroidered curtains, stained-glass windows and paintings on the pendentives depicting civic virtues personified by leading figures from Czech history.

Hybernská

Directly opposite the Obecní dům stands a haughty Neoclassical building, **U hybernů** (The Hibernians), built as a customs office in the Napoleonic period, on the site of a Baroque church which belonged to an order of Irish Franciscans who fled Tudor England (hence its name) – it's currently a theatre. If you walk down **Hybernská** from here, you'll pass the Art Nouveau former **Hotel Central** on the right. Designed by Dryák and Bendelmayer (who built the *Grand Hotel Evropa* on Wenceslas Square) and dating from 1900, its gilded decoration stands out amid its plainer nineteenth-century neighbours.

Opposite the hotel is the **Lidový dům**, headquarters of the Czech Social Democratic Party (ČSSD), which was forcibly amalgamated with the Communist

Party shortly after the 1948 coup. The party regained its independence in 1989, and is once more the country's main centre-left political party. In January 1912, a small backroom in the building was given over to a congress of the exiled Russian Social Democratic Labour Party (RSDLP). The RSDLP was deeply divided, and the meeting poorly attended, with only fourteen voting delegates present (all but two of them Bolsheviks), and **Lenin** himself in the chair. The Communists turned the whole place into a vast museum dedicated to Lenin, and, in a nice twist of fate, the building now houses the American Center for Culture and Commerce.

A little further down Hybernská, a wrought-iron canopy held up by slim green pillars marks the entrance to Prague's first train station, **Masarykovo nádraží**, opened in 1845 and still much as it was then – a modest, almost provincial affair compared to the flamboyant Art Nouveau Praha hlavní nádraží. On the opposite side of Hybernská is the former **Café Arco**, once a favourite of Kafka (who worked nearby), and the circle of Prague-German writers known as the "Arconauts". The café was pretty faithfully reconstructed in the 1990s, though it failed to recapture the *fin de siècle* glory days and has since closed.

Senovážné náměstí

South of Masarykovo nádraží, down Dlážděná, is the old hay market, **Senovážné náměstí**, packed out with parked cars and a couple of market stalls. Its most distinguished feature is the **Jindřišská věž**, the freestanding fifteenth-century belfry of the nearby church of **sv Jindřich** (St Henry), whose digitally controlled, high-pitched bells ring out every fifteen minutes, and play an entire medley every four hours. In contrast to every other surviving tower in Prague, the Jindřišská věž has been imaginatively and expensively restored and now contains a café, restaurant, shop, exhibition space and, on the tenth (and uppermost) floor, a small **museum** (April–Oct Mon–Fri 9am–7pm, Sat & Sun 10am–7pm; Oct–March closes 6pm; 60Kč) on Prague's hundred-plus towers, with a good view across the city's rooftops.

Jubilejní synagoga (Jubilee synagogue)

The **Jubilejní synagoga**, a short way up Jeruzalémská from Senovážné náměstí (April–Oct daily except Sat 1–5pm; 80Kč or combined ticket with Josefov sights, see p.103), was named in honour of the sixtieth year of the Emperor Franz-Joseph I's reign in 1908. Built in an incredibly colourful Moorish style similar to that of the Španělská synagoga in Josefov, but with a touch of Art Nouveau, the synagogue is definitely worth the thirty-minute guided tour. The Hebrew quote from Malachi on the facade strikes a note of liberal optimism: "Do we not have one father? Were we not created by the same God?"

Na poříčí

Running roughly parallel with Hybernská, to the north of Masarykovo nádraží, is the much busier street of **Na poříčí**, an area that, like sv Havel in Staré Město, was originally settled by German merchants. Kafka spent most of his working life as a frustrated and unhappy clerk for the Arbeiter-Unfall-Versicherungs-Anstalt (Workers' Accident Insurance Company), in the grand nineteenth-century building at no. 7. A little further along the street at no. 15, there's more faded *fin de siècle* architecture at the **Café Imperial**, which has miraculously retained its utterly over-the-top ceramic tiling from 1914 (see p.193).

On the opposite side of the street, at no. 24, is a much more unusual piece of corporate architecture, the **Banka legií** (Mon–Fri 9am–5pm) – now a branch of the ČSOB – one of Pavel Janák's rare Rondo-Cubist efforts from the early 1920s. Set into the bold smoky-red moulding is a striking white marble frieze by Otto Gutfreund, depicting the epic march across Siberia undertaken by the Czechoslovak Legion and their embroilment in the Russian Revolution (see p.237). You're free to wander into the main banking hall on the ground floor, which, though marred by the current bank fittings, retains its curved glass roof and distinctive red-and-white marble patterning. The glass curtain-walled **Bílá labuť** (White Swan) department store, opposite, is a good example of the functionalist style which Janák and others went on to embrace in the late 1920s and 1930s.

As a lively shopping street, Na poříčí seems very much out on a limb, as do the cluster of hotels at the end of the street, and around the corner in **Těšnov**. The reason behind this is the now defunct Těšnov train station, which was demolished in the 1960s to make way for the monstrous Wilsonova flyover.

Muzeum Prahy (Prague museum)

On the far side of the Wilsonova flyover, Antonín Balšánek's purpose-built neo-Renaissance mansion, housing the Muzeum hlavního města Prahy (Museum of the City of Prague), better known simply as the **Muzeum Prahy** (Tues–Sun 9am–6pm; first Thurs of month 9am–8pm; 100Kč; ⓦ www.muzeumprahy.cz), managed to survive the 1960s redevelopment. Inside, there's an ad hoc collection of the city's art, a number of antique bicycles and usually an intriguing temporary exhibition on some aspect of the city. The museum's prize possession, though, is the **Langweilův model**, a paper model of Prague which Antonín Langweil completed in the 1830s. It's a fascinating insight into early nineteenth-century Prague – predominantly Baroque, with the cathedral incomplete and the Jewish quarter "unsanitized" – and, consequently, has served as one of the most useful records for the city's restorers. The most surprising thing, of course, is that so little has changed.

Poštovní muzeum and Ministry of Transport

North of Na poříčí, close to the riverbank of nábřeží Ludvíka Svobody, is the **Poštovní muzeum** (Postal Museum; Tues–Sun 9am–6pm; 100Kč; ⓦ www.cpost .cz), housed in the Vávrův dům, an old mill on Nové mlýny, near one of Prague's many water towers. The first floor contains a series of jolly nineteenth-century wall paintings of Romantic Austrian landscapes, and a collection of drawings on postman themes. The real philately is on the ground floor – a vast international collection of stamps arranged in vertical pull-out drawers. The Czechoslovak issues are historically and artistically interesting, as well as of appeal to collectors. Stamps became a useful tool in the propaganda wars of the last century; even such short-lived ventures as the Hungarian-backed Slovak Soviet Republic of 1918–19 and the Slovak National Uprising of autumn 1944 managed to print special issues. Under the First Republic, the country's leading artists, notably Alfons Mucha and Max Švabinský, were commissioned to design stamps, some of which are excep-tionally beautiful.

The distinctive, glass-domed 1920s building – now the **Ministry of Transport** – further east along the embankment, holds a special place in the country's history. Under the Communists, it was the former headquarters of the Party's Central Committee, where Dubček and his fellow reformers were arrested in August 1968, before being spirited away to Moscow for "frank and fraternal" discussions.

Jungmannovo náměstí

Back at Wenceslas Square, if you head west from Můstek (see p.114), before you hit Národní třída, you pass through **Jungmannovo náměstí**, named for Josef Jungmann (1772–1847), a prolific writer, translator and leading light of the Czech national revival, whose pensive, seated statue was erected here in 1878. This small, ill-proportioned square boasts an unrivalled panoply of Czech architectural curiosities, ranging from Emil Králíček and Matěj Blecha's unique **Cubist streetlamp** (and seat) from 1912, beyond the Jungmann statue in the eastern corner of the square, to the gleaming, functionalist facade of the former **ARA department store** (now the ČSOB), built in the late 1920s on the corner of Perlova and ulica 28 října (October 28 Street, commemorating the foundation of the First Republic).

Palác Adria

Diagonally opposite the ARA department store is the Jungmannovo náměstí's most imposing building, the chunky, vigorously sculptured **Palác Adria**. It was designed in the early 1920s by Pavel Janák and Josef Zasche, with sculptural extras by Otto Gutfreund and a central *Seafaring* group by Jan Štursa. Janák was a pioneering figure in the short-lived, prewar Czech Cubist movement; after the war, he and Josef Gočár attempted to create a national style of architecture appropriate for the newly founded republic. The style was dubbed "Rondo-Cubism" – semicircular motifs are a recurrent theme – though the Palác Adria owes as much to the Italian Renaissance as it does to the new national style.

Constructed for the Italian insurance company Reunione Adriatica di Sicurità – hence its current name – the building's *pasáž* retains its wonderful original portal featuring sculptures by Bohumil Kafka, depicting the twelve signs of the zodiac. The theatre in the basement of the building was once a studio for the multimedia **Laterna magika** (Magic Lantern) company. In 1989, it became the underground nerve centre of the Velvet Revolution, when Občanské fórum (Civic Forum) found temporary shelter here shortly after their inaugural meeting on the Sunday following the November 17 demonstration. Against a stage backdrop for Dürenmatt's *Minotaurus*, the Forum thrashed out tactics in the dressing rooms and gave daily press conferences in the auditorium during the crucial fortnight before the Communists relinquished power.

Church of Panna Maria Sněžná

Right beside the Cubist streetlamp on Jungmannovo náměstí is the medieval gateway of the Franciscan church of **Panna Maria Sněžná** (St Mary of the Snows; ⓦpms.ofm.cz), once one of the great landmarks of Wenceslas Square, but now barely visible from any of the surrounding streets. To enter the church, go through the archway beside the Austrian Cultural Institute, behind the statue of Jungmann, and across the courtyard beyond. Like most of Nové Město's churches, the Panna Maria Sněžná was founded by Charles IV, who envisaged a vast coronation church on a scale comparable with the St Vitus Cathedral, on which work had just begun. Unfortunately, the money ran out shortly after completion of the chancel; the result is curious – a church which is short in length, but equal to the cathedral in height. The thirty-metre-high, prettily painted vaulting – which collapsed on the Franciscans who inherited the half-completed building in the seventeenth century – is awesome, as is the gold and black Baroque main altar which touches the ceiling. To get an idea of the intended scale of the finished structure, take a stroll through the **Františkanská zahrada**, to the south of the church; these gardens make a lovely hideaway from Nové Mesto's bustle, marred only by the intrusive modern garden furniture.

Národní třída

The eastern half of **Národní** is lined with shops, galleries and clubs, all of which begin to peter out as you near the river. On the right-hand side is an eye-catching duo of Art Nouveau buildings, designed by Osvald Polívka in 1907–08. The first, at no. 7, was built for the **pojišťovna Praha** (Prague Savings Bank), hence the beautiful mosaic lettering above the windows advertising *život* (life insurance) and *kapital* (loans), as well as help with your *důchod* (pension) and *věno* (dowry). Next door, the slightly more ostentatious **Topičův dům**, headquarters of Československý spisovatel, the official state publishers, provides the perfect accompaniment, with a similarly ornate wrought-iron and glass canopy.

Opposite, the convent and church of **sv Voršila** (St Ursula) are distinguished by the rare sight (in this part of town) of a tree – in this case sticking straight out of the base of the white facade. When it was completed in 1678, this was one of the first truly flamboyant Baroque buildings in Prague, and its white stucco and frescoed interior have been restored to their original state.

Národní divadlo (National Theatre) and Café Slavia

Overlooking the Vltava at the end of Národní, is the gold-crested **Národní divadlo** (Ⓦ www.narodni-divadlo.cz), proud symbol of the Czech nation. Refused money from the Habsburg state coffers, Czechs of all classes dug deep into their pockets to raise funds for the venture themselves. The foundation stones, gathered from various historically significant sites in Bohemia and Moravia, were laid in 1868 by the historian and politician František Palacký and the composer Bedřich Smetana; the architect, Josef Zítek, spent the next thirteen years on the project. In June 1881, the theatre opened with a premiere of Smetana's opera *Libuše*. In August of the same year, fire destroyed everything except the outer walls. Within two years the whole thing was rebuilt – even the emperor contributed this time – under the supervision of Josef Schulz, and it opened once more to the strains of *Libuše*. Smetana attended both of the theatre's opening nights, even though the organizers failed to send him any tickets and he had to blag his way in on each occasion. The grand portal on the north side of the theatre is embellished

▲ National Theatre

with suitably triumphant allegorical figures, and, inside, every square inch is taken up with paintings and sculptures by leading artists of the Czech national revival.

Standing behind the Národní divadlo, and in dramatic contrast with it, is the theatre's modern extension, the glass box of the **Nová scéna**, designed by Karel Prager, the leading architect of the Communist era, and completed in 1983. It's one of those buildings most Praguers love to hate – it was described by one Czech as looking like "frozen piss" – though compared to much of Prague's Communist-era architecture, it's not that bad. Just for the record, the lump of molten rock in the courtyard is a symbolic evocation of *My Socialist Country*, by Malejovský.

The **Café Slavia**, opposite the theatre, has been a favourite haunt of the city's writers, dissidents and artists (and, inevitably, actors) since the days of the First Republic. The Czech avant-garde movement, Devětsil, led by Karel Teige, used to hold its meetings here in the 1920s; the meetings are recorded for posterity by another of its members, the Nobel prize-winner Jaroslav Seifert, in his *Slavia Poems*. The café has been carelessly modernized since those arcadian days, but it still has a great riverside view and Viktor Oliva's *Absinthe Drinker* canvas on the wall.

Vodičkova and around

Of the many roads which head down towards Karlovo náměstí from Wenceslas Square, **Vodičkova** is probably the most impressive, running southwest for 500m from Wenceslas Square. You can catch several trams along this route, though there are a handful of buildings worth checking out on the way, so you may choose to walk.

The first, **U Nováků**, is impossible to miss, thanks to Jan Preisler's mosaic of bucolic frolicking (its actual subject, *Trade and Industry*, is confined to the edges of the picture), and Osvald Polívka's curvilinear window frames and delicate, ivy-like ironwork – look out for the frog-prince holding up a windowsill. Built for the Novák department store in the early 1900s, for the past sixty years it has been a cabaret hall, restaurant and café all rolled into one; sadly, the original interior fittings have long since been destroyed. Further along, set back from the street, stands the

Milena Jesenská

The most famous "Minervan" was **Milena Jesenská**, born in 1896 into a Czech family whose ancestry stretched back to the sixteenth century. Shortly after leaving school, she was confined to a mental asylum by her father when he discovered that she was having an affair with a Jew. On her release, she married the Jewish intellectual, **Ernst Pollak**, and moved to Vienna, where she took a job as a railway porter to support the two of them. While living in Vienna, she sent her Czech translation of one of **Franz Kafka**'s short stories to his publisher; Kafka wrote back himself, and so began their intense, mostly epistolary, relationship. Kafka described her later as "the only woman who ever understood me", and with his encouragement she took up writing professionally. Tragically, by the time Milena had extricated herself from her disastrous marriage, Kafka, still smarting from three failed engagements with other women, had decided never to commit himself to anyone else; his letters alone survived the war, as a moving testament to their love.

Milena returned to Prague in 1925, and moved on from writing exclusively fashion articles to critiques of avant-garde architecture, becoming one of the city's leading journalists. She married again, this time to the prominent functionalist architect **Jaromír Krejcar**, but later, a difficult pregnancy and childbirth left her addicted to morphine. She overcame her dependency only after joining the Communist Party, but was to quit after the first of Stalin's show trials in 1936. She continued to work as a journalist in the late 1930s, and wrote a series of articles condemning the rise of Fascism in the Sudetenland.

When the Nazis rolled into Prague in 1939, Milena's Vinohrady flat had already become a centre for resistance. For a while, she managed to hang onto her job, but her independent intellectual stance and provocative gestures – for instance, wearing a yellow star as a mark of solidarity with her Jewish friends – soon attracted the attentions of the Gestapo and, after a brief spell in the notorious Pankrác prison, she was sent to **Ravensbrück**, the women's concentration camp near Berlin, where she died of kidney failure in May 1944.

imposing neo-Renaissance **Minerva girls' school**, covered in bright-red sgraffito. Founded in 1866, it was the first such institution in Prague, and was notorious for the antics of its pupils, the "Minervans", who shocked bourgeois Czech society with their experimentations with fashion, drugs and sexual freedom (see box above).

As Vodičkova curves left towards Karlovo náměstí, **Lazarská**, meeting point of the city's night trams, leads off to the right. At the bottom of this street is **Diamant**, completed in 1912 by Emil Králíček, and so called because its prismatic Cubist style is reminiscent of the facets of a diamond. The geometric sculptural reliefs on the facade, the main portal and the frame enclosing a Baroque statue of St John of Nepomuk on Spálená are worth viewing.

Karlovo náměstí

Once Prague's biggest square, **Karlovo náměstí**'s impressive proportions are no longer so easy to appreciate, being obscured by a tree-planted public garden and cut in two by the busy thoroughfare of Ječná. It was created by Charles IV as Nové Město's cattle market (Dobytčí trh) and used by him for the grisly annual public display of his impressive collection of saintly relics, though now it actually signals the southern limit of the city's main commercial district and the beginning of predominantly residential Nové Město.

The **Novoměstská radnice**, or New Town Hall, at the northeastern corner of the square sports three impressive triangular gables embellished with intricate blind tracery. It was built, like the one on Staroměstské náměstí, during the reign of King John of Luxembourg, though it has survived rather better, and is now one of the finest Gothic buildings in the city. It was here that Prague's **first defenestration** took place on July 30, 1419, when the radical Hussite preacher Jan Želivský and his penniless religious followers stormed the building, mobbed the councillors and burghers and threw twelve or thirteen of them (including the mayor) out of the town hall windows onto the pikes of the Hussite mob below, who clubbed any survivors to death. Václav IV, on hearing the news, suffered a stroke and died just two weeks later. So began the long and bloody Hussite Wars. After the amalgamation of Prague's separate towns in 1784, the building was used solely as a criminal court and prison. Nowadays, you can visit the site of the defenestration, and climb to the top of the tower (mid-April to mid-Oct Tues–Sun 10am–6pm; 50Kč; ⓦ www.novomestskaradnice.cz) for a view over central Prague.

Following the defeat of Protestantism two centuries later, the Jesuits were allowed to demolish 23 houses on the east side of the square to make way for their college (now one of the city's main hospitals) and the accompanying church of **sv Ignác** (St Ignatius), begun in 1665 by Carlo Lurago and Paul Ignaz Bayer. The statue of St Ignatius, which sits above the tympanum surrounded by a sunburst, caused controversy at the time, as until then only the Holy Trinity had been depicted in such a way. The church, modelled, like so many Jesuit churches, on the Gesù in Rome, is quite remarkable inside, a salmon-pink and white confection, with lots of frothy stucco-work and an exuberant powder-pink pulpit dripping with gold drapery, cherubs and saints.

At no. 40, at the southern end of the square, is the so-called **Faustův dům** (Faust House), an apricot and grey late Baroque building with a long and diabolical history of alchemy. An occult priest from Opava owned the house in the fourteenth century and, two hundred years later, the English alchemist and international con-man Edward Kelley was summoned here by the eccentric Emperor Rudolf II to turn base metal into gold. The building is also the traditional setting for the Czech version of the Faust legend, with the arrival one rainy night of a penniless and homeless student, Jan Šťastný (meaning lucky, or in Latin *Faustus*). Finding money in the house, he decides to keep it – only to discover that it was put there by the Devil, who then claims his soul in return. Seemingly unperturbed by the history of the site, a pharmacy (*lekárna*) now occupies the ground floor.

Cathedral of sv Cyril and Metoděj (Heydrich Martyrs' Monument)

West off Karlovo náměstí, down noisy Resslova, is the Orthodox cathedral of **sv Cyril and Metoděj** (Tues–Sun: March–Oct 10am–5pm; Nov–Feb 10am–4pm; 60Kč), originally constructed for the Roman Catholics by Bayer and Dientzenhofer in the eighteenth century, but since the 1930s the main base of the Orthodox Church in the Czech Republic. Amid all the traffic, it's extremely difficult to imagine the scene here on June 18, 1942, when seven **Czechoslovak secret agents** involved in the most dramatic assassination of World War II (see box, p.128) were besieged in the church by hundreds of Waffen SS. Acting on the basis of a tip-off by one of the Czech resistance who turned himself in, the Nazis surrounded the church just after 4am and fought a pitched battle for over six hours, trying explosives, flooding and any other method they could think of to drive the men out of their stronghold in the crypt. Eventually, all seven agents

The assassination of Reinhard Heydrich

The assassination of **Reinhard Heydrich** in 1942 was the only attempt the Allies ever made on the life of a leading Nazi. It's an incident which the Allies have always billed as a great success in the otherwise rather dismal seven-year history of the Czech resistance. But, as with all acts of brave resistance during the war, there was a price to be paid. Given that the reprisals meted out to the Czech population were entirely predictable, it remains a controversial, if not suicidal, decision to have made.

The target, Reinhard Tristan Eugen Heydrich, was a talented and upwardly mobile anti-Semite (despite rumours that he was partly Jewish himself), a great organizer and a skilful concert violinist. He was a late recruit to the Nazi Party, signing up in 1931, after having been dismissed from the German Navy for dishonourable conduct towards a woman. However, he swiftly rose through the ranks of the SS to become second in command after Himmler, and in the autumn of 1941 he was appointed **Reichsprotektor** of the puppet state of Böhmen und Mähren – effectively, the most powerful man in the Czech Lands. Although his rule began with brutality, it soon settled into the tried and tested policy which Heydrich liked to call *Peitsche und Zucker* (literally, "whip and sugar").

On the morning of May 27, 1942, as Heydrich was being driven by his personal bodyguard, *Oberscharführer* Klein, in his open-top Mercedes from his manor house north of Prague to his office in Hradčany, three Czechoslovak agents (parachuted in from England) were taking up positions in the northeastern suburb of Libeň. The first agent gave the signal as the car pulled into Kirchmayer Boulevard (now V Holešovičkách). Another agent, a Slovak called **Gabčík**, pulled out a Sten gun and tried to shoot, but the gun jammed. Rather than driving out of the situation, Heydrich ordered Klein to stop the car and attempted to shoot back. At this point, the third agent, **Kubiš**, threw a hand grenade at the car. The blast injured Kubiš and Heydrich, who immediately leapt out and began firing at Kubiš. Kubiš, with blood pouring down his face, jumped on his bicycle and fled downhill. Gabčík meanwhile pulled out a second gun and exchanged shots with Heydrich, until the latter collapsed from his wounds. Gabčík fled into a butcher's, shot Klein – who was in hot pursuit – in the legs and escaped down the backstreets.

Meanwhile, back at the Mercedes, a baker's van was flagged down by a passer-by, but the baker refused to get involved. Eventually, a small truck carrying floor polish was commandeered and Heydrich taken to the Bulovka hospital. Heydrich died eight days later from shrapnel wounds and was given full Nazi honours at his **Prague funeral**; the cortege passed down Wenceslas Square, in front of a crowd of thousands. As the home resistance had forewarned, revenge was quick to follow. The day after Heydrich's funeral, the village of **Lidice** was burnt to the ground and its male inhabitants murdered; two weeks later the men and women of Ležáky suffered a similar fate.

The plan to assassinate Heydrich had been formulated in the early months of 1942 by the Czechoslovak **government-in-exile** in London, without consultation with the Czech Communist leadership in Moscow, and despite fierce opposition from the resistance within Czechoslovakia. Since it was clear that the reprisals would be horrific (thousands were executed in the aftermath), the only logical explanation for the plan is that this was precisely the aim of the government-in-exile's operation – to forge a solid wedge of resentment between the Germans and Czechs. In this respect, if in no other, the operation was ultimately successful.

committed suicide rather than give themselves up. There's a plaque at street level on the south wall commemorating those who died, and an exhibition on the whole affair situated in the crypt itself, which has been left pretty much as it was; the entrance is underneath the church steps on Na Zderaze.

Along the embankment

Magnificent turn-of-the-twentieth-century mansions line the Vltava's right bank, almost without interruption, for some 2km from the Charles Bridge south to the rocky outcrop of Vyšehrad. It's a long walk, even just along the length of **Masarykovo** and **Rašínovo nábřeží**, though there's no need to do the whole lot in one go: you can hop on a tram (#17 or #21) at various points, drop down from the embankments to the waterfront itself, or take a boat (April–Oct daily every 20min) to one of the two islands, Střelecký ostrov, or Slovanský ostrov, better known as Žofín.

Most of the ornate buildings along the waterfront itself are private residential apartments, and therefore inaccessible. One exception is the Art Nouveau concert hall, **Hlahol** (Ⓦwww.hlahol.cz), at Masarykovo nábřeží 16, built for the Hlahol men's choir in 1903–06, and designed by the architect of the main train station, Josef Fanta, with a pediment mural by Mucha and statues by Šaloun – check the listings magazines or the posters outside the hall for details of forthcoming concerts.

The islands

Access to either of the two islands in the central section of the Vltava is from close to the Národní divadlo. The first, **Střelecký ostrov**, or Shooters' Island, is where the army held their shooting practise, on and off, from the fifteenth until the nineteenth century. Closer to the left bank, and accessible via most Legií (Legion's Bridge), it became a favourite spot for a Sunday promenade, and is still popular, especially in summer. The first Sokol festival took place here in 1882 (see p.75), and the first May Day demonstrations in 1890.

The second island, **Slovanský ostrov**, came about as a result of the natural silting of the river in the eighteenth century. It's commonly known as **Žofín**, after the island's very yellow cultural centre, built in 1835 and named for Sophie, the mother of Emperor Franz-Joseph I. By the late nineteenth century the island had become one of the city's foremost pleasure gardens, where, as the composer Berlioz remarked, "bad musicians shamelessly make abominable music in the open air and immodest young males and females indulge in brazen dancing, while idlers and wasters…lounge about smoking foul tobacco and drinking beer." On a decent day, things seem pretty much unchanged from those heady times. Concerts, balls and other social gatherings take place here in the cultural centre, and there's a decent beer garden round the back; rowing boats can be rented in the summer.

At the southern tip of Slovanský ostrov stands the onion-domed **Šítek water tower**, which provided a convenient lookout post for the Czech secret police, whose job it was to watch over Havel's nearby flat (see p.130). Close by, spanning the narrow channel between the island and the riverbank, is the striking white functionalist box of the **Mánes** art gallery (Tues–Sun 10am–6pm; Ⓦwww.galeriemanes.cz). Designed in open-plan style by Otakar Novotný in 1930, the gallery is named after Josef Mánes, a traditional nineteenth-century landscape painter and Czech nationalist, and puts on consistently interesting contemporary exhibitions; in addition there's a café and an upstairs restaurant, suspended above the channel.

Tančící dům (Dancing House) to Výtoň

South of the Mánes gallery, Masarykovo nábřeží becomes **Rašínovo nábřeží,** named after Alois Rašín, who was sentenced to death for treason during World War I, went on to become the interwar Minister of Finance and was assassinated by an anarchist in 1923. The most striking building on the embankment is the

Tančící dům (Dancing House) or "Fred and Ginger", after the shape of the building's two towers, which look vaguely like a couple ballroom dancing. Designed by the Canadian-born Frank Gehry and the Yugoslav-born Vlado Milunič, the building was all the more controversial as it stands next door to no. 77, an apartment block built at the turn of the century by Havel's grandfather, where, until the early 1990s, Havel and his first wife, Olga, lived in the top-floor flat.

Further along the embankment, at **Palackého náměstí**, the buildings retreat for a moment to reveal Stanislav Sucharda's remarkable Art Nouveau **Monument to František Palacký**, the great nineteenth-century Czech historian, politician and nationalist. Like the Hus Monument, which was unveiled three years later, this mammoth project – fifteen years in the making – had missed its moment by the time it was finally completed in 1912, and found universal disfavour. The critics have mellowed over the years, and nowadays it's appreciated for what it is – an energetic and inspirational piece of work. Ethereal bronze bodies, representing the world of the imagination, shoot out at all angles, contrasting sharply with the plain stone mass of the plinth and below, the giant, grimly determined, seated figure of Palacký himself, representing the real world.

If you continue along the embankment to the very southern edge of Nové Město you'll come to a freestanding square building sunk below the level of the embankment. This is **Výtoň**, an attractive, sixteenth-century former customs house which now houses a pub and, in the timber-framed attic above it, a small **museum** (Tues– Sun 10am–6pm; 30Kč) telling the history of the Podskalí area – literally "under the rocks", ie Vyšehrad – with a model of the old embankment. There's also a fascinating video of one of the last *voroplavba* (log rafts) to come down the Vltava, before the river was dammed in the 1950s.

Emauzy to the Botanická zahrada

Behind Palackého náměstí, on **Vyšehradská**, the intertwined concrete spires of the **Emauzy monastery** are an unusual modern addition to the Prague skyline. The monastery was one of the few important historical buildings to be damaged in the last war, in this case by a stray Anglo-American bomb – the story goes that the pilot thought he was over Dresden. Charles IV founded the monastery for Croatian Benedictines, who used the Old Slavonic liturgy (hence its Czech name, Klášter na Slovanech, or "Monastery at the Slavs"), but after the Battle of Bílá hora it was handed over to the more mainstream Spanish Benedictines, who renamed it after Emmaus. The cloisters can be visited (June–Sept Mon–Sat 11am–5pm; Oct–May Mon–Fri 11am–5pm; 30Kč) and contain some extremely valuable Gothic frescoes.

Rising up behind Emauzy is one of Kilian Ignaz Dientzenhofer's little gems, the church of **sv Jan Nepomucký na skalce** (St John of Nepomuk on the Rock), perched high above Vyšehradská, with a facade that displays the plasticity of the Bavarian's Baroque style in all its glory. Heading south, Vyšehradská descends to a junction, where you'll find the entrance to the **Botanická zahrada** (daily: Feb & March 10am–5pm; April–Aug 10am–7.30pm, Sept & Oct 10am–6pm, Nov–Jan 10am–4pm; free), the university's botanic garden, laid out in 1897 on a series of terraces up the other side of the hill. Though far from spectacular, the garden is one of the few patches of green in this part of town, and the 1930s greenhouses (*skleníky*) have been restored to their former glory.

Ke Karlovu

Ke Karlovu is a quiet street just east of the botanical gardens, that heads south to the edge of Nové Město. The only busy spot is Na bojišti, a sidestreet to the north where you'll find **U kalicha** (www.ukalicha.cz), the pub immortalized in the opening passages of the consistently popular comic novel, *The Good Soldier Švejk*, by Jaroslav Hašek. In the story, on the eve of World War I, Švejk (*Schweik* to the Germans) walks into *U kalicha*, where a plain-clothes officer of the Austro-Hungarian constabulary is sitting drinking and, after a brief conversation, finds himself arrested in connection with the assassination of Archduke Ferdinand. Whatever the pub may have been like in Hašek's day (and even then, it wasn't his local), it's now unashamedly oriented towards reaping in the euros, and about the only authentic thing you'll find inside – albeit at a price – is the beer.

Vila Amerika (Muzeum Antonína Dvořáka)

A more rewarding place of pilgrimage, set back from the road behind wrought-iron gates, is the salmon-pink **Vila Amerika** (April–Sept Tues, Wed & Fri–Sun 10am–1.30pm & 2–5pm, Thurs 11am–3.30pm & 4–7pm; Oct–March Tues–Sun 10am–1.30pm & 2–5pm; 50Kč; Wwww.nm.cz), now a museum devoted to Czech composer, **Antonín Dvořák** (1841–1904), who lived for a time on nearby Žitná. Even if you've no interest in Dvořák, the house itself is a delight, designed for the upwardly mobile Count Michna as a minuscule Baroque summer palace around 1720 and one of Kilian Ignaz Dientzenhofer's most successful secular works. Easily the most famous of all Czech composers, for many years Dvořák had to play second fiddle to Smetana in the orchestra at the Národní divadlo, where Smetana was the conductor. Among the various items of memorabilia are Dvořák's golden honorary degree gown from Cambridge and some furniture from his Žitná flat. However, the tasteful period rooms, with the composer's music wafting in and out and the tiny garden dotted with Baroque sculptures, compensate for what the display cabinets may lack. Occasional concerts take place upstairs, in the velky sál, with its *trompe l'oeil* frescoes.

▲ Vila Amerika

Muzeum Policie ČR

At the southern end of Ke Karlovu, the former Augustinian monastery of Karlov is now the **Muzeum Policie ČR** (Tues–Sun 10am–5pm; 30Kč; Ⓦwww.mvcr.cz). Under the Communists, the most famous exhibit was undoubtedly Brek, the stuffed German Shepherd Dog who saw twelve years' service on border patrols, intercepted sixty "law-breakers" and was twice shot in action. Brek has been mothballed, and the current exhibition concentrates on road and traffic offences, and the force's latest challenges: forgery, drugs and murder. Sadly, there's not much information in English, but it's still mildly diverting, in particular the exhibits on the Iron Curtain, the display of Czech police motorbikes through the ages, the parade of European police uniforms and the gruesome section on forensic science. For the kids, there's a mini road layout for go-karts (dětské dopravní hřiště; Thurs 1–3pm, Sat & Sun 10am–noon & 2–4pm; 10Kč).

Na Karlově church

Attached to the museum is the monastic church of **Na Karlově**, founded by Charles IV (of course), designed in imitation of Charlemagne's tomb in Aachen and quite unlike any other church in Prague. If it's open, you should take a look at the musty interior, which was remodelled in the sixteenth century by Bonifaz Wohlmut. The stellar vault has no central supporting pillars – a remarkable feat of engineering for its time, and one which gave rise to numerous legends about the architect being in league with the devil. The later Baroque fittings are just as arresting, with polychrome figures dotted about on every cornice – check out Pontius Pilate and Christ above the south door, and beneath them, a set of holy stairs, and an underground Bethlehem grotto (Betlémské jeskyně).

From outside the church, there's a great view south across the Botič valley, to a small cluster of skyscraper hotels and the low-lying, supremely ugly **Kongresové centrum Praha** (Prague Congress Centre; Ⓦwww.kcp.cz), the country's biggest conference and concert venue, originally used for Communist Party congresses; to the right is the fortress of Vyšehrad. Vyšehrad metro is on the other side of the Nuselský most, the flyover bridge; alternatively, you can walk down to the bottom of the valley and catch a tram (#7, #18 or #24).

Vyšehrad and the eastern suburbs

The fortress of **Vyšehrad**, just to the south of Nové Město, was one of the earliest points of settlement in Prague, and is by far the most enticing of Prague's outlying sights. Its cemetery contains the remains of Bohemia's artistic elite; the ramparts afford superb views over the river; and below the fortress, there are several examples of **Czech Cubist** architecture.

By the end of his reign in 1378, Charles IV had laid out his city on such a grand scale that it wasn't until the Industrial Revolution hit Bohemia in the mid-nineteenth century that Prague began to spread beyond the boundaries of the medieval town. The first suburbs were planned to the east of the old town, with public parks and grid street plans; twentieth-century suburbs have tended to grow with less grace, trailing their tenements and high-rise *paneláky* across the hills, and swallowing up existing villages on the way. Of the eastern suburbs, **Vinohrady** and **Žižkov** best retain their individual late nineteenth-century identities, which makes them worth checking out on even a short visit to the city; they also contain one or two specific sights to guide your wandering.

Vyšehrad

At the southern tip of Nové Město, around 3km south of the city centre, the rocky red-brick fortress of **VYŠEHRAD** (Ⓦ www.praha-vysehrad.cz) – literally "High Castle" – has more myths attached to it than any other place in Bohemia. According to Czech legend, this is the place where the Slav tribes first settled in Prague, where the "wise and tireless chieftain" Krok built a castle, and whence his youngest daughter **Libuše** went on to found Praha (Prague) itself. Alas, the archeological evidence doesn't bear this claim out, but it's clear that **Přemysl Vratislav II** (1061–92), the first Bohemian ruler to bear the title "king", built a royal palace here to get away from his younger brother who was lording it in the Hrad. Within half a century the royals had moved back to Hradčany, into a new palace, and from then on Vyšehrad began to lose its political significance.

The fortress enjoyed something of a renaissance under Emperor Charles IV, who wished to associate his own dynasty with that of the early Přemyslids. A system of walls was built to link the fortress to the newly founded Nové Město,

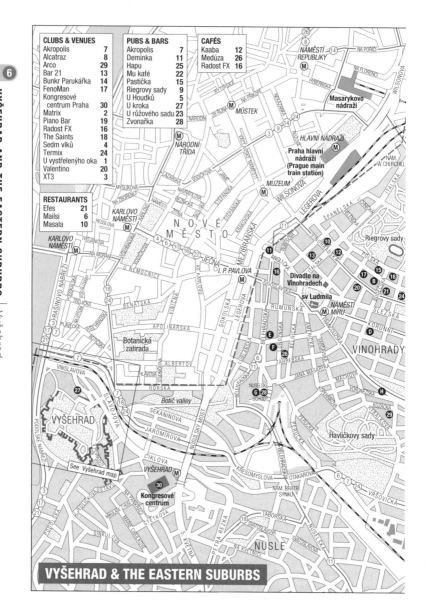

VYŠEHRAD & THE EASTERN SUBURBS

CLUBS & VENUES
Akropolis	7
Alcatraz	8
Arco	29
Bar 21	13
Bunkr Parukářka	14
FenoMan	17
Kongresové centrum Praha	30
Matrix	2
Piano Bar	19
Radost FX	16
The Saints	18
Sedm vlků	4
Termix	24
U vystřeleného oka	1
Valentino	20
XT3	3

PUBS & BARS
Akropolis	7
Deminka	11
Hapu	25
Mu kafé	22
Pastička	15
Riegrovy sady	9
U Houdků	5
U kroka	27
U růžového sadu	23
Zvonařka	28

CAFÉS
Kaaba	12
Medúza	26
Radost FX	16

RESTAURANTS
Efes	21
Mailsi	6
Masala	10

and it was decreed that the *králová cesta* (coronation route) should begin from here. Those fortifications were destroyed by the **Hussites** in 1420, but the hill was settled again over the next two hundred years. In the mid-seventeenth century, the Habsburgs turfed everyone out and rebuilt the place as a fortified barracks, only to tear it down in 1866 to create a public park. By the time the **Czech national revival** movement became interested in Vyšehrad, only the

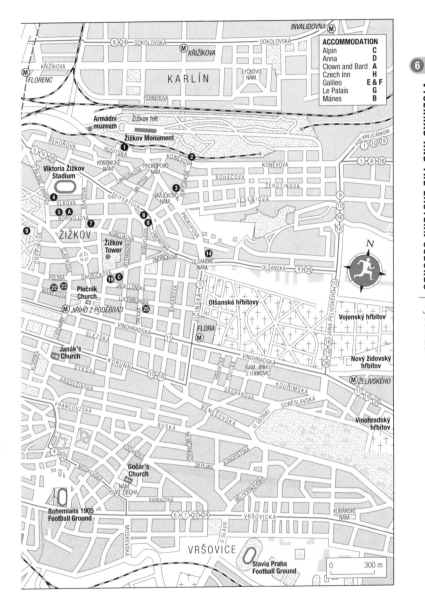

red-brick fortifications were left as a reminder of its former strategic importance; they rediscovered its history and its legends, and gradually transformed it into a symbol of Czech nationhood. Today, Vyšehrad makes for one of the most rewarding trips away from the human congestion of the city, a perfect afternoon escape and a great place from which to watch the evening sun set behind the Hrad.

VYŠEHRAD

Cihelná brána	a
Táborská brána	b
Information centre	c
sv Petr and Pavel	d
Slavín monument	e
Galerie Vysehrad	f
sv Martin	g
sv Vavrinec	h
Premysl and Libuse	i
Lumír and Písen	j
Záboj and Slavoj	k
Ctirad and Sárka	l
Nájemný obytný dům (Chocol)	m
Nájemný obytný dům (Belada)	n
Kovařovicova vila	o
Rodinný trojdům	p

0   100 m

PUB
U kroka   1

Vyšehrad Ⓜ ▼

The fortress

There are several **approaches to the fortress**: if you've come by one of the trams (#3, #7, #17 or #21) which trundle along the waterfront to stop Výtoň, you can either wind your way up Vratislavova and enter through the Cihelná brána (**a**), or take the steep stairway from Rašínovo nábřeží that leads up through the trees to a small side entrance in the west wall. Alternatively, from Vyšehrad metro station, walk west past the ugly Kongresové centrum Praha, and enter through the Táborská brána (**b**) and Leopoldova brána (**c**), between which there's an **information centre** (daily: April–Oct 9.30am–6pm; Nov–March 9.30am–5pm). Vyšehrad is perfect for a picnic, though *Café Citadella* in the southwestern corner of the ramparts is convenient for food and drink, as are the pubs in the streets below the fortress.

Church of sv Petr and Pavel

Standing by the western entrance to Vyšehrad Cemetery is the blackened sandstone basilica of **sv Petr and Pavel** (**d**), rebuilt in the 1880s by Josef Mocker in neo-Gothic style on the site of an eleventh-century basilica. The twin open-work spires are now the fortress's most familiar landmark, and the bells play a slice of Dvořák's *Cello Concerto* on the hour. Inside, you can admire the church's Art Nouveau murals, which cover every available surface (Tues–Thurs & Sat 9am–noon & 1–5pm, Fri 9am–noon, Sun 10am–noon & 1–5pm; 30Kč).

Vyšehradský hřbitov (Vyšehrad Cemetery)

One of the first initiatives of the national revival movement was to establish the **Vyšehradský hřbitov** (daily: March, April & Oct 8am–6pm; May–Sept 8am–7pm; Nov–Feb 8am–5pm; Ⓦwww.slavin.cz), which spreads out to the north and east of the church. It's a measure of the part that artists and intellectuals played in the foundation of the nation, and the regard in which they are still held, that the most prestigious graveyard in the city is given over to them: no soldiers, no politicians, not even the Communists managed to muscle their way in here (except on artistic merit). Sheltered from the wind by its high walls, lined on two sides by delicate arcades, it's a tiny cemetery (reflecting, as it were, the size of the nation) filled with well-kept graves, many of them designed by the country's leading sculptors.

To the uninitiated only a handful of figures are well known, but for the Czechs the place is alive with great names (there's a useful plan of the most notable graves at the entrance nearest the church). Ladislav Šaloun's grave for **Antonín Dvořák** (1841–1904), situated under the arches, is one of the more showy ones, with a mosaic inscription, studded with gold stones, glistening behind wrought-iron railings. **Bedřich Smetana** (1824–84), who died twenty years earlier, is buried in comparatively modest surroundings near the Slavín monument (see p.138). The *Pražské jaro* festival begins with a procession from his grave to the Obecní dům, on the anniversary of his death (May 12).

Other graves that attract (mostly Czech) pilgrims are those of the nineteenth-century writer **Božena Němcová**, in the shadow of the church's east end, and playwright **Karel Čapek**, whose grave faces the arcades – he coined one of the two Czech words to have entered the English language, "robot" (the other is "pistol"). Several graves of lesser-known individuals stand out artistically, too: in particular, František Bílek's towering statue of *Sorrow* on the grave of the writer Václav Beneš Třebízský, which aroused a storm of protest when it was first unveiled; Bohumil Kafka's headstone for Dr Josef Kaizl, with a woman's face peeping out from the grave; and Karel Hladík's modern *Cathedral* sculpture, which sits above his own grave.

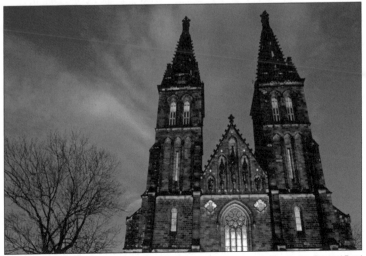

▲ Church of sv Petr and Pavel

The focus of the cemetery, though, is the **Slavín monument (e)**, a big, bulky stele built in 1893 to a design by Antonín Wiehl, covered in commemorative plaques and topped by a sarcophagus and a statue representing Genius. It's the communal resting place of more than fifty Czech artists, including the painter **Alfons Mucha**, the sculptors Josef Václav Myslbek and Ladislav Šaloun, the architect Josef Gočár and the opera singer **Ema Destinnová**.

The grave of the Romantic poet **Karel Hynek Mácha** was the assembly point for the demonstration on November 17, 1989, which triggered the Velvet Revolution. This was organized to commemorate the fiftieth anniversary of the Nazi attack on Czech higher education institutions in 1939. Student protests against the German occupation reached a peak on October 28, 1939, when violent clashes resulted in the death of medical student **Jan Opletal**; his funeral, on November 11, was accompanied by more violent disturbances. On November 17, the Nazis took the initiative, executing various student leaders, packing thousands off to the camps and shutting down all Czech higher education institutes. Fifty years later, in 1989, the cemetery was the gathering point for a 50,000-strong crowd who attempted to march from here to Wenceslas Square.

The rest of the fortress

The next best thing to do after a stroll around the cemetery is to head off and explore the **Kasematy,** or dungeons (daily: April–Oct 9.30am–6pm; Nov–March 9.30am–5pm; 30Kč), which you enter via the **Cihelná brána (a)**. After a short guided tour of a section of the underground passageways underneath the ramparts, you enter a vast storage hall, which shelters several of the original statues from the Charles Bridge, and, when the lights are switched off, reveals a camera obscura image of a tree.

The rest of the deserted fortress makes for a pleasant afternoon meander; you can walk almost the entire length of the ramparts, which give some superb views out across the city. **Galerie Vyšehrad** (daily: April–Oct 9.30am–6pm; Nov, Dec & March 9.30am–5pm) is a small art gallery housed in one of the bastions (**f**), which puts on temporary exhibitions. The heavily restored rotunda of **sv Martin (g)** – one of a number of Romanesque rotundas scattered across Prague – is the sole survivor of the medieval fortress built by Vratislav II in the eleventh century; it's only open for services. The foundations of the basilica of **sv Vavřinec (h)**, from the same period, can be seen nearby.

If the weather's good, though, time is probably better spent lounging on the patch of grass to the south of the church, where there are regular outdoor concerts on summer Sundays. Dotted about the grass are the gargantuan **Myslbek statues** that used to grace the nearby bridge, Palackého most. Four couples are dotted across the green, all taken from Prague legends: *Přemysl and Libuše* (**i**), the husband and wife team who founded Prague and started Bohemia's first royal dynasty, the Přemyslids; *Lumír and Píseň* (**j**), the legendary Czech singer and his muse, Song; *Záboj and Slavoj* (**k**), two mythical Czech warriors; and *Ctirad and Šárka* (**l**), for whose story, see the box on p.156.

Czech Cubism in Vyšehrad

Even if you harbour only a passing interest in modern architecture, it's worth seeking out the cluster of **Cubist villas** below the fortress in Vyšehrad. Whereas Czech Art Nouveau was heavily influenced by the Viennese Secession, it was Paris rather than the imperial capital that provided the stimulus for the short-lived but extremely productive Czech Cubist movement. In 1911, the Skupina výtvarných umělců, or SVU (Group of Fine Artists), was founded in Prague, and quickly became the movement's organizing force. **Pavel Janák** was the SVU's chief

Cubist and Rondo-Cubist buildings elsewhere in Prague

Prague's unique Cubist and Rondo-Cubist buildings are scattered right across the city. Here is a checklist of where to find the best examples of the style away from Vyšehrad.

Staré Město
Gočár's **Dům U černé Matky boží** p.93

Nové Město
Janák and Zasche's **Palác Adria** p.123
Janák's **Banka legií** p.121
Blecha and Králíček's **lamppost** p.123
Králíček's **Diamant** p.126

theorist, **Josef Gočár** its most illustrious exponent, but **Josef Chochol** was the most successful practitioner of the style in Prague.

Cubism is associated mostly with painting, and the unique contribution of its Czech offshoot was to apply the theory to **furniture** (some of which is on permanent display at the Muzeum českého kubismu; see p.93) and **architecture**. In Vyšehrad alone, Chochol completed three buildings, close to one another below the fortress, using prismatic shapes and angular lines to produce the sharp geometric contrasts of light and dark shadows characteristic of Cubist painting. Outside the Czech Republic, only the preparatory drawings by the French architect Duchamp-Villon for his (unrealized) *Maison Cubiste* can be considered remotely similar.

The SVU's plans were cut short by World War I, after which Janák and Gočár attempted to establish a specifically Czechoslovak style of architecture incorporating prewar Cubism. The style was dubbed **Rondo-Cubism** since the prismatic moulding had been replaced by semicircular motifs, but only a few projects got off the ground before Czech architects turned to the functionalist ideals of the international modernist movement.

The buildings

The most impressive example of Czech Cubist architecture, brilliantly exploiting its angular location, is Chochol's **nájemný obytný dům (m)**, an apartment block at Neklanova 30, begun in 1913 for František Hodek and now housing a restaurant on its ground floor. Further along Neklanova, at no. 2, there's Antonín Belada's **nájemný obytný dům (n)**, with its Cubist facade, and around the corner is the most ambitious project of the lot – Chochol's **Kovařovicova vila (o)**, which backs onto Libušina. From the front, on Rašínovo nábřeží, you can appreciate the clever, slightly askew layout of the garden, designed right down to its zigzag garden railings. Further along the embankment is Chochol's largest commission, the **Rodinný trojdům (p)**, a large building complex with a heavy mansard roof, a central "Baroque" gable with a pedimental frieze and room enough for three families.

Vinohrady

Southeast of Nové Město is the predominantly late nineteenth-century district of **VINOHRADY**, Prague's most resolutely bourgeois suburb, with two spacious parks – **Riegrovy sady**, to the north, and **Havlíčkovy sady**, to the south – and a fabulous array of turn-of-the-twentieth-century apartment buildings. In terms of conventional sightseeing, however, the area is definitely low priority, though there are a few places here (and in neighbouring Žižkov) worth a visit, most of them quick and easy to reach by metro.

Náměstí Míru

If Vinohrady has a centre, it's the leafy square of **náměstí Míru**, a good introduction to the aspirations of this confident, bourgeois neighbourhood. At its centre stands the brick-built basilica of **sv Ludmila**, designed by Josef Mocker in the late 1880s in a severe neo-Gothic style, though the interior furnishings have the odd flourish of Art Nouveau. In front of the church is a statue commemorating the **Čapek brothers**, writer Karel and painter Josef, both local residents, who together symbolized the golden era of the interwar republic. Karel died of pneumonia in 1938, shortly after the Nazi invasion, while Josef perished in Belsen seven years later. Two more buildings on the square deserve attention, the most flamboyant being the **Divadlo na Vinohradech**, built in 1907, using Art Nouveau and neo-Baroque elements in equal measure. More subdued, but equally ornate inside and out, is the district's former **Národní dům**, a grandiose neo-Renaissance edifice from the 1890s housing a ballroom/concert hall and restaurant.

From náměstí Míru, block after block of tenements, each clothed in its own individual garment of sculptural decoration, form a grid plan of grand bourgeois avenues stretching eastwards to the city's great cemeteries (see opposite). If the weather's nice, you could stroll your way down Mánesova to Plečnik's church. However, distances are deceptive, and you may prefer to take the metro.

Plečnik's church

Vinohrady's other main square, **náměstí Jiřího z Poděbrad**, halfway between náměstí Míru and the cemeteries, contains Prague's most celebrated modern church, **Nejsvětějšího Srdce Páně** (Most Sacred Heart of Our Lord), built in 1928 by Josip Plečnik, the Slovene architect responsible for much of the remodelling of the Hrad (see box, p.46). It's a marvellously eclectic and individualistic work, employing a sophisticated potpourri of architectural styles: a Neoclassical pediment and a great slab of a clock tower with a giant transparent face in imitation of a Gothic rose window, as well as the bricks and mortar of contemporary Constructivism. Plečnik also had a sharp eye for detail; look out for the little gold crosses inset into the brickwork like stars, inside and out, and the celestial orbs of light suspended above the heads of the congregation. If you can collar the priest, it may be possible to climb the clock tower.

Janák and Gočár's functionalist churches

Further afield are two, more uncompromisingly modernist, churches. The first is the **Husův sbor** (Hussite Church), three blocks south of Plečnik's church down U vodárny, on the corner of Dykova. Built in the early 1930s by Pavel Janák, the church's most salient feature is its freestanding hollow tower, which encloses a corkscrew spiral staircase and is topped by a giant copper chalice, symbol of the Hussite faith. A memorial on the wall commemorates the church's pioneering role in the Prague Uprising against the Nazis in May 1945, when it served as a Czech resistance headquarters.

Josef Gočár's equally severe, functionalist church of **sv Václav** built around the same time, lies a kilometre or so southeast on náměstí Svatopluka Čecha;

take tram #4 or #22 from náměstí Míru or the bottom of U vodárny to the Čechovo náměstí stop. Here it forms the centrepiece of a sloping green square, with a distinctive stepped roof rising up from a slender, smoothly rendered eighty-metre-high tower.

Žižkov

Though they share much the same architectural heritage, **ŽIŽKOV**, unlike neighbouring Vinohrady, is a traditionally working-class area, and was a Communist Party stronghold between the wars, earning it the nickname "Red Žižkov". Nowadays its peeling turn-of-the-twentieth-century tenements are home to a large proportion of Prague's Romany community, and it boasts more pubs and brothels per head than any other district in Prague. The main reason for venturing into Žižkov is to visit its two landmarks – ancient (Žižkov Hill) and modern (the TV tower) – and the city's main cemeteries, at the eastern end of Vinohradská.

Žižkov TV tower

At 216m in height, the Televizní vysílač, or **Žižkov TV tower** (daily 10am–11.30pm; 150Kč; ⓦ www.tower.cz), is the tallest building in Prague. Close up, it's an intimidating futuristic piece of architecture, made all the more disturbing by the addition of several statues of giant babies crawling up the sides, courtesy of artist David Černý. Begun in the 1970s in a desperate bid to jam West German television transmissions, the tower became fully operational only in the 1990s. In the course of its construction, however, the Communists saw fit to demolish part of a nearby Jewish cemetery which had served the community between 1787 and 1891; a small section survives to the northwest of the tower. From the fifth-floor café or the viewing platform on the eighth floor, you can enjoy a **spectacular view** across Prague. To get to the tower, take the metro to Jiřího z Poděbrad and walk northeast a couple of blocks – it's difficult to miss.

Olšany cemeteries

Approaching from the west, the first and the largest of Prague's vast cemeteries – each of which is bigger than the entire Jewish quarter – is the **Olšanské hřbitovy** (Olšany cemeteries; daily dawn to dusk), originally created for the victims of the

Jaroslav Seifert of Žižkov

The Czech Nobel prize-winning poet **Jaroslav Seifert** (1901–86) was born and bred in the Žižkov district. He was one of the founding members of the Czecho-slovak Communist Party, and in 1920 helped found Devětsil, the most daring and provocative avant-garde movement of the interwar republic. Always accused of harbouring bourgeois sentiments, Seifert and several other Communist writers were expelled from the Party when Gottwald and the Stalinists hijacked the Party at the Fifth Congress in 1929. After the 1948 coup, he became *persona non grata*, though he rose to prominence briefly during the 1956 Writers' Union congress, when he attempted to lead a rebellion against the Stalinists. He was a signatory of Charter 77, and in 1984, amid much controversy, he became the one and only Czech to win the Nobel Prize for Literature.

1680 plague epidemic. The perimeter walls are lined with glass cabinets, stacked like shoeboxes, containing funereal urns and mementoes, while the graves themselves are a mixed bag of artistic achievements, reflecting the funereal fashions of the day as much as the character of the deceased. The cemeteries are divided into districts and crisscrossed with cobbled streets; at each gate there's a map, and an aged janitor ready to point you in the right direction.

The cemeteries' two most famous incumbents are an ill-fitting couple: **Klement Gottwald**, the country's first Communist president, whose remains were removed from the mausoleum on Žižkov Hill in 1962 after the embalming went wrong; and **Jan Palach**, the philosophy student who set light to himself in January 1969 in protest at the Soviet occupation. More than 750,000 people attended Palach's funeral, and, in an attempt to put a stop to the annual vigils at his graveside, he was reburied in his home town, 60km outside Prague. His place was taken by an unknown woman, Maria Jedličková, who for the next seventeen years had her grave covered in flowers instead. Finally, in 1990, Palach's body was returned to the Olšany cemeteries; you'll find it just to the east of the main entrance on Vinohradská (metro Flora).

To the east of the Olšany cemeteries and usually totally deserted, is the **Vojenský hřbitov** (Military Cemetery; daily dawn to dusk); the entrance is 200m up Jana Želivského, on the right (metro Želivského). Its centrepiece is the monument to the 436 Soviet soldiers who lost their lives on May 9, 1945 in the liberation of Prague, surrounded by a small, tufty meadow dotted with simple white crosses. Nearby, the graves of Czechs who died fighting for the Habsburgs on the Italian front in World War I are laid out in a semicircle. There are even some Commonwealth war graves here, mostly (though not exclusively) British POWs who died in captivity.

Nový židovský hřbitov (New Jewish Cemetery)

Immediately south of the Military Cemetery is the **Nový židovský hřbitov** (April–Sept Mon–Thurs & Sun 9am–4.30pm, Fri 9am–2.30pm; Oct–March Mon–Thurs & Sun 9am–3.30pm, Fri 9am–1.30pm; 50Kč), founded in the 1890s, when the one by the Žižkov TV tower (see p.141) was full; it was designed to last for a century, with room for 100,000 graves. It's a melancholy spot, particularly so in the east of the cemetery, where large empty allotments wait in vain to be filled by the generation that perished in the Holocaust. In fact, the community is now so small that it's unlikely the graveyard will ever be full. Most people come here to visit **Franz Kafka**'s grave, 400m east along the south wall and signposted from the entrance. He is buried, along with his mother and father (both of whom outlived him), beneath a plain headstone; the plaque below commemorates his three sisters who died in the camps.

Žižkov Hill

Žižkov hill (also known as Vítkov hill) is the thin green wedge of land that separates Žižkov from Karlín, the grid-plan industrial district to the north. From its westernmost point, which juts out almost to the edge of Nové Město, is the definitive panoramic view over the city centre. It was here, on July 14, 1420, that the Hussites enjoyed their first and finest victory at the **Battle of Vítkov**, under the inspired leadership of the one-eyed general, Jan Žižka (hence the name of the district). Ludicrously outnumbered by more than ten to one, Žižka and his fanatically motivated troops thoroughly trounced Emperor Sigismund and his papal forces. To reach Žižkov Hill, walk or take bus #133 or #175 from Florenc metro station to U památníku stop.

Armádní muzeum (Army museum)

On the right as you climb Žižkov Hill is the **Armádní muzeum** (Army Museum; Tues–Sun 10am–6pm; free; ⓦ www.vhu.cz), guarded by a handful of tanks, howitzers and armoured vehicles. Czech military victories may be few and far between, but the country has a long history of manufacturing top-class weaponry for world powers (Semtex is probably their best-known export). It's no coincidence that of the two Czech words to have made it into the English language, one is "pistol" (from *pišťále*, a Hussite weapon); the other is "robot" (from Karel Čapek's play *R.U.R.*). The museum covers the period from 1914 to 1945, and contains a balanced account of both world wars, including the fate of the Czechoslovak Legion, the Heydrich assassination (see box, p.128) and the 1945 Prague Uprising.

Národní památník (National Monument)

The chief reason for ascending Žižkov Hill is to visit the giant concrete **Národní památník** (Wed–Sun 10am–6pm; 110Kč; ⓦ www.nm.cz), which houses a fascinating museum on the history of Czechoslovakia from its foundation in 1918 to its disintegration in 1992. Despite its overblown totalitarian aesthetics, inside and out, the monument was actually begun in the late 1920s as a memorial to the Czechoslovak Legion who fought against the Habsburgs – the gargantuan equestrian statue of the mace-wielding Žižka, which fronts the monument, is reputedly the largest in the world. The building eventually became a Communist mausoleum: presidents Gottwald, Zápotocký and Svoboda were all buried here, along with the obligatory Unknown Soldier and various other Party hacks. Gottwald himself was originally pickled and embalmed (à la Lenin), but a fire damaged his corpse so badly that the leader had to be cremated in 1962. In 1990, the remaining bodies were cremated and quietly reinterred in the Olšany cemeteries.

From the south side of the monument, you enter the central hall, which has engaging displays on the great political turning points in **Czech twentieth-century history**: the 1938 Munich Agreement, the 1948 Communist coup, the 1968 Prague Spring and the 1989 Velvet Revolution. Along the sides are cabinets filled with historical artefacts from the Sudetenland, the Sokol, Scout and Communist Pioneer movements, as well as the hiking subculture known as *tramping*. The Kolumbárium where the Communist leaders were once interred now commemorates famous (non-Communist) Czechs of the last century. There's plenty of social realist decor for fans of Communist kitsch – the best stuff is in the marble apsidal Síň osvobození (Liberation Hall), where the **Tomb of the Unknown Soviet Soldier** resides, surrounded by mosaic depictions of heroic World War II combatants. In the basement, you can inspect the state-of-the-art 1950s technology that failed to preserve Gottwald's remains and the remnants of his sarcophagus.

Holešovice and the western suburbs

The points of interest in Prague's northern and western suburbs, on the left bank of the Vltava, are spread over a much larger area than those east of the river. The suburbs themselves are also far more varied: some, like Holešovice and parts of Smíchov, date from the late nineteenth century, whereas Dejvice and Střešovice were laid out between the wars as well-to-do garden suburbs. The left bank also boasts a great deal more greenery, including the city's largest public park, Stromovka. All this goes to make up a fascinating patchwork of communities, which few tourists bother to see. It's worth the effort, though, if only to remind yourself that Prague doesn't begin and end at the Charles Bridge.

There are several specific sights in each suburb that can lend structure to your meandering. The single most important sight is the **Veletržní palác** in **Holešovice**, which houses the country's finest modern art collection. Other sights – for

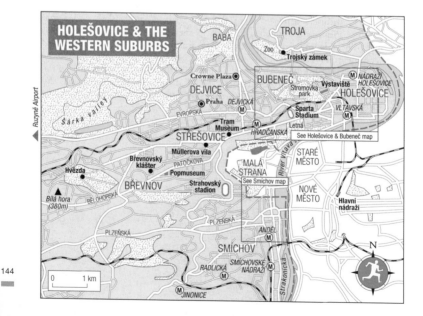

instance the functionalist villas in **Dejvice** and **Střešovice** – are of more specialized interest; some, such as the exquisite Renaissance chateau of **Hvězda**, deserve to be better known, and some areas, like **Smíchov**, give an interesting slice of downtown Prague that most tourists don't get to see.

Holešovice and Bubeneč

The late nineteenth- and early twentieth-century districts of **HOLEŠOVICE** and **BUBENEČ**, tucked into a huge U-bend in the Vltava, have little in the way of truly magnificent architecture, but they do have some grandiose apartment blocks and a huge swathe of former factories that are slowly being converted for use as nightclubs, galleries and flats. The area also boasts two huge splodges of green: to the south, **Letná**, overlooking the city centre, and to the north, **Stromovka**, bordering the Výstaviště funfair and international trade fair grounds. Holešovice is also home to the **Veletržní palác**, Prague's impressive modern art museum.

Letná

A high plateau hovering above the city, the flat green expanse of the **LETNÁ** plain has long been the traditional assembly point for invading and besieging armies. It was laid out as a public park in the mid-nineteenth century and used under the Communists as the site of their **May Day parades**. For these, thousands of citizens were dragooned into marching past the south side of the city's main football ground, the Sparta stadium, where the old Communist cronies would take the salute from a giant red podium. In November 1989, the largest demo of the Velvet Revolution took place here, with nearly a million people gathering to support the

▲ The view from Letná

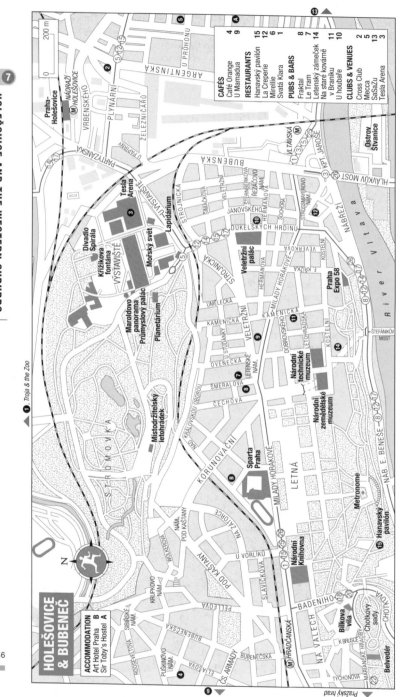

HOLEŠOVICE & BUBENEČ

ACCOMMODATION
Art Hotel Praha	B
Sir Toby's Hostel	A

CAFÉS
Café Orange	4
U Mamadua	9

RESTAURANTS
Hanavský pavilón	15
La Creperie	12
Mirellie	6
Svatá Klara	1

PUBS & BARS
Fraktal	8
Le Tram	7
Letenský zámeček	14
Na staré kovárně	11
v Braníku	
U houbaře	10

CLUBS & VENUES
Cross Club	2
Mecca	5
SaSaZu	13
Tesla Arena	3

▲ Troja & the Zoo

▲ Pražský hrad

general strike. In 1990 the road by the football stadium was renamed after Milada Horáková, the Socialist politician executed in a Communist show trial in 1950.

Letná's – indeed Prague's – most infamous monument is one which no longer exists. The **Stalin monument**, the largest in the world, was once visible from almost every part of the city: a 30-metre-high granite sculpture portraying a procession of Czechs and Russians being led to Communism by the Pied Piper figure of Stalin, but popularly dubbed *tlačenice* (the crush) because of its resemblance to a Communist-era bread queue. Designed by Jiří Štursa and Otakar Švec, it took six hundred workers five hundred days to erect the 14,200-ton monster. Švec committed suicide shortly before it was unveiled, as his wife had done three years previously, leaving all his money to a school for blind children, since they at least would not have to see his creation. It was eventually revealed to the cheering masses on May 1, 1955, but within a year, Khrushchev had denounced his predecessor. After pressure from Moscow, the monument was blown to smithereens by a series of explosions spread over a fortnight in 1962. All that remains above ground is the statue's vast concrete platform and steps, on the southern edge of the Letná plain, now graced with David Černý's symbolic giant red **metronome**; it's also a great viewpoint, with the central stretch of the Vltava glistening in the afternoon sun.

Visible to the west of the metronome is the **Hanavský pavilón**, a café-restaurant (see p.196) that looks rather like a Russian Orthodox church. It was devised by Count Hanavský as a showpiece of wrought-ironwork for the 1891 Prague Exhibition, and is executed in a flamboyant style which anticipated the arrival of Art Nouveau a few years later.

Národní technické muzeum

Occupying a seminal functionalist 1930s building on Kostelní, the **Národní technické muzeum** (National Technical Museum; ⓦ www.ntm.cz) is, despite its rather dull title, a surprisingly interesting museum. The whole place has been closed for renovation for a number of years, but it is scheduled to reopen in late 2011. The showpiece hangar-like main hall contains an impressive gallery of motorbikes, Czech and foreign, and a wonderful collection of old planes, trains and automobiles from Czechoslovakia's industrial heyday between the wars when the country's Škoda cars and Tatra soft-top stretch limos were really something to brag about. The oldest car in the collection is Laurin & Klement's 1898 Präsident, more of a motorized carriage than a car; the museum also boasts the oldest Bugatti in the world. Other displays trace the development of early photography, and feature a collection of some of Kepler's and Tycho Brahe's astronomical instruments.

Národní zemědělské muzeum (National agricultural museum)

Occupying an almost identical 1930s building to the west, the **Národní zemědělské muzeum** (National Agricultural Museum; Tues–Sun 9am–5pm; 60Kč; ⓦ www.nzm.cz) contains probably one of the finest displays of tractors that you're ever likely to see. Among the domestic workhorses by Škoda and Zetor, there's a Lanz Bulldog, one of the most popular interwar German tractors, with its distinctive, easy-to-maintain hot bulb engine, and a very fetching American MrCormick-Deering tractor in lilac and red livery. Several upstairs galleries are given over to temporary exhibitions throughout the year, and outside there's a small city farm with hens, very large rabbits and a couple of Wallachian sheep (called Cecilka and Dorotka).

Veletržní palác (Trade Fair Palace)

Situated at the corner of Dukelských hrdinů and Veletržní, some distance from the nearest metro station, the **Veletržní palác** (Tues–Sun 10am–6pm; 200Kč, after 4pm 100Kč; Ⓦ www.ngprague.cz) gets nothing like the number of visitors it should. Not only does the building house the Národní galerie's excellent **nineteenth- and twentieth-century art** collection, but it's also an architectural sight in itself. A seven-storey building constructed in 1928 by Oldřich Tyl and Josef Fuchs, it is Prague's ultimate functionalist masterpiece, not so much from the outside, but inside, where its gleaming white vastness is suitably awesome. Even the normally hypercritical Le Corbusier, who visited the building the year it was completed, was impressed: "Seeing the Trade Fair Palace, I realized how to make large buildings, having so far built only several relatively small houses on a low budget."

The main exhibition hall is once more used for trade fairs, with the Národní galerie confined to the north wing. Nevertheless, the gallery is both big and bewildering, stretching over six floors, and virtually impossible to view in its entirety (audioguides in English are included in the admission price). Special exhibitions occupy the ground and fifth floors; the most popular section is the **French art** collection on the third floor. From the ground floor you can stare up at the glass-roofed atrium, a glorious space for wacky modern pieces of art, overlooked by six floors of balconies.

To reach the Veletržní palác by public transport, catch tram #14 from náměstí Republiky, tram #12 from Malostranská metro, tram #17 from Staroměstská metro or tram #12 or #15 from Nádraží Holešovice to the Veletržní stop. For somewhere to eat nearby, *U houbaře* (The Mushroom), opposite the museum is a good pub (see p.202), or there's *Ouky Douky*, a café-bar and secondhand bookshop, one block east at Janovského 14.

First floor: foreign art

As good a place as any to start is the bluntly entitled **Foreign Art** exhibition that occupies the first floor. There are one or two gems here, beginning with **Gustav Klimt**'s mischievous *Virgins*, a mass of naked bodies and tangled limbs painted over in psychedelic colours, plus one of the square landscapes he used to like painting during his summer holidays in the Salzkammergut.

Egon Schiele's mother came from the South Bohemian town of Český Krumlov, the subject of a tiny, gloomy, autumnal canvas, *Dead Town*. The gallery also owns one of Schiele's most popular female portraits, wrongly entitled *The Artist's Wife*, an unusually graceful and gentle watercolour of a seated woman in green top and black leggings. In contrast, *Pregnant Woman and Death* is a morbidly bleak painting, in which Schiele depicts himself as both the monk of death and the life-giving mother.

Look out, too, for two canvases by **Edvard Munch**, and for **Oskar Kokoschka**'s typically vigorous landscapes, dating from his brief stay in Prague in the 1930s, when the political temperature got too hot in Austria.

Second floor: Czech art 1930–2000

On the second floor, the section covering **Czech art from 1930 to 2000** gives a pretty good introduction to the country's artistic peaks and troughs. To be honest, though, there's too much stuff here – paintings, sculptures and installations – to take in at one go. Below are one or two highlights.

First off, there's a wild kinetic-light sculpture by **Zdeněk Pešánek**, a world pioneer in the use of neon in art, who created a stir at the 1937 Paris Expo with a neon fountain. Devětsil, the most important avant-garde art movement in the interwar republic, is represented here by **Toyen** (Marie Čermínová) and her lifelong companion **Jindřich Štyrský**, and by abstract photographic works. Avant-garde photography featured strongly in Devětsil's portfolio, and there are several fine abstract works on display, as well as some beautiful "colour tests" and graphics by Vojtěch Preissig, and a few short experimental films from the 1930s. One Czech artist who enthusiastically embraced Surrealism was **Josef Šíma**, who settled permanently in Paris in the 1920s; several of his trademark floating torsos and cosmic eggs are displayed here.

Fans of Communist kitsch should make their way to the small **Socialist Realism** section, with works such as the wildly optimistic *We Produce More, We Live Better*, and Eduard Stavinoha's cartoon-like *Listening to the Speech of Klement Gottwald, Feb 21, 1948*. There's a great model and drawing of a Tatra 603, the limo of choice for Party apparatchiks in the 1950s, yet clearly inspired by American car design. Note, too, the model of Otakar Švec's now demolished Stalin statue, which once dominated central Prague (see p.147). Nearby is the allegorical *Large Meal* by Mikuláš Medek, who was banned from exhibiting his works under the Communists. Opposite, there's a whole section on the **1958 Brussels Expo**, in which Czechoslovakia won several awards, and which, in a sense, signalled the beginning of the slow thaw in censorship.

In the 1960s, **performance art** (*umění akce*) was big in Czechoslovakia, and it, too, has its own section. Inevitably, it's difficult to recapture the original impact of some of the "happenings" – the photographs of Milan Knížak asking passers-by to crow have lost some of their immediacy. Other photos, such as those of Zorka Ságlová's *Laying out Nappies near Sudoměř*, give you a fair idea of what you missed, and Vladimír Boudník's theory of "explosionalism" would appeal to most small boys. Other works, such as Eva Kmentová's *Footprints*, betray their ephemeral intentions by being reproduced in a gallery: her plastercasts were originally exhibited for one day only in 1970 before being signed and given away.

The gallery owns several works by **Jiří Kolář** – pronounced "collage" – who, coincidentally, specializes in collages of random words and reproductions of other people's paintings. The rest of the contemporary Czech art collection is interesting enough, if taken at a canter. **Ivan Kafka**'s phallic *Potent Impotency* installation should raise a smile, and there's the occasional overtly political work such as *Great Dialogue* by Karel Nepraš, in which two red figures lambast each other at close quarters with loudspeakers. It's also worth venturing out onto the balcony, where you'll find, among other things, models of a few of the great landmarks of Czechoslovak Communist architecture and examples from the 1990s, a set design by the innovative **Divadlo Drak** (a puppet company from Hradec Králové) from 1976 and some of **Josef Koudelka**'s famous photographs from the 1968 invasion.

Third floor: nineteenth- and twentieth-century French art

On the third floor is the ever popular **French art** collection, which features anyone of note who hovered around Paris in the fifty years from 1880 onwards.

The collection kicks off with several works by **Auguste Rodin**, particularly appropriate given the ecstatic reception that greeted the Prague exhibition of his work in 1902. Rodin's sculptures are surrounded by works from the advance guard of Impressionism: Courbet, Delacroix, Corot, Sisley and early Monet and Pissarro. There's a characteristically sunny, *Provençal Green Wheat* by **Vincent van Gogh**, and *Moulin Rouge* by Toulouse Lautrec, with Oscar Wilde looking on. Nearby, the loose brushwork and cool turquoise and emerald colours of **Auguste Renoir**'s *Lovers* are typical of the period of so-called High Impressionism. *Bonjour Monsieur Gauguin* is a tongue-in-cheek tribute to Courbet's painting of a similar name, with **Paul Gauguin** donning a suitably Bohemian beret and overcoat. Also on display is the only known self-portrait by **Henri Rousseau**, at once both confident and comical, the artist depicting himself, palette in hand, against a boat decked with bunting and the recently erected Eiffel Tower.

There's also a surprisingly good collection of works by **Pablo Picasso**, including several paintings and sculptures from his transitional period (1907–08), and lots of examples from the height of his Cubist period in the 1910s; his *Landscape with Bridge* from 1909 uses precisely the kind of prisms and geometric blocks of shading that influenced the Czech Cubist architects. In addition, there are a couple of late paintings by **Paul Cézanne**, a classic *pointilliste* canvas by Georges Seurat and Cubist works by Braque. *Joaquine,* painted by **Henri Matisse** in 1910–11 is a first-rate portrait, in which both Fauvist and Oriental influences are evident. Look out too for **Marc Chagall**'s *The Circus,* a typically mad work from 1927, and a rare painting by **Le Corbusier** himself, which clearly shows the influence of Fernand Léger, one of whose works hangs close by.

Third and fourth floors: Czech art 1890–1930

Visitors to the **Czech art 1890–1930** collection are confronted by **Otakar Švec**'s life-sized *Motorcyclist,* a great three-dimensional depiction of the optimistic speed of the modern age. Out on the third-floor balcony, there's a feast of architectural drawings, scenography and industrial design from typewriters and vacuum cleaners to wooden aeroplane propellers. Highlights include Josef Čapek's costume and set designs for Janáček's operas, and a model of the Müllerova vila (see p.155).

Chronologically, you're probably best off starting on the fourth floor, where there are several wood sculptures by **František Bílek**, one of the country's finest sculptors – for a more comprehensive insight into his anguished art, you should visit the Bílkova vila (see p.57). **Jan Preisler**'s mosaics and murals, which feature on Art Nouveau buildings all over Prague, tend to be ethereal and slightly detached, whereas his oil paintings, like the cycle of *Black Lake* paintings displayed here, are more typically melancholic, and reveal the influence of the Norwegian painter Edvard Munch.

The most successful Czech exponent of moody post-Impressionism was **Antonín Slavíček**, whose depictions of Prague remain perennially popular, as do his landscapes ranging from the Klimt-like *Birch Mood* to paintings such as *In the Rain*, which are full of foreboding. There are a couple of oils by **Alfons Mucha**, both classic long and narrow poster designs, one an unfinished version of the *Gismonda* poster for Sarah Bernhardt that propelled the artist to fame in Paris in 1894. To see more of Mucha's works, visit his museum in Nové Město (see p.118).

The fourth-floor collection ends in a foyer area, known rather wonderfully (on each floor) as the Respirium, where sculptures by **Stanislav Sucharda** and **Jan Štursa**, two of the most important Czech Art Nouveau artists, dominate. On the balcony, you can see models and drawings by *fin de siècle* architects such as **Jan Kotěra**, Balšánek, Polívka and Oldřich, plus several exquisite iridescent Lötz vases from Klašterský Mlýn to admire.

On the third floor, there's a whole series of works by **František Kupka**, who was Czech by birth, but lived and worked in Paris from 1895. Kupka was one of the first artists in the Western world to exhibit abstract paintings. His seminal *Fugue in Two Colours (Amorpha)*, one of two abstract paintings Kupka exhibited at the Salon d'Automne in 1912, is displayed here, along with some earlier, pre-abstract paintings (a couple of self-portraits, a family portrait, a Matisse-like portrait of a Parisian cabaret actress and *Piano Keys – Lake*, a strange, abstracted, though by no means abstract, work from 1909) plus a pretty comprehensive selection of his later abstract and cosmic works. As you leave the Kupka section, don't miss the small side-room displaying the photographic work of **František Drtikol**, whose Art Deco nudes made him internationally famous.

The Edvard Munch retrospective exhibited in Prague in 1905 prompted the formation in 1907 of the first Czech modern art movement, Osma (The Eight), one of whose leading members was **Emil Filla**, whose *Ace of Hearts* and *Reader of Dostoyevsky* – in which the subject appears to have fallen asleep, though, in fact, he's mind-blown – are both firmly within the Expressionist genre. However, it wasn't long before several of the Osma group were beginning to experiment with Cubism. Filla eventually adopted the style wholesale, helping found the Cubist SVU in 1911. **Bohumil Kubišta**, a member of Osma, refused to follow suit, instead pursuing his own unique blend of Cubo-Expressionism, typified by the wonderful self-portrait, *The Smoker*, and by the distinctly Fauvist *Players*.

To round out the Czech Cubist picture, there's furniture and ceramics (and even a Cubist chandelier) by Gočár, Janák and Chochol, as well as sculptures by **Otto Gutfreund**, a member of SVU, whose works range from the Cubo-Expressionist *Anxiety* (1911–12) to the more purely Cubist *Bust* (1913–14). Further on in the gallery there are examples of Gutfreund's later super-realist, technicolour sculptures from the 1920s.

Josef Čapek, brother of the playwright, is another Czech clearly influenced by Cubism, as seen in works such as *Accordion Player*, but, like Kubišta, Čapek found Filla's doctrinaire approach difficult to take, and he left SVU in 1912. Another artist who stands apart from the crowd is **Jan Zrzavy**, who joined SVU, but during a long career pursued his own peculiarly individual style typified by paintings such as his 1909 self-portrait, in which he appears Chinese, and *Valley of Sorrow*, his own personal favourite, painted while still a student, and depicting a magical, imaginary and very stylized world.

Výstaviště (Exhibition Grounds)

Five minutes' walk north from the Veletržní palác, up Dukelských hrdinů, takes you right to the front gates of the **Výstaviště** (Tues–Fri 2–10pm, Sat & Sun 10am–10pm; 20Kč or free), a motley assortment of buildings, created for the 1891 Prague Exhibition, which have served as the city's main trade fair arena and funfair ever since. From 1948 until the late 1970s, the Communist Party held its rubber-stamp congresses in the flamboyant stained-glass and wrought-iron **Průmyslový palác** at the centre of the complex.

The grounds are at their busiest on the weekend, particularly in the summer (during which there's sometimes a small entrance charge), when hordes of Prague families descend on the place to down hot dogs, drink beer and listen to traditional brass band music. Apart from the annual trade fairs and special exhibitions, there are a few permanent attractions. These include the city's **Planetárium** (times vary; 50–150Kč; Ⓦ www.planetarium.cz), which has static displays and shows films, but doesn't have telescopes (for which you need to go to the Štefánikova hvězdárna; see p.77); the **Maroldovo panorama** (April–Oct Tues–Fri 2–5pm, Sat & Sun 10am–5pm; 25Kč), a giant diorama of the 1434 Battle of Lipany (see p.232); **Mořský svět** (daily 10am–7pm; 240Kč; Ⓦ www.morsky-svet.cz), an aquarium full of countless colourful tropical fish, a few rays and some sea turtles; and **Lunapark**, a run-down funfair and playground for kids.

In the long summer evenings, there's also an open-air cinema (*letní kino*), and hourly evening performances by the **Křižíkova fontána**, dancing fountains devised for the 1891 Exhibition by the Czech inventor František Křižík, which perform a music and light show (with live dancers; 200Kč) to packed audiences. For the current schedule, ask at the tourist office, or check the website (Ⓣ 220 103 224, Ⓦ www.krizikovafontana.cz).

Lapidárium

Výstaviště also contains the Národní muzeum's **Lapidárium** (Tues–Sun noon–6pm; 40Kč; ⓦ www.nm.cz) – immediately on the right as you enter – official depository for the city's sculptures, which are under threat either from demolition or from the weather. It's actually a much overlooked collection, ranging from the eleventh to the nineteenth century, arranged chronologically over the course of eight rooms.

The first couple of rooms contain a host of salvaged medieval treasures, such as the slender columns decorated with interlacing from the Romanesque basilica that stood on the site of the city's cathedral. Some of the statues saved from the perils of Prague's polluted atmosphere, such as the bronze equestrian statue of **St George**, will be familiar if you've visited Prague Castle; others are more difficult to inspect close up in their original sites, for example the figures from the towers of the Charles Bridge; and there are even copies here, too, such as the busts from the triforium of St Vitus Cathedral.

One of the most outstanding sights is the remains of the **Krocín fountain**, in room 3, a highly ornate Renaissance work in red marble, which used to grace the Staroměstské náměstí, but failed to hold water and was eventually dismantled in 1862. The angels smiting devils, now displayed in room 5, are all that could be rescued from the **Marian Column**, which also used to stand on Staroměstské náměstí, after it had been attacked as a symbol of oppression by marauding Czech nationalists in 1918. Many of the original statues from the **Charles Bridge** are in room 6, as well as the ones that were fished out of the Vltava after the flood of 1890. The sculptural group commissioned by the Jesuits is particularly good, featuring their founder St Ignatius centre stage, surrounded by figures and animals representing all four known continents.

Several pompous imperial monuments that were bundled off into storage after the demise of the Habsburgs in 1918 round off the museum's collection in room 8. One of the first to be removed was the equestrian bronze statue of **Francis I**, which used to sit under the neo-Gothic baldachin that still stands on Smetanovo nábřeží. By far the most impressive, however, is the bronze statue of **Marshall Radecký**, scourge of the 1848 revolution, carried aloft on a shield by eight Habsburg soldiers, a monument which used to stand on Malostranské náměstí.

Stromovka

To the west of Výstaviště lies the *královská obora*, or royal enclosure, more commonly known as **Stromovka**, originally laid out as hunting grounds for the noble occupants of the Hrad, and – again thanks to Count Chotek – now Prague's largest and leafiest public park. If you're heading north to Troja and the city zoo, a stroll through the park is by far the most pleasant approach. If you want to explore a little more of the park, head west sticking to the park's southern border and you'll come to a water tunnel, built by the surrealist court painter Giuseppe Arcimboldo as part of Rudolf II's ambitious horticultural scheme to carry water from the Vltava to the lakes he created a little to the north.

Further west still is Stromovka's main sight, the **Místodržitelský letohrádek**, one of the earliest neo-Gothic structures in the city, begun way back in 1805. Originally conceived as a royal hunting chateau, it served as the seat of the governor of Bohemia until 1918 and now houses the Národní muzeum's periodicals collection (closed to the public). To continue on to Troja and the zoo, head north under the railway, over the canal and on to the Císařský ostrov (Emperor's Island) – and from there to the right bank of the Vltava.

Troja

Though still well within the municipal boundaries, the suburb of **TROJA**, across the river to the north of Holešovice and Bubeneč, still has a distinctly country feel to it. Its most celebrated sight is Prague's only genuine **chateau**, or **zámek**, perfectly situated against a hilly backdrop of vines. Troja's other attraction is the city's enormously popular **zoo**.

Trojský zámek (Troja chateau)

The **Trojský zámek** (April–Oct Tues–Thurs, Sat & Sun 10am–6pm, Fri 1–6pm; 120Kč; Ⓦwww.ghmp.cz) was designed by Jean-Baptiste Mathey for the powerful Šternberg family towards the end of the seventeenth century. Despite renovation and a rusty red repaint, its plain early Baroque facade is no match for the action-packed, blackened figures of giants and titans who battle it out on the chateau's monumental balustrades. The highlights of the **interior** are the gushing frescoes depicting the victories of the Habsburg Emperor Leopold I (1657–1705) over the Turks, which cover every inch of the walls and ceilings of the grand hall. You also get to wander through the chateau's pristine, trend-setting, French-style formal **gardens**, the first of their kind in Bohemia.

The zoo

On the other side of U trojského zámku, which runs along the west wall of the chateau, is the city's capacious **zoo** (daily: March 9am–5pm; April, May, Sept & Oct 9am–6pm; June–Aug 9am–7pm; Nov–Feb 9am–4pm; 150Kč; Ⓦwww.zoopraha.cz). Founded in 1931 on the site of one of Troja's numerous hillside vineyards, the zoo has had a lot of money poured into it and now has some very imaginative animal enclosures. All the usual animals are on show here – including elephants, hippos, giraffes, zebras, big cats and bears – and kids, at least, will enjoy

▲ Troja chateau

themselves. A bonus in the summer is the fact you can take a chairlift (*lanová dráha*) from the duck pond over the enclosures to the top of the hill, where the prize exhibits – a rare breed of miniature horse known as Przewalski – hang out. Other highlights include the red pandas, the giant tortoises, the Komodo dragons and the bats that actually fly past your face in the Twilight Zone.

Botanická zahrada Prahy (Botanic gardens)

Another reason for coming out to Troja is to visit the city's **Botanická zahrada Prahy** (daily: March & Oct 9am–5pm; April 9am–6pm; May–Sept 9am–7pm; Nov–Feb 9am–4pm; April–Oct 50Kč; ⓦ www.botanicka.cz), hidden in the woods to the north of the *zámek*. The botanic gardens feature a vineyard, a Japanese garden, several glasshouses and great views over Prague. Hidden in the woods a little higher up the hill there's also a spectacular, new, curvaceous greenhouse, **Fata Morgana** (same hours but Tues–Sun only; 120Kč), with butterflies flitting about amid the desert and tropical plants. Fata Morgana, incidentally, means "mirage" in Czech.

Dejvice and the northwest suburbs

Spread across the hills to the northwest of the city centre are the leafy garden suburbs of **Dejvice** and neighbouring **Střešovice**, peppered with fashionable modern villas built in the first half of the twentieth century for the upwardly mobile Prague bourgeoisie and commanding magnificent views across the north of the city. Dejvice is short on conventional sights, but interesting to explore all the same; Střešovice has one compelling attraction, the **Müllerova vila**, a perfectly restored functionalist house designed by Adolf Loos. Some 4km further west, the valley of **Šárka** is about as far as you can get from an urban environment without leaving the city. To the south of Šárka is the battlefield of **Bílá hora**, and **Hvězda**, a beautiful park containing a pretty star-shaped chateau.

Dejvice

DEJVICE was planned and built in the early 1920s for the First Republic's burgeoning community of civil servants and government and military officials. Its enormous, unappealing main square, **Vítězné náměstí** (metro Dejvická), is unavoidable if you're planning to explore any of the western suburbs, since it's a major public transport interchange. There's nothing much of note in this central part of Dejvice, though you can't help but notice the former **Hotel International** (now the *Crowne Plaza*) at the end of Jugoslávských partyzánů, a Stalinist skyscraper that is disturbingly similar to the universally loathed Palace of Culture in Warsaw. For followers of socialist-realist chic, however, its workerist motifs merit closer inspection – you can even stay there (see p.184). To get there, take tram #8 from metro Dejvická two stops to the Podbaba terminal.

Baba

Dejvice's most intriguing villas are located to the north in **Baba** (bus #131 from metro Hradčanská), a model neighbourhood of 33 functionalist houses, each individually commissioned and built under the guidance of one-time Cubist and born-again functionalist Pavel Janák. A group of leading architects affiliated to the Czech Workers' Alliance, inspired by a similar project in Stuttgart, initiated what was, at the time, a radical housing project to provide simple, single-family villas. The idea was to use space and open-plan techniques rather than expensive materials to create a luxurious living space.

Despite the plans of the builders, the houses were mostly bought up by Prague's artistic and intellectual community. Nevertheless, they have stood the test of time better than most utopian architecture, not least because of the fantastic site – facing south and overlooking the city. Some of them remain exactly as they were when first built, others have been radically altered, but as none of them is open to the public you'll have to be content with surreptitious peeping from the following streets: Na ostrohu, Na Babě, Nad Paťankou and Průhledová. To see the inside of a – albeit luxury – functionalist house, you need to head for the Müllerova vila (see below).

Muzeum MHD (Transport Museum)

Prague's public transport museum, **Muzeum MHD** (April to mid-Nov Sat & Sun 9am–5pm; 35Kč; Ⓦ www.dpp.cz), is housed in a 1909 tram shed on the border of Střešovice and Hradčany at Patočkova 4 – to get there take tram #1, #2, #15, #18 or the historic tram #91 (see p.27) to Vozovna Střešovice. The oldest exhibit is a horse tram from 1886, but the majority of the vehicles here are municipal trams from the last century, sporting the cream and red livery introduced in 1908. There are one or two buses and trolleybuses too and an exhibition covering everything from funiculars to the Soviet-built metro.

Müllerova vila

The most famous of Prague's interwar villas is the **Müllerova vila** (Müller Haus), or Loosova vila, at Nad hradním vodojemem 14, in Střešovice, to the southwest of Dejvice. Designed by the Brno-born architect, **Adolf Loos** – regarded by many as one of the founders of modern architecture – and Karel Lhota, and completed in 1930 (after planning permission had been refused ten times), it was one of Loos's few commissions, a typically uncompromising box, wiped smooth with concrete rendering, its window frames picked out in yellow. It's nothing to look at from the outside – Loos believed that "a building should be dumb on the outside and reveal its wealth only on the inside" – but if you've any interest in modernist architecture, then a trip out here is an absolute must. To visit the house, you must phone in advance as only seven people are allowed on each **guided tour** (Tues, Thurs, Sat & Sun: April–Oct 9am, 11am, 1pm, 3pm & 5pm; Nov–March 10am, noon, 2pm & 4pm; 300Kč, plus 100Kč extra for an English guide; ☏ 224 312 012, Ⓦ www .mullerovavila.cz). To reach the house, take tram #1 or #18 from metro Hradčanská, four stops to Ořechovka.

The Müller family were extremely wealthy, and spared no expense when it came to the interior furnishings. They lived here, with numerous servants, until the 1948 Communist coup, after which they were granted a single room, while the rest of the house was turned into offices. Dr Müller was given a job as a stoker in the house's boiler room, where he died in 1951 in an accident; Mrs Müller continued to live in the boudoir until her death nearly twenty years later. In the 1990s, the house was given back to the Müllers and then bought off them by the City of Prague Museum, who have restored it to something like its original state.

Loos's most famous architectural concept was the *Raumplan*, or open-plan design, at its most apparent in the living room, which is overlooked by the dining room on the mezzanine level and, even higher up, by the boudoir, itself a *Raumplan* in miniature. The house is decorated throughout in the rich materials and minimal furnishings that were Loos's hallmark: green and white Cipolino marble columns, with an inset aquarium in the living room and mahogany panelling for the dining room ceiling. The "American kitchen" was state-of-the-art in the 1930s, as was the use of lino for the floor and walls of the children's room, and there are two lifts in the centre of the house – one for people, one for food. Other highlights include the his 'n' hers dressing rooms off the master bedroom and the Japanese-style summer dining room, which opens out onto the roof terrace overlooking Prague Castle.

Šárka

If you've had your fill of postcards and crowds, take tram #20 or #26 from metro Dejvická to the last stop and walk north down into the **Šárka valley**, a peaceful limestone gorge that twists eastwards back towards Dejvice. The first section (Divoká Šárka) is particularly dramatic, with grey-white crags rising up on both sides – it was here that Šárka plunged to her death (see box below). Gradually the valley opens up, with a grassy meadow to picnic on, and an **open-air swimming pool** nearby (see p.224), both fairly popular with Czechs on summer weekends. There are various points further east from which you can pick up a city bus back into town, depending on how far you want to walk. The full walk to where the Šárka stream flows into the Vltava, just north of Baba, is about 6–7km all told, though none of it is particularly tough going.

Šárka and Ctirad

The Šárka valley takes its name from the Amazonian **Šárka**, who, according to Czech legend, committed suicide here sometime back in the last millennium. The story begins with the death of Libuše, the founder and first ruler of Prague. The women closest to her, who had enjoyed enormous freedom and privilege in her court, refused to submit to the new patriarchy of her husband, Přemysl. Under the leadership of a woman called Vlasta, they left Vyšehrad and set up their own proto-feminist, separatist colony called Děvín, on the opposite bank of the river.

They scored numerous military victories over the men of Vyšehrad, but never managed to finish off the men's leader, a young warrior called **Ctirad**. In the end they decided to ensnare him and tied one of their own warriors naked to a tree, sure in the knowledge that Ctirad would take her to be a maiden in distress and come to her aid. Šárka offered to act as the decoy, luring Ctirad into the ambush, after which he was tortured and killed. However, in her brief meeting with Ctirad, Šárka fell madly in love with him and, overcome with grief at what she had done, threw herself off the aforementioned cliff. And just in case you thought the legend has a feminist ending, it doesn't. Roused by the cruel death of Ctirad, Přemysl and the lads had a final set-to with Vlasta and co., and butchered the lot of them.

Hvězda, Bílá hora and Břevnov

A couple of kilometres southwest of Dejvice, trams #1, #2 and #18 terminate close to the main entrance to the hunting park of **Hvězda** (Tues–Sun: April & Oct 10am–5pm; May–Sept 10am–6pm; 30Kč; Ⓦ www.pamatniknarodnihopisemnictvi .cz), one of Prague's most beautiful and peaceful parks. Wide, soft, green avenues of trees radiate from a bizarre star-shaped building (*hvězda* means "star"), which was designed by Archduke Ferdinand of Tyrol for his wife in 1555. Inside, there's a small exhibition on the Battle of Bílá hora, which took place nearby (see box below). It's the building itself, though – decorated with delicate stuccowork and frescoes – that's the real reason for venturing inside; it makes a perfect setting for the chamber music concerts occasionally staged here.

A short distance southwest of Hvězda is the once entirely barren limestone summit of **Bílá hora** (White Mountain), accessible from Hvězda through one of the many holes in the park's southern perimeter wall. It was here in 1620 that the first battle of the Thirty Years' War took place, sealing the fate of the Czech nation for the following three hundred years. In little more than an hour, the Protestant forces of the "Winter King" Frederick of Palatinate were roundly beaten by the Catholic troops of the Habsburg Emperor Ferdinand II. As a more or less direct consequence, the Czechs lost their aristocracy, their religion, their scholars and, most importantly, the remnants of their sovereignty. There's nothing much to see now, apart from the small monument (*mohyla*), and a pilgrims' church, just off Nad

The Battle of Bílá hora

The **Battle of Bílá hora** (White Mountain) may have been a skirmish of minor importance in the Thirty Years' War, but for the Czechs it was to have devastating consequences. The victory of the Catholic forces of Habsburg Emperor **Ferdinand II** in 1620 set the seal on the Czech Lands for the next three hundred years, prompting an emigration of religious and intellectual figures that relegated the country to a cultural backwater for most of modern history. The defeat also heralded the decimation of the Bohemian and Moravian aristocracy, which meant that, unlike their immediate neighbours, the Poles and Hungarians, the Czechs had to build their nineteenth-century national revival around writers and composers, rather than counts and warriors.

The 28,000 Catholic soldiers – made up of Bavarians, Spanish, German and French troops (among them the future philosopher, René Descartes) – outnumbered the 21,000-strong Czech, Hungarian and German Protestant army, though the latter occupied the strategic chalky hill to the west of Prague. Shortly after noon on November 8 the imperial troops (under the nominal command of the Virgin Mary) began by attacking the Protestants' left flank, and, after about an hour, prompted a full-scale flight. The Protestant commander, Christian von Anhalt, went hot-foot back to the Hrad, where he met the Czech king, **Frederick of Palatinate**, who was late for the battle, having been delayed during lunch with the English ambassador.

Frederick, dubbed the "Winter King" for his brief reign, had once tossed silver coins to the crowd, and entertained them by swimming naked in the Vltava, while his wife, Elizabeth, daughter of James I of England, had shocked Prague society with her expensive dresses, her outlandish hairdo, and her plunging décolletage. Now, abandoned by their allies, the royal couple gathered up the crown jewels and left Prague in such a hurry they almost forgot their youngest son – later to become the dashing Prince Rupert of the English Civil War – who was playing in the nursery. The city had no choice but to surrender to the Catholics, who spent a week looting the place, before executing 27 of the rebellion's leaders on Staroměstské náměstí.

višňovkou. This was erected by the Catholics to commemorate the victory, which they ascribed to the timely intercession of the Virgin Mary – hence its name, **Panna Maria Vítězná** (St Mary the Victorious). To get to Bílá hora from the centre of town, take tram #22 from metro Malostranská to the western terminus, then walk up Nad višňovkou and across the field.

If you've time to spare before heading back into town, it's worth making the five minutes' walk east of the park, down Zeyerova alej, to the idyllic Baroque monastery of **Břevnovský klášter** (guided tours Sat & Sun: April–Oct 10am, 2 & 4pm; Nov–March 10am & 2pm; 50Kč). Founded as a Benedictine abbey by St Adalbert, tenth-century bishop of Prague, it was worked over in the eighteenth century by both Christoph and Kilian Ignaz Dientzenhofer, and bears their characteristic interconnecting ovals, inside and out. To get there from the city centre, take tram #22 to the Břevnovský klášter stop.

Close by the monastery is the compellingly obscure **Popmuseum** (Wed–Sun 4–8pm; 80Kč; Ⓦ www.popmuseum.cz), at Bělohorská 150, on the opposite side of Patočkova. Here, you can sit down and listen to a whole load of scratchy recordings and bootlegs of Czech bands from the late 1950s and 1960s heyday of Czech underground rock (or *bigbít* as it's known in Czech). Against the odds, the locals fought for the right to party, and there's a vast array of memorabilia on display, from old tickets and promo material to a *Daily Mirror* article on Manfred Mann's 1965 Czech tour, and a home-made amp called Samuel, so famous (in Czechoslovakia) it had a band named after it. You can also try out their ancient Czech electric guitars and instruments.

Smíchov

Historically, **SMÍCHOV** is a late nineteenth-century working-class suburb, whose skyline is peppered here and there with satanic chimneys some of which still dutifully belch out smoke. It was home (until recently) of the Tatra factory that produced trams for the Communist bloc, and is still home to the city's largest brewery, which produces the ubiquitous **Staropramen**. The centre, however, around metro Anděl, has been transformed in the past couple of decades, and is endowed with big new glassy malls. To the west, as the suburb gains height, the tenements give way to another of Prague's sought-after villa quarters. To the north, Smíchov borders Malá Strana and, officially at least, takes in a considerable part of the woods of **Petřín**, south of the Hladová zed'.

Downtown Smíchov, around metro Anděl, is now totally dominated by the glasshouse of French architect, Jean Nouvel's shopping complex, **Zlatý Anděl**, which has an angel (*anděl*) from Wim Wenders' film *Wings of Desire*, etched into the glass. Hidden away behind Zlatý Anděl, up Plzeňská, is Smíchov's former **synagogue** (now a bookshop). Built in 1863 to serve the local wealthy Jewish business folk, it was remodelled in the 1930s in functionalist style, and sports unusual crenellations on the roof – only the Hebrew inscription on the ground floor gives any indication of its former use.

The district's traditional heart is **náměstí 14 října**, a short walk from metro Anděl up Štefánikova. The Art Nouveau Národní dům, and the adjacent market hall (now converted into a bland supermarket), both erected around 1906, have seen better days, but the neo-Renaissance **church of sv Václav** (Mon–Fri 6.15am–noon, Sat 7.15–11am, Sun 7.30–11am), built in the 1880s and overlooking

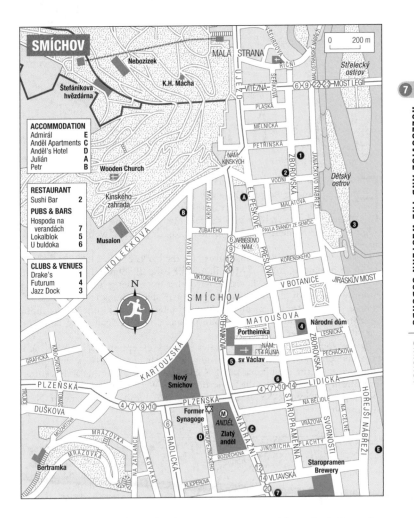

the square, is worth a visit. The gloomy interior is a jewel box of rich Byzantine decoration, with gilded mosaics, huge Ionic pillars of red Swedish granite and a coffered ceiling. The stained-glass windows in the nave feature strikingly tall, colourful portrayals of the Apostles and there's a wonderfully Turkish-looking gilded pulpit, with a tent-like tester.

Out from the city

ew capital cities can boast such extensive unspoilt tracts of woodland so near at hand as Prague. Once you leave the half-built high-rise estates of the outer suburbs behind, the traditional provincial feel of **Bohemia** (Čechy) immediately makes itself felt. Many towns and villages still huddle below the grand residences of their former lords, their street layout little changed since medieval times.

To the north, several such chateaux grace the banks of the Vltava, including the wine-producing town of **Mělník**, on the Labe (Elbe) plain. Further north is **Terezín**, the wartime Jewish ghetto that is a living testament to the Holocaust. One of the most obvious day-trip destinations is to the east of Prague: **Kutná Hora**, a medieval silver-mining town with one of the most beautiful Gothic churches in the country, and a macabre gallery of bones in the suburb of Sedlec.

To the south, the **Konopiště** chateau boasts exceptionally beautiful and expansive grounds. Southwest of Prague, a similar mix of woods and rolling hills surrounds the popular castle of **Karlštejn**, a gem of Gothic architecture, dramatically situated above the River Berounka. West of Prague, **Lidice**, razed to the ground by the SS, is another town that recalls the horror of Nazi occupation.

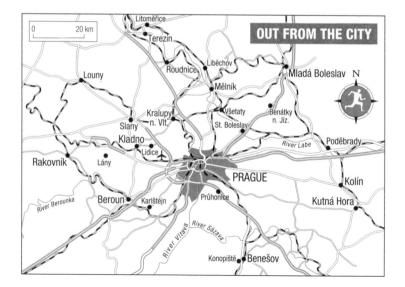

Mělník

Occupying a spectacular, commanding site at the confluence of the Vltava and Labe rivers, **MĚLNÍK**, 33km north of Prague, lies at the heart of Bohemia's tiny wine-growing region. The town's history goes back to the ninth century, when it was handed over to the Přemyslids as part of Ludmila's dowry when she married Prince Bořivoj. From that time until the fifteenth century it became the seat of the widowed queens. It was here that Ludmila introduced her heathen grandson Václav (later to become St Wenceslas; see box, p.49) to the joys of Christianity. Viticulture became the town's economic mainstay when the Emperor Charles IV, aching for a little of the French wine of his youth, introduced grapes from Burgundy (where he was also king).

The old town

Mělník's greatest monument is its Renaissance chateau, or **zámek** (daily 10am–5pm; 90Kč; ⓌWwww.lobkowicz-melnik.cz), perched high above the flat plains and visible for miles around. Apart from during World War II and under the Communists, the building has been owned by the Lobkowicz family since 1753. Visitors get to see a handful of the chateau's magnificently proportioned rooms, which are filled with porcelain, old maps and Old Masters, and which also provide great views out over the plain. You can also visit the castle **wine cellars** (daily 10am–5pm; 40Kč), finishing up with samples of plonk (extra charge); the Ludmila rosé is the most sought-after Mělník wine, though the vineyards produce red and white, too.

Below the chateau, vines cling to the south-facing terraces, as the land plunges into the river below. From Mělník's onion-domed church of **sv Petr and Pavel** (Tues–Fri 9.30am–4pm, Sat & Sun 10am–12.30pm & 1.15–4pm; 30Kč), next door to the chateau, there's an even better view of the rivers' confluence (to the left) and the subsidiary canal (straight ahead), once so congested with vessels that

▲ The chateau at Mělník

traffic lights had to be introduced to avoid accidents. You can climb the **tower** (10am–1pm & 1.30–6pm; 40Kč) for an even better view and visit the compellingly macabre **ossuary**, or *kostnice* (Tues–Fri 9.30am–4pm, Sat & Sun 10am–12.30pm & 1.15–4pm; 30Kč), filled with more than 10,000 bones of medieval plague victims, fashioned into weird and wonderful skeletal shapes by students in the early part of the nineteenth century.

The rest of the old town is pretty small, but it's pleasant enough for a casual stroll. One half of the main square, **náměstí Míru**, is arcaded Baroque and typical of the region, and there's an old medieval gateway nearby, the Pražská brána, which has been converted into an art gallery.

Practicalities

There's no direct **train service** to Mělník from Prague, so you'll need to take the train from Praha hlavní nádraží to Všetaty and change there; connections are pretty good and the journey should take around an hour. There is also a regular **bus service** which leaves from metro Nádraží Holešovice and Florenc (stand 19) and takes fifty minutes. On arrival at Mělník **bus station**, to reach the older part of town, simply head up Krombholcova in the direction of the big church tower. The **train station** is still further from the old town, a couple of blocks northeast of the bus station, down Jiřího z Poděbrad.

As for **food and drink**, the *Zámecká restaurace* (closed Mon) is as good a place as any to sample some of the local wine (and enjoy the view). With equally good views is the *Stará škola* restaurant, behind the church; otherwise, you could try *Na hradbách*, on náměstí Míru, which serves up big portions of rabbit and game, with local wines, in a cosy brick and wood-panelled interior and a little courtyard.

Terezín

The old road from Prague to Berlin passes through the fortress town of **TEREZÍN** (Theresienstadt), just over 60km northwest of the capital. Purpose-built in the 1780s by the Habsburgs to defend the northern border against Prussia, it was capable of accommodating 14,500 soldiers and hundreds of prisoners. In 1941, the population was ejected and the whole town turned into a **Jewish ghetto** (ⓦ www.pamatnik-terezin.cz), and used as a transit camp for Jews whose final destination was Auschwitz.

Hlavní pevnost (Main Fortress)

Although the **Hlavní pevnost** (Main Fortress) has never been put to the test in battle, Terezín remains intact as a garrison town. Today, it's an eerie, soulless place, built to a dour eighteenth-century grid plan, its bare streets empty apart from the residual civilian population and visitors making their way between the various museums and memorials. As you enter, the red-brick zigzag fortifications are still an awesome sight, though the huge moat has been given over to allotments.

Muzeum Ghetta (Ghetto Museum)

The first place to head for is the **Muzeum Ghetta** (daily: April–Oct 9am–6pm; Nov–March 9am–5.30pm; 160Kč; combined ticket 200Kč), which opened in 1991. After the war, the Communists had followed the consistent Soviet line by

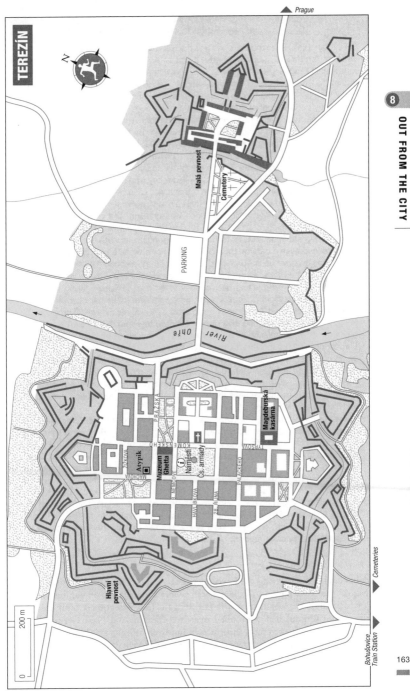

TEREZÍN

N

▲ Prague

Malá pevnost

Cemetery

PARKING

River Ohře

Hlavní pevnost

Atypik

Muzeum Ghetta

Náměstí
Čs. armády

Magdeburská kasárna

PRAŽSKÁ

ŽIŽKOVA

VODNÍ

NÁDRAŽNÍ

B. NĚMCOVÉ

HAVLÍČKOVA

28. ŘÍJNA

PALACKÉHO

200 m

0

◀ Bohušovice,
   Train Station

◀ Cemeteries

A brief history of the ghetto

In October 1941, Reinhard Heydrich and the Nazi high command decided to turn the whole of Terezín into a **Jewish ghetto**. It was an obvious choice: fully fortified, close to the main Prague–Dresden railway line, and with an SS prison already established in the Malá pevnost (Small Fortress) nearby. The original inhabitants of the town – fewer than 3500 people – were moved out, and transports began arriving at Terezín from many parts of central Europe. Within a year, nearly 60,000 Jews were interned here in appallingly overcrowded conditions; the monthly death rate rose to 4000. In October 1942, the first transport left for **Auschwitz**. By the end of the war, 140,000 Jews had passed through Terezín; fewer than 17,500 remained when the ghetto was finally liberated on May 8, 1945. Most of those in the camp when the Red Army arrived had been brought to Terezín on forced marches from other concentration camps. Even after the liberation, typhus killed many who had survived this far.

One of the perverse ironies of Terezín is that it was used by the Nazis as a cover for the real purpose of the *Endlösung*, or "final solution", devised at the Wannsee conference in January 1942 (at which Heydrich was present). The ghetto was made to appear self-governing, with its own council or *Judenrat*, its own bank printing (worthless) ghetto money, its own shops selling goods confiscated from the internees on arrival and even a café on the main square. For a while, a special "Terezín family camp" was even set up in Auschwitz, to continue the deception. The deportees were kept in mixed barracks, allowed to wear civilian clothes and – the main purpose of the whole thing – send letters back to their loved ones in Terezín telling them they were OK. After six months' "quarantine", they were sent to the gas chambers.

Despite the fact that Terezín was being used by the Nazis as cynical propaganda, the ghetto population turned their **unprecedented freedom** to their own advantage. Since the entire population of the Protectorate (and Jews from many other parts of Europe) passed through Terezín, the ghetto had an enormous number of outstanding Jewish artists, musicians, scholars and writers (many of whom subsequently perished in the camps). Thus, in addition to the officially sponsored activities, countless clandestine cultural events were organized in the cellars and attics of the barracks: teachers gave lessons to children, puppet theatre productions were put on and literary evenings were held.

Towards the end of 1943, the so-called *Verschönerung,* or **"beautification"**, **of the ghetto** was implemented, in preparation for the arrival of the International Red Cross inspectors. Streets were given names instead of numbers, and the whole place was decked out as if it were a spa town. When the **International Red Cross** asked to inspect one of the Nazi camps, they were brought here and treated to a week of Jewish cultural events. A circus tent was set up in the main square; a children's pavilion erected in the park; numerous performances of Hans Krása's children's opera, *Brundibár* (Bumble Bee), staged; and a jazz band, called the Ghetto Swingers, performed in the bandstand on the main square. The Red Cross visited Terezín twice, once in June 1944, and again in April 1945; both times the delegates filed positive reports.

deliberately underplaying the Jewish perspective on Terezín. Instead, the emphasis was on the Malá pevnost (see opposite), where the majority of victims were not Jewish, and on the war as an anti-fascist struggle, in which good (Communism and the Soviet Union) had triumphed over evil (fascism and Nazi Germany). The current museum's extremely informative and well-laid-out exhibition attempts to do some justice to the extraordinary and tragic events which took place here between 1941 and 1945, including background displays on the measures which led inexorably to the *Endlösung*. There's also a fascinating video (with English subtitles) showing clips of the Nazi propaganda film shot in Terezín – *Hitler Gives the Jews a Town* – intercut with harrowing interviews with survivors.

Magdeburská kasárna (Magdeburg Barracks)

To the south of the ghetto, the **Magdeburská kasárna** (times as for Muzeum Ghetta; 160Kč; combined ticket 200Kč), former seat of the Jewish self-governing council, or *Freizeitgestaltung*, has been turned into a fascinating museum concentrating on the remarkable artistic life of Terezín. First off, however, there's a reconstructed women's dormitory with three-tier bunks, full of luggage and belongings, to give an idea of the cramped living conditions endured by the ghetto inhabitants. The first exhibition room has displays on the various Jewish musicians who passed through Terezín, including Pavel Haas, a pupil of Janáček; Hans Krása, a pupil of Zemlinsky; and Karel Ančerl, who survived the Holocaust to become conductor of the Czech Philharmonic. The final exhibition room concentrates on the writers who contributed to the ghetto's underground magazines. The rooms in between, however, are given over to the work of Terezín's numerous artists, many of whom were put to work by the SS, who set up a graphics department here; headed by cartoonist Bedřich Fritta, it produced visual propaganda showing how smoothly the ghetto ran. In addition, there are many clandestine works, ranging from portraits of inmates to harrowing depictions of the cramped dormitories and the transports. These provide some of the most vivid and deeply affecting insights into the reality of ghetto life in the whole of Terezín, and it was for this "propaganda of horror" that several artists, including Fritta, were eventually deported to Auschwitz.

Malá pevnost (Small Fortress)

On the other side of the River Ohře, east down Pražská, lies the **Malá pevnost** (daily: April–Oct 8am–6pm; Nov–March 8am–4.30pm; 160Kč; combined ticket 200Kč), built as a military prison in the 1780s, at the same time as the main fortress. The prison's most famous inmate was the young Bosnian Serb, **Gavrilo Princip**, who assassinated Archduke Ferdinand in Sarajevo in 1914, and who was interned and died here during World War I. In 1940 it was turned into an **SS prison** by Heydrich and, after the war, it became the official memorial and museum of Terezín. The majority of the 32,000 inmates who passed through the prison were active in the resistance (and, more often than not, Communists). Some 2500 inmates perished here, while another 8000 died subsequently in the concentration camps. The vast cemetery laid out by the entrance contains the graves of over 2300 individuals, plus numerous other corpses of unidentified victims, and is rather insensitively dominated by a large Christian cross, plus a smaller Star of David.

There are guides (some of whom are survivors of Terezín) to show you around, or else you can simply use the brief guide to the prison in English, and walk around yourself. The infamous Nazi refrain *Arbeit Macht Frei* (Work Brings Freedom) is daubed across the entrance on the left, which leads to the exemplary washrooms, still as they were when built for the Red Cross tour of inspection. The rest of the camp has been left empty but intact, and graphically evokes the cramped conditions under which the prisoners were kept, half-starved and badly clothed, subject to indiscriminate cruelty and execution. The prison's main **exhibition** is housed in the SS barracks opposite the luxurious home of the camp *Kommandant* and his family. A short documentary, intelligible in any language, is regularly shown in the cinema that was set up in 1942 to entertain the SS guards.

Practicalities

Terezín is about an hour's **bus** ride from Prague's Florenc terminal – buses leave from stand 17 – and therefore easy to visit on a day-trip. The nearest **train station** is at Bohušovice nad Ohří (on the main Prague–Děčín line), 2km south of the fortress. The only acceptable **restaurant** in the centre is the simple but clean *Atypik* on Máchova, one block west of the museum.

Kutná Hora

For 250 years or so, **KUTNÁ HORA** (Kuttenberg) was one of the most important towns in Bohemia, second only to Prague, thanks to the silver deposits in the area. At the end of the fourteenth century its population was equal to that of London, its shantytown suburbs straggled across what are now green fields, and its ambitious building projects set out to rival those of the capital itself. Today, Kutná Hora is a small provincial town with a population of just over 20,000, but the monuments dotted around it, its superb Gothic cathedral and the remarkable monastery and ossuary in the suburb of **Sedlec**, make it one of the most enjoyable of all possible day-trips from Prague. In addition to the new influx of tourists, Kutná Hora has also benefited from a large injection of cash from the American tobacco giant Philip Morris, which runs the local tobacco factory.

▲ Kutná Hora

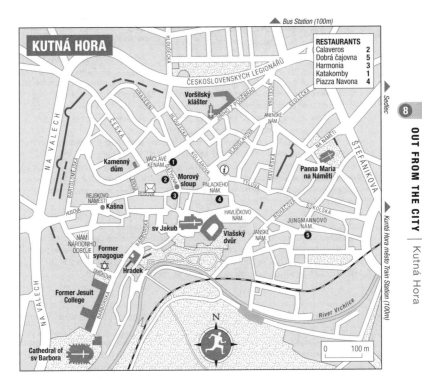

Vlašský dvůr and around

The small, unassuming houses that line the town's medieval lanes and main square, **Palackého náměstí**, give little idea of Kutná Hora's former glories. A narrow alleyway on the south side of the square, however, leads to leafy Havlíčkovo náměstí, on which stands the **Vlašský dvůr** (Italian Court), originally conceived as a palace by Václav II, and for three centuries the town's bottomless purse. It was here that Florentine minters produced the Prague Groschen (*pražské groše*), a silver coin widely used throughout central Europe until the nineteenth century. The building itself has been mucked about with over the years, most recently – and most brutally – by nineteenth-century restorers, who left only the fourteenth-century oriel window (capped by an unlikely looking wooden onion dome) and the miners' fountain unmolested. The original workshops of the minters have been bricked in, but the outlines of their little doors and windows are still visible in the courtyard. On the thirty-minute **guided tour** (daily: March & Oct 10am–5pm; April–Sept 9am–6pm; Nov–Feb 10am–4pm; 80Kč) – available in English – you get to see some silver Groschen, learn about the minters' hard life and admire the medieval royal chapel, which shelters a superb full-relief fifteenth-century altarpiece depicting the Death of Mary, and which was spectacularly redecorated in 1904 with Art Nouveau murals.

Outside the court is a statue of the country's founder and first president, **T.G. Masaryk**; twice removed – once by the Nazis and once by the Communists – it has now been returned to its pride of place for the third time. Before you leave, take a quick look in the court gardens, which descend in steps to the Vrchlice valley. This is undoubtedly Kutná Hora's best profile, with a splendid view over to the Cathedral of sv Barbora (see below).

Behind the Vlašský dvůr is **sv Jakub** (St James), the town's oldest church, begun a generation or so after the discovery of the silver deposits. Its grand scale is a clear indication of the town's quite considerable wealth by the fourteenth century, though in terms of artistry it pales in comparison with Kutná Hora's other ecclesiastical buildings. The leaning tower is a reminder of the precarious position of the town, the church's foundations being prone to subsidence from the disused mines below.

Hrádek

To see some of actual mines, head for the **Hrádek** (April & Oct Tues–Sun 9am–5pm; May, June & Sept 9am–6pm; July & Aug Tues–Sun 10am–6pm; Nov Sat & Sun 10am–4pm; ☎327 512 159, ⓦwww.cms-kh.cz), an old fort which was used as a second mint. There are now two guided tours to choose from, each setting off every half-hour. On the "Town of Silver" (*Město stříbra*; 60Kč), which takes around an hour, you get to go round the silver museum; more fun is the "Way of Silver" (*Cesta stříbra*; 110Kč), which takes half an hour longer, you can don period miner's garb of white coat, helmet and torch, and follow a guide through narrow sections of the medieval mines that were discovered beneath the fort in the 1960s – some of which tunnel over 100m below the surface. The mine tour is very popular, so advance booking is advisable.

Cathedral of sv Barbora

Kutná Hora's **Cathedral of sv Barbora** (April–Oct daily 9am–6pm; Nov–March 10am–4pm; 50Kč) is arguably the most spectacular and moving ecclesiastical building in central Europe. Not to be outdone by the great monastery at Sedlec (see opposite) or the St Vitus Cathedral in Prague, the miners of Kutná Hora began financing the construction of a great Gothic cathedral of their own, dedicated to

St Barbara, the patron saint of miners and gunners. The foundations were probably laid by Peter Parler in the 1380s, but work was interrupted by the Hussite Wars, and the church remained unfinished until the late nineteenth century, despite being worked on in the intervening centuries by numerous architects, including Master Hanuš, Matouš Rejsek and Benedikt Ried.

The approach road to the cathedral, Barborská, is lined with a parade of gesticulating Baroque saints and cherubs that rival the sculptures on the Charles Bridge; and on the right-hand side is the palatial seventeenth-century former **Jesuit College**. The cathedral bristles with pinnacles, finials and flying buttresses which support its most striking feature, a **roof** of three tent-like towers added in the sixteenth century, culminating in unequal, needle-sharp spires.

Inside, cold light streams through the numerous plain-glass windows, illuminating the lofty **nave** and Ried's playful ribbed vaulting, which forms branches and petals stamped with coats of arms belonging to Václav II and the local miners' guilds. The wide spread of the five-aisled nave is remarkably uncluttered: the multi-tiered tester of the Gothic pulpit – half-wood, half-stone – creeps tastefully up a central pillar; matching black and gold Renaissance confessionals lie discreetly in the north aisle; while nearby the filigree work on the original Gothic choirstalls echoes the cathedral's exterior. Look up, and you'll see virtually an entire chamber orchestra of gilded putti disporting themselves over the Baroque organ case.

The **ambulatory** boasts an array of early twentieth-century stained glass, but it's the medieval frescoes preserved in the southernmost chapels that really stand out. In the Smíšek Chapel, there's a wonderful orchestra of angels in the vaulting and a depiction of the Queen of Sheba on one of the walls. Two chapels further along is the Minters' Chapel, its walls decorated with fifteenth-century frescoes showing the Florentines at work.

The rest of the town

There are a few minor sights worth seeking out in the rest of the town. On Rejskovo náměstí, the squat, polygonal **Kašna** (fountain), built by Rejsek in 1495, strikes a very odd pose: peppered with finials and replete with blind arcading, it was actually designed as the decorative casing for a reservoir and now houses a roofless shop selling sculptures (Ⓦ www.nemeth.cz).

At the bottom of the sloping Šultyskovo náměstí is a particularly fine **Morový sloup** (plague column), giving thanks for the end of the plague of 1713. Around the corner from the top of the square is the **Kamenný dům**, built around 1480, with an oriel window and a steep gable covered in an ornate sculptural icing – it now contains the local museum (Tues–Sun: April & Oct 9am–5pm; May, June & Sept 9am–6pm; July & Aug 10am–6pm; Nov 10am–4pm; 40Kč).

A couple of blocks down Poděbradova stands Kilian Ignaz Dientzenhofer's unfinished Ursuline convent, or **Voršilský klášter** (April & Oct Sat & Sun 9am–4pm; May–Sept Tues–Sun 9am–5.30pm; free). Only three sides of the convent's ambitious pentagonal plan were actually finished, its neo-Baroque church being added in the late nineteenth century while sv Barbora was being restored.

Sedlec

From Kutná Hora's inner ring road, buses #1 and #4 run 3km northeast to **SEDLEC**, once a separate village but now a suburb of the town. Adjoining Sedlec's defunct eighteenth-century Cistercian monastery (now the largest tobacco factory in Europe, owned by Philip Morris) is the fourteenth-century church of **Nanebevzetí Panny Marie** (April–Oct Mon–Sat 9am–noon & 1–5pm; 30Kč), imaginatively redesigned in the eighteenth century by Giovanni Santini, who specialized in melding Gothic with Baroque. Here, given a plain French Gothic church gutted during the Hussite Wars, Santini set to work on the vaulting, adding his characteristic sweeping stucco rib patterns, relieved only by the occasional Baroque splash of colour above the chancel steps.

Cross the main road, following the signs, and you come to the monks' graveyard, where an ancient Gothic chapel – again redesigned by Santini – leans heavily over the entrance to the macabre subterranean **kostnice** (daily: March & Oct 9am–5pm; April–Sept 8am–6pm; Nov–Feb 9am–4pm; 50Kč; Ⓦwww.kostnice .cz), the mother of all ossuaries, full to overflowing with human bones. When holy earth from Golgotha was scattered over the graveyard in the twelfth century, all of Bohemia's nobility wanted to be buried here and the bones mounted up until there were more than 40,000 complete sets. In 1870, worried about the ever-growing piles, the authorities commissioned František Rint to do something creative with them. He rose to the challenge and moulded out of bones four giant bells, one in each corner of the crypt, designed wall-to-ceiling skeletal decorations, including the Schwarzenberg coat of arms, and, as the centrepiece, put together a chandelier made out of every bone in the human body. Rint's signature (in bones) is at the bottom of the steps.

Practicalities

The simplest way to get to Kutná Hora is to take a **bus** from stand 2 of Prague's Florenc bus station (1hr 15min) to the bus station which is just northeast of the old town. Fast **trains** from Prague's hlavní nádraží take around an hour (some involve a change at Kolín – not to be confused with Kolín zastávka). The main **train station** (Kutná Hora hlavní nádraží) is a long way out of town, near Sedlec; bus #1 or #4 will take you into town, or there's usually a shuttle train service ready to leave for Kutná Hora město train station, near the centre of town.

The town has a highly efficient system of orientation signs and, at almost every street corner, a pictorial list of the chief places of interest (beware, though, that the train station signposted is not the main one). The town's **tourist office** is on Palackého náměstí (April–Oct Mon–Fri 9am–6.30pm, Sat & Sun 9am–5pm; Nov–March Mon–Fri 9am–5pm; ☏327 512 873, Ⓦwww.kutnahora.cz), with another small office by the cathedral.

For **eating and drinking**, you're spoilt for choice: *Piazza Navona* is an excellent pizzeria, run by an Italian, with outdoor tables on Palackého náměstí; alternatively, try *Harmonia* on Husova, which serves up traditional Czech dishes and also has an outdoor terrace, or *Calaveros*, a Czech-Mex themed restaurant in a lovely Renaissance house on Šultysova. There's also a branch of the reliable teahouse chain, *Dobrá čajovna*, on Junmannovo náměstí.

Konopiště

The popularity of **Konopiště** (April & Oct Tues–Fri 9am–noon & 1–3pm, Sat & Sun 9am–noon & 1–4pm; May–Aug Tues–Sun 9am–noon & 1–5pm; Sept Tues–Fri 9am–noon & 1–4pm, Sat & Sun 9am–5pm; Nov Sat & Sun 9am–noon & 1–3pm; 130–200Kč; Ⓦwww.zamek-konopiste.cz), with a quarter of a million visitors passing through its portcullis every year, is surpassed only by the likes of Karlštejn (see p.172). Though Karlštejn looks more dramatic from the outside, Konopiště is the more interesting of the two. Coach parties from all over the world home in on this Gothic chateau, which is stuffed with dead animals, weaponry and hunting trophies. Most interesting are its historical associations: King Václav IV was imprisoned by his own nobles in the chateau's distinctive round tower, and the **Archduke Franz Ferdinand**, heir to the Habsburg throne, lived here with his wife, Sophie Chotek, until their assassination in Sarajevo in 1914. In addition to remodelling the chateau into its current appearance, the archduke shared his generation's voracious appetite for hunting, eliminating all living creatures foolish enough to venture into the grounds. However, he surpassed all his contemporaries by recording, stuffing and displaying a significant number of the 171,537 birds and animals he shot between the years 1880 and 1906, the details of which are recorded in his *Schuss Liste* displayed inside.

There's a choice of three **guided tours**. The first tour, *I okruh*, explores the period interiors, which contain some splendid Renaissance cabinets and lots of Meissen porcelain, while the *II okruh* takes you through the chapel, past the stuffed bears and deer teeth, to the assorted lethal weapons of one of the finest armouries in Europe. Both of these tours cost 130Kč each, take roughly 45 minutes, and, you'll be relieved to know, include the hunting trophies. The *III okruh* – which takes an hour, costs 200Kč and is restricted to just eight people per tour – concentrates on the personal apartments of the archduke and his wife. Due to the fact that Sophie was a mere countess, and not an archduchess, the couple were shunned by the Habsburg court in Vienna, and hid themselves away in Konopiště. Occasionally there are tours in English, French and German, too, so ask at the box office before you sign up or phone ahead and book one (☏301 721 366), though they cost extra.

Even if you don't fancy a guided tour, there are plenty of other things to do in Konopiště. In the main courtyard of the chateau, you can pop into the purpose-built **Střelnice** (shooting range; 30Kč), where the archduke used to hone his skills as a marksman against moving mechanical targets, all of which have been lovingly restored. Tucked underneath the south terrace is the **Muzeum sv Jiří** (30Kč), which is stuffed to the gunwales with artefacts from Franz Ferdinand's collection – from paintings to statuettes and trinkets relating to St George, the fictional father of medieval chivalry, with whom the archduke was obsessed. Much the best reason to come to Konopiště, though, is to explore its extensive **zámecký park**, which boasts a marked red path around the largest lake, sundry statuary, an unrivalled rose garden with a café, several greenhouses (*skleníky*; 35Kč) and a deer park. There are also regular one-hour displays of **falconry** in the chateau's grounds (April & Oct Sat & Sun 10am–noon & 2–4pm, May–Sept Tues–Sun same times) in English and Czech.

Practicalities

To get to Konopiště take a fast (50min) or slow (1hr 5min) **train** from Praha hlavní nádraží to Benešov u Prahy; the chateau is a pleasant two-kilometre walk west of the train station along either the red- or yellow-marked path – the red one is marginally more through the woods (buses are relatively infrequent). If the weather's fine, you might as well come equipped with a picnic, though there are several basic **food** stalls by the main car park, and decent Czech dishes available in the nineteenth-century *Stará Myslivna*, on the path to the castle, and in the bistro in the main courtyard. Back in Benešov, you can while away some time before your train departs at the *Galerijní čajovna* teahouse on Malé náměstí.

Karlštejn

KARLŠTEJN is a small ribbon village, strung out along one of the tributaries of the Berounka. No doubt once pretty, today it boasts a pricey golf course and is jam-packed with tacky souvenir stands and tourists – over a quarter of a million a year – visiting its superbly positioned **hrad** (Tues–Sun: March & Nov 9am–noon & 1–3pm; April & Oct 9am–noon & 1–4pm; May, June & Sept 9am–5pm; July & August 9am–6pm; ☎311 681 617, ⓦwww.hradkarlstejn.cz), which occupies a defiantly unassailable position above the village. Designed in the fourteenth century by Matthias of Arras for Emperor Charles IV as a giant safe-box for the imperial crown jewels and his large personal collection of precious relics, it quickly became Charles's favourite retreat from the vast city he himself had masterminded. Women were strictly forbidden to enter the castle, and the story of his third wife Anna's successful break-in (in drag) became one of the most popular Czech comedies of the nineteenth century.

Ruthlessly restored in the late nineteenth century, the castle now looks much better from a distance, with its giant wedge towers rising above a series of castellated walls. Most of the rooms visited on the guided tour (*okruh I*; 50min; 150Kč) contain only the barest of furnishings, the empty spaces taken up by uninspiring displays on the history of the castle. Theoretically, the top two chambers would make the whole trip worthwhile: unfortunately, on the basic

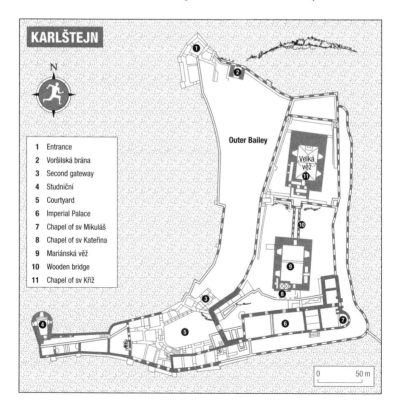

KARLŠTEJN

N

1 Entrance
2 Voršilská brána
3 Second gateway
4 Studniční
5 Courtyard
6 Imperial Palace
7 Chapel of sv Mikuláš
8 Chapel of sv Kateřina
9 Mariánská věž
10 Wooden bridge
11 Chapel of sv Kříž

Outer Bailey

Velká věž

0   50 m

guided tour, you can only look into (but not enter) the emperor's residential **Mariánská věž**. It was here that Charles shut himself off from the rest of the world, with any urgent business passed to him through a hole in the wall of the tiny ornate chapel of **sv Kateřina**.

The castle's finest treasure, the **Chapel of sv Kříž**, connected by a wooden bridge that leads on from here to the highest point of the castle, the **Velká věž**, is only open to those who book the longer tour in advance (*okruh II*; June–Oct only; 1hr 10min; 300Kč). In the emperior's day, only a select few could enter this gilded treasure-house, whose six-metre-thick walls contain 2200 semi-precious stones and 128 breathtakingly beautiful fourteenth-century painted panels, by the masterful Master Theodoric, Bohemia's greatest fourteenth-century painter (a small selection of his panels are exhibited in Prague's Anežský klášter). The imperial crown jewels, once secured here behind nineteen separate locks, were removed to Hungary after an abortive attack by the Hussites, while the Bohemian jewels are now stashed away in the cathedral in Prague.

If you're feeling energetic, you could go to the popular flooded quarry, **Malá Amerika**, a couple of kilometres away, a nice spot for a swim. Getting there is tricky: either take the red-marked path from near the castle, and head off northwest through the woods at *U dubu* (you may need to ask a local to point you in the right direction), or head west down the track, which comes off the road between Mořina and Bubovice.

Practicalities

Trains for Karlštejn leave Prague's Smíchovské nádraží roughly every hour, and take about 35 minutes to cover the 28km. The village is ten minutes' walk across the river from the station, and it's a further fifteen- to twenty-minute climb up to the castle entrance. If you're looking for somewhere to grab a beer and a bite to **eat**, try the attractive, hunting-lodge-style *U Janů*, which has an outdoor terrace, or the *Koruna*, both on the main street. Alternatively, bring a picnic with you and eat by the banks of the river.

Lidice

The small mining village of **LIDICE**, 18km northwest of Prague, hit world headlines on June 10, 1942, at the moment when it ceased to exist. On the flimsiest pretext, it was chosen as scapegoat for the assassination of the Nazi leader Reinhard Heydrich (see box, p.128). All 173 men from the village were rounded up and shot by the SS, the 198 women were sent to Ravensbrück concentration camp, and the 89 children either went to the camps, or, if they were Aryan enough, were packed off to "good" German homes, while the village itself was burnt to the ground.

Knowing all this as you approach Lidice makes the modern village seem almost perversely unexceptional. At the end of the straight, tree-lined main street, 10 června 1942 (June 10, 1942), there's a dour concrete memorial with a small but horrific **museum** (daily: March 9am–5pm; April–Oct 9am–6pm; Nov–Feb 9am–4pm; 80Kč) where you can watch a short film about Lidice, including footage shot by the SS themselves as the village was burning. The spot where the old village used to lie is just south of the memorial, now merely smooth green pasture punctuated with a few simple reminders and a chilling bronze memorial depicting the 82 local children who never returned.

After the massacre, the "Lidice shall live" campaign was launched and villages all over the world began to change their name to Lidice. The first was Stern Park Gardens, Illinois, soon followed by villages in Mexico and other Latin American countries. From Coventry to Montevideo, towns twinned themselves with Lidice, so that rather than "wiping a Czech village off the face of the earth" as Hitler had hoped, the Nazis created an international symbol of anti-fascist resistance.

To reach Lidice, catch one of the regular buses from outside metro Dejvická in Prague, opposite the *Hotel Diplomat*, getting off at the turn-off to the village on the main road.

Listings

Listings

Accommodation

C ompared to the price of beer, **accommodation** in Prague is very expensive. If you're looking for a double and can pay around 4000Kč (€150) a night then you'll find plenty of choice. At the other end of the scale, there are numerous hostels charging as little as 400Kč (€15) for a bed. However, there's a chronic shortage of decent, inexpensive to middle-range places. You can, however, get some very good deals – and undercut the often exorbitant rack rates – by booking online well in advance. Given that Prague can be pretty busy all year round, it's not a bad idea to book ahead in any case. Prices are at their very highest over public holidays such as New Year, but drop by as much as a third in July and August, and sometimes by half in the low season between November and February.

Apartments and accommodation agencies

If you're looking for an apartment or you arrive in Prague without having booked a room, there are several **accommodation agencies** you can turn to, most of which will book you into either a hotel or pension, and some of which can also help you find a hostel bed or a private room in an apartment. Before agreeing to part with any money, be sure you know exactly where you're staying and check about transport to the centre – some places can be a long way out of town.

Apartments in Prague ☎251 512 502, UK ☎020/8133 6353, US ☎1303/800 0858; Ⓦapartments-in-prague.org. Good choice of self-catering apartments spread across the old town, all with free wi-fi.

AVE ☎251 551 011, Ⓦwww.praguehotellocator.com. AVE offers a selection of hotels, pensions, apartments and hostel beds. You can book in advance online or on arrival at the airport (daily 7am–9pm) and both international train stations.

PIS Ⓦwww.prague-info.cz. You can book everything from hotels to hostels in advance online, or book through one of the city's PIS tourist offices (see p.38) when you arrive.

RENTeGO ☎224 323 734, Ⓦwww.rentego.com. Good selection of self-catering apartments in the old town. Book online and get the keys or eCode sent to you.

Stop City Vinohradská 24, Vinohrady ☎222 521 233, Ⓦwww.stopcity.com; metro Muzeum or Náměstí Míru (daily: April–Oct 9am–9pm; Nov–March 10am–8pm). Friendly agency that can book you into hotels, pensions and private rooms at very reasonable rates.

Travel.cz Divadelní 24, Nové Město; metro Národní třída; ☎800 800 722, UK ☎0808/120 2320, US ☎1-877/744 1222; Ⓦwww.travel.cz (daily: June–Aug 8am–10pm; Sept–May 8am–8pm). Well-established, upmarket travel agency that can book you into hotels, pensions and apartments in Prague, and help with accommodation outside Prague, too.

Hotels and pensions

Prague offers everything from big multinational chain **hotels** to attractive **pensions** furnished with real antiques in the old town. The vast majority of rooms have en-suite bathrooms and TVs, with continental breakfast either included in the price or offered as an optional extra. There's no hard and fast rule as to what constitutes a hotel and what a pension, and it's certainly not reflected in the price. Standards overall are still somewhat variable, with "service with a snarl" and sheer incompetence still encountered here and there. As a result, it's really worth considering a **self-catering** apartment – occasionally known as a "residence".

Prague postal districts

If you're thinking of booking a room in advance or planning a long-term stay, it's as well to know a little about the merits, or otherwise, of Prague's various areas and **postal districts** (see map opposite). From 1960 to 1990, Prague was divided into ten districts and most Praguers refer to their area either by name, or by the old postal districts, which still appear on street signs and on addresses.

Prague 1 Prague 1 covers all of the old city on both sides of the river, and half of Nové Město, and consequently is generally the most expensive part of the capital in which to stay. However, anything in this area will be within easy walking distance of the main sights, and will save you a lot of hassle.

Prague 2 Prague 2 is another prime central area, taking in the southern half of Nové Město and western half of Vinohrady, a nineteenth-century des res with good metro connections.

Prague 3 The less salubrious, eastern half of Vinohrady in Prague 3 is nevertheless well served by the metro; Žižkov, on the other hand, is an edgier, working-class district, connected to the centre only by trams.

Prague 4 Covers a wide area in the southeast of the city, stretching from half-decent, predominantly nineteenth-century suburbs such as Nusle, Podolí and Braník to the grim high-rise *paneláky* of Chodov and Háje. However, even if you find yourself in the latter two areas, you can at least be sure of quick metro connections to the city centre.

Prague 5 Vast area in the hilly southwest of the city, with clean air and attractive family villas predominating and a metro line running through some of it. The area closest to the city is Smíchov, a vibrant, late nineteenth-century district, with cheaper than average rooms.

Prague 6 The perfect, hilly villa district to the north of the centre, a favourite with foreign embassies and their staff (not to mention Havel himself). The metro goes only as far as Dejvická, however, which means that only Dejvice and Bubeneč enjoy really fast connections with the centre.

Prague 7 The nineteenth-century suburb of Holešovice in the northeast is well served by the metro and trams. Troja, home to numerous ad hoc campsites, is almost bucolic, and correspondingly difficult to get to.

Prague 8 The grid-plan streets of nineteenth-century Karlín are close to the centre and well served by the metro, which extends as far as Libeň; the rest of the area is not so aesthetically pleasing, though the metro reaches out into Kobylisy.

Prague 9 Dominated by factories, Prague 9, in the northeast of the city, is something of a last resort; however, with good metro connections, it's at least easy enough to get into town.

Prague 10 Beware of Prague 10, which extends right into the countryside; areas like Strašnice and Vršovice in the southeast of the city are slightly closer to the centre of things and served, in part, by the metro.

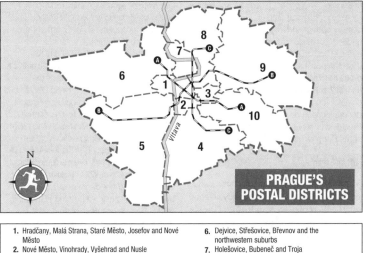

PRAGUE'S POSTAL DISTRICTS

1. Hradčany, Malá Strana, Staré Město, Josefov and Nové Město
2. Nové Město, Vinohrady, Vyšehrad and Nusle
3. Vinohrady and Žižkov
4. Nusle, Podolí, Braník, Krč and the southeastern suburbs
5. Smíchov and the southwestern suburbs
6. Dejvice, Střešovice, Břevnov and the northwestern suburbs
7. Holešovice, Bubeneč and Troja
8. Karlín, Libeň and the northern suburbs
9. Vysočany and the northeastern suburbs
10. Vršovice, Strašnice and the eastern suburbs

With plenty of centrally located hotels, there's really no need to stay out in the suburbs unless you're on a very tight budget. The quietest central areas to stay in are on the hilly left bank in Malá Strana and Hradčany, though there's more choice, and more nightlife, in Staré Město and Nové Město. All prices quoted are for the **cheapest double room** available in high season, which may mean without private bath or shower in the less expensive places – again, these rates may be slashed if you book in advance.

Hradčany

Hradčany is obviously a great area to stay in, right by the castle, although there are few accommodation options. It's also extremely quiet, is accessible only by tram or on foot (uphill), and boasts only a limited number of places to eat and drink. For locations see map, p.42.

Domus Henrici Loretánská 11 ☎ 220 511 369, ⓦ www.domus-henrici.cz; tram #22 to Pohořelec. Stylish, discreet hotel in a fabulous location, with just eight rooms/apartments, some with splendid views. Run in conjunction with *Domus Balthasar* on Mostecká, by the Charles Bridge. Free wi-fi. Doubles from 4400Kč.

Questenberk Úvoz 15 ☎ 220 407 600, ⓦ www.questenberk.cz; tram #22 to Pohořelec. From the outside, this hotel looks like a Baroque chapel, but inside it's been totally modern-ized. Rooms are smart but plain, though the views from some are superb. Doubles from 3000Kč.

Savoy Keplerova 6 ☎ 224 302 430, ⓦ www.savoyhotel.cz; tram #22 to Pohořelec. Super-luxury hotel on the western edge of Hradčany, concealed behind a pretty Art Nouveau facade and famous for its large marble bathrooms. This is one of Prague's finest, and as a result is popular with visiting celebs. Doubles from 4500Kč.

U krále Karla (King Charles) Úvoz 4 ☎ 257 532 869, ⓦ www.romantichotels.cz; tram #22 to Pohořelec. Possibly the most tastefully exquisite of all the small luxury hotels in the castle district, with beautiful antique furnishings and stained-glass windows. Situated at the top of Nerudova, it's a steep walk from the nearest tram stop, however. Doubles from 4000Kč.

U raka (The Crayfish) Černínská 10 ☎ 220 511 100, ⓦ www.romantikhotel-uraka.cz; tram #22

to Brusnice. The perfect hideaway, six double rooms in a little half-timbered, eighteenth-century cottage in Nový Svět. No children under 12 or dogs and advance reservation a must. Doubles from 3500Kč.

U zlatého koníčka (The Golden Horse) Úvoz 8 ☎603 841 790, ⊛www.goldenhorse.cz; tram #22 to Pohořelec. Small, plain, clean, en-suite rooms at real bargain prices in a perfect location on the way up to the Hrad. Breakfast is served in the brick-vaulted cellar. Doubles from 2350Kč.

Malá Strana

Malá Strana is a beautiful area, and, with the exception of a few key streets, relatively traffic-free and quiet. Pretty much all of the most attractive and memorable places to stay in Prague are concentrated here, and as a result, it's pricey; however, there are one or two bargains, for which it's worth booking ahead. The nearest metro station for all the places listed below is Malostranská, though some will require a further tram ride on tram #12, #20 or #22. For locations see map, p.66.

Alchymist Grand Hotel Tržiště 19 ☎257 286 011, ⊛www.alchymisthotel.com; tram #12, #20 or #22 to Malostranské náměstí. Total decadent luxury abounds in this sixteenth-century palace which has been tastefully converted into a secluded spa hotel, complete with Indonesian masseuses and an indoor pool. Doubles from 9000Kč.

Aria Tržiště 9 ☎225 334 111, ⊛www.ariahotel.net; tram #12, #20 or #22 to Malostranské náměstí. Prague's most popular boutique hotel, this superbly stylish, contemporary place has a stunning roof terrace and music-themed floors (and rooms) from jazz and rock to classical and opera. Breakfast is extra. Doubles from 5000Kč.

Castle Steps Nerudova 10 ☎257 216 337 (plus numerous international toll-free numbers), ⊛www.castlesteps.com; tram #12, #20 or #22 to Malostranské náměstí. This is without doubt Malá Strana's most amazing bargain: a variety of beautifully furnished rooms and apartments, some with unbeliev-able views, some with shared facilities, others with self-catering facilities, dotted around the vicinity. There's no reception as such, but an office where you check in (with free internet access. A fairly rudimentary vegan breakfast is served in a cellar (with free internet access) on Úvoz until 11am. Doubles from 1500Kč.

Dientzenhofer Nosticova 2 ☎257 316 830, ⊛www.dientzenhofer.cz; tram #12, #20 or #22 to Malostranské náměstí. Birthplace of the eponymous architect Kilian Ignác Dientzen-hofer and a very popular and unpretentious pension, as it's one of the few reasonably priced places (anywhere in Prague) to have wheelchair access. Doubles from 3200Kč.

Dům U velké boty (The Big Shoe) Vlašská 30 ☎257 532 088, ⊛www.dumuvelkeboty .cz; tram #12, #20 or #22 to Malostranské náměstí. The sheer discreetness of this pension, in a lovely old building in the quiet backstreets, is one of its main draws. Run by a very friendly couple, who speak good English, it has a series of cosy rooms with genuine antiques, some en suite, some not. Breakfast is extra. Doubles from 3000Kč.

Lundborg U lužického semináře 3 ☎257 011 911, ⊛www.lundborg.cz; metro Malostranská. Very stylish Swedish-run apartment suites with Baroque painted ceilings and tasteful furnishings, as well as jacuzzis and free internet access in every room. Situated in the thick of it, right by the Charles Bridge tower. Suites from 6000Kč.

Neruda Nerudova 44 ☎257 535 557, ⊛www .hotelneruda-praha.cz; tram #12, #20 or #22 to Malostranské náměstí. Stylish hotel a fair walk up Nerudova, with a funky, glass-roofed foyer, lots of natural stone and smart, minimalist modern decor in the rooms. Doubles from 3000Kč.

Nosticova Nosticova 1 ☎257 312 513, ⊛www .nosticova.com; tram #12, #20 or #22 to Malostranské náměstí. Baroque house with ten beautifully restored apartments replete with antique furnishings, sumptuous bathrooms and small kitchens, on a peaceful square not far from the Charles Bridge. Apartments from 7500Kč.

Sax Jánský vršek 3 ☎257 531 268, ⊛www .hotelsax.cz; tram #12, #20 or #22 to Malostranské náměstí. Perfectly located in the backstreets off Nerudova, this hotel has gone for a remarkably convincing groovy retro 1960s look, but it's also a very well-run, well-equipped place with a DVD library and free wi-fi. Doubles from 3500Kč.

U červeného lva (The Red Lion) Nerudova 41 ☎257 533 832, ⊛www.hotelredlion.com; tram #12, #20 or #22 to Malostranské náměstí.

The service can be variable, but the price is good and the decor is outstanding: original seventeenth-century wooden ceilings throughout, complemented by tasteful furnishings, parquet flooring and rugs. Doubles from 3000Kč.

U Karlova mostu Na Kampě 15 ☏ 234 652 808, ⓦ www.archibald.cz; tram #12, #20 or #22 to Malostranské náměstí. Situated on a lovely tree-lined square, just off the Charles Bridge, the rooms in this former brewery (now a pub-restaurant) have real character, despite the modern fittings. Doubles from 5500Kč.

U zlaté studně (The Golden Well) U zlaté studně 4 ☏ 257 011 213, ⓦ www.goldenwellhotel.com; metro Malostranská. The location is pretty special: tucked into the terraces below Prague Castle, next to the terraced gardens, with incredible views across the rooftops. The rooms aren't half bad either, with lots of original ceilings, and there's a good restaurant attached, with a wonderful summer terrace. Doubles from 4500Kč.

U zlatých nůžek (The Golden Scissors) Na Kampě 6 ☏ 257 530 473, ⓦ www .uzlatychnuzek.com; tram #12, #20 or #22 to Malostranské náměstí. Ten pleasant rooms with parquet flooring, the odd beam and simple modern furnishings on Kampa island, close to the Charles Bridge. Doubles from 2875Kč.

Staré Město

Staré Město is right in the centre of things, with lots of pubs and restaurants to choose from, all within easy walking distance. Inexpensive places to stay are few and far between, but there are several moderately priced options – here, more than anywhere, it's essential to book ahead. For locations see map, p.80.

Arcadia Old Town Kožná 6 & 13 ☏ 224 922 040, ⓦ www.arcadiaoldtown.com; metro Můstek. A cosy set of apartments right in the heart of the labyrinth of streets south of Old Town Square. Decor is bright, cheerful and modern. Doubles from 3400Kč.

Buddha Bar Hotel Jakubská 8 ☏ 221 776 300, ⓦ www.buddha-bar-hotel.cz; metro Náměstí Republiky. Supremely stylish, central boutique hotel with an oriental slant to the decor and ambience – the rooms have all mod cons including free wi-fi. Doubles from 6000Kč.

Černá liška (The Black Fox) Mikulášská 2 ☏ 224 232 250, ⓦ www.cernaliska.cz; metro Staroměstská. Well-appointed rooms, all with lovely wooden floors, some with incredible views on to Old Town Square, quieter ones at the back. Doubles from 3700Kč.

Černý slon (Black Elephant) Týnská 1 ☏ 222 321 521, ⓦ www.hotelcernyslon.cz; metro Náměstí Republiky. Another ancient building tucked away off Old Town Square by the north portal of the Týn church, now tastefully converted into a very comfortable small hotel. Doubles from 3900Kč.

Cloister Inn Konviktská 14 ☏ 224 211 020, ⓦ www.cloister-inn.com; metro Národní třída. Pleasant, well-equipped hotel housed in a nunnery in one of the backstreets; the rooms are simply furnished with modern fittings, free wi-fi, and the location is good – see also the *Unitas*. Doubles from 2500Kč.

Grand Hotel Bohemia Kralodvorská 4 ☏ 224 804 111, ⓦ www.grandhotelbohemia.cz; metro Náměstí Republiky. Possibly the most elegant luxury hotel in the old town, just behind the Obecní dům, with some very tasty Art Nouveau decor and all the amenities you'd expect from an Austrian outfit. Doubles from 3500Kč.

Grand Hotel Praha Staroměstské náměstí 22 ☏ 221 632 556, ⓦ www.prague-residence.cz; metro Staroměstská/Můstek. If you want a room overlooking the astronomical clock on Old Town Square, then book in here, well in advance. There are beautiful antique furnishings, big oak ceilings, but only a very few rooms, including a single, as well an attic suite for four. Doubles from 4000Kč.

Josef Rybná 20 ☏ 221 700 111, ⓦ www .hoteljosef.com; metro Náměstí Republiky. Prague's top designer hotel exudes modern professionalism, the lobby is a symphony in off-white efficiency and the rooms continue the crisply maintained minimalist theme. Doubles from 3500Kč.

Pachtův Palace Karoliny Světlé 20 ☏ 234 705 111, ⓦ www.pachtuvpalace.com; metro Národní třída. Former Baroque palace, now luxury hotel, in the heart of the old town, with charming and efficient staff, rooms and suites decked in a blend of antique and repro furniture. Doubles from 5000Kč.

Paříž U Obecního domu 1 ☏ 222 195 195, ⓦ www.hotel-paris.cz; metro Náměstí Republiky. Setting for Bohumil Hrabal's *I Served the King of England*, this is a good top-notch hotel with plenty of *fin de siècle* atmosphere surviving. Doubles from 4500Kč.

Residence Řetězová Řetězová 9 ☏222 221 800, ⓦwww.residenceretezova.com; metro Staroměstská. Attractive apartments of all sizes, with kitchenettes, wooden or stone floors, Gothic vaulting or wooden beams and repro furnishings throughout. Apartments from 3000Kč.

Savic Jilská 7 ☏224 248 555, ⓦwww.savic.eu; metro Národní třída. This hotel, in the heart of the old town, has retained plenty of period features: painted ceilings, vaulting, exposed beams and the like. Staff are as helpful as can be and the buffet breakfast is superb. Doubles from 3700Kč.

U medvídků (The Little Bears) Na Perštýně 7 ☏224 211 916, ⓦwww.umedvidku.cz; metro Národní třída. The rooms above this famous Prague pub are plainly furnished, quiet considering the locale and therefore something of an old town bargain; booking ahead essential. Doubles from 3500Kč.

U tří bubnů (The Three Drums) U radnice 8–10/14 ☏224 214 855, ⓦwww.utribubnu.cz; metro Staroměstská. Small hotel just off Old Town Square with five tastefully furnished rooms, either with original fifteenth-century wooden ceilings or lots of exposed beams. No lift but plenty of stairs. Free wi-fi. Doubles from 3600Kč.

▲ *Grand Hotel Evropa*

U zlatého jelena (The Golden Stag) Štupartská 6 ☏222 317 237, ⓦwww.hotel-u-zlateho-jelena .cz; metro Náměstí Republiky. Inexpensive little pension with spacious rooms very simply furnished with parquet flooring and repro ironwork. Doubles from 3600Kč.

Unitas Bartolomějská 9 ☏224 211 020, ⓦwww .unitas.cz; metro Národní třída. Set in a Franciscan nunnery, the *Unitas* offers both simple twins and bargain dorm beds in its *Art Prison* hostel (see p.184). No smoking or drinking. Doubles from 2000Kč.

Nové Město

Nové Město covers a large and very varied area of the city. The streets just to the south of Národní, and to the east of Náměstí Republiky, are within walking distance of the old town. For places in the nether regions, you'll need to hop on a tram or metro to get into the centre of town. For locations see map, p.112.

Alcron Štěpánská 40 ☏222 820 000, ⓦwww.radissonblu.com; metro Muzeum/ Můstek. Giant 1930s luxury hotel, just off Wenceslas Square, which has been superbly restored to its former Art Deco glory by the Radisson chain. Double rooms here are without doubt the most luxurious and tasteful you'll find in Nové Město. Free wi-fi. Doubles from 5000Kč.

Grand Hotel Evropa Václavské náměstí 25 ☏224 215 387, ⓦwww.evropahotel.cz; metro Muzeum. Sumptuously decorated in Art Nouveau style, and potentially the most wonderful hotel in Prague, this place is still run like an old Communist behemoth – a blast from the past in every sense. The doubles with shared facilities (and without breakfast) on the student floor are only 800Kč each. Doubles from 1600Kč.

Hotel 16 – U sv Kateřiny Kateřinská 16 ☏224 920 636, ⓦwww.hotel16.cz; tram #4, #6, #10, #16 or #22 to Štěpánská. Really friendly, family-run hotel offering small, plain but clean en-suite rooms. There's a small terraced garden at the back and botanic gardens nearby. Doubles from 2900Kč.

Icon Hotel V jámě 6 ☏221 634 100, ⓦwww .iconhotel.eu; metro Můstek. Modern designer hotel, whose white-walled rooms are equipped with large, handmade Hästens beds. All day à la carte breakfast will suit late risers. Doubles from 4700Kč.

Imperial Na poříčí 15 ☎246 011 600, ⓌWWW .hotel-imperial.cz; metro Náměstí Republiky. Despite describing itself as Art Deco, this place is actually more of an Art Nouveau masterpiece. Built in 1914, the public rooms are dripping with period ceramic friezes; the rest of the hotel is standard twenty-first-century luxury. Doubles from 5500Kč.

Na zlatém kříži (The Golde Cross) Jungmannovo náměstí 2 ☎224 219 501, Ⓦwww.antikhotels .com; metro Můstek. Small hotel in a very tall (no lift), narrow building just a step away from the bottom of Wenceslas Square. Rooms are spacious – especially the suites – and decked out in tasteful modern furnishings. Doubles from 2500Kč.

Palace Panská 12 ☎224 093 181, ⓌWWW .palacehotel.cz; metro Můstek. Luxury five-star hotel just off Wenceslas Square, renowned for its excellent service and facilities – rooms are spotless and the buffet breakfast is top-class. Doubles from 4500Kč.

Salvator Truhlářská 10 ☎222 312 234, ⓌWWW .salvator.cz; metro Náměstí Republiky. Very good location for the price, just a minute's walk from Náměstí Republiky, with small but clean rooms (the cheaper ones with shared facilities), set around a courtyard. Good buffet breakfast; friendly staff; free wi-fi. Doubles from 2300Kč.

U šuterů Palackého 4 ☎224 948 235, ⓌWWW .usuteru.cz; metro Můstek/Národní třída. With elegant modern furnishings, wooden floors, and some lovely vaulted ceiling, this small pension is a very good-value choice in a decent location between Národní and Wenceslas Square. Staff are very helpful and the downstairs restaurant is great. Doubles from 2400Kč.

Vyšehrad and the eastern suburbs

Vinohrady is a pleasant nineteenth-century suburb, a few metro or tram stops east of Wenceslas Square. **Žižkov** is a more run-down area, best-known for its riotous pubs and ethnically mixed population; it has no metro, but several tram routes run through it. For locations see map, p.134.

Alpin Velehradská 25, Žižkov ☎222 726 751, Ⓦwww.alpin.cz; metro Jiřího z Poděbrad. Clean, bare, bargain rooms on the border between Vinohrady and Žižkov; it's a short hop on the tram to get into town. Doubles from 1700Kč.

Anna Budečská 17, Vinohrady ☎222 513 111, Ⓦwww.hotelanna.cz; metro Náměstí Míru. Plain, but smartly appointed rooms, warm friendly staff and a decent location make this a popular choice in Vinohrady, with trams and the metro close by. Free wi-fi. Doubles from 2500Kč.

Arco Donská 13, Vinohrady ☎271 740 734, Ⓦwww.arco-guesthouse.cz; tram #4 or #22 to Krymská. Gay-friendly guesthouse just a short tram ride from the centre of town. Furnishings are plain and modern, with all rooms en suite. Internet and wi-fi available. Doubles from 1200Kč.

Galileo Bruselská 3, Vinohrady ☎222 500 222, Ⓦwww.hotel-galileo-prague.com; tram #6 or #11 to Bruselská. Chic, modern hotel furnished with style, offering apartments as well as en-suite doubles. Doubles from 2600Kč.

Le Palais U Zvonařky 1, Vinohrady ☎234 634 111, Ⓦwww.palaishotel.cz; tram #6 or #11 to Bruselská. Plush late nineteenth-century hotel overlooking the Nusle valley, with the Belle Epoque theme continued throughout the lobby and rooms. Doubles from 4000Kč.

Mánes Mánesova 46, Vinohrady ☎603 104 121, Ⓦwww.penzionmanes.cz; tram #11 to Vinohradská tržnice or metro Náměstí Míru. Clean and modern inside, very cheap and close to a tram stop and a lovely local park. Doubles from 1900Kč.

Holešovice and the western suburbs

Holešovice is another pleasant late nineteenth-century residential suburb, within easy walking distance of a lot of greenery, and with good metro and tram connections. **Dejvice** is a spacious residential interwar suburb, with garden villas on its fringes and a metro. **Smíchov** is a late nineteenth-century district, which has been rejuvenated in recent years and is only a short tram or metro ride from the centre.

Admirál Hořejší nábřeží, Smíchov ☎257 321 302, Ⓦwww.admiral-botel.cz; metro Anděl; see map, p.159. The best of Prague's antiquated "botels" (floating hotels) is moored in Smíchov. Cabins are tiny but fittings modern and seasickness impossible. Doubles from 3000Kč.

Anděl Apartments Nádražní 114, Smíchov ☎257 215 679, Ⓦwww.venturapraha.cz; metro Anděl; see map, p.159. Modern apartments right opposite Anděl metro in the heart of Smíchov.

183

Spotlessly clean and very quiet considering the location. Doubles from 1750Kč.

Anděl's Hotel Stroupežnického 21, Smíchov ☎296 889 688, Ⓦwww.andelshotel.com; metro Anděl; see map, p.159. Ultra-modern mega-hotel in the heart of newly renovated Smíchov. The lobby exudes fashionable designer minimalism, as do the well-equipped rooms; the buffet breakfast is enormous. Doubles from 4000Kč.

Art Hotel Praha Nad Královskou oborou 53, Bubeneč ☎233 101 331, Ⓦwww.arthotel.cz; tram #1, #15, #25 or #26 to Sparta; see map, p.146. Sharp modern hotel, sprinkled with contemporary art, in a quiet neighbourhood, close to Stromovka park and Výstaviště. Doubles from 5000Kč.

Crowne Plaza Koulova 15, Dejvice ☎296 537 111, Ⓦwww.crowneplaza.cz; tram #8 to Podbaba. See map, p.144. Prague's classic 1950s Stalinist wedding-cake hotel, with its dour socialist realist friezes and large helpings of marble, is now run by Austrians. Doubles from 2000Kč.

Julián Elišky Peškové 11, Smíchov ☎257 311 150, Ⓦwww.julian.cz; tram #6, #9, #12 or #20 to Švandovo divadlo; see map, p.159. Large luxurious hotel a short tram ride from Malá Strana. All the usual facilities, plus mini-kitchens and a nice lounge with a real fire. Doubles from 3400Kč.

Petr Drtinova 17, Smíchov ☎257 314 068, Ⓦwww.hotelpetr.cz; tram #6, #9 or #12 to Kinského zahrada; see map, p.159. Situated on a leafy street at the foot of Petřín hill, close to Malá Strana. It doesn't look that promising from the outside, but is modern and pleasant inside. Doubles from 3600Kč.

Praha Sušická 20, Dejvice ☎224 342 650, Ⓦwww.htlpraha.cz; tram #2, #20 or #26 Hadovka; see map, p.144. The old Party VIP hotel, where the likes of Ceauçescu once stayed. The building itself is an appropriately grotesque 1980s concrete palace, though each room has a balcony with a wonderful view over to the Hrad. It's a bit of a walk from the tram stop, so most guests take a taxi. Doubles from 4000Kč.

Hostels

There are a fair few **hostels** in Prague which cater for the large number of backpackers who hit the city all year round – and these are supplemented further by a whole host of more transient, high-season-only hostels. Visit Ⓦwww.hostel-world.com to see the whole range and read hostellers' reviews. Only a few stand out from the crowd and they're recommended below. Prices in hostels usually start from around 400Kč for a bed in a dormitory.

A tiny handful of Prague hostels give discounts to HI (Hostelling International; Ⓦwww.hihostels.com) and can be booked via the HI's online booking service, including the **Travellers' Hostels**, whose chain of hostels is particularly popular with US students. Its main booking office is at Dlouhá 33, Staré Město (☎224 826 662, Ⓦwww.travellers.cz), where there is also a hostel (see opposite).

Art Prison Bartolomějská 9, Staré Město ☎224 230 603, Ⓦart-prison.prague-hostels.cz; metro Národní třída; see map, p.80. Set in a Franciscan nunnery – and part of *Pension Unitas* – this hostel offers both simple twins and bargain dorm beds in converted secret police prison cells (Havel was kept in P6). Twins from 1260Kč.

Clown and Bard Bořivojova 102, Žižkov ☎222 716 453, Ⓦwww.clownandbard.com; tram #5, #9 or #26 to Husinecká; see map, p.134. Žižkov hostel that attracts backpackers who like to party. Still, it's clean, undeniably cheap, stages events and has laundry facilities and free wi-fi. Veggie breakfast extra. Doubles from 1200Kč, dorm beds from 300Kč.

Czech Inn Francouzská 76, Vinohrady ☎267 267 600, Ⓦwww.czech-inn.com; tram #4 or #22 to Jana Masaryka; see map, p.134. Upbeat, designer hostel that feels and looks like a hotel, with friendly and helpful staff and a choice of dormitories and private rooms. Doubles from 1600Kč, dorm beds from 400Kč.

Klub Habitat Na Zderaze 10, Nové Město ☎224 918 252; metro Karlovo náměstí; see map, p.112. Perfectly serviceable, clean, charity-run hostel in a great location south of Národní. Breakfast included; free internet. Dorm beds from 450Kč.

Miss Sophie's Melounová 3, Nové Město ☎296 303 530, Ⓦwww.miss-sophies.com;

Czech Beer

Beer's no doubt a heavenly gift, it chases away worries and troubles and imparts strength and courage.

From Smetana's opera *The Bartered Bride*

The Czechs drink more beer than anyone else in the world, downing approximately a pint a day for every man, woman and child in the country – in fact, more beer is drunk here than water. The drink's history is deeply embedded in the national culture: after all, this is the country that invented the first Pilsner, or golden lager, as well as being home to the world's most prized hops from Žatec (Saaz). Others beers just don't get a look in, with imported beer accounting for just one percent of the domestic market.

A short history of beer

The Czechs' greatest claim to beer fame is that they invented the world's original Pilsner beer. The real story is a bit more complicated than that. By the late 1830s, the German-speaking inhabitants of **Plzeň** (Pilsen), 90km west of Prague, were disgruntled with the local beer, a top-fermented, dark, cloudy brew of dubious quality. In disgust, they founded the *Bürgerliche Brauhaus*, and employed a Bavarian brewer, Josef Groll, who, on October 5, 1842, produced the world's first lager, a bottom-fermented beer stored in cool caves. The pale Moravian malt, the Žatec (Saaz) hops and the local soft water produced a clear, golden beer that caused a sensation. At the same time, cheap, mass-produced glass appeared on the market, which showed off the new beer's colour and clarity beautifully. The new rail network meant that the drink could be transported all over central Europe, and Pilsner-style beers became all the rage.

Brewing methods remained traditional until the fall of Communism, after which the larger breweries almost all

Dark beer ▲

U Vejvodů ▲

Waiter at U Fleků ▼

Czech beer terms

čepované pivo – draught beer
černé – dark-coloured beer
kvasnicové pivo – yeast beer
lahvové pivo – bottled beer
malé pivo – small beer, served as 0.3l
nefiltrované – unfiltered (cloudy) beer
nepasterované – unpasteurized beer
pivo – beer, served as 0.5l
polotmavé – a "half-dark" beer
pšeničné pivo – wheat beer
řezané – "cut" beer, a mixture of light and dark beers
světlé – light-coloured beer
tmavé – dark-coloured beer
točené pivo – draught beer

The pivnice experience

The classic Czech **pivnice**, or pub, is a straightforward affair: wooden tables, benches, beermats and an endless supply of beer. There's rarely any music and, apart from the odd game of cards or dominoes, drinking (though not necessarily getting drunk) is the chief pursuit. It's common practice in Prague pubs to share a table with others. **Je tu volno?** (Is this seat free?) is the standard question. Waiter service is the norm – just sit down and place a beermat in front of you, and soon enough a waiter will walk round with a tray of frothing mugs, slap one down and give you a paper tab on which he or she will keep a tally of your consumption. Raise your glass to your companions, say **na zdraví** (cheers) and start drinking. As you near the end of the glass, before you've even begun to worry about catching the waiter's eye, you'll be served another – **ještě jednou?** (another one?) he or she will ask. At which point it becomes clear why Czechs don't go in for pub crawls – you need a serious strength of will (and a clear head) to get up and leave. Most pubs also serve traditional Czech food. When you want to leave, simply say **zaplatím, prosím** ("I'll pay, please"), and your tab will be totted up. Round up the bill to the nearest few crowns and, on leaving, bid your neighbours farewell (**na shledanou**).

▲ Barman at Pivovarský dům

▼ Pub sign

opted for modernization: pasteurization, de-oxidization, rapid maturation and carbon dioxide injections – which resulted in longer shelf-life, less taste and more fizz. The republic's smaller breweries were either swallowed up or went to the wall. By the mid-1990s, there were just sixty Czech breweries left, with the biggest (except Budvar) owned by multinationals. However, in the last decade a new breed of microbreweries has sprung up, eschewing modern technology and producing some of the tastiest, most individual brews you'll ever encounter.

U medvídků ▲

Prague pub interior ▲

U Fleků ▼

Ten great Prague pubs

▸▸ **Hospoda na verandách** This is the gargantuan Staropramen brewery, which serves a lovely unfiltered kvasnicové pivo (wheat beer). **See p.202**

▸▸ **Klášterní pivovar** The monks were always at the forefront of beer-making, and the Strahov monastery in Hradčany is continuing the tradition with its own St Norbert beers. **See p.198**

▸▸ **Letenský zámeček** Probably the city's best beer garden, with views from the heights of Letná right down the Vltava. **See p.202**

▸▸ **Novoměstský pivovar** Labyrinthine, modern microbrewery that produces a misty 11° home brew, plus classic Czech pub food. **See p.200**

▸▸ **Pivovarský dům** Prague's most popular microbrewery pub produces some weird brews – from nettle beer to chocolate – but the regular light, dark and wheat beers are the ones to plump for. **See p.200**

▸▸ **U Bulovky** Prague's most impressive microbrewery is hidden in the suburbs, but well worth the journey for its wide range of traditionally brewed beers. **See p.202**

▸▸ **U černého vola (The Black Ox)** A real traditional pub in the heart of the castle district of Hradčany. Long benches, simple decor and mugs of Velkopopovický kozel. **See p.198**

▸▸ **U Fleků** This may be the ultimate tourist trap, but for the pub's legendary dark chocolatey 13° lager it's worth it. **See p.201**

▸▸ **U medvídků (The Little Bears)** Traditional medieval beer hall in the centre of town, serving well-kept Budvar beer from České Budějovice. **See p.199**

▸▸ **U Pinkasů** A traditional Czech *pivnice*, where Pilsner Urquell was first served in Prague – it now serves the brewery's excellent unpasteurized beer. **See p.201** metro I. P. Pavlova; see map, p.112. The most central of Prague's smart new designer hostels offering everything from cheap dorm beds to fully equipped apartments. Dorm beds from 400Kč, doubles from 1790Kč.

Ritchie's Karlova 9 & 13, Staré Město ☎222 221 229, ⓦwww.ritchieshostel.cz; metro Staroměstská; see map, p.80. In the midst of the human river that is Karlova, this old town hostel has no in-house laundry or cooking facilities, but it's clean and accommodation ranges from en-suite doubles to twelve-bed dorms. Doubles from 1500Kč, dorm beds 300Kč.

Rosemary Růžová 5, Nové Město ☎222 211 124, ⓦwww.praguecityhostel.cz; metro Můstek or Hlavní nádraží; see map, p.112. Clean, modern hostel a short walk from the main train station, Praha hlavní nádraží. Three- to twelve-bed mixed dorms, plus doubles with or without en-suite/kitchen facilities. Communal kitchen and free internet. Dorms from 400Kč, doubles from 1300Kč.

Sir Toby's Hostel Dělnická 24, Holešovice ☎246 032 610, ⓦwww.sirtobys.com; tram #1, #3, #5, #12, #15 or #25 to Dělnická; see map, p.146. Out in Holešovice, but among the most welcoming, characterful and efficiently run hostels in the city, and the centre is only a tram ride away. Dorm beds from 260Kč, doubles from 1450Kč.

Sokol Nosticova 2, Malá Strana ☎257 007 397, ⓦwww.sokol-cos.cz; tram #12, #20 or #22 to Hellichova; see map, p.66. Shambolic student hostel with crowded dorms, plus a communal kitchen and a beer terrace in a great location in Malá Strana; the entrance is on Všehrdova. Doubles from 700Kč, dorm beds 350Kč.

Travellers Hostel Dlouhá 33, Staré Město ☎224 826 662, ⓦwww.travellers.cz; metro Náměstí Republiky; see map, p.80. Very centrally located party hostel (although it's not the cleanest of places), situated above the *Roxy* nightclub, and the main booking office for a network of hostels – if there's not enough room here, staff will find you a bed in one of their other central branches. Dorm beds from 300Kč, doubles from 1400Kč.

Týn Týnská 19, Staré Město ☎224 828 519, ⓦwww.hosteltyn.com; metro Náměstí Republiky; see map, p.80. Prague's most centrally located hostel is a very basic affair, located in a quiet courtyard (with a veggie Indian café in it) a stone's throw from Old Town Square. Doubles from 1240Kč, six-bed dorms 420Kč.

Vesta Wilsonova 8, Nové Město ☎224 225 790, ⓦvesta.prague-hostels.cz; metro Hlavní nádraží; see map, p.112. The ultimate last resort if you arrive at the main train station (Praha hlavní nádraží) late at night, this hostel is in the south tower of the station itself; functional doubles from 900Kč, and you can ask (and pay) for sole occupancy.

Campsites

Prague abounds in **campsites** – there's a whole rash of them in Troja – and most are relatively easy to get to by public transport. Facilities, on the whole, are rudimentary and badly maintained, but the prices reflect this, starting at around 350Kč for a tent and two people.

Džbán SK Aritma, Nad lávkou 5, Vokovice ☎235 358 554, ⓦwww.camp.cz/dzban; tram #20 or #26 to Nad Džbánem; 15min from the tram stop and 4km west of the centre, near the Šárka valley. Large field with tent pitches, bungalows, shop, restaurant, tennis courts, lake swimming and gym. Open all year.

Herzog Trojská 161, Troja ☎283 850 472, ⓦwww.campherzog.cz; bus #112 from metro Nádraží Holešovice. Good location, one of several along the road to Troja chateau, situated in a large, shady back garden. Open all year.

Kotva U ledáren 55, Braník ☎244 466 085, ⓦwww.kotvacamp.cz. The oldest, and nicest, site, with a riverside location twenty minutes by tram south of the city. Hostel and caravan accommodation is available too. Take tram #3, #17 or #21 to Nádraží Braník. Open all year.

Sokol Troja Trojská 171a, Troja ☎233 542 908, ⓦwww.camp-sokol-troja.cz; bus #112 from metro Nádraží Holešovice. Larger than *Herzog* and slightly further away from the Troja chateau and zoo, but well organized, with kitchen, laundry and restaurant on site. Open all year.

Cafés and restaurants

C zech food tends to be meaty, hearty and filling, and while it's fun to sample Czech cuisine, you could spend a whole week eating out in Prague and never go near a dumpling, should you so wish. There is, however, now a vast range of **restaurants** serving up everything from Afghan to sushi (though remember, you're a long way from the sea). With the Czech crown going from strength to strength, prices in the city's restaurants are at or above the EU average – the quality of the food and the service sometimes still has some catching up to do. Not surprisingly, places in the main tourist areas tend to be overpriced – venture instead into the backstreets and you're more likely to find better service, better value and perhaps even better food. Another option is to head for a **pub** (see Chapter 11), where you can be sure of cheap, typical, Czech dishes.

At the beginning of the twentieth century, Prague boasted a **café** society to rival that of Vienna or Paris. Communism put paid to that sort of bourgeois nonsense, but a handful of classic Habsburg-era haunts have survived – or been resurrected – and have since been joined by a whole range of new places from designer cafés to rarified teahouses. Like the Austrians who once ruled over them, the Czechs have a grotesquely sweet tooth, and the more traditional cafés offer a wide range of **cakes**; others offer a whole range of snacks from soup and sandwiches to rolls and wraps. **Coffee** follows the Italian model, but is generally not as strong. **Tea** is drunk weak and without milk, although you'll usually be given a glass of boiling water and a tea bag so you can do your own thing – for milk, say "*s mlékem*".

Most places have an English **menu**; for help in deciphering Czech menus, see p.269. Watch out for extras: you will often be charged a **cover charge** for bread, music and for everything you touch, including the almonds you thought were courtesy of the house. When **tipping**, simply round the bill up to the nearest 10Kč or 20Kč.

Czech cuisine

Czech cuisine has an inherent predilection for pork, gravy, dumplings and pickled cabbage and a peculiar aversion to fresh vegetables (other than potatoes) and salads. So it's never going to top the league table of the world's great cuisines, but it does have one or two dishes worth sampling.

Czechs aren't big on starters, with the exception of **soup** (*polévka*), one of the country's culinary strong points. Main dishes are overwhelmingly based on **meat** (*maso*), usually pork (*vepřové*), sometimes beef (*hovězí*). The difficulty lies in decoding names such as *klášterní tajemství* (literally "mystery of the monastery", but actually just a filet of beef) or even a common dish like *Moravský vrabec* (literally "Moravian sparrow", but actually just roast pork). **Fish** (*ryby*) is generally listed separately, or along with chicken (*drůbez*) and other fowl like duck (*kachna*). River

Cheap eats and quick snacks

The most obvious snack in Prague is, of course, a *párek*, or **hot dog**, a dubious-looking frankfurter (traditionally two – *párek* means a pair), dipped in mustard and served in a white roll (*v rohlíku*).

Pastries (*pečivo*) are available from Prague's bakeries (*pekářství* or *pekárna*). Traditional Czech pastry (*koláč*) is more like sweet bread, dry and fairly dense with only a little condiment to flavour it, such as almonds (*oříškový*), poppy seed jam (*mákový*), plum jam (*povidlový*) or a kind of sour-sweet curd cheese (*tvarohový*). Czechs occasionally dabble in **sandwiches** – a reliable city-wide chain is *Paneria* (see p.192; Ⓦ www.paneria.cz), which specializes in providing sandwiches, toasted panini and pastries for Prague's hungry office workers; the most central branches are at Kaprova 3 and Maiselova 4 (both metro Staroměstská). Traditionally, the Czechs went in for artistically presented open sandwiches known as *chlebíčky* – with combinations of gherkins, cheese, salami, ham and aspic – but the baguette, panini and wrap are now in the ascendancy.

Obviously the usual multinational burger chains have their outlets splattered all over Prague. For something uniquely Czech, head for *Havelská Koruna*, Havelská 21 (metro Můstek), an authentic no-frills, self-service *jídelna* serving **Czech comfort food** classics such as *sekaná*, goulash and *zelí*, all for under 50Kč (you pay at the exit).

Whatever the season, Czechs love to have a daily fix of **ice cream** (*zmrzlina*), traditionally dispensed from window kiosks in the sides of buildings. There are several proper ice-cream parlours, too, some with seating, serving authentic Italian *gelato*.

For **markets** and **food shops**, including, delis, patisseries, bakeries and ice-cream shops, see p.219.

---

trout (*pstruh*) and carp (*kapr*) – the traditional dish at Christmas – are the cheapest and most widely available fish, and are usually served, grilled or roasted, in delicious buttery sauces or breadcrumbs.

Side dishes (*přílohy*) are usually potatoes (*brambory*), though with meat dishes you'll more often be served **dumplings** (*knedlíky*), one of the mainstays of Bohemian cooking and nothing like English dumplings, more like a heavy white bread. The ubiquitous *obloha* is the Czech version of a **salad**: a bit of tomato, cucumber and lettuce, or cabbage (*zelí*), often swimming in a slightly sweet, watery dressing.

With the exception of *palačinky* (pancakes), filled with chocolate or fruit or cream, Czechs don't go in for **desserts** (*moučníky*). They prefer to eat their ice cream on the street and their cakes in the cafés or cake shops.

Hradčany

For locations see map, p.42.

Cafés

Malý Buddha Úvoz 46; tram #12, #20 or #22 to Malostranské náměstí. Typical Prague teahouse decor, with a Buddhist altar in one corner and (mainly) vegetarian Vietnamese snacks on the menu. A very useful haven just down from the Hrad. Tues–Sun 1–10.30pm.

U zavěšenýho kafe (The Hanging Café) Úvoz 6 Ⓦ www.uzavesenyhokafe.cz; tram #12, #20 or #22 to Malostranské náměstí. A pleasant, smoky crossover café/pub, serving cheap beer and traditional Czech food in a handy spot near the Hrad. A "hanging coffee" is one that has been paid for by the haves for the have-nots who drop in. Daily 11am–midnight.

Restaurants

U císařů (The Emperor) Loretánská 5 ☏ 220 518 484, Ⓦ www.ucisaru.cz; tram #22 to Pohořelec. Upmarket medieval place serving up hearty meaty Czech dishes, as well as trout, butterfish and fondue for 400Kč and upwards. Daily 9am–1am.

187

U ševce Matouše (The Cobbler Matouš)
Loretánské náměstí 4 ☎ 220 514 536; tram #22
to Pohořelec. Large steak and chips, for
around 300Kč, is the speciality of this
former cobbler's, which is one of the few
half-decent places to eat in the castle
district. Bottled beer only. Daily 11am–4pm
& 6pm–11pm.

Villa Richter Staré zámecké schody 6 ☎ 257 219
079, ⓦ www.villarichter.cz; metro Malostranská.
Set amidst the castle vineyards, just outside
the Black Tower (Černá věž), this place has
three separate places one on top of the
other: the *Piano Nobile* serves up classy
fish, rabbit and wild boar dishes
(600–700Kč); below, the *Piano Terra*
specializes in Bohemian standards
(150–300Kč); and *Panorama Pergola* is the
perfect place to sample some Czech wines
and soak in the view. Tues–Sun 10am–6pm.

Malá Strana

For locations see map, p.66.

Cafés

Bohemia Bagel Lázeňská 19 ⓦ www
.bohemiabagel.cz; tram #12, #20 or #22 to
Malostranské náměstí. Malá Strana branch of
the successful self-service chain (and expat
favourite) situated close to Charles Bridge,
serving filled bagels, all-day breakfasts,
soup and chilli. Daily 7.30am–7pm.

Café Savoy Vítězná 5 ☎ 257 311 562,
ⓦ www.ambi.cz; tram #6, #9, #12, #20 or
#22 to Újezd. The *Savoy* is a classic,
L-shaped Habsburg-era café from 1893
with a superb, neo-Renaissance ceiling; you
can have just have a coffee or a snack if
you want, but it doubles as a very good
restaurant, with mains (including lots of
seafood) for 350Kč and above. Mon–Fri
8am–10.30pm, Sat & Sun 9am–10.30pm.

Cukrkávalimonáda Lázeňská 7; tram #12, #20 or
#22 to Malostranské náměstí. Very professional
and well-run café, serving good brasserie-
style dishes, as well as coffee and croissants,
with tables overlooking the church of Panna
Maria pod řetězem. Daily 8.30am–8pm.

Pekářství v Karmelitské Karmelitská 20; tram
#12, #20 or #22 to Hellichova. This is a classic
cheap Czech bakery, just off Malostranské
náměstí, with a café attached where you
can wash down your cakes, pastries and
rolls with a coffee. Mon–Sat 7am–7pm, Sun
10am–6pm.

U knofličků (The Little Button) Újezd 17; tram
#12, #20 or #22 to Hellichova. A quaint, slightly
chintzy, new *cukrárna* (patisserie) selling ice
cream, cakes, coffee and traditional
chlebíčky (open sandwiches). Mon–Fri
9am–6.30pm, Sat & Sun 10am–6.30pm.

U zeleného čaje (The Green Tea) Nerudova 19;
tram #12, #20 or #22 to Malostranské náměstí.
Great little smoke-free stop-off for a pot of
tea or a veggie snack en route to or from
Prague Castle; the only problem is getting a
place at one of the four tables. Daily
11am–10pm.

Restaurants

Bar Bar Všehrdova 17 ☎ 257 312 246, ⓦ www
.bar-bar.cz; tram #6, #9, #12, #20 or #22 to
Újezd. Unpretentious cellar restaurant that
specializes in savoury (mostly veggie)
pancake dishes (around 125–140Kč) and
sweet crêpes/*palačinky* (80Kč) on offer. Free
wi-fi. Mon–Thurs & Sun noon–midnight, Fri
& Sat noon–2am.

Café de Paris Maltezské náměstí 4 ☎ 603
160 718; tram #12, #20 or #22 to Hellichova.
This is a cosy, family-run restaurant based on
the famous *Café de Paris* in Geneva. The
menu is very short and the signature dish is
beef entrecôte 280Kč in a creamy sauce
composed to a secret recipe (there's a tofu
version available, too). Daily noon–midnight.

David Tržiště 21 ☎ 257 533 109, ⓦ www.restaurant
-david.cz; tram #12, #20 or #22 to Malostranské
náměstí. Tip-top service is guaranteed at this
small, formal, family-run restaurant, which
specializes in doing classic Bohemian cuisine
full justice. The best deal is the three-course
fixed menu, which starts at 600Kč. Daily
11.30am–11pm.

Hergetová cihelna Cihelná 2b ☎ 296 826 103,
ⓦ www.kampagroup.com; metro Malostranská.
Slick, smart restaurant serving up tiger
prawn starters (385Kč), plus tasty pasta and
risotto (250–300Kč), and the odd traditional
Czech dish (200–400Kč). The riverside
summer terrace overlooks Charles Bridge.
Daily 11.30am–1am.

Kampa Park Na Kampě 8b ☎ 296 826 102,
ⓦ www.kampagroup.com; metro Malostranská.
Pink house exquisitely located right by the
Vltava on Kampa Island, with a superb fish
and seafood menu (mains 600–900Kč),
top-class service and tables outside in
summer. Daily 11.30am–1am.

Nebozízek (Little Auger) Petřínské sady 411
☎ 257 515 329, ⓦ www.nebozizek.cz; tram #6,

#9, #12, #20 or #22 to Újezd. Situated at the halfway stop on the Petřín funicular. The view from *Nebozízek* is superb; there's an outdoor terrace and a traditional Czech menu heavy with game dishes from 300Kč. Daily 11am–11pm.

Noi Újezd 19 ☎257 311 411, ⒲www .noirestaurant.cz; tram #12, #20 or #22 to Hellichova. A stylish, atmospheric restaurant dishing out some of the tastiest, spiciest Thai food in Prague (mains 200–300Kč), though it's not great for veggies. There's a lovely courtyard patio round the back. Daily 11am–1am.

Pálffý palác Valdštejnská 14 ☎257 530 522, ⒲www.palffy.cz; metro Malostranská. The restaurant occupies a grand candle-lit room on the first floor of an old Baroque palace, and features a wonderful outdoor terrace from which you can survey the red rooftops of Malá Strana. The international menu is renowned for its venison (main courses 500–700Kč). Daily 11am–11pm.

Rybářský klub U sovových mlýnů 1 ☎257 534 200, ⒲www.rybklub.cz; tram #6, #9, #12, #20 or #22 to Újezd. Freshwater fish – carp, catfish, zander and others – baked, grilled or deep-fried in breadcrumbs for around 250–400Kč are served up at this unpretentious riverside restaurant situated in the park on Kampa Island. Daily noon–11pm.

U malé velryby Nebovidská 6 ☎257 214 703, ⒲www.umalevelryby.cz; tram #12, #20 or #22 to Hellichova. Herb-encrusted salmon, succulent steaks and duck (around 300Kč) are all turned out to perfection by the chef at this simple modern restaurant. There's also a tapas menu and freshly baked bread. Mon–Sat 11am–11pm, Sun 11am–8pm.

U sedmi Švábů (The Seven Swabians) Janský vršek 14 ☎257 531 455, ⒲www.svabove.cz; metro Malostranská. Named after the Grimm brothers' tale, this torch-lit tavern serves up traditional Czech beer and food (150–300Kč) to the occasional accompaniment of medieval shenanigans from fire breathing to sword fighting. Daily 11am–11pm.

Staré Město

For locations see map, p.80.

Cafés

Au Gourmand Dlouhá 10 ⒲www.augourmand .cz; metro Náměstí Republiky. Beautifully tiled

French boulangerie, patisserie and *traiteur* selling wickedly delicious pastries – take-away or eat-in. Branch at Rytířská 22 (metro Můstek). Mon–Fri 8am–7pm, Sat 8.30am–7pm, Sun 9am–7pm.

Bakeshop Praha Kozí 1 ⒲www .bakeshop.cz; metro Náměstí Republiky. Top-class expat bakery serving excellent bread, sandwiches and wraps (100–200Kč), as well as tarts and cakes, which you can either take away or wash down with coffee whilst reading the papers. Daily 7am–7pm.

Beas Týnská 19 ⒲www.beas-dhaba.cz; metro Malostranská/Náměstí Republiky. Bright, modern Indian veggie café through the courtyard off Týnská, offering simple, authentic dosas and thalis served on traditional metal trays. Mon–Fri 11am–8pm, Sat noon–8pm, Sun noon–6pm.

Bohemia Bagel II Masná 2 ⒲www .bohemiabagel.cz; metro Staroměstská. Staré Město branch of the successful self-service bagel bar, just off Staroměstské náměstí, with unlimited coffee refills and an internet café attached. Mon–Fri 7am–midnight, Sat & Sun 8am–midnight.

Chez Marcel Haštalská 12; metro Náměstí Republiky. Effortlessly chic French café-bistro. A good place to grab a coffee or a *tarte tatin*, read a French magazine or eat some moderately priced brasserie staples. Mon–Fri 8am–1am, Sat & Sun 9am–1am.

Country Life Melantrichova 15 ⒲www .countrylife.cz; metro Můstek. Self-service café behind the health-food shop of the same name: pile up your plate with hot or cold dishes and salad and pay by weight. Mon–Thurs 10.30am–8pm, Fri 9am–3pm, Sun noon–6pm. There's another branch at Jungmannova 1, Nové Mesto (Mon–Fri only).

Cream & Dream Husova 12 ⒲www.cream -dream.com; metro Staroměstská. Multinational *gelateria* chain that serves up some of the best ice cream in Prague, with real fruit and no artificial rubbish. Daily 11am–10pm.

Érra Konviktská 11; metro Národní třída. Vaulted cellar café in the backstreets off Betlémské náměstí that's popular with a fashionable mixed straight/gay crowd. Tasty salads and snacks on offer too. Daily 10am–midnight.

▲ *Grand Café Orient*

Classic, cheap, smoky, studenty, Czech café, serving good coffee and with lots of books and newspapers to browse through and free wi-fi. Mon–Fri 8am–midnight, Sat & Sun noon–midnight.

Literární kavárna Řetězová 10 ⓦwww .knihytynska.cz; metro Staroměstská. Relaxed café in the centre of the old town, attached to a bookshop, offering draught beers, cheap food and occasional happenings. Mon–Fri noon–11pm, Sat & Sun 5–11pm.

Montmartre Řetězová 7; metro Staroměstská. Classic, small, barrel-vaulted café, the "*Montik*" was once a famous First Republic dance and cabaret venue, frequented by the likes of Werfel, Jesenská and Hašek. Mon–Fri 9am–11pm, Sat & Sun noon–11pm.

Siva Masná 8 ⓦwww.siva.cajiky.cz; metro Náměstí Republiky. A fair stab at a teahouse cellar-den complete with hookah pipes, scatter cushions and passable attempts at Arab snacks. Mon–Fri noon–11.30pm, Sat 2–11.30pm, Sun 2–10pm.

U Bakaláře Celetná 13; metro Staroměstská/ Náměstí Republiky. Basic Czech food – it won't win any culinary prizes – in a typical old-style restaurant, served up to sustain the local students. Daily 10am–10pm.

U čarodějek Rámová 4 ⓦwww.restaurace -ucarodejek.mysteria.cz; metro Náměstí Republiky. Cosy, vaulted, self-styled *literární kavárna*, this place serves simple snack dishes for around 100kč, and is a popular lunchtime spot with local office workers. Daily 11am–11pm.

Grand Café Orient Ovocný trh 19; metro Náměstí Republiky. This superb reconstruction of a famous Cubist café from 1911, on the first floor of the Museum of Czech Cubism, dishes up cakes, pancakes and coffee. Mon–Fri 9am–10pm, Sat & Sun 10am–10pm.

Havelská Koruna Havelská 21; metro Můstek. Popular no-frills, self-service Czech *jídelna* with wooden booths, serving comfort food classics such as *sekaná*, goulash and *zelí*, all for under 50Kč; you pay at the exit – not for the faint-hearted. Daily 10am–8pm.

Krásný ztráty (Lovely Losses) Náprstkova 10 ⓦwww.krasnyztraty.cz; metro Staroměstská.

Restaurants

Ariana Rámová 6 ☎222 323 438, ⓦkabulrest.sweb.cz; metro Náměstí Republiky. Welcoming Afghan restaurant

---

Breakfast

Many Czechs get up so early in the morning (often around 6am) that they don't have time to start the day with anything more than a quick cup of coffee. As a result, the whole concept of **breakfast** (*snídaně*) as such is alien to the Czechs. Most hotels will serve the "continental" basics of tea, coffee, rolls and cold cheese and meat, but for a real hearty breakfast, you need to go to one of the many places in the city that cater for expats in search of an American-style **brunch**.

Where to go for:

• **An early coffee and a light snack**: *Bakeshop Praha* (see p.219), *Bohemia Bagel* (see p.188) or *Cukrávalimonáda* (see p.188).

• **Continental-style breakfasts**: *Louvre* (see p.194) or *Obecní dům* (see p.193).

• **The full English breakfast** or **American brunch**: *U malého Glena* (see p.206).

Czech meat consumption remains high so it's hardly suprising then that **vegetarianism** is still a minority sport. Nevertheless, there are one or two excellent vegetarian restaurants, plenty of pizzerias and a good selection of expat places that always have one or two veggie options.

Even in traditional Czech places, most menus have a section called *bezmasa* (literally "without meat") – don't take this too literally, though, for it simply means the main ingredient is not dead animal; dishes like *omeleta se šunkou* (ham omelette) can appear under these headings. The staple of Czech vegetarianism is *smažený sýr*, a slab of melted cheese deep-fried in breadcrumbs and served with tartar sauce (*tartarská omačka*) – beware, though, as it's sometimes served *se šunkou* (with ham). Other types of cheese can also be deep-fried, as can other vegetables: *smažené žampiony* (mushrooms) and *smaženy květák* (cauliflower). Emergency veggie standbys which most Czech pubs will knock up for you without too much fuss include *knedlíky s vejci* (dumplings and scrambled egg) or *omeleta s hráskem* (pea omelette).

Veggie phrases to remember are *"jsem vegeterián/vegeteriánka. máte nejaké bezmasa?"* (I'm a vegetarian. Is there anything without meat?). For emphasis, you could add *"nejím maso nebo ryby"* (I don't eat meat or fish).

Exclusively vegetarian places include: **Albio** (see p.193), **Beas** (see p.189), **Country Life** (see p.189), **Lehká hlava** (see below), **Malý Buddha** (see p.187), **Radost FX** (see p.196) and **U Góvindy** (see p.193).

---

serving up authentic spicy kebabs and veggie dishes (180–250Kč) a stone's throw from the Old Town Square. Daily 11am–11pm.

Bellevue Smetanovo nábřeží 18 ☏222 221 443, ⓦwww.bellevuerestaurant.cz; metro **Národní třída**. The view of Charles Bridge and the Hrad is outstanding, the setting is very formal and the international cuisine is imaginatively prepared – the only drawback is that main courses are 500–700Kč and you need to book ahead. Daily noon–3pm & 5.30–11pm.

Divinis Týnská 21 ☏222 325 440, ⓦwww .divinis.cz; metro **Staroměstská**. Elegant rustic Italian restaurant where the beautifully presented dishes are exceptionally good value at around 200Kč. Mon–Sat 5pm–1am.

Kabul Karoliny Světlé 14 ☏224 235 452, ⓦwww.kabulrestaurant.cz; metro **Staroměstská** or **Náměstí Republiky**. Small Afghan café-restaurant that serves up homely, simple grilled meats, aubergine and okra dishes (150–300Kč), with hot poppy-seed covered flat bread. Daily noon–11pm.

Kogo Havelská 27 ☏224 214 543, ⓦwww.kogo .cz; metro **Můstek**. Divided into two intimate spaces by a passageway, and with a small courtyard out back, this place offers decent pasta, pizza and salads for around 250Kč, served by courteous and efficient waiters. Several branches across Prague. Mon–Fri 8am–11pm, Sat & Sun 9am–11pm.

La Dégustation Bohême Bourgeoise Haštalská 18 ☏222 311 234, ⓦwww.ladegustation.cz; metro **Staroměstská**. One of Prague's most upmarket restaurants; make sure you're hungry before you make a reservation and choose between three tasting menus (1850–2650Kč), each made up of seven courses and seven *amuse-bouches*, all inspired by Czech cuisine. Mon, Fri & Sat 6pm–midnight, Tues–Thurs noon–2.30pm.

La Finestra Platnéřská 13 ☏222 325 325, ⓦwww.lafinestra.cz; metro **Staroměstská**. Congenial Italian restaurant serving really good traditional dishes (300–500Kč) using fresh seasonal produce. Mon–Sat noon–11pm, Sun noon–10pm.

Lehká hlava (Clear Head) Boršov 2 ☏222 220 665, ⓦwww.lehkahlava.cz; metro **Staroměstská**. Exotic cave-like vegetarian restaurant, just off Karoliny Světlé, offering tapas, soups, salads and Mediterranean dishes for 125–175Kč. Even though it's hardly a formal restaurant, it's wise to book ahead. Mon–Fri 11.30am–11.30pm, Sat & Sun noon–11.30pm.

Lokál Dlouhá 33 ☏222 316 265 ⓦwww .ambi.cz; metro **Náměstí Republiky**. Vast corridor of a restaurant, decked out in sleek, minimalist decor, with waiters in formal long white aprons. They serve traditional – but excellent – Czech pub food for around 100Kč, plus unpasteurized Pilsner Urquell. Free wi-fi. Mon–Fri 11am–1am, Sat noon–1am, Sun noon–10pm.

Maitrea Týnská ulička 6 ☎ 222 711 631, Ⓦ www.restaurace-maitrea.cz; metro Staroměstská or Náměstí Republiky. Larger, more luxurious branch of *Lehká hlava*, a den of stylish Buddhist calm serving global vegetarian dishes (125–150Kč). Mon–Fri 11.30am–11.30pm, Sat & Sun noon–11.30pm.

Mlýnec Novotného lávka 9 ☎ 221 082 208, Ⓦ www.mlynec.cz; metro Staroměstská. A pricey place (which has occasionally garnered Michelin stars) with a fabulous riverside terrace overlooking the Charles Bridge and the Hrad. Czech staples like crispy duck are interspersed with Asian fusion dishes. Mains 500–700Kč. Daily noon–3pm & 5.30–11pm.

Orange Moon Rámová 5 ☎ 222 325 119, Ⓦ www.orangemoon.cz; metro Náměstí Republiky. Popular, unpretentious Burmese restaurant that cooks up spicy curries from all over the subcontinent for around 200Kč, washed down with Czech beer. Daily 11.30am–11.30pm.

Stoleti Karoliny Světlé 21 ☎ 222 220 008, Ⓦ www.stoleti.cz; metro Národní třída. Imaginative Czech cuisine named after stars of film and stage served in an unstuffy, simply furnished restaurant. Mains around 200Kč. Daily noon–midnight.

V zátiší (Still Life) Liliová 1 ☎ 222 221 155, Ⓦ www.vzatisi.cz; metro Národní trída. Exquisitely prepared international cuisine with fresh vegetables, fresh pasta and regular non-meat dishes, all served in nouvelle cuisine-sized portions in a space the size of a living room. Fixed menus for around 900Kč. Daily noon–3pm & 5.30–11pm.

Josefov

For locations see map, p.100.

Cafés

Nostress Dušní 10; metro Náměstí Republiky. Despite the tacky name, this smart, Belgian-owned café is actually a great place in which to unwind amidst the eclectic designer furniture. Decent salads and snacks on offer too. Daily 10am–midnight.

Paneria Kaprova 3 Ⓦ www.paneria.cz; metro Staroměstská. Central branch of a large chain of Czech bakeries specializing in sandwiches, toasted panini and pastries. Branches across Prague. Daily 8am–8pm.

Rudolfinum Alšovo nábřeží 12; metro Staroměstská. Gloriously grand nineteenth-century café on the first floor of the old parliament building – you don't have to visit the gallery to go to the café. Tues–Sun 10am–6pm.

Restaurants

Dinitz Bílková 12 ☎ 222 313 308, Ⓦ www.dinitz .cz; metro Staroměstská. Kosher restaurant offering Middle Eastern snacks, sandwiches, pasta, salads (200–250Kč) and steaks (350–500Kč). Daily except Sat 11.30am–10.30pm.

King Solomon Široká 8 ☎ 224 818 752, Ⓦ www .kosher.cz; metro Staroměstská. Sophisticated kosher restaurant which serves big helpings of international dishes and traditional Jewish specialities: a three-course set menu (with a beer) costs around 550Kč. Daily except Fri & Sat noon–11pm.

Le Café Colonial Široká 6 ☎ 224 818 322, Ⓦ www.lecafecolonial.cz; metro Staroměstská. Conveniently situated informal café/formal restaurant right opposite the Klausen Synagogue. The colonial theme isn't overplayed, though the vast French-based menu has a touch of Chinese and Indian. Pasta and risotto for under 200Kč; other main courses 200–400Kč. Daily 10am–midnight.

Les Moules Pařížská 19 ☎ 222 315 022, Ⓦ www.lesmoules.cz; metro Staroměstská. Part of a chain of wood-panelled Belgian brasseries which flies in fresh mussels and serves them up for around 460Kč a kilo, with French fries and Belgian beers. Daily 11.30am–midnight.

Pizzeria Rugantino Dušní 4 ☎ 222 318 172, Ⓦ www.rugantino.cz; metro Staroměstská. This pizzeria, just off Dlouhá, is the genuine article: an oak-fired oven, gargantuan thin bases and numerous toppings to choose from (130–220Kč). Mon–Sat 11am–11pm, Sun noon–11pm.

Pravda (Truth) Pařížská 17 ☎ 222 326 203, Ⓦ www.pravdarestaurant.cz; metro Staroměstská. Chic brasserie with attentive service and an excellent global menu ranging from Cajun to Vietnamese, including home-made pasta dishes and French-style salads. Main dishes 500–600Kč. Daily noon–1am.

▲ *Pravda* restaurant

Northern Nové Město and Václavské náměstí

For locations see map, p.112.

Cafés

Albio Truhlářská 18–20; metro Náměstí Republiky. Prague's most committed organic vegetarian/vegan café (at the back of the deli/bakery) serves a whole range of healthy dishes from wholewheat pasta and noodles to filled baguettes and (vegetarians be warned) fish. Mon–Sat 11am–10pm.

Archa Na poříčí 26, ⓦ www.archatheatre.cz; metro Náměstí Republiky/Florenc. Designer café-bar belonging to the Prague's cutting-edge theatre venue of the same name, with big fishbowl windows for people-watching. Light snacks only; free wi-fi. Mon–Fri 9am–10.30pm, Sat 10am–10pm, Sun noon–10pm.

Dahab Soukenická 4, ⓦ www.dahab.cz; metro Náměstí Republiky. *Dahab* gives you the full harem monty, with drapery galore, cushions and carpets, hookahs for hire, plus a Middle Eastern snacky menu. Mon–Fri 11am–1am, Sat 2pm–3am, Sun 2pm–midnight.

Dobrá čajovna Václavské náměstí 14 ⓦ www .tea.cz; metro Můstek/Muzeum. Mellow, rarefied teahouse, with an astonishing variety of teas (and a few Middle Eastern snacks) served by waiters who slip by silently in their sandals. Mon–Fri 10am–9.30pm, Sat & Sun 2–9.30pm.

Grand Hotel Evropa Václavské náměstí 25 ⓦ www.evropahotel.cz; metro Můstek/Muzeum. This sumptuous Art Nouveau café has all its original fittings, but has reached a new low in ambience and service. For architectural curiosity only. Daily 9.30am–11pm.

Hájek Havlíčkova 15; metro Náměstí Republiky. *Chlebíčky* (open sandwiches), coffee and cakes in a bright ice-cream parlour of a place. Mon–Fri 7.30am–7pm, Sat 9am–7pm, Sun 11am–7pm.

Imperial Na poříčí 15 ⓦ www.cafeimperial.cz; metro Náměstí Republiky. Built in 1914, and featuring the most incredible ceramic friezes on its walls, pillars and ceilings, the *Imperial* is a must for fans of outrageously sumptuous Art Nouveau decor. You can just come for a coffee, but they also serve breakfast, light lunches and full-on main dishes for 300Kč or so. Daily 7am–11pm.

Lucerna Vodičkova 36 ⓦ www.lucerna.cz; metro Můstek/Muzeum. Wonderfully lugubrious *fin de siècle* café-bar on the first floor, en route to the cinema of the same name, with lots of faux marble and windows overlooking the Lucerna *pasáž*. Free wi-fi. Daily 10am–midnight.

Millhouse Sushi – Kaitan Na příkopě 22 ⓦ www.millhouse-sushi.cz; metro Můstek. Minimalist conveyor-belt sushi at the back of the Slovanský dům. Choose all-you-can-eat from the conveyor belt, or order some of the grills or *nigiri* on offer. Daily 11am–11pm.

Obecní dům Náměstí Republiky 5; metro Náměstí Republiky. The vast *kavárna* (café), with its famous fountain, is a glittering Art Nouveau period piece – an absolute aesthetic treat. Food is nice enough, but most folk come here for a coffee and a little something from the cake trolley. Daily 7.30am–11pm.

Tramvaj Václavské náměstí; metro Můstek. Two vintage no. 11 trams stranded in the middle of Wenceslas Square (where they used to run) have been converted into a café – a convenient spot for coffee and easy to locate. Mon–Sat 9am–midnight, Sun 10am–midnight.

U Góvindy Soukenická 27; metro Náměstí Republiky. Daytime Hare Krishna (Haré Kršna in Czech) restaurant with very basic decor, serving organic Indian veggie dishes for just 85Kč. Mon–Sat noon–5pm.

Restaurants

Červená tabulka (Red Tablet) Lodecká 4 ☎224 810 401, ⓦ www.cervenatabulka.cz; metro Náměstí Republiky. Famed for its duck in gingerbread sauce and its wide choice of fish and seafood, this little villa restaurant delivers attentive service and has a slightly offbeat, cosy interior. Mains 300–450Kč. Daily 11.30am–11pm.

Francouzská restaurace Náměstí Republiky 5 ☎ 222 002 770, ⓦ www.obecni-dum.cz; metro Náměstí Republiky. The Art Nouveau decor in this cavernous Obecní dům restaurant is absolutely stunning, but the French-style main dishes, though proficient enough, are very, very expensive (600–950Kč), as are the drinks. Daily 11.30am–4pm & 6–11pm.

Hybernia Hybernská 7 ☎ 222 226 004, ⓦ www .hybernia.cz; metro Můstek. Busy restaurant, with a nice outdoor terrace out the back; specializes in *špíz* (needles), aka kebabs, but also serves good-value Czech food and pasta dishes (150–350Kč). Mon–Fri 8am–11.30pm, Sat & Sun 10.30am–11.30pm.

Modrý zub (Blue Tooth) Jindřišská 5 ☎ 222 212 622, ⓦ modryzub.com; metro Můstek. Good-value Thai rice and noodle dishes (175–275Kč) in a place that has a modern wine-bar feel to it – popular with Wenceslas Square shoppers. Daily 11am–11pm.

🏃 **Pizza Nuova** Revoluční 1, ☎ 222 803 308, ⓦ www.ambi.cz; metro Náměstí Republiky. Decent, spacious, stylish upstairs pizza and pasta place, with great views of the trams wending their way through Náměstí Republiky. Pizzas go for around 200Kč; pasta dishes for a little less. Daily 11.30am–11.30pm.

Plzeňská restaurace Obecní dům, náměstí Republiky 5 ☎ 222 002 770, ⓦ www.obecni -dum.cz; metro Náměstí Republiky. Decent Czech pub-restaurant in the cellar of the Obecní dům, cheaper than the French restaurant upstairs, with main dishes from 300Kč, but not quite the same aesthetic experience. Daily 11am–11pm.

Siam Orchid Na poříčí 21 ☎ 222 319 410, ⓦ www.siamorchid.cz; metro Náměstí Republiky. Upstairs in a *pasáž* near the *Bílá labuť*, this is a great place serving cheap but tasty Thai dishes from spicy salads to fried tofu – most dishes are around 180Kč. Daily 10am–10pm.

U sádlů (The Lard) Klimentská 2 ☎ 224 813 874, ⓦ www.usadlu.cz; metro Náměstí Republiky. Deliberately over-the-top themed medieval banqueting hall offering a hearty Czech menu, with classics such as roast pork knuckle and goulash (200–400Kč) helped down with lashings of frothing Budvar. Daily 11am–11.30pm.

🏃 **Zahrada v opeře (Opera Garden)** Legerova 75 ☎ 224 239 685, ⓦ zahradavopere.cz; metro Můstek. Striking modern interior and beautifully presented food from around the world at democratic prices. Huge salads for just 150Kč; main dishes for 200–500Kč; and, if you have any room, creative desserts for 125Kč. Free wi-fi. Daily 11.30am–1am.

Zvonice (Belltower) Jindřišská věž, Jindřišská ☎ 224 220 028, ⓦ www.restaurantzvonice.cz; metro Můstek. Atmospheric restaurant on the sixth and seventh floors of a medieval belltower. Weekday lunch menu for under 300Kč, but traditional Czech main dishes in the evening start at around 500Kč. Daily 11.30am–midnight.

Southern Nové Město and Národní

For locations see map, p.112.

Cafés

Café 35 – Institut Français Štěpánská 35 ⓦ www.ifp.cz; metro Muzeum. Housed in Prague's Institut Français, you can be sure of great coffee and fresh French pastries – plus of course the chance to pose with a French newspaper. Free wi-fi. Mon & Fri 8.30am–8pm, Sat 10am–2pm.

Cafeterapie Na Hrobci 3; tram #3, #7, #16, #17 or #21 ⓦ www.cafeterapie.o1.cz. Small, simply furnished café that serves up nice healthy Mediterranean-influenced salads, sandwiches, toasties and a few hot dishes. Mon–Fri 10am–10pm, Sat & Sun noon–10pm.

Globe Pštrossova 6 ⓦ www.globebookstore.cz; metro Národní třída/Karlovo náměstí. Large, buzzing café, at the back of the English-language bookstore of the same name that's a popular expat hangout, but enjoyable nevertheless, with live music on Friday and Saturday evenings. Free wi-fi and terminals available at 1Kč/minute. Daily 9.30am–1am.

🏃 **Louvre** Národní 22; metro Národní třída. Turn-of-the-twentieth-century café with a long pedigree, and still a very popular refuelling spot for Prague's shoppers. Dodgy colour scheme, but high ceiling, mirrors, daily papers, decent, inexpensive food, lots of cakes, a billiard hall and window seats overlooking Národní. Mon–Fri 8am–11.30pm, Sat & Sun 9am–11.30pm.

Marathon Černá 9; metro Národní třída. Smoky, self-styled "library café" in the university's

1920s-style religious faculty, hidden in the backstreets south of Národní. Mon–Fri 10am–10pm.

St Tropez Vodičkova 11; metro Národní třída/ Můstek. Light and airy family-run French patisserie inside the U Nováků building on Vodičkova. Mon–Fri 8am–7pm, Sat & Sun 9.30am–7pm.

Shabu Palackého 11; metro Národní třída/ Můstek. Tiny little café down a passageway, serving an interesting selection of Balkan snacks such as grilled aubergine and *burek*. Daily 11am–11pm.

Slavia Smetanovo nábřeží 2 ⓦwww.cafeslavia .cz; metro Národní třída. This famous 1920s riverside café (see p.125) pulls in a mixed crowd from shoppers and tourists to old-timers and the pre- and post-theatre mob. Come here for a coffee and the view, not the food or the service. Daily 9am–11pm.

U sv Vojtěcha (St Adalbert) Vojtěšská 14; metro Karlovo náměstí. Lively coffee place not far from the Národní divadlo and Žofín, with big windows that open out onto the street in summer. Mon–Fri 8am–11pm, Sat 10am–10pm, Sun 10am–8pm.

Velryba (The Whale) Opatovická 24; metro Národní třída. Classic student café – smoky, loud and serving cheap Czech food (lots of veggie options) and a ridiculously wide range of malt whiskies. Daily 11am–midnight.

Restaurants

Céleste Rasínovo nábřeží 80 ⓣ222 984 160, ⓦwww.celesterestaurant.cz; metro Karlovo náměstí. Restaurant on the seventh floor of the Tančící dům (Dancing House), with spectacular views across to Prague Castle; food is traditional French but with an agreeably fresh and light touch. Mains 500–700Kč. Mon–Sat noon–2.30pm & 6.30–10.30pm.

Cicala Žitná 43 ⓣ222 210 375, ⓦtrattoria.cicala .cz; metro I.P. Pavlova. Very good family-run Italian basement restaurant specializing (mid-week) in fresh seafood (from 300Kč). There's also a wide range of pasta (180–240Kč) and an appetizing antipasto selection. Mon–Sat 11.30am–10.30pm.

Čínská restaurace po sečuánsku Národní 25 ⓣ224 085 331, ⓦtrattoria.cicala.cz; metro I.P. Pavlova. Hidden inside the Palác Metro *pasáž*, this is an inexpensive, unpretentious Sichuan restaurant dishing up steaming plates of authentic Chinese food for 150–250Kč. Daily 10am–11pm.

Dynamo Pštrossova 29 ⓣ224 932 020; metro Národní třída. Fashionable little spot with eye-catching retro-1960s designer decor; inexpensive veggie and pasta dishes (125–150Kč) and steaks and Czech dishes for around 200Kč. Daily 11.30am–midnight.

Lemon Leaf Myslíkova 14 ⓣ224 919 056, ⓦwww.lemon.cz; metro Karlovo náměstí. Clean and bright Thai restaurant, serving up spicy meat and fish curries (170–250Kč). The weekday lunchtime menus (100–130Kč) are very popular as is the all-you-can-eat weekend brunch (240Kč). Mon–Thurs 11am–11pm, Fri 11am–12.30am, Sat 12.30pm–12.30am, Sun 12.30pm–11pm.

Pizzeria Kmotra (Godmother) V jirchářích 12 ⓣ224 934 100, ⓦwww.kmotra.cz; metro Národní třída. This inexpensive, brick-vaulted basement pizza place is popular, and justifiably so – if possible, book a table in advance. Pizzas 110–160Kč. Daily 11am–midnight.

Posezení u Čiriny Navrátilova 6 ⓣ222 231 709; metro Karlovo náměstí. A little family-run place, with only a handful of tables inside, leather benches in cosy wooden alcoves and a summer terrace. Classic Slovak home cooking for around 200Kč. Mon–Sat 11am–11pm.

Střelecky ostrov Střelecký ostrov ⓣ603 775 662, ⓦwww.streleckyostrov.cz; tram #6, #9, #12, #20 or #22. The kitchen here serves up classic Czech cuisine (mains from around 300Kč), but it's the location – on an island in the Vltava, with an outdoor terrace overlooking the National Theatre – that pulls in the punters. Mon–Sat 11am–11pm.

Žofín Garden Slovanský ostrov ⓣ774 774 774, ⓦwww.zofingarden.cz; metro Karlovo náměstí. Located on the island nearest the National Theatre, *Žofín* serves up beautifully presented pizzas and barbecued dishes for under 200Kč.

Vyšehrad and the eastern suburbs

For locations see map, p.134.

Cafés

Kaaba Mánesova 20, Vinohrady; metro Náměstí Míru. This stylish ice-cream parlour of a café attracts a young trendy crowd with its funky mismatched 1950s repro chairs and tables. Serves breakfast, open sandwiches, salads, soup and toasties. Mon–Fri 8am–10pm, Sat 9am–10pm, Sun 10am–10pm.

Medúza Belgická 17, Vinohrady ⓦ www.meduza .cz; metro Náměstí Míru. A cool young crowd hangs out in this deliberately faded, inexpensive café, which puts artworks and photography by local artists on its walls and serves breakfast and *palačinky* (pancakes) all day. Free wi-fi. Mon–Fri 10am–1am, Sat & Sun noon–1am.

Radost FX Café Bělehradská 120, Vinohrady ⓦ www.radostfx.cz; metro I.P. Pavlova. The veggie dishes at this expat favourite are filling and all under 200Kč; the decor is decadent and there's a dance soundtrack (with live DJs at the weekend). Despite all this, *Radost* can be a disappointing culinary experience. Free wi-fi. Daily 11am–midnight.

Restaurants

Efes Vinohradská 63, Vinohrady ☎ 222 250 015, ⓦ www.masala.cz; metro Náměstí Míru/Jiřího z Poděbrad. Honest Turkish grilled meats for under 200Kč with all the trimmings, *cacik*, hummus and fresh bread – veggie dishes like *ayvar*, or bulgar wheat and aubergine, are also available. Mon–Sat 11.30am–11pm.

Mailsi Lipanská 1, Žižkov ☎ 222 717 783; metro Jiřího z Poděbrad. Prague's only Pakistani restaurant is a friendly, unpretentious Punjabi place that's great for a comfort curry for around 300Kč, as hot as you can handle. The decor includes a wall of built-in aquariums. Daily noon–3pm & 6pm–midnight.

🏃 **Masala** Mánesova 13, Vinohrady ☎ 773 555 652, ⓦ www.masala.cz; metro Náměstí Míru. This North Indian restaurant is justifiably popular with the local expats. The Tandoori kebabs and kormas (160–260Kč) are authentically spicy and the naan bread is homemade. The Jain brothers who run it are genuinely friendly. Mon–Fri 11.30am–10.30pm, Sat & Sun 12.30–10.30pm.

Holešovice and the western suburbs

See map, p.146, unless otherwise stated.

Cafés

🏃 **Café Orange** Puškinovo náměstí 13, Bubeneč; metro Dejvická. Brightly

decorated café with seats outside overlooking a quiet residential square and good pasta dishes, bruschetta snacks, fresh juice and ice cream on the menu. Mon–Sat 10am–11pm, Sun 11am–3pm.

U Mamadua Milady Horákové 54, Holešovice ⓦ www.umamadua.cz; tram #1, #15, #25 or #26 to Letenské náměstí. Suburban downstairs den of a teahouse with scatter cushions to collapse on, internet access and Thai massage. Daily 11am–10pm.

Restaurants

Hanavský pavilon Letenské sady 173, Letná ☎ 233 323 641, ⓦ www.hanavskypavilon.cz; tram #1, #8, #18 or #20 to Chotkovy sady. Highly ornate wrought-iron Art Nouveau pleasure pavilion high above the Vltava, with stunning views from the terrace; Czech and international mains 350–500Kč. Daily 11am–1am.

La Crêperie Janovského 4, Holešovice ☎ 220 878 040, ⓦ www.lacreperie.cz; metro Vltavská. Small, unpretentious, inexpensive French-run crêperie (with a kids' play area) serving buckwheat *galette* and sweet and savoury pancakes (for around 120Kč), washed down with Breton cider. Daily 9am–11pm.

Mirellie V.P. Čkalova 14, Bubeneč ☎ 222 959 999, ⓦ www.mirellie.cz; metro Dejvická/ Hradčanská. Something of a find in the backstreets of Bubeneč, *Mirellie* produces decent Mediterranean pizza, pasta and risotto dishes for under 200Kč. Daily 11am–11pm.

🏃 **Sushi Bar** Zborovská 49, Smíchov ☎ 603 244 882, ⓦ www.sushi.cz; tram #6, #9, #12, #20 or #22 to Újezd; see map, p.159. Modern sushi bar in the part of Smíchov just south of Malá Strana. The sushi and sashimi set dishes are delicious, but the cost can mount up, with each morsel 100–350Kč. Daily noon–10pm.

Svatá Klara (St Clare) U Trojského zámku 35, Troja ☎ 233 540 173, ⓦ www.svataclara.cz; bus #112 from metro Nádraží Holešovice. Formal, evening-only restaurant, first opened in 1679, in a romantic wine-cave setting near the zoo. Specializes in fondues and Czech game dishes from 500Kč. Daily 7pm–1am.

Pubs and bars

As in most European capitals, the **pub and bar** scene in Prague is enormously diverse, with everything from expat American-style bars and "Irish" pubs to swish, modern cocktail bars. Even the traditional Czech pub (*pivnice*) has had something of a makeover, with smarter decor, prompter service and a wider range of food. Smoky, male-dominated pubs, primarily designed for drinking copious quantities of Czech beer by the half-litre, survive here and there, particularly away from the centre. Whatever their faults, Czech *pivnice* remain deeply embedded in the local culture, and to sample that, you need to sample the amber nectar. Food, where served, tends to be of the traditional Czech variety (for more on Czech cuisine, see p.186) – cheap and filling, but long-term abuse could ultimately shorten your life by a couple of years.

Alcohol

Alcohol consumption among Czechs has always been high. It doubled in the 1970s and the Czechs have remained on top of the world league table of beer consumption ever since. That said, it's a problem that seldom spills out onto the streets; violence in pubs is uncommon and the only obnoxious drunks you're likely to see in public are British tourists on a stag or hen outing.

Czech **beer** (*pivo*) ranks among the best in the world and the country remains the true home of most of the lager drunk around the world today. Beer is served by the half-litre; if you want anything smaller, you must specifically ask for a *malé pivo* (0.3l). The average jar is medium strength, usually about 4.2 percent alcohol. Somewhat confusingly, the Czechs class their beers using the **Balling scale**, which measures the original gravity, calculated according to the amount of malt and dissolved sugar present before fermentation. The most common varieties are 10° (*desítka*), which are generally slightly weaker than 12° (*dvanáctka*). Light beer (*světlé*) is the norm, but many pubs also serve a slightly sweeter dark variety (*tmavé* or *černé*) – or you can have a mixture of the two (*řezané*).

Czech **wine** (*víno*) will never win over as many people as its beer, but since the import of French and German vines in the fourteenth century a modest selection of medium-quality wines has been produced. The main wine region is South Moravia, though a little is produced around the Bohemian town of Mělník (see p.161). Most domestic wine is pretty drinkable – *Veltlínské zelené* (Grüner Veltliner) is a good, dry white – and rarely much more than 60Kč a bottle in shops, while the best stuff is only available from a good wine shop (see p.219) or private wine cellar, hundreds of which still exist out in the wine-growing regions. A Czech speciality to look out for is **burčák**, a very young, fizzy, sweet, misty wine of varying (and

For more on beer and pubs in Prague see our **Czech beer** colour section.

Czech breweries

The most famous Czech beer is **Pilsner Urquell**, known to the Czechs as Plzeňský Prazdroj, the original bottom-fermented Pils from Plzeň (Pilsen), a city 80km southwest of Prague. Plzeň also boasts the **Gambrinus** brewery, whose domestic sales actually exceed those of Pilsner Urquell. The other big Bohemian brewing town is České Budějovice (Budweis), home to the country's biggest-selling export beer, **Budvar**, a mildly flavoured brew for Bohemia but still leagues ahead of Budweiser, the German name for Budvar that was adopted by American brewers, Anheuser-Busch in 1876 (and a cause of litigious grief ever since).

The biggest brewery in the country is Prague Breweries (majority-owned by British beer giants, Bass), whose Smíchov brewery produces **Staropramen** (meaning "ancient spring"), a typical Bohemian brew with a mild hoppy flavour. Some Staropramen is also produced at the Holešovice brewery, better known for its popular, dark **Měšťan** beer. The city's other brewery is in the southern suburb of **Braník**; it produces a light, malty brew. Beers worth seeking out include the award-winning, hoppy and slightly bitter **Velkopopovický kozel**, and Bohemian brews Bernard and Pelhřimov, both of which are unpasteurized. Wheat beer (*pšeničné pivo*) and yeast beer (*kvasnicové pivo*) are both becoming more popular, but so, rather worryingly, is **Velvet**, a dark, bland, electrically pumped ale produced by Prague Breweries in Ostrava, and its more Guinness-like cousin, **Kelt**.

often very strong) alcoholic content, which appears on the streets in the vintage harvest season in September.

The home production of brandies is a national pastime. The most renowned of the lot is **slivovice**, a plum brandy originally from the border hills between Moravia and Slovakia. You'll probably also come across *borovička*, a popular Slovak firewater, made from juniper berries, and *myslivec*, a rough brandy with a firm following. There's also a fair selection of intoxicating herbal concoctions: *fernet* is a dark-brown bitter drink, known as *bavorák* (Bavarian beer) when it's mixed with tonic, while *becherovka* is a supposedly healthy herbal spirit from the Bohemian spa town of Karlovy Vary, with a very unusual, almost medicinal taste.

Although illegal in some parts of Europe, **absinthe** has enjoyed something of a renaissance in Prague. The preferred poison of Parisian painters and poets in the 1920s, absinthe is a nasty green spirit made from fermented wormwood – it even gets a biblical mention in Revelation: "and the name of the star is called Wormwood: and the third part of the waters became wormwood; and many men died of the waters, because they were made bitter." St John wasn't wrong: at up to 170 degrees proof, it's dangerous stuff and virtually undrinkable neat. To make it vaguely palatable, you need to set light to an absinthe-soaked spoonful of sugar, and then mix the caramelized mess with the absinthe.

Hradčany

For locations see map, p.42.

Klášterní pivovar (Monastery brewery) Strahovské nádvoří 1; tram #22 to Pohořelec. Tourist-friendly monastic brewery, offering their own pricey light and dark St Norbert beers and Czech pub food. Daily 10am–11pm.

U černého vola (The Black Ox) Loretánské náměstí 1; tram #22 to Pohořelec. Great traditional Prague pub doing a brisk business providing the popular light beer Velkopopovický kozel in huge quantities to thirsty local workers, plus a few basic pub snacks. Daily 10am–10pm.

Malá Strana

For locations see map, p.66.

Baráčnická rychta Na tržišti 23 (down a narrow passageway leading south off Nerudova); tram #12, #20 or #22 to Malostranské náměstí. *Všebaráčnická rychta* (as it's also known) is a smoke-free backstreet *pivnice* hidden away in the cobbled streets south of Nerudova – at night, approach from Tržiště. Daily noon–midnight.

Jo's Bar Malostranské náměstí 7; tram #12, #20 or #22 to Malostranské náměstí. *Jo's* is the city's original American expat/backpacker hangout. It no longer has quite the same vitality but remains a good place to hook up with other travellers. There's also a club, *Jo's Garáž*, downstairs. Daily 11am–2am.

Latin Art Café Janský vršek 2; tram #12, #20 or #22 to Malostranské náměstí. A Latino hideout, decked out with Botero prints and tucked away in the backstreets, this café-bar is worth seeking out to hear some great Latin American live music. Free wi-fi. Daily 2pm–5am.

St Nicholas Café Tržiště 10; tram #12, #20 or #22 to Malostranské náměstí. A well-dressed older crowd of Czechs and expat diplomatic folk come to this small, vaulted cellar bar for live music, pizza and Pilsner. Mon–Fri 4pm–2am, Sat & Sun 1pm–1am.

Tato kojkej Kampa Park; tram #6, #9, #12, #20 or #22 to Újezd. Not a bad pub considering its touristy location right by the Charles Bridge. Reasonably priced Pilsner Urquell, Czech pub food and the occasional accordionist. Daily 10am–midnight.

U hrocha (The Hippo) Thunovská 10; tram #12, #20 or #22 to Malostranské náměstí. A close-knit bunch of locals fill this small, smoky Czech *pivnice* close to the British embassy, serving Pilsner Urquell. Daily 11am–11pm.

U kocoura (The Cat) Nerudova 2; tram #12, #20 or #22 to Malostranské náměstí. The most famous Czech pub on Nerudova inevitably attracts tourists, but the locals come here too for the Pilsner Urquell and the Budvar, plus the obvious Czech stomach-fillers. Daily 11am–11pm.

U malého Glena (Little Glenn's) Karmelitská 23; tram #12, #20 or #22 to Malostranské náměstí. Smart-looking pub/jazz bar that attracts a fair mixture of Czechs and expats thanks to its better-than-average food and live music in the basement. Daily 8.30am–2am.

Staré Město

For locations see map, p.80.

Blatnička Michalská 5; metro Můstek. Long-established wine shop where you can drink straight from the barrel, take away or head next door to the popular basement *vinárna* for more wine and inexpensive snacks. Daily 11am–11pm.

Kozička Kozí 4 ⓦ www.kozicka.cz; metro Staroměstská. Busy, designer bare-brick cellar bar with cheap Czech food, tucked away just a short walk from Staroměstské náměstí. Mon–Fri noon–4am, Sat 6pm–4am, Sun 7pm–3am.

Molly Malone's U Obecního dvora 4 ⓦ www .mollymalones.cz; metro Staroměstská. The best of Prague's Irish pubs, with real Irish staff, an open fire, draught Kilkenny and Guinness and decent Irish-themed food. Free wi-fi. Mon–Thurs & Sun 11am–1am, Fri & Sat 11am–2am.

U medvídků (The Little Bears) Na Perštýně 7 ⓦ www.umedvidku.cz; metro Národní trída. A Prague beer hall going back to the thirteenth century and still much the same as it always was (make sure you turn right when you enter, and avoid the bar to the left). The Budvar comes thick and fast, and the food is reliably Bohemian. Mon–Fri 11am–11pm, Sat 11.30am–11pm, Sun 11.30am–10pm.

U Rudolfina Křížovnická 10; metro Staroměstská. A proper Czech *pivnice* serving beautifully kept Pilsner Urquell and typical pub grub, very close to the Charles Bridge. Daily 11am–11pm.

U Vejvodů Jilská 4 ⓦ www.restauraceuvejvodu.cz; metro Národní třída. This atmospheric vaulted

▲ Barman pouring a beer

Czech pub menus

In pubs and inexpensive restaurants, the **menu** (*jídelní lístek*), which should be displayed outside, is often in Czech only and deciphering it without a grounding in the language can be quite a feat. Just bear in mind that the general rule is for the right-hand column to list the prices, while the far left column often gives you the estimated weight of every dish in grammes.

The menu is usually divided into various sections beginning with *předkrmy* (starters) or *polévky* (soups), followed by the main courses: *jídla na objednávku* (food to order), *hotová jídla* (ready-made food, which should arrive quickly), *drůbež a ryby* (fowl and fish) and, if you're lucky, *bezmasa* (vegetarian dishes). Side dishes are listed under *přílohy*; puddings, where available, are listed under the heading *moučníky*.

beer hall is now one of Pilsner Urquell's very successful chain of pubs, serving upmarket pub food. Mon–Thurs 10am–3am, Fri & Sat 10am–4am, Sun 10am–2am.

U zlatého tygra (The Golden Tiger) Husova 17; metro Staroměstská. Small central *pivnice* always busy with locals and tourists trying to get a seat; the late writer and bohemian, Bohumil Hrabal, was a semi-permanent resident. Daily 3pm–midnight.

Josefov

For locations see map, p.100.

Barock Pařížská 24 ⓦ www.barockrestaurant .cz; metro Staroměstská. This is the café-bar of choice for the upwardly mobile locals who shop on fashionable Pařížská – the tagline is the cringe-inducing "delicious meal and beautiful women". Daily 10am–1am.

Kolkovna V kolkovně 8 ⓦ www.kolkovna.cz; metro Staroměstská. Justifiably popular with passing tourists, this Pilsner Urquell pub has plush new decor, excellent pub food and unpastuerized Pilsner on tap. Daily 11am–midnight.

Tretter's V kolkovně 3 ⓦ www.tretters.cz; metro Staroměstská. Wonderfully smart and sophis-ticated (but not exclusive) American cocktail bar, with very professional staff and a celebrity air about the place. Live jazz (Tues). Daily 7pm–3am.

Nové Město

For locations see map, p.112.

American Bar Obecní dům, náměstí Republiky 5; metro Náměstí Republiky. Underused and pricey, the bar in the basement of the Obecní dům is nevertheless another archi-tectural treat from 1911. Daily 11am–11pm.

Billiard Centrum V cípu 1 ⓦ www .billiardcentrum.cz; metro Můstek. Den of table football, table tennis, bowling, snooker and pool, with Černá hora beer to quench your thirst. Daily 1pm–2am.

Branický sklípek Vodičkova 26; metro Můstek. Convenient downtown pub (aka *U Purkmistra*) decked out like a pine furniture showroom, serving typical Czech food, and jugs of Prague's Braník beer. The rough and ready *Branická formanka* next door opens and closes earlier. Mon–Fri 9am–11pm, Sat & Sun 11am–11pm.

Bredovský dvůr Politických vězňů 12; metro Můstek/Muzeum. Popular, brick-vaulted city pub, off Wenceslas Square, serving standard pub fare washed down with Pilsner Urquell or Velkopopovický kozel. Mon–Sat 11am–midnight, Sun 11am–11pm.

Novoměstský pivovar Vodičkova 20 ⓦ www .npivovar.cz; metro Národní třída. Microbrewery which serves its own well-tapped misty 11° home brew, plus Czech food, in a series of bright, sprawling modern beer halls. Mon–Fri 10am–11.30pm, Sat 11.30am–11.30pm, Sun noon–10pm.

Pivovarský dům Corner of Lipová/Ječná; metro Karlovo náměstí. Busy micro-brewery dominated by big, shiny copper vats, serving gorgeous light, mixed and dark unfiltered beer (plus banana, coffee and wheat varieties), and standard Czech pub dishes (including the classic pivný sýr). Daily 11am–11.30pm.

Potrefená husa (The Wounded Goose) Jiráskovo náměstí 1; metro Karlovo náměstí. Staropramen's chain of smart pubs, serving decent pub food, have proved very popular; this one's in a cosy, brick-lined cellar near the Tančící dům (Dancing House). Daily 11.30am–1am.

U bubeníčků (The Little Drummer) Myslíkova 8 ⓦ www.ububenicku.cz; metro Karlovo náměstí. Good, unpretentious place to down a few halves of Pilsner Urquell and eat some simple Czech cuisine after visiting the Mánes gallery. Daily 11am–11pm.

U Fleků Křemencova 11 ⓦ www.ufleku.cz; metro Karlovo náměstí. Famous medieval brewery where the unique dark 13° beer, Flek, has been brewed and consumed since 1499. Seats over five hundred German tourists at a go, serves short measures (0.4l), slaps an extra charge on for the music and still you might have to queue to get in. The only reason to visit is to sample the beer, which you're best off doing during the day. Daily 9am–11pm.

U havrana (The Crow) Hálkova 8 ⓦ www.uhavrana.cz; metro I.P. Pavlova. Surprisingly unseedy all-night pub serving food and Kozel beer throughout the night. Mon–Fri 5pm–5am, Sat & Sun 6pm–5am.

U kruhu (The Wheel) Palackého 21; metro Národní třída. Proper Czech pub, serving Plzeň beers and Velkopovický kozel, with its own garden courtyard out front. Mon–Fri 10am–10pm, Sat & Sun 2–10pm.

U Pinkasů Jungmannovo náměstí 16; ⓦ www.upinkasu.cz; metro Můstek. Famous as the pub where Pilsner Urquell was first served in Prague, it still serves excellent unpasteurized beer and classic Czech pub food. Daily 9am–midnight.

Zlatá hvězda (The Golden Star) Ve Smečkách 12 ⓦ www.sportbar.cz; metro Muzeum. The main reason to hit this big, loud pub is to watch the match you want on the numerous satellite TV screens, while quaffing beer and pizza. Mon 11am–midnight, Tues–Thurs 11am–2am, Fri & Sat 11am–3am, Sun noon–midnight.

Vyšehrad and the eastern suburbs

For locations see map, p.134.

🏃 **Akropolis** Kubelíkova 27, Žižkov ⓦ www.palacakropolis.cz; metro Jiřího z Poděbrad. Prague's very popular smoke-filled world music venue is also a great place just to have a drink or a bite to eat as well as listen to live gigs. Daily 7pm–5am.

Demínka Škrétova 1; metro Národní třída. With much of its original grandiose 1880s decor intact – it is Prague's oldest café – Demínka is now run as a pub by Pilsner Urquell, who serve their excellent unpasteurized beer and classic Bohemian cuisine. Daily 11am–11pm.

Hapu Orlická 8, Žižkov; metro Flora. Chilled-out Žižkov cocktail bar without the snooty/ uptight factor, lots of great mixes and comfy sofas in which to sink. Mon–Sat 6pm–2am.

Mu kafé Mánesova 87, Vinohrady; metro Jiřího z Poděbrad. Cool, relaxed vibes at this bare-brick cellar bar with weekend DJs, world music and even improvised theatre. Mon–Fri 1pm–1am, Sat & Sun 1pm–4am.

Pastička (The Mousetrap) Blanická 25, Vinohrady; metro Náměstí Míru. Very popular local Vinohrady pub with cosy wooden booths and a summer beer terrace. Mon–Fri 11am–1am, Sat & Sun 5pm–1am.

Riegrovy sady Riegrovy sady, Vinohrady; metro Jiřího z Poděbrad or tram #11 to Vinohradská tržnice. Unpretentious park café-pub whose beer terrace is popular with the locals. Daily 11am–11pm.

U Houdků Bořivojova 110, Žižkov; tram #5, #9 or #26 to Husinecká. Friendly local pub in the heart of Žižkov with a beer garden, Eggenberg and Budvar on tap and cheap Czech food. Daily 11am–11pm.

U kroka (The Crocodile) Vratislavova 12 Vyšehrad; tram #3, #7, #17 or #21 to Výtoň. Updated Czech pub decor and a "children's corner", but otherwise the usual food and Plzeň beer. Mon–Sat noon–11.30pm, Sun noon–10pm.

U růžového sadu (The Rose Garden) Mánesova 89, Vinohrady ⓦ www.uruzovehosadu.cz; metro Jiřího z Poděbrad. Imaginatively decorated for a Czech pub and perfectly situated if you're visiting the Plečnik Church. Mon–Thurs 10.30am–midnight, Fri & Sat 10.30am–1am, Sun 11.30am–10pm.

🏃 **Zvonařka (The Bell)** Šafaříkova 1, Vinohrady; tram #6 or #11 to Bruselská. The smart modern pub has a summer terrace with great views over the Nuselské schody and Botič valley. Daily 11am–midnight.

Holešovice and the western suburbs

For locations see map, p.146.

🏃 **Fraktal** Šmeralova 1, Holešovice; tram #1, #8, #15, #25 or #26 to Letenské náměstí. Very popular expat cellar bar with ad hoc funky furnishings, exhibitions and occasional live music, plus a beer garden and kids' play area outside. Daily 11am–1am.

Klášterní šenk Markétská 1, Břevnov; tram #15 or #22 to Břevnovský klášter. Smart pub within the precincts of Břevnov's Benedictine monastery, with both a real fire inside and tables out, plus a menu of classic Czech dishes. Daily 11am–11.30pm.

Le Tram Šmeralova 12, Holešovice; tram #1, #8, #15, #25 or #26 to Letenské náměstí. One for the tram enthusiasts: a small, late-night bar decorated with tram seats and notices. Daily 8pm–5am.

Letenský zámeček Letenské sady, Holešovice ⓦ www.letenskyzamecek.cz; tram #1, #8, #15, #25 or #26 to Letenské náměstí. The beer garden, with its great views down the Vltava, is cheap and popular with the locals (the restaurant inside has gone upmarket and is less remarkable). Daily 11am–11.30pm.

Na staré kovárně v Braníku (The Old Black-smith's in Braník) Kamenická 17, Holešovice; tram #1, #8, #15, #25 or #26 to Kamenická. Nicely refurbished pub that's popular with the local youth, with Czech–Mex menu, Plzeň beers and good music. Mon–Sat 11am–1am, Sun 11.30am–11.30pm.

U Bulovky Bulovka 17, Libeň ⓦ www .pivovarubulovky.cz; tram #10, #24 or #25 to Bulovka. Prague's finest microbrewery, run by expat ex-punk František Richter, whose beers are brewed old-style. The pub is way out in the suburbs, but worth the ride. Mon–Thurs 11am–11pm, Fri 11am–midnight, Sat noon–midnight, Sun noon–11pm. Not marked on maps.

U houbaře (The Mushroom) Dukelských hrdinů 30; tram #5 from metro Náměstí Republiky to Veletržní. Comfortable local pub, directly opposite the Veletržní palác, serving Pilsner Urquell and inexpensive Czech pub food. Daily 11am–midnight.

Smíchov

For locations see map, p.159.

Hospoda na verandách Nádražní 90; metro Anděl. The busy Staropramen brewery tap, and therefore the place to taste Prague's most popular beer – try the pub's unique unfiltered yeast beer (*kvasnak*) too. Mon–Thurs & Sun 11am–midnight, Fri & Sat 11am–1am.

Lokalblok náměstí 14 října 10 ⓦ lokalblok.cz; metro Anděl. Groovy modernist bar on the ground floor with a climbing wall in the basement. Mon–Fri 11am–1am, Sat & Sun 4pm–1am.

U buldoka (The Bulldog) Preslova 1 ⓦ www .ubuldoka.cz; metro Anděl. Great, offbeat Smíchov pub serving Gambrinus and classic Czech pub food, with live sport and occasional DJ nights and live music in the psychedelic cellar. Mon–Thurs & Sat 11am–midnight, Fri 11am–1am.

Clubs and live music

A dedicated minority of Praguers, including many of the city's expats and tourists, are keen to party until the wee small hours. The city has a good selection of late-night drinking holes (see chapter 11), but only a handful of dedicated dance **clubs**. What Prague really excels in, however, is in the sheer variety of venues from the quirky to the tacky, which host a whole range of events from DJ nights to all sorts of **live music gigs** from Czech reggae to thrash. In addition, a surprising array of world music bands find their way to Prague, along with some big names from the US and UK (for classical music, opera and theatre see chapter 13). Note that, due to Prague's strict music licensing laws, clubs in residential districts (and that includes much of the city centre) are under constant threat of closure, so don't be surprised if some of those listed below have fallen by the wayside.

Drink **prices** in clubs and venues are inevitably higher than in pubs, but the hike-up is usually relatively modest and entry to most late-night places is rarely extortionate. To find out about the city's up-and-coming events, check the **listings** sections in *Prague Post* or the Czech listings monthly *Culture in Prague/ Česká kultura*, and keep your eyes peeled for flyers and posters. To buy **tickets** in advance, try one of the agencies such as Ticketpro, which has branches all over the city, with outlets in the Staroměstská radnice (Old Town Hall), Staroměstské náměstí, Staré Město (Mon–Fri 9am–6pm, Sat & Sun 9am–5pm; Ⓦwww .ticketpro.cz), as well as at Rytířská 31, Staré Město (Mon–Sat 9am–9pm), and in the Lucerna *pasáž*, Štěpánská 61, Nové Město (Mon–Fri noon–4pm & 4.30–8.30pm).

Clubs and small live venues

Abaton Na Košince 8, Libeň Ⓦwww .prostorabaton.cz; metro Palmovka. Large, cavernous factory venue in the suburbs that hosts some of the city's best raves and gigs.

Akropolis Kubelíkova 27, Žižkov Ⓦwww .palacakropolis.cz; tram #5, #9 or #26 to Lipanská; see map, p.134. This old Art Deco theatre is Žižkov's most popular club venue – it's also a great place to just have a drink or a bite to eat, as well as checking out the DJ nights or the live gigs. Cover charge from 100Kč upwards. Bar Mon–Thurs 11am–12.30am, Fri 11am–1.30am, Sat & Sun 3pm–12.30am. Venue doors open 7pm.

Bunkr Parukářka Olšanské náměstí 40, Žižkov Ⓦwww.parukarka.eu; tram #5, #9 or #26 to Olšanské náměstí; see map, p.134.

Graffiti-covered former Communist nuclear fallout shelter now converted into a club, with a climbing wall and lots of techno tunes. Cover charge from 50Kč upwards. Fri & Sat 9pm–late.

Chapeau Rouge Jakubská 2, Staré Město Ⓦwww.chapeaurouge.cz; metro Náměstí Republiky; see map, p.80. Centrally located, multifloor, good-time club, with a blood-red bar on the ground floor (free entry) and two dancefloors above featuring either DJs or live bands. Cover charge 50–100Kč. Mon– Thurs noon–late, Fri–Sun 4pm–late.

Cross Club Plynární 23, Holešovice Ⓦcrossclub .cz; metro Nádraží Holešovice; see map, p.146. Ad hoc labyrinthine club on several floors, decked out in arty industrial decor, out near Nádraží Holešovice. The DJs on each floor cater to different music tastes from techno to ambient. Cover charge 50–100Kč. Daily 2pm–2am or later.

Futurum Zborovská 7, Smíchov Ⓦ www .musicbar.cz; metro Anděl; see map, p.159. Smíchov's turn-of-the-century Národní dům is the unlikely home of this impressive, hi-tech club which hosts Czech bands and DJs playing anything from retro nights to house. Cover charge 100Kč and upwards. Daily 8pm–1am.

Karlovy lázně Smetanovo nábřeží 198, Staré Město Ⓦ www.karlovylazne.cz; metro Staroměstská; see map, p.80. Mega, hi-tech club on four floors of an old bathhouse by the Charles Bridge; techno on the top floor, progressively more retro as you descend to the café on the ground floor. Cover charge from 50Kč upwards. Daily until 5am.

Klub Lávka Novotného lavka 1, Staré Město Ⓦ www.lavka-nights.cz; metro Staroměstská; see map, p.80. Cheesy disco with go-go girls and a great riverside terrace overlooking the Charles Bridge and the Hrad. Cover charge 100Kč upwards. Daily 10pm–5am.

Lucerna music bar Vodičkova 36, Nové Město Ⓦ www.musicbar.cz; metro Můstek; see map, p.112. Not to be confused with the big venue of the same name, this is an unsophisticated, sweaty cellar bar in the Lucerna *pasáž* that hosts all sorts of gigs as well as themed discos. Cover charge from 100Kč upwards. Daily 8/9pm–3am.

Matrix Koněvova 13, Žižkov Ⓦ www.matrixklub .cz; metro Florenc; see map, p.134. No frills Žižkov club with an inexpensive bar and a basic menu of drum'n'bass and jungle, but whose programme includes everything from live indie bands to heavy metal. Check the website before setting out. Cover charge free–100Kč. Doors open at 8pm.

Mecca U Průhonu 3, Holešovice Ⓦ www .mecca.cz; tram #5, #12 or #15 to U Průhonu; see map, p.146. Out in the grid-plan industrial streets of Prague 7, this coolly converted factory is one of the most impressive, professional and popular clubs in Prague. Café/restaurant Mon–Thurs 10am–11pm, Fri & Sat 10am–6am; club Mon–Thurs 8pm–2am, Fri & Sat 8pm–6am.

N11 Národní třída 11, Nové Město Ⓦ www.n11 .cz; metro Národní třída; see map, p.112. Funky, medium-sized, central club with several bars, a reasonable restaurant, a decent sound system and DJs who play a whole range of dance tunes from hip-hop to

Latin, plus the occasional live act. Cover charge free–150Kč. Tues–Thurs & Sun 8pm–4am, Fri & Sat 7pm–5am.

Nebe (Heaven) Křemencova 10, Nové Město Ⓦ www.nebepraha.cz; metro Národní třída; see map, p.112. A simple formula: a brick-vaulted cocktail bar with a reasonably priced drinks menu and DJs that pump out dance music from the last three or four decades. Cover charge 70–150Kč. Tues–Sat 8pm–4am.

Popocafépetl @ Újezd Újezd 19, Malá Strana Ⓦ www.popocafepetl.cz; tram #12, 20 or #22 to Hellichova; see map, p.66. Part of a chain of popular cafés, this one is slightly different as it has a dancefloor – the programme ranges from DJs spinning retro dance hits to live gypsy bands and Latino nights. Cover charge free–100Kč. Daily 4pm–late.

Radost FX Bělehradská 120, Vinohrady Ⓦ www.radostfx.cz; metro I.P. Pavlova; see map, p.134. This spacious, comfortable club is the longest-running all-round dance venue in Prague, with house and techno keeping the expats happy. Cover charge 150–250Kč. Thurs–Sat 10pm–4am.

Roxy Dlouhá 33, Staré Město Ⓦ www.roxy .cz; metro náměstí Republiky; see map, p.80. The centrally located *Roxy* is a great little venue: a laid-back, rambling old theatre with an interesting programme of events from arty films and exhibitions to exceptional live acts and top DJ nights. Cover charge free–400Kč. Daily from 7pm.

SaSaZu Bubenské nábřeží 38, Holešovice Ⓦ www.sasazu.cz; metro Vltavská; see map, p.146. Prague's biggest, slickest, newest venue is housed in Holešovice's vast market complex and includes a pan-Asian restaurant, a major venue for live gigs and a nightclub.

Sedm vlků (Seven Wolves) Vlkova 7, Žižkov Ⓦ www.sedmvlku.cz; tram #5, #9 or #26 from metro náměstí Republiky to Husinecká; see map, p.134. Club-bar with a penchant for reggae, hard house, techno and drum 'n' bass whose resident DJs make the most of the impressive sound system. No cover charge. Mon–Sat 5pm–3am.

Studio 54 Hybernská 38, Nové Město; metro Náměstí Republiky; see map, p.112. This late-late dance venue is a useful place to know about if you want the night to continue well into the early hours. Cover charge 100Kč. Thurs 5am–9am, Sat & Sun 5am–1pm.

U vystřeleného oka (The Shot-Out Eye) U božích bojovníků 3, Žižkov ⓦ www.uvoka.cz; tram #5, #9 or #26 to Lipanská; see map, p.134. Big, loud, smoky, heavy-drinking pub just south of Žižkov Hill, off Husitská, with unusually good (occasionally live) indie rock playing and lashings of Měšťan beer, plus absinthe chasers. Free entry. Mon–Sat 4.30pm–1am.

Újezd Újezd 18, Malá Strana; tram #6, #9, #12, #20 or #22 to Újezd; see map, p.66. Long-standing, popular indie venue with a very small stage and a very smoky atmosphere. Free entry. Daily until 4am.

Vertigo Havelská 4, Staré Město ⓦ www.vertigo -club.cz; metro Můstek; see map, p.80. Very central club with a decent dancefloor and sound system, and an eclectic rota of themed nights. Free entry. Daily until 4am.

XT3 Rokycanova 29, Žižkov ⓦ www.xt3.cz; tram #5, #9 or #26 to Lipanská; see map, p.134. A young Czech crowd flock to this Žižkov club for the mix of cheap beer, hip-hop, reggae and live music. Cover charge 50–100Kč. Daily until 3am.

Large live venues

Kongresové centrum Praha (Prague Congress Centre) 5 května 65, Vyšehrad ⓦ www.kcp.cz; metro Vyšehrad; see map, p.134. Revamped (but still very ugly) 1970s concrete monstrosity used for the old Communist Party congresses.

Lucerna Vodičkova 36, Nové Město ⓦ www .lucpra.com; metro Můstek; see map, p.112. Without doubt the best venue in Prague, a gilded turn-of-the-century ballroom with balconies, situated in the Lucerna *pasáž*.

Malostranská beseda Malostranské náměstí 21, Malá Strana ⓦ www.malostranska-beseda.cz; tram #12, #20 or #22 to Malostranské náměstí; see map, p.66. Malá Strana's old town hall attracts lots of Czechs, due to its long history. The programme is a great mixture of rock, roots and jazz. Cover charge from 100Kč upwards. Gigs usually start at 8.30pm.

O2 Arena Ocelářská 2, Libeň ⓦ www.o2arena .cz; metro Českomoravská. 18,000-capacity indoor arena used for ice hockey and big-name US and UK artists from Madonna to Mötley Crüe.

Strahovský stadion Strahovská, Břevnov; bus #176 from metro Karlovo náměstí; see map, p.144. The largest stadium in the world can hold an incredible 250,000 spectators so you're only going to see the like of the Stones here.

Tesla Arena Za elektrárnou 1, Bubeneč ⓦ www .tesla-arena.cz; tram #5, #12, #14 or #17 to Výstaviště; see map, p.146. The sponsors may change, but the awful acoustics don't, at this ice hockey stadium, which doubles as one of Prague's biggest indoor venues.

Výstaviště (Exhibition Grounds) U Výstaviště, Holešovice ⓣ 266 727 411; tram #5, #12, #14 or #17 to Výstaviště; see map, p.146. The 1891 Exhibition Hall at Výstaviště is an atmospheric aircraft hangar of a place to watch a band, even if the acoustics aren't up to much.

Jazz clubs

Prague has a surprisingly long indigenous jazz tradition, and is home to a handful of good jazz clubs. With little money to attract acts from abroad, the artists are almost exclusively Czech and tend to do virtually the entire round of venues each month. The one exception is *AghaRTA*, which attracts a few big names each year. More often than not it's a good idea to book a table – particularly *AghaRTA* and *Reduta*.

AghaRTA Jazz Centrum Železná 16, Staré Město ⓣ 222 211 275, ⓦ www.agharta.cz;

▲ *AghaRTA Jazz Centrum*

metro Můstek; see map, p.80. Probably the best jazz club in Prague, with a good mix of Czechs and foreigners and a consistently good programme of gigs, plus a round-the-year festival that brings in some top acts. Cover charge 250Kč. Daily 7pm–1am.

Blues sklep Liliová 9, Staré Město ☎774 624 677, Ⓦwww.bluessklep.cz; metro Staroměstská; see map, p.80. Old town cellar club that puts on live jazz, flamenco, ragtime and blues from 9pm to midnight. Cover charge 250Kč. Daily 7pm–2.30am.

Charles Bridge Jazz Club Saská 3, Malá Strana ☎257 220 820, Ⓦwww.jazzblues.cz; tram #12, #20 or #22 to Malostranské náměstí; see map, p.66. The city's priciest jazz venue pulls in lots of tourists due to its central venue, but puts on a decent selection of music nevertheless, with the emphasis on jazz and funk. Daily 7pm–midnight.

Jazz Dock Janáčkovo nábřeží 2, Smíchov ☎774 058 838, Ⓦwww.jazzdock.cz; tram #6, #9, #12 or #20 to Švandovo divadlo; see map, p.159. Floating jazz bar with ten-metre long bar and river views. Gigs begin around 10pm,

with jam sessions afterwards and Dixieland on Sundays. Cover charge 150Kč. Daily 11am–4am.

Reduta Národní 20, Nové Město ☎224 933 487, Ⓦwww.redutajazzclub.cz; metro Národní třída; see map, p.112. Prague's best-known jazz club – Bill Clinton played his sax here in front of Havel – obviously attracts a very touristy crowd, but also some decent acts. Gigs daily from 9.30pm; box office open from 3pm.

U malého Glena (Little Glen's) Karmelitská 23, Malá Strana ☎257 531 717, Ⓦwww.malyglen .cz; tram #12, #20 or #22 to Malostranské náměstí; see map, p.66. Tiny downstairs stage worth checking out for its eclectic mix of Latin jazz, be-bop and blues. Live music 9.30pm–1am.

U staré paní (The Old Lady) Michalská 9, Staré Město ☎224 228 090, Ⓦwww.jazzlounge.cz; metro Můstek or Národní třída; see map, p.80. Cellar club but with modern decor, the programme here ranges from blues and cool jazz to Latin and big band. Cover charge 100–250Kč. Daily 7pm–2am. Live music starts at 9pm.

Gay and lesbian Prague

Prague has a small but well-established **gay and lesbian scene**, with its spiritual heart in leafy Vinohrady and neighbouring Žižkov. For up-to-date listings check out Ⓦprague.gayguide.net and Ⓦwww.praguesaints.cz. You'll also find useful flyers at the places listed below. For a gay-friendly place to stay *Arco* (see p.183) is a good option.

Alcatraz Bořivojova 58, Žižkov ☎222 711 458, Ⓦklubalcatraz.webnode.cz; tram #5, #9 or #26 to Lipanská; see map, p.134. A rubber and leather cellar club with dark-rooms and glory holes and much more besides. Entry 80Kč. Daily 9pm–4am.

Babylonia Martinská 6, Staré Město ☎224 232 304, Ⓦwww.saunababylonia.cz; metro Národní třída; see map, p.80. Prague's most centrally located gay sauna, with steam baths, pools and massage on offer. Entry 200–300Kč. Daily 2pm–3am.

Bar 21 Římská 21, Vinohrady ☎724 254 048; metro Náměstí Míru; see map, p.134. Small local gay club-bar in a cosy Vinohrady cellar. Entry free. Daily 4pm–4am.

Drake's Zborovská 50, Smíchov ☎257 326 828, Ⓦwww.drakes.cz; tram #6, #9, #12, #20 or #22 to Újezd; see map, p.159. Very cruisey, labyrinthine gay club with lots of late-night

action, strip shows and dark rooms. Entry 500Kč. Open 24hr.

FenoMan Blanická 28, Vinohrady ☎603 740 263, Ⓦwww.fenomanclub.cz; metro Náměstí Míru; see map, p.134. Small cellar bar-club in the Vinohrady gay quarter attracting a mostly local crowd, but with a very useful late licence. Entry free. Mon, Tues, Thurs & Sun 5pm–5am, Wed, Fri & Sat 5pm–9am.

Friends Bartolomějská 11, Staré Město ☎224 236 772; metro Národní třída; see map, p.80. Mixed gay cellar club-bar in the centre of the old town, with regular Friday lesbian nights. Daily 6pm–3am.

JampaDampa V tůních 10, Nové Město ☎739 592 099, Ⓦwww.jampadampa.cz; metro Muzeum or I.P. Pavlova; see map, p.112. Currently the city's most popular and friendly lesbian café/club, with dancing and karaoke and other one-off events. Café daily 4pm–late; club 10pm–late.

Piano Bar Milešovská 10, Žižkov ☎ 222 727 496, ⓦ www.pianobar.sweb.cz; metro Jiřího z Poděbrad; see map, p.134. Relaxed bar with billiards, a piano and an older, mostly gay, mostly local crowd. Daily 5pm–midnight.

The Saints Polská 32, Vinohrady ☎ 222 250 326, ⓦ www.praguesaints.cz; metro Náměstí Míru or Jiřího z Poděbrad; see map, p.134. Small gay bar run by British expats that attracts an older gay crowd (both genders) – a good place to go if you want to find out about the scene. Daily 7pm–4am.

Termix Třebízského 4a, Vinohrady ☎ 222 710 462, ⓦ www.club-termix.cz; metro Jiřího z Poděbrad; see map, p.134. Stylish mixed gay/lesbian club, with lots of dancing, as well as chill-out and dark rooms. Entry free. Wed–Sun 8pm–5am.

Tingl Tangl Karoliny Světlé 12, Staré Město ☎ 224 238 278, ⓦ www.tingltangl.cz; tram #6, #9, #17, #18, #21 or #22 to Národní divadlo; see map, p.80. Bar/club/restaurant with regular drag acts followed by DJs. Mon–Sat 8pm–5am. Entry free. Cabaret Wed, Fri & Sat 9.30pm; 250Kč.

U Rudolfa Mezibranská 3, Nové Město ☎ 605 872 492; metro Muzeum; see map, p.112. Straightforward Czech gay pub just off Wenceslas Square. Mon–Fri 2pm–2am, Sat & Sun 4pm–2am.

Valentino Vinohradská 40, Vinohrady ☎ 222 513 491, ⓦ www.club-valentino.cz; metro Náměstí Míru; see map, p.134. Easily the city's biggest, most popular gay club, with two dancefloors, two dark rooms, four bars and outdoor tables in the summer. Entry free. Daily 11am–late.

CLUBS AND LIVE MUSIC | Gay and lesbian Prague

The arts

A longside the city's numerous cafés, pubs and clubs, there's a rich **cultural life** in Prague. **Classical music** is everywhere in the city, especially in the summer, when the streets, churches, palaces, opera houses, concert halls and even the gardens are filled with the strains of music. Mozart had strong links with the city, and of course the Czechs themselves produced four top-drawer classical composers. In addition, Prague boasts three opera houses, five excellent orchestras and a couple of festivals that attract top-class international artists.

Even if you don't understand Czech, the **theatre** scene here is so diverse that there's usually something worth catching aimed at an English-speaking audience. For a start, Prague has a strong tradition of mime, "black light theatre" (see p.211) and puppetry. As for **film**, many cinemas show movies in their original language, and new Czech films often get a showing with English subtitles. Rock, pop and jazz gigs are covered in the previous chapter.

Prague has an impressive array of **art galleries** housing the country's permanent collection from medieval to contemporary art, as well as staging temporary blockbuster exhibitions. In a photogenic city like Prague, it may come as little surprise that the city also boasts an impressive roster of **photography** galleries.

Tickets

If you can obtain **tickets online** or from the box office (*pokladna*) of the venue concerned, then all well and good. If a performance is sold out (*vyprodáno*), stand-by tickets are often available at the venue around an hour before the start of the performance. Alternatively, you may still be able to get a ticket from one of the city's numerous **ticket agencies** such as Ticketpro (Ⓦwww.ticketpro.cz) which has branches all over the city, with outlets in the Staroměstská radnice (Old Town Hall), Staroměstské náměstí, Staré Město (Mon–Fri 9am–6pm, Sat & Sun 9am–5pm; Ⓦwww.ticketpro.cz), as well as at Rytířská 31, Staré Město (Mon–Sat 9am–9pm), and in the Lucerna *pasáž*, Štěpánská 61, Nové Město (Mon–Fri noon–4pm & 4.30–8.30pm). Ticket **prices**, with a few notable exceptions, are good value, ranging between 200Kč and 600Kč.

Listings and information

The English-language **listings** in *Prague Post* (Ⓦwww.praguepost.com) are selective, but they do at least pick out the events that may be of particular interest to the non-Czech speaker, and list all the major venues and their addresses. Also in English is the monthly handout *Culture in Prague* (Ⓦwww.ceskakultura.cz) – published in Czech as *Česká kultura* – available from any PIS office (see p.38).

Classical music, opera and ballet

Folk songs lie at the heart of Czech music and have found their way into much of the country's traditional repertoire of **classical music**, of which the Czechs are justifiably proud, having produced four composers of international stature – Dvořák, Janáček, Smetana and Martinů – and a fifth, Mahler, who, though German-speaking, was born in Bohemia. If the music of Mozart appears rather too often in the city's monthly concert programme, it's partly because the tourists love him, but also because of his special relationship with Prague (see p.65).

The city boasts three large-scale theatres where opera is regularly staged, and has several resident orchestras, the most illustrious of which are the **Czech Philharmonic** (Česká filharmonie), which is based at the Rudolfinum, and the **Prague Symphony Orchestra** (Symfonický orchestr hl. m. Prahy), whose home is the Smetanova síň in the Obecní dům. The country continues to produce top-class conductors, a host of singers and virtuoso violinists, and the city's musical heritage (and outstanding beauty) ensures a regular supply of international stars.

By far the biggest annual event is the Pražské jaro or **Prague Spring** festival (see p.32), the country's most prestigious **international music** festival. The main venues are listed below, but keep an eye out for concerts in the city's churches and palaces, gardens and courtyards (the main ones are listed separately below); evening performances tend to start fairly early, either at 5pm or 7pm. All the major venues close down for most of July and August.

The major venues

Národní divadlo (National Theatre) Národní 2, Nové Město ☎ 224 901 448, ⓦ www.narodni -divadlo.cz; metro Národní třída. Prague's grandest nineteenth-century theatre is the living embodiment of the Czech national revival movement, and continues to put on a wide variety of mostly, though by no means exclusively, Czech plays, plus opera and ballet. Worth visiting for the decor alone. The Nová scéna is the theatre's modern second stage. Some productions have English surtitles. Box office daily 10am–6pm.

Obecní dům – Smetanova síň náměstí Republiky 5, Nové Město ☎ 222 002 101, ⓦ www.obecni -dum.cz; metro Náměstí Republiky. This fantastically ornate Art Nouveau concert hall is where the Prague Spring festival usually kicks off, and is also home to the excellent Prague Symphony Orchestra (ⓦ www.fok .cz). Box office daily 10am–6pm.

Rudolfinum Alšovo nábřeží 12, Staré Město ☎ 227 059 352, ⓦ www.rudolfinum.cz; metro Staroměstská. A truly stunning neo-Renaissance concert hall from the late nineteenth century that's home base for the Czech Philharmonic (ⓦ www.ceskafilharmonie.cz). The Dvořákova síň is the large hall; the Sukova síň is the chamber concert hall. Box office Mon–Fri 10am–6pm.

Státní opera Praha (Prague State Opera) Wilsonova 4, Nové Město ☎ 224 227 266, ⓦ www.opera.cz; metro Muzeum. A sumptuous nineteenth-century opera house, built by the city's German community, which once attracted star conductors such as Mahler and Zemlinsky. Nowadays, it's the number two venue for

▲ Stavovské divadlo

opera. Most productions have English surtitles Box office Mon–Fri 10am–5.30pm, Sat & Sun 10am–noon & 1–5.30pm.
Stavovské divadlo (Estates Theatre) Ovocný trh 1, Staré Město ☎224 902 322, ⓦwww .narodni-divadlo.cz; metro Můstek. Prague's oldest opera house, which witnessed the premiere of Mozart's *Don Giovanni*, hosts a mixture of opera, ballet and straight theatre (with simultaneous headphone translation available). Some productions have English surtitles. Box office daily 10am–6pm.

Concert venues

Anežský klášter (Convent of sv Anežka) U milosrdných 17, Staré Město ☎221 879 270; metro Náměstí Republiky. This branch of the Národní galerie puts on regular chamber concerts, often featuring music by the big

four Czech composers, in the convent's atmospheric Gothic chapel (see p.94).
Atrium na Žižkově Čajkovského 12, Žižkov; ☎221 721 838; tram #5, #9 or #26 to Lipanská. A most unlikely location, this Baroque chapel sits deep in the heart of Žižkov, staging a regular (though not daily) programme of chamber music.
Bazilika sv Jakub (St James) Malá Štupartská 6, Staré Město ☎224 828 816; metro Náměstí Republiky. Choral church music, sung Mass and Prague's finest organ, used for regular recitals (see Church of sv Jakub, p.93).
Chrám sv Mikuláše (St Nicholas) Staroměstské náměstí, Staré Město ☎224 190 994; metro Staroměstská. This whitewashed Baroque church on the edge of Staroměstské náměstí, used for singing recitals and choral concerts, should not be confused with the

Cultural institutes

The various national cultural institutions put on a wide variety of artistic offerings throughout the year.
Austrian Cultural Institute (Rakouský kulturní fórum) Jungmannovo náměstí 18, Nové Město ☎221 181 777, ⓦwww.beia.gv.at/kultur/prag; metro Můstek. Very good exhibitions of Austrian art, plus the odd concert, film and talk. Gallery Mon–Fri 10am–5pm.
British Council (Britská rada) Bredovský dvůr, Politických vězňů 13, Nové Město ☎221 991 160, ⓦwww.britishcouncil.cz; metro Můstek/Muzeum. Various lectures and events all year, plus temporary exhibitions, newspapers, magazines and a reading room. Mon–Thurs 8am–8pm, Fri 8am–5pm, Sat 8.30am–1pm.
Goethe Institut Masarykovo nábřeží 32, Nové Město ☎221 962 111, ⓦwww.goethe .de/prag; metro Národní třída. Weekly film showings and more frequent lectures; small exhibition space and library. Tues–Fri 1–7pm, Sat 10am–2pm.
Hungarian Cultural Centre (Maďarské kulturní středisko) Rytířská 25–27, Staré Město ☎224 222 424, ⓦwww.magyarintezet.hu; metro Můstek. Weekly film showings and regular exhibitions and concerts. Mon–Thurs 10am–6pm, Fri 10am–2pm.
Institut Français (Francouzský institut) Štěpánská 35, Nové Město ☎221 401 011, ⓦwww.ifp.cz; metro Muzeum. Great exhibitions and a great café, with croissants and *journaux*. Also puts on screenings of classic French films, plus lectures and even the odd concert. *Café 35* (see p.194): Mon–Fri 8.30am–8pm, Sat 10am–2pm.
Instituta Italiana di Cultura (Italský kulturní institut) Šporkova 14, Malá Strana ☎257 090 681, ⓦwww.iic-praga.cz; tram #12 #20 or #22 to Malostranské náměstí. Exhibitions, films and events are staged in various locations including the wonderful Baroque chapel on Vlašská. Mon–Fri 9am–1pm & 3–6pm, Fri 9am–1pm.
Instituto Cervantes (Španělské kulturní centrum) Na Rybníčku 6, Nové Město ☎221 595 211, ⓦpraga.cervantes.es; metro I.P. Pavlova. Regular programme of concerts and films in Spanish, plus a library. Tues & Thurs 9.30am–12.30pm & 1.30–7pm, Wed 12.30–7pm, Fri & Sat 9.30am–2pm.
Polish Institute (Polský institut) Malé náměstí 1, Staré Město ☎224 214 708, ⓦwww .polskyinstitut.cz; metro Muzeum. Weekly film showings, occasional concerts and lectures. Mon–Thurs 10am–5pm, Fri 10am–3pm.

church of the same dedication in Malá Strana. (see Church of sv Mikuláš, p.90).

Kostel sv Mikuláše (St Nicholas) Malostranské náměstí, Malá Strana ☎257 534 215; tram #12 #20 or #22 to Malostranské náměstí. Prague's most sumptuous Baroque church is the perfect setting for choral concerts and organ recitals (see Church of sv Mikuláš, p.68).

Kostel sv Šimona a Judy (St Simon & Jude) Dušní, Staré Město ☎222 321 352; metro Náměstí Republiky. Deconsecrated *trompe l'oeil* church, where the Prague Symphony Orchestra runs chamber music concerts.

Lichtenštejnský palác (Liechtenstein Palace) Malostranské náměstí 13, Malá Strana ☎257 534 206; metro Malostranská. The Czech Academy of Music (HAMU) lives here (see p.65) and puts on chamber concerts and string quartets inside and out in the courtyard.

Lobkovický palác (Lobkowicz Palace) Jiřská 3, Hradčany ☎233 311 925, ⓦwww .lobkowiczevents.cz; metro Malostranská. Baroque and Renaissance concerts are held in the palace's main, frescoed hall at the eastern edge of Prague Castle (see p.55).

Pražský hrad (Prague Castle) Hradčany ☎224 373 424, ⓦwww.kulturanahrade.cz; tram #22 to Pražský hrad. There's a regular and varied music programme laid on at the castle, using venues ranging from the Renaissance Míčovna (Ball Game Court) in the Královská zahrada (Royal Gardens) to the spectacularly ornate Španělský sál (Spanish Hall).

Zrcadlová kaple (Mirrored Chapel) Klementinum, Mariánské náměstí, Staré Město ☎221 663 111; metro Staroměstská. Regular chamber and organ concerts held in the Klementinum's beautifully atmospheric pink Baroque chapel of mirrors (see p.86).

Theatre

Theatre (*divadlo*) has always had a special place in Czech culture – after all, the first post-Communist Czech president, Václav Havel, was a playwright – and the theatre scene continues to thrive. With a steady supply of tourists and expats as potential audience, there are now several English-language theatre companies based in Prague. Ticket prices start at around 100Kč and are available online or from the venues themselves, or for considerably more from the ticket agencies listed on p.208.

Prague also has a strong tradition of **mime** and "**Černé divadlo**" or "black light theatre" (visual trickery created by "invisible" actors dressed all in black), ranging from the classical style of the late Ladislav Fialka and his troupe to the more experimental work of Boris Polívka. However, along with Prague's long-running multimedia company, Laterna magika, many of these shows are now deliberately geared towards tourists, and can make for disappointing viewing.

Puppet theatre (*loutkové divadlo*) also has a long indigenous folk tradition, as an art form for both adults and children, and is thriving partly thanks to its accessibility to non-Czech audiences. Avoid the never-ending performances of Mozart's *Don Giovanni* in period costume, specifically aimed at passing tourists, and sample one of the other companies instead. Unfortunately, few theatres maintain the traditional puppets-only set-up, instead featuring live actors in their productions, many of which can be very wordy, making the shows less accessible if you don't speak the language.

Selected theatres

The Stavovské divadlo (see p.94) and the Národní divadlo (p.124) both put on plays as well as opera and ballet. Below is a selection of Prague's other main theatres.

Alfred ve dvoře Fr Křížka 36, Holešovice ☎233 376 997, ⓦwww.alfredvedvore.cz; tram #12, #14 or #17 to Veletržní. Experimental theatre founded in 1997 by mime theatre guru, Ctibor Turba; puts on non-verbal and mime performances and also hosts occasional student dramas. Tickets available in advance from Divadlo v Celetné, Celetná 17 (Mon–Fri 10am–7.30pm, Sat & Sun noon–7.30pm).

Black Light Theatre of Prague (Černé divadlo Jiřího Srnce) Reduta, Národní 20, Nové Město ☎602 291 572, ⓦwww.blacktheatresrnec.cz;

metro Národní třída. One of the founders of Laterna magika and inventors of "black light" theatre, Jiří Srnec puts on shows, some of which are a cut above the competition. Box office daily 10am–6pm.

Divadlo Archa Na poříčí 26, Nové Město ☎ 221 716 333, ⓦ www.archatheatre.cz; metro Florenc. By far the most exciting, innovative venue in Prague, with two very versatile spaces, plus an art gallery and a café. The programming includes music, dance and theatre, with an emphasis on new and experimental work. English subtitles or translation often available. Box office Mon–Fri 10am–6pm, plus 2hr before performance.

Divadlo Image Pařížská 4, Staré Město ☎ 222 329 191, ⓦ www.imagetheatre.cz; metro Staroměstská. One of the more innovative and entertaining of Prague's ubiquitous "black light theatre" venues. Box office Mon–Fri 9am–8pm, Sat & Sun 10am–8pm.

Divadlo na zábradlí Anenské náměstí 5, Staré Město ☎ 222 868 868, ⓦ www.nazabradli.cz; metro Staroměstská. Václav Havel's old haunt and a centre of absurdist theatre back in the 1960s, the Divadlo na zábradlí is still a provocative rep theatre, with a wide variety of shows (in Czech) and a lively bar. Box office Mon–Fri 2–8pm, Sat & Sun 2hr before performance.

Duncan Centre Branická 41, Braník ☎ 244 461 342, ⓦ www.duncanct.cz; tram #3, #17 or #21 to Přístaviště. Occasional dance performances by resident and visiting artists at this theatre based in a school for contemporary dance in the southern suburb of Braník.

Laterna magika (Magic Lantern) Nová scéna, Národní 4, Nové Město ☎ 224 931 482, ⓦ www.laterna.cz; metro Národní třída. The National Theatre's Nová scéna, one of Prague's most modern and versatile stages, is the main base for Laterna magika, founders of multi-media and "black light" theatre way back in 1958. Their slick productions continue effortlessly to pull in crowds of tourists. Box office daily 10am–6pm.

Ponec Husitská 24a, Žižkov ☎ 222 721 531, ⓦ www.divadloponec.cz; metro Hlavní nádraží

or Florenc. Former cinema, now an innovative dance venue and centre for the annual Tanec Praha dance festival in May/June. Box office Mon–Fri 5–8pm and 1hr before performance.

Roxy – NoD Dlouhá 33, Staré Město ☎ 222 826 330, ⓦ nod.roxy.cz; metro Náměstí Republiky. Experimental (and often very quirky) theatre staged on the first floor of the Roxy cultural complex. Box office daily 10am–6am.

Švandovo divadlo Štefánikova 57, Smíchov ☎ 257 318 666, ⓦ www.svandovodivadlo.cz; tram #6, #9, #12 or #20 to Švandovo divadlo. Pioneering, exciting and experimental, Švandova is a great place to sample the Prague theatre scene; all productions are in Czech (with English surtitles), there's a great bar and often gigs too. Box office Mon–Fri 11am–2pm & 2.30–7pm, Sat & Sun 5–7pm.

Puppet theatre

Divadlo minor Vodičkova 6, Nové Město ☎ 222 231 351, ⓦ www.minor.cz; metro Karlovov náměstí. The former state puppet theatre puts on children's shows most days, plus adult shows on occasional evenings – sometimes with English subtitles. Box office Mon–Fri 10am–1.30pm & 2.30–8pm, Sat & Sun 11am–8pm.

Divadlo Spejbla a Hurvínka Dejvická 38, Dejvice ☎ 224 316 784, ⓦ www.spejbl-hurvinek.cz; metro Dejvická/Hradčanská. Features the indomitable marionette duo, Spejbl and Hurvínek, created by Josef Skupa at one of the few puppets-only theatres in the country. Box office Tues–Fri 10am–2pm & 3–6pm, Sat & Sun 1–5pm.

Národní divadlo marionet Žatecká 1, Staré Město ☎ 222 324 565, ⓦ www.riseloutek.cz; metro Staroměstská. This company's rather dull marionette version of Mozart's *Don Giovanni* (ⓦ www.mozart.cz) has been going for years, but it also puts on more interesting kids' shows at the weekends. Box office Wed 3.30–6pm and 1hr before performance.

Film

The **cinema** (*kino*) remains relatively inexpensive (around 100–150Kč a ticket) and popular in Prague. Hollywood blockbusters form a large part of the weekly schedule, but the Czech film industry continues to chug along, turning out films that do well domestically, and occasionally even achieving international distribution. Foreign films are more often than not shown in their original language with subtitles (*titulky*) – beware dubbing (*dabing*) and live translation (*s překl*). And thanks to Prague's large expat community, some Czech films are occasionally shown with English subtitles – for a comprehensive rundown of the week's films, see the monthly *Culture in Prague/Česká kultura* (Ⓦ www.ceskakultura.cz). Film titles are nearly always translated into Czech, so you'll need to have your wits about you to identify films such as *Užívej si, co to jde* as Woody Allen's *Whatever Works*.

The city's main **cinemas** have traditionally been concentrated around Wenceslas Square. The list below is confined to the best screens, plus Prague's art-house film clubs, where you may need to buy an annual membership card (*roční legitimace*) in order to purchase tickets. Keep a look out, too, for films shown at the various foreign cultural institutions around town (see p.210), and for the summer-only open-air *letní kino*, which is held on the Střelecký ostrov (Ⓦ www.letnak.cz). The nearest Prague comes to a film festival is the annual **Days of European Film** (Ⓦ www.eurofilmfest.cz), which takes place over two weeks in April.

Aero Biskupcova 31, Žižkov ☎ 271 771 349, Ⓦ www.kinoaero.cz; tram #9, #10, #16 or #19 to Biskupcova. Crumbling art-house cinema that shows rolling mini-festivals, retrospectives and independent movies. They also run Bio Oko in Holešovice and Světozor, just off Wenceslas Square in Nové Město.

Bio Konvikt – Ponrepo Bartolomějská 11, Staré Město ☎ 226 211 866, Ⓦ www.bio-ponrepo.cz; metro Národní třída. Really old classics from the black-and-white era, dug out from the National Film Archives. Membership cards (150Kč) can only be bought Mon–Fri 3–6pm, and you need to bring a photo.

Evald Národní 28, Nové Město ☎ 221 105 225, Ⓦ www.cinemart.cz; metro Národní třída. Prague's most centrally located art-house cinema shows a discerning selection of new releases interspersed with plenty of classics.

Kino MAT Karlovo náměstí 19, Nové Město ☎ 224 915 765, Ⓦ www.mat.cz; metro Karlovo náměstí. Tiny café and cinema popular with the film crowd, with an eclectic programme of shorts, documentaries and Czech films with English subtitles. Entrance is on Odborů.

Lucerna Vodičkova 36, Nové Město ☎ 224 216 972, Ⓦ www.lucerna.cz; metro Můstek. Without doubt the most ornate commercial cinema in Prague, with the best café-bar, all decked out in Moorish style by Havel's grandfather, in the *pasáž* the family once owned.

Palace – Slovanský dům Na příkopě 22, Nové Město ☎ 257 181 212, Ⓦ www.palacecinemas.cz; metro Můstek. The most central of Prague's new multiplex cinemas – it regularly shows new Czech releases with English subtitles.

The visual arts

The Národní galerie (National Gallery) or NG runs the city's main **permanent art collections**, in the Anežský klášter, Jiřský klášter, palác Kinských, Schwarzenberský palác, Šternberský palác and Veletržní palác, each of which is described in detail in the guide section. Most of these galleries also give over space for **temporary exhibitions**, and there are several others which only ever stage special exhibitions. *Prague Post* has selective listings, and there's a list of foreign cultural institutes, which also put on regular exhibitions (see p.210), but as ever you'll find the fullest listings in the Czech monthly listings magazine *Culture in Prague/Česká kultura*.

Dozens of **commercial galleries** have sprung up in the past twenty years or so, only a handful of which can be relied on regularly to show interesting stuff; below is a selection of the best. Look out, too for the various **Prague Biennales** – the city has, in the past, staged more than one in a single year. As in Venice, but on a fraction of the budget, the exhibitions attract contemporary artists and curators from all over the world.

Exhibition spaces

České muzeum výtvarných umění (Czech Museum of Fine Art) Husova 19–21, Staré Město ⓦ www.cmvu.cz; metro Staroměstská. Showcases retrospectives of twentieth-century Czech and (occasionally) foreign artists. Tues–Sun 10am–6pm.

DOX Poupětova 1, Holešovice ⓦ www .doxprague.org; tram #5, #12, #15, to Ortenovo náměstí. Big, new, privately financed contemporary art gallery housed in a former metal factory in the industrial east side of Holešovice – expect lots of interesting and provocatively entitled shows. Mon 10am–6pm, Wed–Fri 11am–7pm, Sat & Sun 10am–6pm.

Dům U kamenného zvonu Staroměstské náměstí 13, Staré Město ⓦ www.ghmp.cz; metro Staroměstská. The Prague City Gallery puts on a real range of Czech retrospectives, from Baroque to avant garde, in the small Gothic rooms and courtyard of this ancient building (see p.91). Tues–Sun 10am–6pm.

Galerie Hollar Smetanovo nábřeží 6, Staré Město ⓦ www.hollar.cz; metro Národní třída. The main exhibition space for Czech graphic artists is situated on the noisy river embankment, but there are plenty of old prints for sale. Tues–Sun 10am–1pm & 2–6pm.

Galerie Jaroslava Fragnera Betlémské náměstí 5a, Staré Město ⓦ www.gjf.cz; metro Národní třída. Small gallery that puts on exhibitions on an architectural theme. Tues–Sun 10am–6pm.

Mánes Masarykovo nábřeží 250, Nové Město; ⓦ www.galeriemanes.cz; tram #17 or #21/metro Karlovo náměstí. White functionalist building spanning a channel in the Vltava, with an open-plan gallery and a tradition of excellent exhibitions of contemporary art and photography. Tues–Sun 10am–6pm.

Městská knihovna (Municipal Library) Mariánské náměstí 1, Staré Město ⓦ www .citygalleryprague.cz; metro Staroměstská. Exhibitions at this central Prague City Gallery space are usually devoted to Czech or central European artists and photographers and are well worth checking out. Tues–Sun 10am–6pm.

Obecní dům náměstí Republiky 5, Nové Město ⓦ www.obecni-dum.cz; metro Náměstí Republiky. Exhibitions on a *fin de siècle* theme in the luscious surroundings of the Art Nouveau Obecní dům (see p.119). Daily 10am–6pm.

Pražský hrad (Prague Castle) Hradčany ⓦ www .kulturanahrade.cz; tram #22 to Pražský hrad. Prague Castle has several temporary exhibition spaces, the most impressive of which is the Císařská konírna, Rudolf II's former stables. Tues–Sun 10am–6pm.

Rudolfinum Alšovo nábřeží 12, Staré Město ⓦ www.galerierudolfinum.cz; metro Staroměstská. This magnificent late nineteenth-century arts complex has one of the few galleries in Prague that can take large-scale international art and photography exhibitions. Tues–Sun 10am–6pm, Thurs until 8pm.

Staroměstská radnice Staroměstské náměstí, Staré Město ⓦ www.ghmp.cz; metro Staroměstská. The town hall has populist exhibitions (often photography) on the ground floor and contemporary artists on the first floor. Tues–Sun 10am–6pm.

UPM 17 listopadu 2, Staré Město; ⓦ www.upm .cz; metro Staroměstská. The UPM, the city's museum of applied art (see p.108), owns some of the finest Czech art in the world, and puts on consistently excellent temporary exhibitions. Tues–Sun 10am–6pm.

Valdštejnská jízdárna (Waldstein Stables) Valdštejnská 3, Malá Strana ⓦ www.ngprague .cz; metro Malostranská. Some of the Národní galerie's most popular exhibitions – from retrospectives of Old Masters to twentieth-century Czech greats – are staged in these former stables by Malostranská metro station. Tues–Sun 10am–6pm.

Veletržní palác Dukelských hrdinů 47, Holešovice ⓦ www.ngprague.cz; tram #5, #12 or #17 to Veletržní. Prague's vast modern art museum puts on excellent temporary exhibitions and retrospectives in the ground- first- and fifth-floor galleries (see p.148). Tues–Sun 10am–6pm.

Commercial galleries

AM 180 Bělehradská 45, Vinohrady ⓦ www .am180.org; tram #11 or #16 to Bruselská/metro I.P. Pavlova. This youthful arts collective put on exhibitions drawn from their members, and changed every two or three weeks. Mon–Thurs 1–7pm.

Futura Holečkova 49, Smíchov ⓦ www .futuraproject.cz; tram #6, #9, #10 or #16 to Bertramka. Futura remains at the top of the city's commercial art galleries. The courtyard features David Černy's *Brownnosers* sculpture, and the interior has several exhibition spaces ranging from the classic white cube to atmospheric cellars; there are also separate studios in Karlín. Wed–Sun 11am–6pm.

Galerie Display Bubenská 3, Holešovice ⓦ www.display.cz; metro Vltavská. Excellent contemporary gallery that puts on an experimental range of exhibitions, shows films and encourages artistic debate. Wed–Sun 3–6pm.

Galerie Jiří Švestka Biskupský dvůr 6, Nové Město ⓦ www.jirisvestka.cz; metro Náměstí Republiky. Private gallery showcasing young Czech artists and occasionally staging exhibitions by international names. Tues–Sat 11am–6pm.

Galerie Tvrdohlaví Vodičkova 36, Nové Město ⓦ www.tvrdohlavi.cz; metro Můstek. Situated in the Lucerna *pasáž*, this gallery showcases the work of the Tvrdohlaví (Stubborn Ones), a group of provocative Czech artists born in the 1950s and early 1960s. Mon–Fri noon–8pm, Sat & Sun 10am–10pm.

Gambra Černínská 5, Hradčany; tram #22 from metro Malostranská to Brusnice. The gallery of Prague's small but persistent surrealist movement, past and present, hidden in the enchanting backstreets of Hradčany, also provides a window for the works of animator extraordinaire, Jan Švankmajer, and his late wife, the artist Eva Švankmajerová. March–Oct Wed–Sun

noon–6pm; Nov–Feb Sat & Sun noon–5.30pm.

Photographic galleries

Ateliér Josefa Sudka Újezd 30, Malá Strana ⓦ www.sudek-atelier.cz; tram #6, #9, #12, #20 or #22 to Újezd. One of three galleries named after the father of Czech photography, this place is worth a visit if only to sneak a look at Sudek's reconstructed studio, where he executed some of his most famous photographic cycles, and which now contains a smattering of Sudek memorabilia. Tues–Sun noon–6pm.

Galerie Josefa Sudka Úvoz 24, Hradčany ⓦ www.upm.cz; metro Náměstí Republiky. In the house where Sudek lived and worked from 1959 onwards, this gallery puts on excellent exhibitions organized by the UPM. April–Sept Wed–Sun 11am–7pm; Oct–March Wed–Sun 11am–5pm.

Komorní galerie domu Josefa Sudka Maiselova 2, Josefov ⓦ czechpressphoto.cz; metro Staroměstská. Exhibition space used by Czech Press Photo to put on exhibitions of photojournalism. Tues–Sun 11am–6pm.

Langhans Galerie Vodičkova 37, Nové Město; ⓦ www.langhansgalerie.cz; metro Můstek. Just off Wenceslas Square, this former atelier puts on exhibitions drawn from its wonderful archives as well as contemporary Czech works. Tues–Sun 1–7pm.

Shopping

Communist shop assistants were famously rude, and although things have changed enormously, service in Prague's **shops** can sometimes still be surly. For the passing tourist, the typical purchases are in goods like glass, ceramics, cutlery and wooden toys, though the Czechs also continue to produce CDs and books and, of course, smoked meats, salamis and alcohol, at knock-down prices. The backstreets of **Malá Strana**, **Staré Město** and **Nové Město** are good for finding interesting little shops, as long as you steer clear of Karlova, Mostecká and Nerudova, where it's strictly puppets, jester hats, Kafka T-shirts, Russian army gear, Mucha merchandise and *matrioshka* dolls. The multinational franchises have staked out **Pařížská**, **Na příkopě** and **Wenceslas Square**. Shopping malls have really taken off, with **Palladium**, on Náměstí Republiky, the mother of Prague's malls; more interesting are the old-fashioned, interwar covered **pasáže** on and around Wenceslas Square.

Antiques, arts, crafts and glass

Antique shops (*starožitnosti*), **secondhand** junk shops (*bazar*) and bric-a-brac outlets feature all over Prague. There are few bargains in the ones in the main tourist districts, but elsewhere you may find some inexpensive curios. Shops selling **glass** (*sklo*) are all over Prague; the difficulty is finding anything you actually like the look of. For folk arts and crafts, look no further than the Havelská market (see p.219) or the ubiquitous Manufaktura chain listed below.

Antique Music Instruments Pohořelec 7 & 9, Hradčany; tram #15 or #22 to Pohořelec. More than just lutes and old violins, this place also sells icons, Art Nouveau glass, clocks and model trains and cars. Daily 9am–6pm.

Art Deco Michalská 21, Staré Město ⓦ www.artdecogalerie-mili.com; metro Můstek. A stylish antique shop crammed with a wonderful mixture of clothes, hats, mufflers, teapots, glasses, clocks and art from the first half of the last century. Mon–Fri 2–7pm.

Arzenal Valentinská 11, Staré Město ⓦ www .arzenal.cz; metro Staroměstská. Lots of fancy kitchen gear and glassware by leading Czech designer, Bořek Šípek, who helped restore Prague Castle in the 1990s. Mon–Fri 10am–6pm, Sat & Sun 11am–5pm.

Bric a Brac Týnská 7, Staré Město; metro Náměstí Republiky. Absolutely minute antique store, packed to the very rafters with every conceivable trinket. The central location

▲ Interior of Art Deco

means that prices are quite high, but the place is worth visiting for the spectacle alone. The owner also runs a larger place round the corner. Daily 10am–6pm.

Celetná Celetná 15, Staré Město; metro Staroměstská. If you're interested in buying some of the ubiquitous crystal or porcelain that clogs up the city's shop windows, you're sure to get top-quality goods here. Daily 10am–7pm.

Eduard Čapek bazar Dlouhá 32, Staré Město; metro Staroměstská. Opened in 1911 (and privately owned even under the Communists), this place is a relic in itself, selling quality junk from old domestic utensils and battered tea cups to tools and lamps. Daily noon–10pm.

Elíma Jánský vršek 5, Malá Strana ⓦ www.elimashop.cz; tram #12, #20 or #22 to Malostranské náměstí. This tiny little shop in the backstreets sells beautiful, inexpensive, handmade Polish pottery from Bolesławiec (Bunzlau). Daily 10am–6pm.

Granát Turnov Dlouhá 28, Staré Město; metro Náměstí Republiky. The best place to get hold of fiery red Bohemian garnet jewellery from North Bohemia. Mon–Fri 10am–6pm, Sat 10am–1pm.

Kubista Ovocný trh 19, Staré Město ⓦ www.kubista.cz; metro Náměstí Republiky. Beautiful shop housed in the same building as the Museum of Czech Cubism and selling reproductions of some of the museum's exquisite Cubist ceramics, jewellery and furniture. Tues–Sun 10am–6.30pm.

Le Patio Národní 22, Nové Město; metro Národní třída. Stylish café-restaurant that also sells its furnishings from the chairs and chandeliers to the bottle-racks and birdcages. Mon–Fri 8am–11pm, Sat & Sun 10am–11pm.

Manufaktura Melantrichova 17, Staré Město; metro Staroměstská. Czech folk-inspired shop with a fantastic array of wooden toys, painted Easter eggs, straw decorations, honeycomb candles and sundry kitchen utensils. There are branches on Karlova and Jilská (plus many more). Daily 10am–8pm.

Modernista Celetná 12, Staré Město ⓦ www.modernista.cz; metro Náměstí Republiky. Beautiful but pricey emporium selling top-drawer restored Czech furniture and furnishings in the functionalist and Cubist styles popular between the wars and beyond. Daily 11am–7pm.

Marionety Nerudova 51, Malá Strana ⓦ www.marionettes.cz; metro Malostranská. Decent range of marionettes, rod and glove puppets, antique and new. Daily 10am–8pm.

Moser Na příkopě 12, Nové Město ⓦ www.moser-glass.com; metro Můstek. The most famous glass and crystal manufacturers in the country – though you won't find many bargains here. Branch at Malé náměstí 11. Mon–Fri 10am–8pm, Sat & Sun 10am–7pm.

Vetešnictví Vítězná 16, Malá Strana; tram #6, #9, #12, #20 or #22 to Újezd. Proper Prague bric-a-brac shop jam-packed with everything from old metal signs and Communist memorabilia to glassware and porcelain. Daily 10am–4pm.

Books, maps and graphics

Prague is home to numerous English-language bookstores (*knihkupectví*), which thrive on the large expat community. The city is also replete with secondhand bookstores (*antikvariát*), though these are often pricey antiquarian-type places rather than cheap, rambling shops; however, many also stock a good selection of old prints and posters.

Academia Václavské náměstí 34, Nové Město ⓦ www.academia.cz; metro Muzeum/Můstek. One of the best downtown bookstores for Czech books, with a fair selection of English-language books and a café on the first floor. Mon–Fri 9am–8pm, Sat 9.30am–7pm, Sun 9.30am–6pm.

Anagram Týn 4, Staré Město ⓦ www.anagram.cz; metro Náměstí Republiky. Friendly English-language bookstore which has lots of Czech authors in translation and books on Czech politics and culture, plus a small secondhand section. Mon–Sat 10am–8pm, Sun 10am–7pm.

Big Ben Book Shop Malá Štupartská 5, Staré Město ⓦ www.bigbenbookshop.com; metro Náměstí Republiky. Bookstore with a vast selection of fiction and nonfiction, plus cheap paperbacks, kids' books, magazines and papers. Mon–Fri 9am–6.30pm, Sat 10am–5pm, Sun noon–5pm.

Fraktály Betlemské náměstí 5a, Staré Město ⓦ www.fraktaly.cz; metro Staroměstská. Great bookshop with stylish armchairs to collapse into and peruse books on design, architecture and fine art, or a good place to pick up a groovy poster or arty gift. Mon–Sat 10am–8pm, Sun noon–8pm.

The Globe Pštrossova 6 ⓦ www .globebookstore.cz; metro Národní třída/ Karlovo náměstí. The expat bookstore par excellence – both a social centre and superbly well-stocked store, with an adjacent café and friendly staff. Daily 9.30am–1am.

Judaica Široká 7, Josefov; metro Staroměstská. Probably the best stocked of all the places flogging Jewish books to passing tourists, with books and prints, secondhand and new. Daily except Sat 10am–6pm.

Kant Opatovická 26, Nové Město ⓦ www .antik-kant.cz; metro Národní třída. Lots of old books, including a fair few English-language ones, plus a good display of prints. Mon–Fri 10am–6pm.

Kanzelsberger Václavské náměstí 4, Nové Město; metro Můstek ⓦ www.kanzelsberger.cz. Well-stocked four-storey Czech bookshop at the bottom of Wenceslas Square with a café on the first floor. Daily 9am–8pm.

Shakespeare a synové U lužického semináře 10, Malá Strana; metro Malostranská. Don't be deceived by the tiny frontage, this is a wonderful, large, rambling well-stocked English-language bookstore in which to while away some time. Daily 11am–7pm.

Department stores

For most basic goods, you're best off heading for a department store (*obchodní dům*), which will stock most things – including toiletries, stationery and usually an extensive food and drink selection. The prices are low, but so, often, is the quality.

Kotva náměstí Republiky 8, Nové Město; metro Náměstí Republiky. A seminal piece of dreadful brown 1970s architecture, Kotva is a good old-fashioned Czech department store, with prices to suit all pockets. Mon–Fri 9am–8pm, Sat 10am–7pm, Sun 10am–6pm.

My národní Národní 26, Nové Město; metro Národní třída. Prague's premier downtown department store. Its name is a pun on its Communist predecessor (called *Máj*), and it's actually owned by British supermarket chain Tesco, as the basement food hall attests. Mon–Fri 8am–9pm, Sat 9am–8pm, Sun 10am–8pm.

Palladium náměstí Republiky 1 Nové Město; metro Náměstí Republiky ⓦ www .palladiumpraha.cz. The apotheosis of Czech consumerism, this is the country's largest shopping mall, and it occupies the spruced-up former barracks opposite Obecní dům. Mon–Fri 7am–10pm, Sat & Sun 8am–10pm.

Fashion and cosmetics

Ahasver Prokopská 3, Malá Strana ⓦ www .ahasver.com; tram #12, #20 or #22 to Malostranské náměstí. Delightful little shop selling antique gowns and jewellery, as well as paintings, porcelain and glass. Tues–Sun 11am–6pm.

Baťa Václavské náměstí 6, Nové Město; metro Můstek. Functionalist flagship store of Baťa shoe empire with five floors of fancy footwear in a prime position on Wenceslas Square. Mon–Fri 9am–9pm, Sat 9am–8pm, Sun 10am–8pm.

Botanicus Týn 3, Staré Město ⓦ www .botanicus.cz; metro Náměstí Republiky. Czech take on the UK's Body Shop, with a more folksy ambience. Dried flowers, handmade paper and fancy honey are sold alongside natural soaps and shampoos. There are other branches at Truhlářská 10, Nové Město and Vítězná 10, Malá Strana. Daily 10am–6.30pm.

Chez Parisienne Pařížská 8, Josefov; metro Staroměstská. Prague's sexiest lingerie store takes its name from Prague's most fashion-conscious street Pařížská. Mon–Sat 10am–7pm, Sun noon–7pm.

Faux Pas Újezd 26, Malá Strana ⓦ www.fauxpas .cz; tram #6, #9, #12, #20 or #22 to Újezd. At Faux Pas, designer Jolana Izbická goes in for brightly coloured and provocative clothing, as well as stocking one-off pieces by other central European designers. Daily 11am–7pm.

Modes Robes **Benediktská 5, Staré Město;** metro Náměstí Republiky. Women's boutique whose interior is smothered in crazy, arty murals – best of all, you can have a coffee while trying on the clothes. Mon–Fri 10am–7pm, Sat 10am–4pm.

Quasimodo Vintage Fashion **Vladislavova 17, Nové Město; metro Národní třída.** Hidden away in a courtyard, the clothes here are not exclusively vintage, more plain old second-hand, and all the more affordable for it (200–400Kč). Mon–Fri 10am–6pm.

Markets and food and drink stores

Prague is chronically short of good **markets** (*trhy* or *tržiště*) of all types. For bread, butter, cheese, wine and beer, you should simply go to the nearest *potraviny* or supermarket, although these are still a long way from the superstores of the Western world. Christmas markets have now been firmly re-established, and exist from late November onwards at Staroměstské náměstí and Václavské náměstí.

Markets

Havelská **Staré Město; metro Můstek.** The only open-air market, which stretches the full-length of the arcaded street Havelská and sells fruit, flowers, vegetables, CDs, souvenirs and wooden toys. Mon–Fri 8am–6pm, Sat & Sun 9am–6pm.

Shops

Au Gourmand **Dlouhá 10, Staré Město** ⓦ www .augourmand.cz; metro Náměstí Republiky. Beautifully tiled French boulangerie, patisserie and *traiteur* selling wickedly delicious pastries to take away. There are branches at Rytířská 22 and in Palladium. Mon–Fri 8am–7pm, Sat 8.30am–7pm, Sun 9am–7pm.

Bakeshop Praha **V Kolkovně 2, Staré Město** ⓦ www.bakeshop.cz; metro Náměstí Republiky. Top-class expat bakery where you can take away excellent bread, sandwiches, quiches, wraps and entire cakes. Daily 7am–7pm.

Blatnice **Michalská 6, Staré Město; metro Národní třída.** One of the most central places in which to taste and take home Czech *sudová vina* (wine from the barrel). Mon–Fri 10am–6pm.

Cellarius **Štěpánská 61, Nové Město** ⓦ www.cellarius.cz; metro Muzeum. Very well-stocked shop in the Lucerna *pasáž*, where you can taste and take away Czech wines. Mon–Sat 9.30am–8pm, Sun 2–8pm.

Country Life **Melantrichova 15, Staré Město; metro Můstek.** Health food shop selling excellent picnic fodder, organic vegetables, dried fruit and takeaway sandwiches. Mon–Thurs 8.30am–7pm, Fri 8.30am–3/4/6pm, Sun 11am–6pm.

Cream & Dream **Husova 12, Staré Město; metro Staroměstská.** Multinational *gelateria* with lots of fresh fruit in the flavours. Daily 11am–10pm.

Culinaria **Skořepka 9** ⓦ www.culinaria.cz; metro Staroměstská. Prague's first really fancy deli, with lots of imported goods which are difficult to find elsewhere in the city. Mon–Sat 10am–7pm, Sun noon–5pm.

Galerie piva **Lázeňská 15; tram #12, #20 or #22 to Malostranské náměstí.** This is a relatively small shop, but it stocks one of the city's most judicious selection of Czech bottled beers. Mon–Sat 11am–7pm.

Jarmark lahůdky **Vodičkova 30, Nové Město; metro Můstek.** Little Italian deli opposite the restaurant of the same name in the Lucerna *pasáž*. Mon–Fri 9am–8pm, Sat & Sun 9am–6pm.

Koruna Pralines **V jámě 5, Nové Město; metro Můstek.** Top-quality Belgian chocolates – make sure you try the uniquely Czech pralines filled with the national *digestif*, Becherovka. Mon–Fri 9am–8pm, Sat & Sun 9am–6pm.

La Bretagne **Široká 22, Staré Město; metro Staroměstská.** Wide array of fresh fish and seafood available at this centrally located fishmonger's, plus takeaway sushi. Mon–Sat 9.30am–7.30pm.

Monarch **Na Perštýně 15, Staré Město** ⓦ www .monarch.cz; metro Národní třída. Emerging as the city's number-one wine shop (and wine bar), with stock from all over the world as well as local wine – it sells cheese and dried meats, too. Mon–Sat noon–8pm.

Pivní galerie **U Průhonu 9, Holešovice** ⓦ www.pivnigalerie.cz; tram #5, #12 or #15 to U Průhonu. The largest selection of bottled Czech beers in the capital, which you can drink in the shop or take away. All under 30Kč a throw. Tues–Fri noon–7pm.

Music

Czech CDs are priced a little lower than in the West; cassettes and LPs are significantly cheaper. Classical buffs will fare best of all, not just with the Czech composers, but with cheap copies of Mozart, Vivaldi and other favourites on sale at just about every street corner.

Bontonland Palác Koruna, Václavské náměstí 1 Ⓦ www.bontonland.cz; metro Můstek. In the *pasáž* at the bottom of Wenceslas Square, this is Prague's biggest record store, with three floors of rock, folk, jazz and classical CDs, DVDs and video games. Mon–Sat 9am–8pm, Sun 10am–7pm.

Hudební nástroje Náprstkova 10, Staré Město; metro Národní třída Ⓦ www.nastroje-hudebni.cz. Great place to pick up a secondhand Czech instrument from banjos and mandolins to xylophones and accordions. Mon–Sat 10.30am–7pm.

Maximum Underground Jilská 22, Staré Město Ⓦ www.maximum.cz; metro Staroměstská. The best indie record shop in town, very strong on dance music, and also reggae, ragga, punk and world music. Mon–Sat 11am–7pm.

Music antikvariát Národní 25, Nové Město; metro Národní třída. The best secondhand record store in Prague, particularly good for jazz and folk, but also rock/pop – though there's not much in the way of classical. Mon–Sat 10.30am–7pm.

Pohodlí Benediktská 7, Staré Město Ⓦ pohodli.com; metro Jiřího z Poděbrad. The place to go for world music; also stocks a selection of Czech folk music. Mon–Fri noon–7pm.

Toys and children's goods

Hry a hlavolamy Václavské náměstí 38, Nové Město Ⓦ www.hryahlavolamy.cz. A small shop inside the Rokoko *pasáž* which stocks some great wooden puzzles and brainteasers (*hlavolamy*), plus board games. Mon–Fri 10am–7pm, Sat & Sun 11am–5pm.

MPM Myslíkova 19, Nové Město Ⓦ www.mpm.cz; metro Karlovo náměstí. A whole range of kits for making model planes, tanks, trains, ships and cars, and toy soldiers. Mon–Fri 10am–6pm.

Sparky's Havířská 2, Staré Město; metro Můstek. Prague's top dům hraček (House of Toys) on four floors, which stocks everything from the latest high-tech playthings to traditional wooden toys. Mon–Sat 10am–7pm, Sun 10am–6pm.

Truhlář marionety U lužického semináře 5, Malá Strana Ⓦ www.marionety.com; metro Malostranská. Prague is awash with cheap, and frankly quite gawdy, puppets, but the Truhlář family are a cut above the rest. Wooden marionettes off the peg from 1600Kč – bespoke from 12,000Kč. Daily 10am–8pm.

Miscellaneous specialist shops

Centrum Fotoškoda Vodičkova 37, Nové Město; metro Můstek. Big multifloor photography store in the Palác Langhans that has by far the widest range of goods in Prague. Mon–Fri 9am–8pm, Sat 10am–6pm.

Jan Pazdera Vodičkova 28, Nové Město; metro Můstek Ⓦ www.fotopazdera.cz. Truly spectacular selection of old & new cameras, microscopes, telescopes, opera glasses and binoculars. Mon–Fri 10am–6pm, Sat 10am–1pm.

Sparta Praha Betlémské náměstí 7, Staré Město; metro Národní třída. Centrally located football fan shop stocking everything from soccer shirts to ashtrays, mostly for Sparta Praha, but also stocks Slavia Praha, Bohemians and Dukla Praha merchandise. Mon–Thurs 10am–5pm, Fri 10am–4pm.

U Sherlocka Holmese Vodičkova 38, Nové Město; metro Karlovo náměstí. This calls itself a "cigar and pipe shop", but you'll find other sorts of smoking paraphernalia here too, plus plenty of bottles of spirits, including absinthe. Daily 6am–11pm.

Včelařské potřeby Křemencova 8, Nové Město; metro Karlovo náměstí. A beekeeper's paradise, with all the accoutrements required by an apiarist plus a wide selection of honey. Mon & Wed 8.30am–12.30pm & 1–5pm, Tues 9.30am–12.30pm, Thurs 9.30am–12.30pm & 1–6.30pm, Fri 8.30am–2pm.

Sports

or a small nation, the Czechs have a pretty good record when it comes to sporting triumphs: over the past two decades, they have consistently produced world-class tennis players, a strong national **football** team and several of the world's top **ice hockey** players. The two sports that pull in the biggest crowds, by far, are football (soccer) and ice hockey. Getting tickets to watch a particular sport is easy (and cheap) enough on the day – only really big matches sell out. If you want to check forthcoming sports events, read the sports pages in *Prague Post*, or ask at a PIS office. Participating in sports activities is also relatively easy, though the Czechs do not share the Anglo-Saxon obsession with keeping fit and staying healthy.

Football

The Czech national **football** (*fotbal*; soccer) team have enjoyed mixed fortunes since making the final of Euro '96 and the semi-finals of Euro 2004, but failed to qualify for the World Cup in 1998, 2002 and 2010. As with most of the smaller European nations, the best home-grown players seek fame and fortune abroad. As a result, domestic teams usually struggle in European competitions.

The top-flight league, or **První liga**, is currently known as the *Gambrinus liga* (ⓦ www.fotbal.cz); the season runs from August to November and March to May, and matches are usually held on Saturdays. Tickets for domestic games are around 100–150Kč and four-figure crowds remain the norm, but for the moment, however, the best thing about Czech football is the beer.

The most successful club in the country is **Sparta Praha** (ⓦ www.sparta.cz), who have won more league titles than any other club since the Czech league began in 1993. Their traditional working-class fan base is one of the largest in the country and has possibly the worst reputation for racism. They play in claret and white (in honour of Arsenal's original strip) at the 20,850 all-seater Letná stadium, currently known as the Generali Arena (five minutes' walk from metro Hradčanská or take tram #1, #8, #15, #25 or #26); international matches are also regularly played there.

Prague's second most successful team, **Slavia Praha** (ⓦ www.slavia.cz), are Sparta Prague's closest rivals, having won the league in 1996, 2008 and 2009. Slavia have traditionally attracted a smaller, more educated, fan base, and are favourites among the expat community. Their strip is red and white halved shirts and white shorts, and they play in a new 21,000-seater stadium called Eden, in Vršovice (tram #6, #7, #22 or #24 to Slavia).

Viktoria Žižkov (ⓦ www.fkvz.cz), based in the traditionally working-class district of Prague 3, won the league championship for the first and only time in 1928. They have won the Czech cup twice in living memory, but are currently

Fighting amongst the Kangaroos

In 1927, the Czech football club, **AFK Vršovice** went on tour to Australia and were given two kangaroos as a gift. The kangaroos were kept at Prague zoo, and the club renamed itself **Bohemians**, and its nickname (and logo) became **Kangaroos**, or *klokani*. Under the Communists, they attracted a lot of dissident support, and in 1983, the Bohemians enjoyed their finest moment, winning the Czechoslovak league and making it to the semi-finals of the UEFA Cup. However, in 2005, financial mismanagement saw the side relegated to the third tier of Czech football. A club in the northeast of the city, **FC Střížkov**, took a lease out on the name and the distinctive logo, and became **FC Bohemians (Střížkov)**, but when the contract expired refused to give up the Bohemians name, the kangaroo logo or their claim to the club's legacy. Meanwhile back in Vršovice, the original club was saved by its fans and refounded as **Bohemians 1905**. The five-year dispute came to a head in 2010 when Bohemians 1905 were due to play FC Bohemians (Střížkov) in the first division. FC Bohemians (Střížkov) threatened to boycott the game, but instead vented their anger by quadrupling the ticket prices for the away fans. At the return fixture in Vršovice, Střížkov deliberately failed to turn up for the match – the first time this had ever happened in the history of the league – and had 20 points deducted, relegating them to the second division. For the moment, at least, there appears to be an uneasy truce.

see-sawing between the first and second divisions. Viktoria play in red and white vertical stripes and their 5600-seater ground is on Seifertova in Žižkov (tram #5, #9 or #26 to Husinecká); they traditionally play their games on Sunday mornings.

The old army team, **Dukla Praha** (Ⓦ www.fkdukla.cz) – immortalized in the pop song "All I Want for Christmas is a Dukla Prague Away-Kit" by British band Half Man Half Biscuit – were forced to leave the capital in 1997, and merge with Příbram, 60km southwest of Prague. However, in 2006 Dukla Praha were refounded and are now back in the second division. They play at the 18,000-capacity Na Julisce stadium, Dejvice (tram #8 to the Podbaba terminus).

Ice hockey

Ice hockey (*lední hokej*) runs football a close second as the nation's most popular sport. It's not unusual to see kids playing their own form of the game in the street, rather than kicking a football around. The country's best players usually leave to seek fame and fortune in North America's National Hockey League (NHL), but the Czech national team continues to rank among the world's top five hockey nations.

Domestic games take place on Saturdays and can last for anything up to three hours; they are fast and physical and make for cold but compelling viewing. The season starts at the end of September and culminates in the annual World Championships the following summer, when the fortunes of the national side are subject to close scrutiny, especially if pitched against the old enemy Russia, not to mention their former bed-mate and new rival, Slovakia. Tickets for domestic games (60–120Kč) can be bought on the day.

As in football, **Sparta Praha** (Ⓦ www.hcsparta.cz) are one of the country's most successful teams, having won the Extraliga (Ⓦ www.hokej.cz) four times since 2000. Sparta play at the Tesla Arena, next door to the Výstaviště exhibition grounds in Holešovice (metro Nádraží Holešovice). Prague's only other first division team is **Slavia Praha** (ⓦ www.hc-slavia.cz), who have won the league twice, in 2003 and 2008, and play at the O2 Arena in Libeň (metro Českomoravská).

Ice skating

Given the nation's penchant for ice hockey, it's not surprising that **ice skating** (*bruslení*) is Prague's most popular winter activity. Several temporary rinks are set up around the city during the Christmas and New Year period, the most central of which is on Staroměstské náměstí. There's also no shortage of permanent rinks (*zimní stadión*) in the city, although public opening hours are often limited to a few hours at the weekend, plus the city's two reservoirs, Hostivař and Šárka, which regularly freeze over in winter. Most rinks are open from October to April; entry costs around 100Kč and skate rental is 80Kč. The best **indoor skating venue** is Štvanice (Sept–April Mon–Fri, 10am–noon & 3–5.30pm, Wed & Fri also 8–9.30pm, Sat 9am–noon, 2–5pm & 8–10pm, Sun 9am–noon & 2–5pm; ☏ 602 663 449, ⓦ www.stvanice.cz; metro Florenc/Vltavská), an old-fashioned two-rink facility on an island in the Vltava, with skate rental available.

Tennis and squash

For a while, **tennis** was one of the country's most successful exports, with the likes of Martina Navrátilová and Ivan Lendl among the game's all-time greats. The glory days of Czech tennis are over, and Prague is no longer on the ATP tour circuit, but the country still produces a smattering of world-class players. Despite what you might read in the English-speaking press, the former world no. 1, Martina Hingis, and former world no. 5, Daniela Hantuchová, are both of Slovak, not Czech, descent.

If you fancy a quick game yourself, you'll have to bring your own racket and balls with you, or buy them downtown. The most central tennis courts are:

ASB Squash centrum Václavské náměstí 13-15, Nové Město ☏ 224 232 752, ⓦ www.asbsquash .cz; metro Můstek. Only three courts, but this is one of Prague's most central squash centres. Mon–Fri 7am–11pm, Sat & Sun 8am–11pm.

Český Lawn Tennis Klub ostrov Štvanice ☏ 222 316 317, ⓦ www.cltk.cz; metro Florenc/ Vltavská. Floodlit outdoor clay courts and indoor clay and hard tennis courts. Booking essential. Daily 7am–midnight.

Squash Haštal Hastalská 20, Staré Město ☏ 224 828 561, ⓦ www.squash-hastal.cz; metro Náměstí Republiky. Six well-maintained courts in the backstreets of the old town. Mon–Fri 7am–11pm, Sat & Sun 8am–11pm.

Tenisový klub Slavia Praha Letenské sady, Holešovice ☏ 233 374 033, ⓦ www.volny.cz /tkslavia; tram #1, #15, #25 or #26. Indoor and outdoor floodlit clay tennis courts situated opposite the Národní technické muzeum. Daily 7am–9/10pm.

Horse racing

Prague's main racecourse (*závodiště*) is at **Velká Chuchle** (ⓦ www.velka-chuchle.cz), 5km or so south of the city centre; catch bus #172 to Závodiště Chuchle, or bus #129, #241, #243, #244 or #314 to Dostihová, or take an *osobní* train (every 30min) from metro Smíchovské nádraží to **Praha-Velká Chuchle**. Steeplechases and hurdles take place from May to October on Sundays from 2pm. There are also less frequent races at a smaller trotting course on **Cisářský ostrov** (May–Oct only); walk through the Stromovka park and across the river to the island from metro Nádraží Holešovice.

Swimming

The waters of the Vltava, Beroun and Labe are all pretty polluted – the Sázava is marginally better – so for a clean swim it's best to head for one of the city's **swimming** pools (*koupaliště*).

Divoká Šárka Divoká Šárka, Vokovice ☎603 723 501, ⓦkoupaliste-sarka.webnode.cz; tram #20 or #26 to the Divoká Šárka terminus. Idyllically located in a craggy valley to the northwest of Prague, with two small outdoor pools filled with cold but fresh and clean water – great for a full, hot day out. Food and drink and plenty of shade available, too. May to mid-Sept daily 9am–7pm.

Plavecký stadion Podolí Podolská 74, Podolí ☎241 433 952, ⓦwww.pspodoli.cz; tram #3, #16, #17 or #21 to Kublov. The most famous of Prague's outdoor pools, set against a sheltered craggy backdrop, with a children's wading pool and water slide, grass and draught beer. Daily 6am–9.45pm.

YMCA Na poříčí 12, Nové Město ☎224 875 811, ⓦwww.scymca.cz; metro Náměstí Republiky. The YMCA's clean 25-metre indoor pool is the best in central Prague, though you need to check the latest times, as it often closes for private classes. Mon–Fri 6.30/7–8.30am, noon–4pm & 8–9.30pm, Sun 9.30am–8.30pm.

Gyms and saunas

There's no shortage of fitness centres and hotels in Prague with good gyms, saunas and masseurs. Rates are generally lower away from the swish hotels, but hours are erratic so check before you go.

Health Club & Spa InterContinental Praha Pařížská 30, Staré Město ☎296 631 525, ⓦwww.icfitness.cz; metro Staroměstská. Well-equipped gym and friendly staff in this very central and posh hotel. Mon–Fri 6am–11pm, Sat & Sun 8am–10pm.

Hit Fitness Flora Chrudimská 2b, Žižkov ☎267 311 447, ⓦhitfit.cz; metro Flora. Large gym, squash courts, sauna, massage and regular classes – very close to the metro. Mon–Fri 6am–11pm, Sat & Sun 8am–11pm.

YMCA Na poříčí 12, Nové Město ☎224 875 811, ⓦwww.scymca.cz; metro Náměstí Republiky. This modern leisure centre, with gym (*posilovna*), aerobics and pool, is the most central facility available. Mon–Fri 6.30–9.30pm, Sun 10am–8.30pm.

Contexts

Contexts

History

Prague has played a pivotal role in European history – "he who holds Bohemia holds mid-Europe", Bismarck is alleged to have said. As the capital of Bohemia, the city has been fought over and occupied by German, Austrian, French and even Swedish armies. Consequently, it is virtually impossible to write a historical account of Prague without frequent reference to the wider events of European history. Its history as the capital of first Czechoslovakia and now the Czech Republic is, in fact, less than a hundred years old, beginning only with the foundation of the country in 1918. Since then, the country's numerous tragedies, mostly focused on Prague, have been exposed to the world at regular intervals, most notably in 1938, 1948, 1968 and, most happily, in 1989.

Legends

The Czechs have a **legend** for every occasion, and the founding of Bohemia and Prague is no exception. The mythical mound of Říp, the most prominent of the pimply hills in the Labe (Elbe) plain, north of Prague, is where **Čech**, the leader of a band of wandering Slavs, is alleged to have founded his new kingdom, Čechy (Bohemia). His brother Lech, meanwhile, headed further north to found Poland. Some time in the seventh or eighth century AD, **Krok** (aka Pace), a descendant of **Čech**, moved his people south from the plains to the rocky knoll that is now Vyšehrad (literally "High Castle").

Krok was succeeded by his youngest daughter, **Libuše**, the country's first and last female ruler, who, handily enough, was endowed with the gift of prophecy. Falling into a trance one day, she pronounced that the tribe should build a city "whose glory will touch the stars", at the point in the forest where they found an old man constructing the threshold of his house. He was duly discovered on the Hradčany hill, overlooking the Vltava, and the city was named *Praha,* meaning "threshold". However, it wasn't long before Libuše's subjects began to demand that she take a husband. As Cosmas, the twelfth-century chronicler, put it, "resting on her elbow like one who is giving birth, she lay there on a high pile of soft and embroidered pillows, as is the lasciviously wanton habit of women when they do not have a man at home whom they fear". Again she fell into a trance, this time pronouncing that they should follow her horse to a ploughman, with two oxen, whose descendants (the ploughman's, that is) would rule over them. Sure enough, a man called **Přemysl** (which means "ploughman") was discovered, and became the mythical founder of the Přemyslid dynasty which ruled Bohemia until the fourteenth century.

Early history

So much for the legend. According to Roman records, the area now covered by Bohemia was inhabited as early as 500 BC by a Celtic tribe, the **Boii**, who gave their name to the region. Very little is known about the Boii except that around 100 BC they were driven from their territory by a Germanic tribe, the **Marcomanni**, who occupied Bohemia. The Marcomanni were a semi-nomadic people and later proved awkward opponents for the Roman Empire, which wisely chose to use the River Danube as its natural eastern border, thus leaving Bohemia outside the empire.

The disintegration of the Roman Empire in the fifth century AD corresponded with a series of raids into central Europe by eastern tribes: first the **Huns** and later the **Avars**, around the sixth century, settling a vast area including the Hungarian plains and parts of what is now Slovakia. Around the same time, the Marcomanni disappeared from the picture to be replaced by **Slav tribes** who entered Europe from somewhere east of the Carpathian mountains. To begin with, at least, they appear to have been subjugated by the Avars. The first successful Slav rebellion against the Avars seems to have taken place in the seventh century, under the Frankish leadership of **Samo**, though the kingdom he created, which probably included Bohemia, died with him around 658 AD.

The Great Moravian Empire

The next written record of the Slavs in the region isn't until the eighth century, when East Frankish (Germanic) chroniclers report a people known as the **Moravians** as having established themselves around the River Morava, a tributary of the Danube. It was an alliance of Moravians and Franks (under Charlemagne) which finally expelled the Avars from central Europe in 796 AD. This cleared the way for the establishment of the **Great Moravian Empire**, which at its peak included Slovakia, Bohemia and parts of Hungary and Poland. Its significance in political terms is that it was the first and last time (until the establishment of Czechoslovakia, for which it served as a useful precedent) that the Czechs and Slovaks were united under one ruler.

The first attested ruler of the empire, **Mojmír I** (c.830–833), found himself at the political and religious crossroads of Europe under pressure from two sides: from the west, where the Franks and Bavarians (both Germanic tribes) were jostling for position with the Roman papacy; and from the east, where the patriarch of Byzantium was keen to extend his influence across eastern Europe. Mojmír's successor, **Rastislav** (846–70), plumped for Byzantium, and invited the missionaries **Cyril and Methodius** (Metoděj) to introduce Christianity, using the Slav liturgy and Eastern rites. Rastislav, however, was ousted by his nephew, **Svatopluk** (871–94), who helped the Germans capture and blind his uncle. Svatopluk himself was then imprisoned, and, on his release, swapped sides, defeating the Germans on several occasions and declaring himself King of Great Moravia. With the death of Methodius in 885, the Great Moravian Empire fell decisively under the influence of the Roman Catholic Church.

Svatopluk died shortly before the **Magyar invasion** of 896, an event which heralded the end of the Great Moravian Empire and a significant break in Czecho-Slovak history. The Slavs to the west of the River Morava (the Czechs) swore allegiance to the Frankish emperor Arnulf, while those to the east (the Slovaks) found themselves under the yoke of the Magyars. This separation, which continued for the next millennium, underlies the social, cultural and political differences between Czechs and Slovaks, which culminated in the separation of the two nations in 1993.

The Přemyslid dynasty

There is evidence that Bohemian dukes were forced in 806 to pay a yearly tribute of 500 pieces of silver and 120 oxen to the Carolingian empire (a precedent the Nazis were keen to exploit as proof of German hegemony over Bohemia). These early Bohemian dukes "lived like animals, brutal and without knowledge",

The Přemyslid dynasty

Princes

Bořivoj I d. 895
Spytihněv I 895–905
Vratislav I 905–921
Václav I 921–929
Boleslav I 929–972
Boleslav II 972–999
Boleslav III 999–1002
Vladivoj 1002–1003
Jaromir 1003–1012
Ulrich 1012–1034
Břetislav I 1034–1055
Spytihněv II 1055–1061
Vratislav II (king from 1086) 1061–1092
Břetislav II 1092–1110
Bořivoj II 1110–1120
Vladislav I 1120–1125
Soběslav I 1125–1140
Vladislav II (as king, I) 1140–1173
Soběslav II 1173–1189
Otho 1189–1191
Václav II 1191–1192
Otakar I (king from 1212) 1192–1230

Kings

Václav I 1230–1253
Otakar II 1253–1278
Václav II 1278–1305
Václav III 1305–1306

Habsburgs

Rudolf I 1306–1307
Henry of Carinthia 1307–1310

The Luxembourg dynasty

John 1310–1346
Charles I (as emperor, IV) 1346–1378
Václav IV 1378–1419
(Hussite Wars 1419–1434)
Sigismund 1436–1437

Habsburgs

Albert 1437–1439
Ladislav the Posthumous 1439–1457

Czech Hussite

George of Poděbrady 1458–1471

The Jagiellonian dynasty

Vladislav II 1471–1516
Louis I 1516–1526

The Habsburg dynasty

Ferdinand I 1526–1564
Maximilian 1564–1576
Rudolf II 1576–1611
Matthias 1611–1619
Ferdinand II 1619–1637
Ferdinand III 1637–1657
Leopold I 1657–1705
Joseph I 1705–1711
Charles II (as emperor, VI) 1711–1740
Maria Theresa 1740–1780
Joseph II 1780–1790
Leopold II 1790–1792
Franz 1792–1835
Ferdinand IV (I) 1835–1848
Franz Joseph I 1848–1916
Charles III 1916–1918

Presidents

Tomáš Garrigue Masaryk
1918–1935
Edvard Beneš 1935–1938 &
1945–1948
Klement Gottwald 1948–1953
Antonín Zápatocký 1953–1957
Antonín Novotný 1957–1968
Ludvík Svoboda 1968–1975
Gustáv Husák 1975–1989
Václav Havel 1989–1992 &
1993–2003
Václav Klaus 2003–present

according to one chronicler. All that was to change when the earliest recorded Přemyslid duke, **Bořivoj** (852/53–888/89), appeared on the scene. The first Christian ruler of Prague, Bořivoj was baptized, along with his wife Ludmila, in the ninth century by the Byzantine missionaries Cyril and Methodius (see opposite). Other than being the first to build a castle on Hradčany, nothing very certain is known about Bořivoj, nor about any of the other early Premyslid rulers, although there are numerous legends, most famously that of **Prince Václav** (St Wenceslas), who was martyred by his pagan brother Boleslav the Cruel in 929 (see p.49).

Cut off from Byzantium by the Hungarian kingdom, Bohemia lived under the shadow of the **Holy Roman Empire** from the start. In 950, Emperor Otto I led an expedition against Bohemia, making the dukedom officially subject to the empire and its leader one of the seven electors of the emperor. In 973, under Boleslav the Pious (972–99), a bishopric was founded in Prague, subordinate to the archbishopric of Mainz. Thus, by the end of the first millennium, German influence was already beginning to make itself felt in Bohemian history.

The **thirteenth century** was the high point of Přemyslid rule over Bohemia. With Emperor Frederick II preoccupied with Mediterranean affairs and dynastic problems, and the Hungarians and Poles busy trying to repulse the Mongol invasions from 1220 onwards, the Přemyslids were able to assert their independence. In 1212, Otakar I (1192–1230) managed to extract a "**Golden Bull**" (formal edict) from the emperor, securing the royal title for himself and his descendants (who thereafter became kings of Bohemia). Prague prospered, too, benefiting from its position on the central European trade routes. Czechs, Germans, Jews and merchants from all over Europe settled there, and in 1234 the first of Prague's historic five towns, **Staré Město**, was founded to accommodate them.

As a rule, the Přemyslids welcomed **German colonization**, none more so than King Otakar II (1253–78), the most distinguished of the Přemyslid rulers, who systematically encouraged German craftsmen to settle in the kingdom. At the same time, the gradual switch to a monetary economy and the discovery of copper and silver deposits heralded a big shift in population from the countryside to the towns. German immigrants founded whole towns in the interior of the country, where German civic rights were guaranteed them, for example Kutná Hora, Mělník and, in 1257, **Malá Strana** in Prague. Through battles, marriage and diplomacy, Otakar managed to expand his territories so that they stretched (almost) from the Baltic to the Adriatic. In 1278, however, Otakar met his end on the battlefield of Marchfeld, defeated by Rudolf of Habsburg.

The beginning of the fourteenth century saw a series of dynastic disputes – messy even by medieval standards – beginning with the death of Václav II from consumption and excess in 1305. The following year, the murder of his son, the heirless, teenage Václav III, marked the **end of the Přemyslid dynasty** (he had four sisters, but female succession was not recognized in Bohemia). The nobles' first choice of successor, the Habsburg Albert I, was murdered by his own nephew, and when Albert's son, Rudolf I, died of dysentery not long afterwards, Bohemia was once more left without any heirs.

Carolinian Prague

The crisis was finally solved when the Czech nobles offered the throne to **John of Luxembourg** (1310–46), who was married to Václav III's youngest sister. German by birth, but educated in France, King John spent most of his reign participating in foreign wars, with Bohemia footing the bill, and John himself paying for it first with his sight, and finally with his life, on the field at Crécy in 1346.

His son, **Charles IV** (1346–78), was wounded in the same battle, but thankfully for the Czechs lived to tell the tale. It was Charles – Karel to the Czechs – who ushered in Prague's **golden age** (see p.230). Although born and bred in France, Charles was a Bohemian at heart (his mother was Czech and his real name was Václav). In 1344, he had wrangled an archbishopric for Prague, independent of Mainz, and two years later he became not only king of Bohemia, but also, by election, Holy Roman Emperor. In the thirty years of his reign, Charles transformed Prague into the new imperial capital. He established institutions and buildings that still survive today and founded an entire new town, **Nové Město**, to accommodate the influx of students and clergy. He promoted Czech as the official language alongside Latin and German and, perhaps most importantly of all, presided over a period of peace in central Europe while western Europe was tearing itself apart in the Hundred Years' War.

Sadly, Charles's son, **Václav IV** (1378–1419), was no match for such an inheritance. Stories that he roasted an incompetent cook alive on his own spit, shot a monk while hunting and tried his own hand at lopping off people's heads with an axe are almost certainly myths. Nevertheless, he was a legendary drinker, prone to violent outbursts and so unpopular with the powers that be that he was imprisoned twice – once by his own nobles and once by his brother, Sigismund. His reign was also characterized by religious divisions within the Czech Lands and in Europe as a whole, beginning with the **Great Schism** (1378–1417), when rival popes held court in Rome and Avignon. This was a severe blow to Rome's centralizing power, which might otherwise have successfully combated the assault on the Church that was already under way in the Czech Lands towards the end of the fourteenth century.

The Bohemian Reformation

Right from the start, Prague was at the centre of the **Bohemian Reformation**. The increased influence of the Church, and its independence from Mainz established under Charles, led to a sharp increase in debauchery, petty theft and alcoholism among the clergy – a fertile climate for militant reformers like Jan Milič of Kroměříž, whose fiery sermons drew crowds of people to hear him at Prague's Týn church. In Václav's reign, the attack was led by the peasant-born preacher **Jan Hus**, who gave sermons at Prague's Betlémská kaple (see p.96).

Hus's main inspiration was the English reformist theologian John Wycliffe (founder of the Lollard movement), whose heretical works found their way to Bohemia via Václav's sister, Anna, who married King Richard II. Worse still, as far as Church traditionalists were concerned, Hus began to preach in the language of the masses (Czech) against the wealth, corruption and hierarchical tendencies within the Church at the time. A devout, mild-mannered man himself, he became embroiled in a dispute between the conservative clergy, led by Archbishop Zbyněk and backed by the pope, and the Wycliffian Czechs at the university. When Archbishop Zbyněk gave the order to burn the books of Wycliffe, Václav backed Hus and his followers, for political and personal reasons (Hus was, among other things, the confessor to his wife, Queen Sophie).

There can be little doubt that King Václav used Hus and the Wycliffites to further his own political cause. He had been deposed as Holy Roman Emperor in 1400 and, as a result, bore a grudge against the current emperor, Ruprecht of the Palatinate, and his chief backer, Pope Gregory XII in Rome. His chosen battleground was Prague's university, which was divided into four "nations" with equal voting rights: the Saxons, Poles, Bavarians, who supported Václav's enemies, and the Bohemians, who were mostly Wycliffites. In 1409, Václav issued the **Kutná Hora Decree**, which rigged the voting within the university, giving the Bohemian "nation" three votes, and the rest a total of one. The other "nations", who made up the majority of the students and teachers, left Prague in protest.

Three years later the alliance between the king and the Wycliffites broke down. Widening his attacks on the Church, Hus began to preach against the sale of religious indulgences to fund the inter-papal wars, thus incurring the enmity of

Václav, who received a percentage of the sales. In 1412, Hus and his followers were expelled from the university, excommunicated and banished from Prague, and they spent the next two years as itinerant preachers spreading their reformist gospel throughout Bohemia. In 1414, Hus was summoned to the **Council of Constance** to answer charges of heresy. Despite a guarantee of safe conduct from Emperor Sigismund, Hus was condemned to death and, having refused to renounce his beliefs, was burned at the stake on July 6, 1415.

Hus's martyrdom sparked off **widespread riots** in Prague, initially uniting virtually all Bohemians – clergy and laity, peasant and noble (including many of Hus's former opponents) – against the decision of the council, and, by inference, against the established Church and its conservative clergy. The Hussites immediately set about reforming Church practices, most famously by administering communion *sub utraque specie* ("in both kinds", ie bread and wine) to the laity, as opposed to the established practice of reserving the wine for the clergy.

The Hussite Wars: 1419–34

In 1419, Václav inadvertently provoked further large-scale rioting by endorsing the readmission of anti-Hussite priests to their parishes. In the ensuing violence, several councillors (including the mayor) were thrown to their death from the windows of Prague's Novoměstská radnice, in Prague's **first defenestration** (see p.127). Václav himself was so enraged (not to say terrified) by the mob that he suffered a stroke and died, "roaring like a lion", according to a contemporary chronicler. The pope, meanwhile, declared an international crusade against the Czech heretics, under the leadership of Emperor Sigismund, Václav's brother and, since Václav had failed to produce an heir, chief claimant to the Bohemian throne.

Already, though, cracks were appearing in the Hussite camp. The more radical reformers, who became known as the **Táborites** after their south Bohemian base, Tábor, broadened their attacks on the Church hierarchy to include all figures of authority and privilege. Their message found a ready audience among the oppressed classes in Prague and the Bohemian countryside, who went around eagerly destroying Church property and massacring Catholics. Such actions were deeply disturbing to the Czech nobility and their supporters who backed the more moderate Hussites – known as the **Utraquists** or *utrakvisté* (from the Latin *sub utraque specie*) – who confined their criticisms to religious matters.

For the moment, however, the common Catholic enemy prevented a serious split developing amongst the Hussites, and under the inspirational military leadership of the Táborite **Jan Žižka**, the Hussites' (mostly peasant) army enjoyed some miraculous early victories over the numerically superior "crusaders", most notably at the Battle of Vítkov in Prague in 1420. The Bohemian Diet quickly drew up the **Four Articles of Prague**, a compromise between the two Hussite camps, outlining the basic tenets about which all Hussites could agree, including communion "in both kinds". The Táborites, meanwhile, continued to burn, loot and pillage ecclesiastical institutions from Prague to the far reaches of the kingdom.

At the **Council of Basel** in 1433, Rome reached a compromise with the Utraquists over the Four Articles, in return for ceasing hostilities. The peasant-based Táborites rightly saw the deal as a victory for the Bohemian nobility and the status quo, and vowed to continue the fight. However, the Utraquists, now in cahoots with the Catholic forces, easily defeated the remaining Táborites at the **Battle of Lipany**, outside Kolín, in 1434. The Táborites were forced to withdraw to the fortress town of Tábor. Poor old Sigismund, who had spent the best part of his life fighting the Hussites, was only recognized as king in 1436, and died the following year.

Compromise

Despite the agreement of the Council of Basel, the pope refused to acknowledge the Utraquist Church in Bohemia. The Utraquists nevertheless consolidated their position, electing the gifted **George of Poděbrady** first as regent and then king of Bohemia (1458–71). The first and last Hussite king, George – Jiří to the Czechs – is remembered primarily for his commitment to promoting religious tolerance and for his far-sighted, but ultimately futile, attempts to establish some sort of "Peace Confederation" in Europe.

On George's death, the Bohemian Estates handed the crown over to the **Polish Jagiellonian dynasty**, who ruled *in absentia*, effectively relinquishing the reins of power to the Czech nobility. In 1526, the last of the Jagiellonians, King Louis, was decisively defeated by the Turks at the Battle of Mohács, and died fleeing the battlefield, leaving no heir to the throne. The Roman Catholic Habsburg, Ferdinand I (1526–64), was elected king of Bohemia – and what was left of Hungary – in order to fill the power vacuum, marking the **beginning of Habsburg rule** over what is now the Czech Republic. Ferdinand adroitly secured automatic hereditary succession over the Bohemian throne for his dynasty, in return for which he accepted the agreement laid down at the Council of Basel back in 1433. With the Turks at the gates of Vienna, he had little choice but to compromise at this stage, but in 1545 the international situation eased somewhat with the establishment of an armistice with the Turks.

The following year, the Utraquist Bohemian nobility provocatively joined the powerful Protestant Schmalkaldic League in their (ultimately successful) war against the Holy Roman Emperor, Charles V. After a brief armed skirmish in Prague, however, victory initially fell to Ferdinand, who took the opportunity to extend the influence of Catholicism in the Czech Lands, executing several leading Protestant nobles, persecuting the reformist Unity of Czech Brethren, who had figured prominently in the rebellion, and inviting Jesuit missionaries to establish churches and seminaries in the Czech Lands.

Like Václav IV, **Emperor Rudolf II** (1576–1611), Ferdinand's eventual successor, was moody and wayward, and by the end of his reign Bohemia was again rushing headlong into a major international confrontation. But Rudolf also shared characteristics with Václav's father, Charles, in his genuine love of the arts, and in his passion for Prague, which he re-established as the royal seat of power, in preference to Vienna, which was once more under threat from the Turks. He endowed Prague's galleries with the best Mannerist art in Europe, and, most famously, invited the respected astronomts Tycho Brahe and Johannes Kepler and the infamous English alchemists John Dee and Edward Kelley, to Prague (see p.235).

Czechs tend to regard Rudolfine Prague as a second golden age, but as far as the Catholic Church was concerned, Rudolf's religious tolerance and indecision were a disaster. In the early 1600s, Rudolf's melancholy began to veer dangerously close to insanity, a condition he had inherited from his Spanish grandmother, Joanna the Mad. And in 1611, the heirless Rudolf was forced to abdicate by his brother **Matthias**, to save the Habsburg house from ruin. Ardently Catholic, but equally heirless, Matthias proposed his cousin **Ferdinand II** as his successor in 1617. This was the last straw for Bohemia's mostly Protestant nobility, and the following year conflict erupted again.

The Thirty Years' War: 1618–48

On May 23, 1618, two Catholic governors appointed by Ferdinand were thrown out of the windows of Prague Castle (along with their secretary) – the country's **second defenestration** (see p.51) – an event that's now taken as the official beginning of the complex religious and dynastic conflicts collectively known as the **Thirty Years' War**. Following the defenestration, the Bohemian Diet expelled the Jesuits and elected the youthful Protestant "Winter King", Frederick of the Palatinate, to the throne. In the first decisive set-to of the war, on November 8, 1620, the Czech Protestants were utterly defeated at the **Battle of Bílá hora** or Battle of the White Mountain (see p.157) by the imperial Catholic forces under Count Tilly. In the aftermath, 27 Protestant nobles were executed on Prague's Staroměstské náměstí, and the heads of ten of them displayed on the Charles Bridge.

It wasn't until the Protestant Saxons occupied Prague in 1632 that the heads were finally taken down and given a proper burial. The Catholics eventually drove the Saxons out, but for the last ten years of the war Bohemia became the main battleground between the new champions of the Protestant cause – the Swedes – and the imperial Catholic forces. In 1648, the final battle of the war was fought in Prague, when the Swedes seized Malá Strana, but failed to take Staré Město, thanks to stubborn resistance on the Charles Bridge by Prague's Jewish and newly Catholicized student populations.

The Counter-Reformation and the Dark Ages

The Thirty Years' War ended with the **Peace of Westphalia**, which, for the Czechs, was as disastrous as the war itself. An estimated five-sixths of the Bohemian nobility went into exile, their properties handed over to loyal Catholic families from Austria, Spain, France and Italy. Bohemia had been devastated, with towns and cities laid waste, and the total population reduced by almost two-thirds; Prague's population halved. On top of all that, Bohemia was now decisively within the Catholic sphere of influence, and the full force of the **Counter-Reformation** was brought to bear on its people. All forms of Protestantism were outlawed, the education system was handed over to the Jesuits and, in 1651 alone, more than two hundred "witches" were burned at the stake in Bohemia.

The next two centuries of Habsburg rule are known to the Czechs as the **Dark Ages**. The focus of the empire shifted back to Vienna and the Habsburgs' absolutist grip over the Czech Lands catapulted the remaining nobility into intensive Germanization, while fresh waves of German immigrants reduced Czech to a despised dialect spoken only by peasants, artisans and servants. The situation was so bad that Prague and most other urban centres became practically German-speaking cities. By the end of the eighteenth century, the Czech language was on the verge of dying out, with government, scholarship and literature carried out exclusively in German. For the newly ensconced Germanized aristocracy, and for the Catholic Church, of course, the good times rolled and Prague was endowed with numerous Baroque palaces, churches, monasteries and monuments, many of which still grace the city today.

The Enlightenment

After a century of iron-fisted Habsburg rule, dispute arose over the accession of Charles VI's daughter, **Maria Theresa** (1740–80), to the Habsburg throne, and Prague, as usual, found itself at the centre of the battlefield. In November 1741, Prague was easily taken by Bavarian, French and Saxon troops, but the occupation force quickly found itself besieged in turn by a Habsburg army, and in January 1743 was forced to abandon the city. By November 1744, Prague was again besieged, this time by the Prussian army, who bombed the city into submission in a fortnight. After a month of looting, they left the city to escape the advancing Habsburg army. During the Seven Years' War, in 1757, Prague was once more besieged and bombarded by the Prussian army, though this time the city held out, and, following their defeat at the Battle of Kolín, the Prussians withdrew.

Maria Theresa's reign also marked the beginning of the **Enlightenment** in the Habsburg Empire. Despite her own personal attachment to the Jesuits, the empress acknowledged the need for reform, and she followed the lead of Spain, Portugal and France in expelling the order from the empire in 1773. But it was her son, **Joseph II** (1780–90), who, in the ten short years of his reign, brought about the most radical changes to the social structure of the Habsburg lands. His 1781 Edict of Tolerance allowed a large degree of freedom of worship for the first time in over 150 years, and went a long way towards lifting the restrictions on Jews within the empire. The following year, he ordered the dissolution of the monasteries, and embarked upon the abolition of serfdom. Despite all his reforms, Joseph was not universally popular. Catholics – some ninety percent of the Bohemian population by this point – viewed him with disdain, and even forced him to back down when he decreed that Protestants, Jews, unbaptized children and suicide victims should be buried in consecrated Catholic cemeteries. His centralization and bureaucratization of the empire placed power in the hands of the Habsburg civil service, and thus helped entrench the **Germanization** of Bohemia. He also offended the Czechs by breaking with tradition and not bothering to hold an official coronation ceremony in Prague.

The Czech national revival

The Habsburgs' enlightened rule inadvertently provided the basis for the economic prosperity and social changes of the **Industrial Revolution**, which in turn fuelled the Czech national revival of the nineteenth century. The textile, glass, coal and iron industries began to grow, drawing ever more Czechs from the countryside and swamping the hitherto mostly German-speaking towns and cities, including Prague. A Czech working class and even an embryonic Czech bourgeoisie emerged, and, thanks to Maria Theresa's reforms, new educational and economic opportunities were given to the Czech lower classes.

For the first half of the century, the Czech **national revival,** or *národní obrození* was confined to the new Czech intelligentsia, led by philologists like Josef Dobrovský and Josef Jungmann at the Charles University, or Karolinum, in Prague. Language disputes (in schools, universities and public offices) remained at the forefront of Czech nationalism throughout the nineteenth century, only later developing into demands for political autonomy from Vienna. The leading figure of the time was the historian **František Palacký**, a Moravian Protestant who wrote the first history of the Czech nation, rehabilitating Hus and the Czech reformists in the process. He was in many ways typical of the early Czech nation-alists – pan-Slavist, virulently anti-German, but not yet entirely anti-Habsburg.

1848 and all that

The fall of the French monarchy in February **1848** prompted a crisis in the German states and in the Habsburg Empire. The new Bohemian bourgeoisie, both Czech and German, began to make political demands: freedom of the press, of assembly, of religious creeds. In March, when news of the revolutionary outbreak in Vienna reached Prague, the city's Czechs and Germans began organizing a joint National Guard, while the students formed an Academic Legion, in imitation of the Viennese. Eventually, a National Committee of Czechs and Germans was formed, and Prague itself got its own elected mayor.

However, it wasn't long before cracks began to appear in the Czech-German alliance. Palacký and his followers were against the dissolution of the empire and argued instead for a kind of multinational federation. Since the empire contained a majority of non-Germans, Prague's own Germans were utterly opposed to Palacký's scheme, campaigning for unification with Germany to secure their interests. On April 11, Palacký refused an invitation to attend the Pan-German National Assembly in Frankfurt. The Germans immediately withdrew from the National Committee, and Prague's other revolutionary institutions began to divide along linguistic lines. On June 2, Palacký convened a **Pan-Slav Congress**, which met on Prague's Slovanský ostrov, an island in the Vltava. Czechs and Slovaks made up the majority of the delegates, but there were also Poles, Croats, Slovenes and Serbs in attendance.

On June 12, the congress had to adjourn, as fighting had broken out on the streets the previous day between the troops of the local Habsburg commander, **Alfred Prince Windischgrätz**, and Czech protesters. The radicals and students took to the streets of Prague, barricades went up overnight, and martial law was declared. During the night of June 14, Windischgrätz withdrew his troops to the left bank and proceeded to bombard the right bank into submission. On the morning of June 17 the city capitulated – the counter-revolution in Bohemia had begun. The upheavals of 1848 left the absolutist Habsburg Empire shaken but fundamentally unchanged and served to highlight the sharp differences between German and Czech aspirations in Bohemia.

Austria-Hungary: the Dual Monarchy

The Habsburg recovery was, however, short-lived. In 1859, and again in 1866, the new emperor, Franz-Joseph II, suffered humiliating defeats at the hands of the Italians and Prussians, respectively, the latter getting their hands on Prague yet again. In order to buy some more time, the compromise, or *Ausgleich*, of 1867 was drawn up, establishing the so-called **Dual Monarchy** of Austria-Hungary – two independent states united by one ruler.

For the Czechs, the *Ausgleich* came as a bitter disappointment. While the Magyars became the Austrians' equals, the Czechs remained second-class citizens. The Czechs' failure in bending the emperor's ear was no doubt partly due to the absence of a Czech aristocracy that could bring its social weight to bear at the Viennese court. Nevertheless, the *Ausgleich* did mark an end to the absolutism of the immediate post-1848 period, and, compared with the Hungarians, the Austrians were positively enlightened in the wide range of civil liberties they granted, culminating in **universal male suffrage** in 1907.

The Industrial Revolution continued apace in Bohemia, bringing an ever-increasing number of Czechs into the newly founded suburbs of Prague, such as

Smíchov and Žižkov. Thanks to the unfair voting system, however, the German-speaking minority managed to hold onto power in the Prague city council until the 1880s. By the turn of the century, German-speakers made up just five percent of the city's population – fewer than the Czechs in Vienna – and of those more than half were Jewish. Nevertheless, German influence in the city remained considerable, far greater than their numbers alone warranted; this was due in part to economic means, and in part to overall rule from Vienna.

Under Dualism, the Czech *národní obrození* flourished. Towards the end of the century, Prague was endowed with a number of symbolically significant Czech monuments, like the Národní divadlo (National Theatre), the Národní muzeum (National Museum) and the Rudolfinum. Inevitably, the movement also began to splinter, with the liberals and conservatives, known as the **Old Czechs**, advocating working within the existing legislature to achieve their aims, and the more radical **Young Czechs** favouring a policy of non-cooperation. The most famous political figure to emerge from the ranks of the Young Czechs was the Prague university professor **Tomáš Garrigue Masaryk**, who founded his own Realist Party in 1900 and began to put forward the (then rather quirky) concept of closer cooperation between the Czechs and Slovaks.

The Old Czechs, backed by the new Czech industrialists, achieved a number of minor legislative successes, but by the 1890s the Young Czechs had gained the upper hand and conflict between the Czech and German communities became a daily ritual in the boulevards of the capital – a favourite spot for confrontations being the promenade of Na příkopě. Language was also a volatile issue, often fought out on the shop and street signs of Prague. In 1897, the **Badeni Decrees**, which put Czech on an equal footing with German in all dealings with the state, drove the country to the point of civil war, before being withdrawn by the cautious Austrians.

World War I

At the outbreak of **World War I**, the Czechs and Slovaks showed little enthusiasm for fighting alongside their old enemies, the Austrians and Hungarians, against their Slav brothers, the Russians and Serbs. As the war progressed, large numbers defected to form the **Czechoslovak Legion**, which fought on the Eastern Front against the Austrians. Masaryk travelled to the US to curry favour for a new Czechoslovak state, while his two deputies, the Czech Edvard Beneš and the Slovak Milan Štefánik, did the same in Britain and France.

Meanwhile, the Legion, which by now numbered some 100,000 men, became embroiled in the Russian revolutions of 1917, and, when the Bolsheviks made peace with Germany, found itself cut off from the homeland. The uneasy cooperation between the Reds and the Legion broke down when Trotsky demanded that they hand over their weapons before heading off on their legendary **anabasis**, or march back home, via Vladivostok. The soldiers refused and became further involved in the Civil War, for a while controlling large parts of Siberia and, most importantly, the Trans-Siberian Railway, before arriving back to a tumultuous reception in the new republic.

Meanwhile, during the course of the summer of 1918, the Slovaks finally threw in their lot with the Czechs, and the Allies recognized Masaryk's provisional Czechoslovak government. On October 28, 1918, as the Habsburg Empire began to collapse, the first **Czechoslovak Republic** was declared in Prague. In response, the German-speaking border regions (later to become known as the Sudetenland) declared themselves autonomous provinces of the new republic of *Deutsch-Österreich* (German-Austria), which, it was hoped, would eventually unite with Germany itself. The new Czechoslovak government was having none of it, but it took the intervention of Czechoslovak troops before control of the border regions was wrested from the secessionists.

Last to opt in favour of the new republic was **Ruthenia** (also known as Sub-Carpathian Rus or Podkarpatská Rus), a rural backwater of the old Hungarian Kingdom which became officially part of Czechoslovakia by the Treaty of St Germain in September 1919. Its incorporation was largely due to the campaigning efforts of Ruthenian émigrés in the US. For the new republic the province was a strategic bonus, but otherwise a huge drain on resources.

The First Republic

The new nation of Czechoslovakia began postwar life in an enviable economic position – **tenth in the world industrial league table** – having inherited seventy to eighty percent of Austria-Hungary's industry intact. Prague regained its position at the centre of the country's political and cultural life, and in the interwar period was embellished with a rich mantle of Bauhaus-style buildings. Less enviable was the diverse make-up of the country's population – a melange of minorities which would in the end prove its downfall. Along with the six million Czechs and two million Slovaks who initially backed the republic, there were more than three million Germans and 600,000 Hungarians, not to mention sundry other Ruthenians (Rusyns), Jews and Poles.

That Czechoslovakia's democracy survived as long as it did is down to the powerful political presence and skill of **Masaryk**, the country's president from 1918 to 1935, who shared executive power with the cabinet. It was his vision of social democracy that was stamped on the nation's new constitution, one of the most liberal of the time (if a little bureaucratic and centralized), aimed at ameliorating any ethnic and class tensions within the republic by means of universal suffrage, land reform and, more specifically, the Language Law, which ensured bilinguality to any area where the minority exceeded twenty percent.

The elections of 1920 reflected the mood of the time, ushering in the left-liberal alliance of the **Pětka** (The Five), a coalition of five parties led by the Agrarian, Antonín Švehla, whose slogan, "we have agreed that we will agree", became the keystone of the republic's consensus politics between the wars. Gradually all the other parties (except the Fascists and the Communists) – including even Andrej Hlinka's Slovak People's Party and most of the Sudeten German parties – began to participate in (or at least not disrupt) parliamentary proceedings. On the eve of the Wall Street Crash, the republic was enjoying an economic boom, a cultural renaissance and a temporary modus vivendi among its minorities.

The 1930s

The 1929 Wall Street Crash plunged the whole country into crisis. Economic hardship was quickly followed by **political instability**. In Slovakia, Hlinka's People's Party fed off the anti-Czech resentment that was fuelled by Prague's manic centralization, consistently polling around thirty percent, with an increasingly nationalist/separatist message. In Ruthenia, the elections of 1935 gave only 37 percent of the vote to parties supporting the republic, the rest going to the Communists, pro-Magyars and other autonomist groups.

But without doubt the most intractable of the minority problems was that of the Sudeten Germans, who lived in the heavily industrialized border regions of Bohemia and Moravia. Nationalist sentiment had always run high in the Sudetenland, many of whose German-speakers resented having been included in the new republic, but it was only after the Crash that the extremist parties began to make significant electoral gains. Encouraged by the rise of Fascism in Austria, Italy and Germany, and aided by rocketing Sudeten German unemployment, the far-right **Sudeten German Party** (SdP), led by a bespectacled gym teacher called Konrad Henlein, was able to win just over sixty percent of the German-speaking vote in the 1935 elections.

Although constantly denying any wish to secede from the republic, the activities of Henlein and the SdP were increasingly funded and directed from Nazi Germany. To make matters worse, the Czechs suffered a severe blow to their morale with the death of Masaryk late in 1937, leaving the country in the less capable hands of his Socialist deputy, **Edvard Beneš**. With the Nazi annexation of Austria (the *Anschluss*) on March 11, 1938, Hitler was free to focus his attention on the Sudetenland, calling Henlein to Berlin on March 28 and instructing him to call for outright autonomy.

The Munich crisis

On April 24, 1938, the SdP launched its final propaganda offensive in the **Karlsbad Decrees**, demanding (without defining) "complete autonomy". As this would clearly have meant surrendering the entire Czechoslovak border defences, not to mention causing economic havoc, Beneš refused to bow to the SdP's demands. Armed conflict was only narrowly avoided and, by the beginning of September, Beneš was forced to acquiesce to some sort of autonomy. On Hitler's orders, Henlein refused Beneš's offer and called openly for the secession of the Sudetenland to the German Reich.

On September 15, as Henlein fled to Germany, the British prime minister, Neville Chamberlain, flew to Berchtesgaden on his own ill-conceived initiative to "appease" the Führer. A week later, Chamberlain flew again to Germany, this time to Bad Godesburg, vowing to the British public that the country would not go to war (in his famous words) "because of a quarrel in a far-away country between people of whom we know nothing". Nevertheless, the French issued draft papers, the British Navy was mobilized, and the whole of Europe fully expected war. Then, in the early hours of September 30, in one of the most treacherous and self-interested acts of modern European diplomacy, prime ministers Chamberlain (for Britain) and Daladier (for France) signed the **Munich Diktat** with Mussolini and Hitler, agreeing – without consulting the Czechoslovak government – to all of Hitler's demands. The British and French public were genuinely relieved, and Chamberlain flew back to cheering home crowds, waving his famous piece of paper that guaranteed "peace in our time".

The Second Republic

Betrayed by his only Western allies and fearing bloodshed, Beneš capitulated, against the wishes of most Czechs. Had Beneš not given in, however, it's doubtful anything would have come of Czech armed resistance, surrounded as they were by vastly superior hostile powers. Beneš resigned on October 5 and left the country. On October 15, **German troops occupied Sudetenland**, to the dismay of those Sudeten Germans who hadn't voted for Henlein (not to mention the half a million Czechs and Jews who lived there). The Poles took the opportunity to seize a sizeable chunk of North Moravia, while in the short-lived "rump" **Second Republic** (officially known as Czecho-Slovakia), Emil Hácha became president, Slovakia and Ruthenia electing their own autonomous governments.

The Second Republic was not long in existence before it, too, collapsed. On March 15, 1939, Hitler informed Hácha of the imminent Nazi occupation of what was left of the Czech Lands, and persuaded him to demobilize the army, again against the wishes of many Czechs. The Germans encountered no resistance (nor any response from the Second Republic's supposed guarantors, Britain and France) and swiftly set up the Nazi **Protectorate of Bohemia and Moravia**. The Hungarians effortlessly crushed Ruthenia's brief independence, while the Slovak People's Party, backed by the Nazis, declared **Slovak independence**, under the leadership of the clerical fascist Jozef Tiso.

World War II

In the first few months of the occupation, left-wing activists were arrested, and Jews were placed under the infamous Nuremberg Laws, but Nazi rule in the Protectorate was not as harsh as it would later become. The relatively benign, conservative aristocrat, **Baron von Neurath**, was appointed *Reichsprotektor*, though his deputy was the rabid Sudeten German Nazi, Karl Hermann Frank. Then, on October 28 (Czechoslovak National Day), during a demonstration against the Nazi occupiers, **Jan Opletal**, a Czech medical student, was fatally wounded; he died in hospital on November 11. Prague's Czech students held a wake in the pub, *U Fleků*, after which there were further disturbances. Frank used these as an excuse to close down all Czech institutions of higher education, on November 17, executing a number of student leaders and sending over a thousand more off to the camps.

In 1941, Himmler's deputy in the SS, **Reinhard Heydrich**, was made *Reichsprotektor*. More arrests and deportations followed, prompting the Czech government-in-exile to organize the most audacious assassination to take place in Nazi-occupied Europe. In June 1942, Heydrich was fatally wounded by Czech parachutists on the streets of Prague. The reprisals were swift and brutal, culminating in the destruction of the villages of Lidice and Ležáky (see box, p.173). Meanwhile, the "final solution" was meted out to the country's remaining Jews, who were transported first to the ghetto in Terezín, and then on to the extermination camps. The rest of the population were frightened into submission – very few acts of active resistance being undertaken in the Czech Lands until the Prague Uprising of May 1945.

By the end of 1944, Czechoslovak and Russian troops had begun to liberate the country, starting with Ruthenia, which Stalin decided to take as war booty despite having guaranteed to maintain Czechoslovakia's pre-Munich borders. On April 4, 1945, under Beneš's leadership, the provisional National Front, or **Národní fronta**, government – a coalition of Social Democrats, Socialists and Communists – was set up in Košice. By April 18, the US Third Army, under General Patton, had crossed the border in the west, meeting very little German resistance.

On the morning of May 5, the Prague radio station, behind the National Museum, began broadcasting in Czech only. The **Prague Uprising** had officially begun. Luckily for the Czechs, Vlasov's anti-Bolshevik Russian National Liberation Army (see p.246) was in the vicinity and was persuaded to turn on the Germans, successfully resisting the two crack German armoured divisions, not to mention the extremely fanatical SS troops, in and around the capital. Barriers were erected across the city, and an American OSS jeep patrol arrived from Plzeň, which the Third Army were on the point of taking. The Praguers (and Vlasov's men) were pinning their hopes on the Americans. In the end, however, the US military leadership made the politically disastrous decision not to cross the demarcation line that had been agreed between the Allies at Yalta. On May 7, Vlasov's men fled towards the American lines, leaving the Praguers to hold out against the Germans. The following day, a ceasefire was agreed and the Germans retreated, for the most part, and headed, like Vlasov, in the direction of the Americans. The Russians entered the city on May 9, and overcame the last pockets of Nazi resistance.

The Third Republic

Violent reprisals against suspected collaborators and the German-speaking population in general began as soon as the country was liberated. All Germans were immediately given the same food rations as the Jews had been given during the war. Starvation, summary executions and worse resulted in the deaths of countless thousands of ethnic Germans. With considerable popular backing and the tacit approval of the Red Army, Beneš began to organize the forced **expulsion of the German-speaking population**, referred to euphemistically by the Czechs as the *odsun* (transfer). Only those German-speakers who could prove their anti-Fascist credentials were permitted to stay – the Czech community was not called on to prove the same – and by the summer of 1947, nearly 2.5 million Germans had been expelled from the country or had fled in fear. On this occasion, Sudeten German objections were brushed aside by the Allies, who had given Beneš the go-ahead for the *odsun* at the postwar Potsdam Conference. Attempts by Beneš to expel the Hungarian-speaking minority from Slovakia in similar fashion, however, proved unsuccessful.

On October 28, 1945, in accordance with the leftist programme thrashed out at Košice, sixty percent of the country's industry was nationalized. Confiscated Sudeten German property was handed out by the largely Communist-controlled police force, and in a spirit of optimism and/or opportunism, people began to join the Communist Party (KSČ) in droves; membership more than doubled in less than a year. In the **May 1946 elections**, the Party reaped the rewards of its enthusiastic support for the *odsun*, of Stalin's vocal opposition to Munich and of the recent Soviet liberation, emerging as the strongest single party in the Czech Lands with up to forty percent of the vote (the largest ever for a European Communist Party in a multiparty election). In Slovakia, however, they achieved just thirty percent, thus failing to push the Democrats into second place. President Beneš appointed the KSČ leader, **Klement Gottwald**, prime minister of another Národní fronta coalition, with several strategically important cabinet portfolios going to Party members, including the ministries of the Interior, Finance, Labour and Social Affairs, Agriculture and Information.

Gottwald assured everyone of the KSČ's commitment to parliamentary democracy, and initially at least even agreed to participate in the Americans' **Marshall Plan** (the only Eastern Bloc country to do so). Stalin immediately summoned Gottwald to Moscow, and on his return the KSČ denounced the Plan. By the end of 1947, the Communists were beginning to lose support, as the harvest failed, the economy faltered and malpractices within the Communist-controlled Ministry of the Interior were uncovered. In response, the KSČ began to up the ante, constantly warning the nation of imminent "counter-revolutionary plots", and arguing for greater nationalization and land reform as a safeguard.

Then in February 1948 – officially known as **"Victorious February"** – the latest in a series of scandals hit the Ministry of the Interior, prompting the twelve non-Communist cabinet ministers to resign en masse in the hope of forcing Beneš to dismiss Gottwald. No attempt was made, however, to rally popular support against the Communists. Beneš received more than 5000 resolutions supporting the Communists and just 150 opposing them. Stalin sent word to Gottwald to take advantage of the crisis and ask for military assistance – Soviet troops began massing on the Hungarian border. It was the one time in his life when Gottwald disobeyed Stalin; instead, by exploiting the divisions within the Social Democrats, he was able to maintain his majority in parliament. The KSČ took to the streets (and the airwaves), arming "workers' militia" units to defend the country against counter-revolution, calling a general strike and finally, on February 25, organizing the country's biggest ever demonstration in Prague. The same day Gottwald went to an indecisive (and increasingly ill) Beneš with his new cabinet, all Party members or "fellow travellers". Beneš accepted Gottwald's nominees and the most popular Communist coup in Eastern Europe was complete, without bloodshed and without the direct intervention of the Soviets. In the aftermath of the coup, thousands of Czechs and Slovaks fled abroad.

The People's Republic

Following Victorious February, the Party began to consolidate its position, a relatively easy task given its immense popular support and control of the army, police force, workers' militia and trade unions. A **new constitution** confirming the "leading role" of the Communist Party and the "dictatorship of the proletariat" was passed by parliament on May 9, 1948. President Beneš refused to sign it, resigned in favour of Gottwald, and died (of natural causes) shortly afterwards. Those political parties that were not banned or forcibly merged with the KSČ were prescribed fixed-percentage representation within the so-called "multi-party" Národní fronta.

With the Cold War in full swing, the **Stalinization** of Czechoslovak society was quick to follow. In the Party's first Five Year Plan, ninety percent of industry was nationalized, heavy industry (and in particular the country's defence industry) was given a massive boost and compulsory collectivization forced through. Party membership reached an all-time high of 2.5 million, and "class-conscious" Party cadres were given positions of power, while "class enemies" (and their children) were discriminated against. It wasn't long, too, before the Czechoslovak mining "gulags" began to fill up with the regime's political opponents – "kulaks", priests and "bourgeois oppositionists" – numbering more than 100,000 at their peak.

Having incarcerated most of its non-Party opponents, the KSČ, with a little prompting from Stalin, embarked upon a ruthless period of internal blood-letting. As the economy nose-dived, calls for intensified "class struggle", rumours of impending "counter-revolution" and reports of economic sabotage by fifth columnists filled the press. An atmosphere of fear and confusion was created to justify **large-scale arrests of Party members** with an "international" background: those with a wartime connection with the West, Spanish Civil War veterans, Jews and Slovak nationalists.

In the early 1950s, the Party organized a series of Stalinist **show trials** in Prague, the most spectacular of which was the trial of Rudolf Slánský, who had been second only to Gottwald in the KSČ before his arrest. Slánský, Vladimír Clementis, the former KSČ foreign minister, and twelve other leading Party members (eleven of them Jewish, including Slánský) were sentenced to death as "Trotskyist-Titoist-Zionists". Hundreds of other minor officials were given long prison sentences, and only a handful of defendants had the strength of will to endure the torture and refuse to sign their "confessions".

After Stalin

Gottwald died in mysterious circumstances in March 1953, nine days after attending Stalin's funeral in Moscow (some say he drank himself to death). The whole nation heaved a sigh of relief, but the regime seemed as unrepentant as ever. The arrests and show trials continued. Then, on May 30, the new Communist leadership announced a drastic currency devaluation, effectively reducing wages by ten percent, while raising prices. The result was a wave of isolated **workers' demonstrations** and rioting in Plzeň and Prague. Czechoslovak army units called in to suppress the demonstrations proved unreliable, and it was left to the heavily armed workers' militia and police to disperse the crowds and make the predictable arrests and summary executions.

In 1954, in the last of the show trials, Gustáv Husák, the post-1968 president, was given life imprisonment, along with other leading Slovak comrades, though he was one of the few with the strength of will to refuse to sign his confession. So complete were the Party purges of the early 1950s, so sycophantic (and scared) was the surviving leadership, that Khrushchev's 1956 thaw was virtually ignored by the KSČ. An attempted rebellion in the Writers' Union Congress was rebuffed and an enquiry into the show trials made several minor security officials scapegoats for the "malpractices". The genuine mass base of the KSČ remained blindly loyal to the Party for the most part; Prague basked under the largest statue of Stalin in the world, and in 1957 the dull, unreconstructed neo-Stalinist **Antonín Novotný** – subsequently alleged to have been a spy for the Gestapo during the war – became First Secretary and President.

Reformism and invasion

The first rumblings of protest against Czechoslovakia's hardline leadership appeared in the official press in 1963. At first, the criticisms were confined to the country's worsening economic stagnation, but soon developed into more generalized protests against the KSČ leadership. Novotný responded by ordering the belated release and rehabilitation of victims of the 1950s purges, permitting a slight cultural thaw and easing travel restrictions to the West. In effect, he was simply buying time. The half-hearted economic reforms announced in the 1965 **New Economic Model** failed to halt the recession, and the minor political reforms instigated by the KSČ only increased the pressure for greater changes within the Party.

In 1967, Novotný attempted a pre-emptive strike against his opponents. Several leading writers were imprisoned, Slovak Party leaders were branded as "bourgeois nationalists" and the economists were called on to produce results or else forego their reform programme. Instead of eliminating the opposition, though, Novotný unwittingly united them. Despite Novotný's plea to the Soviets, Brezhnev refused to back a leader whom he saw as "Khrushchev's man in Prague", and on January 5, 1968, the young Slovak **Alexander Dubček** replaced Novotný as First Secretary. On March 22, the war hero Ludvík Svoboda dislodged Novotný from the presidency.

1968: The Prague Spring

By inclination, Dubček was a moderate, cautious reformer – the perfect compromise candidate – but he was continually swept along by the sheer force of the reform movement. The virtual **abolition of censorship** was probably the single most significant step Dubček took. It transformed what had been until then an internal Party debate into a popular mass movement. Civil society, for years muffled by the paranoia and strictures of Stalinism, suddenly sprang into life in the dynamic optimism of the first few months of 1968, the so-called **Prague Spring**. In April, the KSČ published their Action Programme, proposing what became popularly known as "socialism with a human face" – federalization, freedom of assembly and expression, and democratization of parliament.

Throughout the spring and summer, the reform movement gathered momentum. The Social Democrat Party (forcibly merged with the KSČ after 1948) re-formed, anti-Soviet polemics appeared in the press and, most famously of all, the writer and lifelong Party member Ludvík Vaculík published his personal manifesto entitled "**Two Thousand Words**", calling for radical de-Stalinization within the Party. Dubček and the moderates denounced the manifesto and reaffirmed the country's support for the Warsaw Pact military alliance. Meanwhile, the Soviets and their hardline allies – Gomulka in Poland and Ulbricht in the GDR – viewed the Czechoslovak developments on their doorstep gravely, and began to call for the suppression of "counter-revolutionary elements" and the re-imposition of censorship.

As the summer wore on, it became clear that the Soviets were planning military intervention. Warsaw Pact manoeuvres were held in Czechoslovakia in late June, a Warsaw Pact conference (without Czechoslovak participation) was convened in mid-July and, at the beginning of August, the Soviets and the KSČ leadership met for **emergency bilateral talks** at Čierná nad Tisou on the Czechoslovak–Soviet border. Brezhnev's hardline deputy, Alexei Kosygin, made his less than subtle threat that "your border is our border", but did agree to withdraw Soviet troops (stationed in the country since the June manoeuvres) and gave the go-ahead to the KSČ's special Party Congress scheduled for September 9.

In the early hours of August 21, fearing a defeat for the hardliners at the forthcoming KSČ Congress, and claiming to have been invited to provide "fraternal assistance", the Soviets gave the order for the **invasion of Czechoslovakia** to be carried out by all the Warsaw Pact forces (only Romania refused to take part). Dubček and the KSČ reformists immediately condemned the invasion before being arrested and flown to Moscow for "negotiations". President Svoboda refused to condone the formation of a new government under the hardliner Alois Indra, and the people took to the streets in protest, employing every form of non-violent resistance in the book. Individual acts of martyrdom, with the self-immolation of **Jan Palach** on Prague's Wenceslas Square, hit the headlines, but casualties were light compared with the Hungarian uprising of 1956 – the cost in terms of the following twenty years was much greater.

Normalization

In April 1969, StB (secret police) agents provoked anti-Soviet riots during the celebrations of the country's double ice hockey victory over the USSR. On this pretext, another Slovak, **Gustáv Husák**, replaced the broken Dubček as First Secretary, and instigated his infamous policy of "**normalization**". More than 150,000 fled the country before the borders closed, around 500,000 were expelled from the Party, and an estimated one million people lost their jobs or were demoted. Inexorably, the KSČ reasserted its absolute control over the state and society. The only part of the reform package to survive the invasion was **federalization**, which gave the Slovaks greater freedom from Prague (on paper at least), though even this was severely watered down in 1971. Dubček, like countless others, was forced to give up his job, working for the next twenty years as a minor official in the Slovak forestry commission.

An unwritten social contract was struck between rulers and ruled during the 1970s, whereby the country was guaranteed a tolerable standard of living (second only to that of the GDR in Eastern Europe) in return for its passive collaboration. Husák's security apparatus quashed all forms of dissent during the early 1970s, and it wasn't until the middle of the decade that an organized opposition was strong enough to show its face. In 1976, the punk rock band **The Plastic People of the Universe** were arrested and charged with the familiar "crimes against the state" clause of the penal code. The dissidents who rallied to their defence – a motley assortment of people ranging from former KSČ members to right-wing intellectuals – agreed to form **Charter 77** (*Charta 77* in Czech), with the purpose of monitoring human rights abuses in the country. One of the organization's prime movers and initial spokespeople was the absurdist Czech playwright **Václav Havel**. Havel, along with many others, endured relentless persecution (including long prison sentences) over the next decade in pursuit of Charter 77's ideals. The initial gathering of 243 signatories had increased to more than 1000 by 1980, and caused panic in the moral vacuum of the Party apparatus, but consistently failed to stir a fearful and cynical populace into action.

The 1980s

In the late 1970s and early 1980s, the inefficiencies of the economy prevented the government from fulfilling its side of the social contract, as living standards began to fall. Cynicism, alcoholism, absenteeism and outright dissent became widespread, especially among the younger (post-1968) generation. The **Jazz Section** of the Musicians' Union, who disseminated "subversive" Western pop music (such as pirate copies of "Live Aid"), highlighted the ludicrously harsh nature of the regime when they were arrested and imprisoned in the mid-1980s. Pop concerts, religious pilgrimages and, of course, the anniversary of the Soviet invasion all caused regular confrontations between the security forces and certain sections of the population. Yet still, a mass movement like Poland's Solidarity failed to emerge.

With the advent of **Mikhail Gorbachev**, the KSČ was put in an extremely awkward position, as it tried desperately to separate *perestroika* from comparisons with the reforms of the Prague Spring. Husák and his cronies had prided themselves on being second only to Honecker's GDR as the most stable and orthodox of the Soviet satellites – now the font of orthodoxy, the Soviet Union, was turning against them. In 1987, **Miloš Jakeš**, the hardliner who oversaw Husák's normalization purges, took over from Husák as General (First) Secretary and introduced *přestavba* (restructuring), Czechoslovakia's lukewarm version of *perestroika*.

The Velvet Revolution

Everything appeared to be going swimmingly for the KSČ as it entered **1989**. Under the surface, however, things were becoming more and more strained. As the country's economic performance worsened, divisions were developing within the KSČ leadership. The protest movement was gathering momentum: even the Catholic Church had begun to voice dissatisfaction, compiling a staggering 500,000 signatures calling for greater freedom of worship. But the twenty-first anniversary of the Soviet invasion produced a demonstration of only 10,000, which was swiftly and violently dispersed by the regime.

During the summer, however, more serious cracks began to appear in Czechoslovakia's staunch hardline ally, the GDR. The trickle of **East Germans fleeing to the West** turned into a mass exodus, with thousands besieging the

The pink tank

Until 1991, **Tank 23** sat proudly on its plinth in Prague's náměstí Sovětských tankistů (Soviet Tank Drivers' Square), one of a number of obsolete tanks generously donated by the Soviets after World War II to serve as monuments to the 1945 liberation. Tank 23 was special, however, as it was supposedly the first tank to arrive to liberate Prague, on May 9, hotfoot from Berlin.

The real story of the liberation of Prague was rather different, however. When the Prague uprising began on May 5, the first offer of assistance actually came from a division of the anti-Communist **Russian National Liberation Army** (**KONR**), under the overall command of **Andrei Vlasov**, a high-ranking former Red Army officer who was instrumental in pushing the Germans back from the gates of Moscow, but who switched sides after being captured by the Nazis in 1942. The Germans were (rightly, as it turned out) highly suspicious of the KONR, and, for the most part, the renegade Russians were kept well away from the real action. In the war's closing stages, the KONR switched sides once more and agreed to fight alongside the Czech resistance, making a crucial intervention against the SS troops who were poised to crush the uprising in Prague. Initially, the Czechs guaranteed Vlasov's men asylum from the advancing Soviets in return for military assistance. In reality, the Czechs were unable to honour their side of the bargain and the KONR finally withdrew from the city late on May 7 and headed west to surrender themselves to the Americans. When the Red Army finally arrived in Prague, many of Vlasov's troops were simply gunned down by the Soviets. Even those in the hands of the Americans were eventually passed over to the Russians and shared the fate of their leader Vlasov who was tried in camera in Moscow and hanged with piano wire on August 2, 1946.

The unsolicited reappearance of Soviet tanks on the streets of Prague in 1968 left most Czechs feeling somewhat ambivalent towards the old monument. And in the summer of 1991, artist **David Černý** painted the tank bubble-gum pink and placed a large phallic finger on top of it, while another mischievous Czech daubed "Vlasov" on the podium. Since the country was at the time engaged in delicate negotiations to end the Soviet military presence in Czechoslovakia, the new regime, despite its mostly dissident leanings, roundly condemned the act as unlawful. Havel, in his characteristically even-handed way, made it clear that he didn't like tanks anywhere, whether on the battlefield or as monuments.

In the end, the tank was hastily repainted khaki green and Černý was arrested under the "crimes against the state" clause of the penal code, which had previously been used by the Communists against several members of the then government. In protest at the arrest of Černý, twelve members of the federal parliament turned up the following day in their overalls and, taking advantage of their legal immunity, repainted the tank pink. Finally, the government gave in, released Černý and removed the tank from public view. There's now no trace of tank, podium or plaque on the square (which has been renamed **náměstí Kinských**). You can, however, still see the tank at the Vojenské technické museum (Military Technical Museum) in Lešany, 40km or so southeast of Prague.

West German embassy in Prague. Honecker, the East German leader, was forced to resign and, by the end of October, nightly mass demonstrations were taking place on the streets of Leipzig and other German cities. The **fall of the Berlin Wall** on November 9 left Czechoslovakia, Romania and Albania alone on the Eastern European stage still clinging to the old truths.

All eyes were now turned upon Czechoslovakia. Reformists within the KSČ began plotting an internal coup to overthrow Jakeš, in anticipation of a Soviet denunciation of the 1968 invasion. In the end, events overtook whatever plans they may have had. On Friday, **November 17**, a 50,000-strong peaceful demonstration organized by the official Communist youth organization was viciously attacked by the riot police. More than one hundred arrests, five hundred injuries and one death were reported (the fatality was later retracted) in what became popularly known as the *masakr* (massacre). Prague's students immediately began an occupation strike, joined soon after by the city's actors, who together called for an end to the Communist Party's "leading role" and a general strike to be held for two hours on November 27.

Civic Forum and the VPN

On Sunday, November 19, on Václav Havel's initiative, the established opposition groups, including Charter 77, met and agreed to form *Občanské fórum*, or **Civic Forum**. Their demands were simple: the resignation of the present hardline leadership, including Husák and Jakeš; an enquiry into the police actions of November 17; an amnesty for all political prisoners; and support for the general strike. In Bratislava, a parallel organization, *Veřejnost' proti nasiliu*, or **People Against Violence** (VPN), was set up to coordinate protest in Slovakia.

On the Monday evening, the first of the really big **nationwide demonstrations** took place – the biggest since the 1968 invasion – with more than 200,000 people pouring into Prague's Wenceslas Square. This time the police held back and rumours of troop deployments proved false. Every night for a week people poured into the main squares in towns and cities across the country, repeating the calls for democracy, freedom and an end to the Party's monopoly of power. As the week dragged on, the Communist media tentatively began to report events, and the KSČ leadership started to splinter under the strain, with the prime minister, **Ladislav Adamec**, alone in sticking his neck out and holding talks with the opposition.

The end of one-party rule

On Friday evening, Dubček, the ousted 1968 leader, appeared alongside Havel, before a crowd of 300,000 in Wenceslas Square, and in a matter of hours the entire Jakeš leadership had resigned. The weekend brought the largest demonstrations the country had ever seen – more than 750,000 people in Prague alone. At the invitation of Civic Forum, Adamec addressed the crowd, only to be booed off the platform. On Monday, November 27, eighty percent of the country's workforce joined the two-hour **general strike**, including many of the Party's previously stalwart allies, such as the miners and engineers. The following day, the Party agreed to an end to one-party rule and the formation of a new "coalition government".

A temporary halt to the nightly demonstrations was called and the country waited expectantly for the "broad coalition" cabinet promised by Prime Minister Adamec. On December 3, another Communist-dominated line-up was announced by the Party and immediately denounced by Civic Forum and the VPN, who called for a fresh wave of demonstrations and another general strike for December 11. Adamec promptly resigned and was replaced by the Slovak Marián Čalfa. On December 10, one day before the second threatened general strike, Čalfa announced his provisional

"**Government of National Understanding**", with Communists in the minority for the first time since 1948 and multiparty elections planned for June 1990. Having sworn in the new government, President Husák, architect of the post-1968 "normalization", finally threw in the towel.

By the time the new Čalfa government was announced, the students and actors had been on strike continuously for over three weeks. The pace of change surprised everyone involved, but there was still one outstanding issue: the election of a new president. Posters shot up all round the capital urging "**HAVEL NA HRAD**" (Havel to the Castle – the seat of the presidency). The students were determined to see his election through, continuing their occupation strike until Havel was officially elected president by a unanimous vote of the Federal Assembly, and sworn in at the Hrad on December 29.

The 1990 elections

Czechoslovakia started the new decade full of optimism for what the future would bring. On the surface, the country had a lot more going for it than its immediate neighbours (with the possible exception of the GDR). The Communist Party had been swept from power without bloodshed, and, unlike the rest of Eastern Europe, Czechoslovakia had a strong interwar **democratic tradition** with which to identify – Masaryk's First Republic. Despite Communist economic mismanagement, the country still had a relatively high standard of living, a skilled workforce and a manageable foreign debt.

In reality, however, the situation was somewhat different. Not only was the country economically in a worse state than most people had imagined, it was also environmentally devastated, and its people were suffering from what Havel described as "post-prison psychosis" – an inability to think or act for themselves. The country had to go through the painful transition "from being a big fish in a small pond to being a sickly adolescent trout in a hatchery". As a result, it came increasingly to rely on its new-found saviour, the humble playwright-president, Václav Havel.

In most people's eyes, "Saint Václav" could do no wrong, though he himself was not out to woo his electorate. His call for the rapid **withdrawal of Soviet troops** was popular enough, but his apology for the postwar expulsion of Sudeten Germans was deeply resented, as was his generous amnesty which eased the country's overcrowded prisons. The amnesty was blamed by many for the huge **rise in crime** in 1990. Every vice in the book – from racism to homicide – raised its ugly head in the first year of freedom.

In addition, there was still a lot of talk about the possibility of "counterrevolution", given the thousands of unemployed StB (secret police) at large. Inevitably, accusations of previous StB involvement rocked each political party in turn in the run-up to the first elections. The controversial **lustrace** (literally "lustration" or cleansing) law, which barred all those on StB files from public office for the following five years, ended the career of many public figures, often on the basis of highly unreliable StB reports.

Despite all the inevitable hiccups, and the increasingly vocal Slovak nationalists, Civic Forum/VPN remained high in the opinion polls. The **June 1990 elections** produced a record-breaking 99 percent turnout. With around sixty percent of the vote, Civic Forum/VPN were clear victors (the Communists won just 13 percent) and Havel immediately set about forming a broad "Coalition of National Sacrifice", including everyone from Christian Democrats to former Communists.

The main concern of the new government was how to transform an outdated command-system economy into a **market economy**. The argument over the speed and model of economic reform eventually caused Civic Forum to split into two main camps: the centre-left Občánské hnutí, or Civic Movement (OH), led by the foreign minister and former dissident Jiří Dienstbier, who favoured a more gradualist approach; and Občánská demokratická strana, the right-wing **Civic Democratic Party** (ODS), headed by the finance minister **Václav Klaus**, whose pronouncement that the country should "walk the tightrope to Thatcherism" sent shivers up the spines of those familiar with the UK in the 1980s.

One of the first acts of the new government was to pass a **restitution law**, handing back small businesses and property to those from whom it had been expropriated after the 1948 Communist coup. This proved to be a controversial issue, since it excluded Jewish families driven out in 1938 by the Nazis, and, of course, the millions of Sudeten Germans who were forced to flee the country after the war. A law was later passed to cover the Jewish expropriations, but the Sudeten German issue remains unresolved.

The Slovak crisis

One of the most intractable issues facing post-Communist Czechoslovakia turned out to be the **Slovak problem**. Having been the victim of Prague-inspired centralization from Masaryk to Gottwald, the Slovaks were in no mood to suffer second-class citizenship any longer. In the aftermath of 1989, feelings were running high in Slovakia, and more than once the spectre of a "Slovak UDI" was threatened by Slovak politicians, who hoped to boost their popularity by appealing to voters' nationalism. Despite the tireless campaigning and negotiating by both sides, a compromise failed to emerge.

The **June 1992 elections** soon became an unofficial referendum on the future of the federation. Events moved rapidly towards the break-up of the republic after the resounding victory of the Movement for a Democratic Slovakia (HZDS), under the wily, populist politician Vladimír Mečiar, who, in retrospect, was quite clearly seeking Slovak independence, though he never explicitly said so during the campaign. In the Czech Lands, the right-wing ODS emerged as the largest single party, under Václav Klaus, who – ever the economist – was clearly not going to shed tears over losing the economically backward Slovak half of the country.

Talks between the two sides got nowhere, despite the fact of opinion polls in both countries consistently showing majority support for the federation. The HZDS then blocked the re-election of Havel, who had committed himself entirely to the pro-federation cause. Havel promptly resigned, leaving the country president-less and Klaus and Mečiar to talk over the terms of the divorce. On January 1, 1993, after 74 years of troubled existence, **Czechoslovakia was officially divided** into two new countries: the Czech Republic and Slovakia.

Czech politics under Klaus

Generally speaking, life was much kinder to the Czechs than the Slovaks in the immediate period following the break-up of Czechoslovakia. While the Slovaks had the misfortune of being led by the increasingly wayward and isolated Mečiar, the Czechs enjoyed a long period of **political stability** under

Klaus, with Havel immediately re-elected as Czech president. Under their guidance, the country jumped to the front of the queue for EU and NATO membership, and was held up as a shining example to all other former Eastern Bloc countries. Prague attracted more foreign investment than anywhere else in the country – plus thousands of American expats into the bargain – and was transformed beyond all recognition, its main thoroughfares lined with brand-new hotels, shops and restaurants.

Klaus and his party, the ODS, certainly proved themselves the most durable of all the new political forces to emerge in the former Eastern Bloc. Nevertheless, in the **1996 elections**, although the ODS again emerged as the largest single party, they failed to gain an outright majority. They repeated the failure again during the first elections for the Czech Senate, the upper house of the Czech parliament. The electorate was distinctly unenthusiastic about the whole idea of another chamber full of overpaid politicians, and a derisory thirty percent turned out to vote in the second round. In the end, however, it was – predictably enough – a series of allegations of corruption over the country's privatization that eventually prompted **Klaus's resignation** as prime minister in 1997.

Political stalemate

The **1998 elections** proved that the Czechs had grown sick and tired of Klaus's dry, rather arrogant, style of leadership. However, what really did for Klaus was that for the first time since he took power, the economy had begun to falter. The **ČSSD**, or Social Democrats, under **Miloš Zeman**, emerged as the largest single party, promising to pay more attention to social issues. Unable to form a majority government, Zeman followed the Austrian example, and decided to make an "**opposition agreement**" with the ODS. This Faustian pact was dubbed the "Toleranzpatent" by the press, after the 1781 Edict of Tolerance issued by Joseph II. The Czech public were unimpressed, seeing the whole deal as a cosy stitch-up, and in 2000, thousands turned out in Wenceslas Square for the *Díky a odejděte* (Thank you, now leave) protest, asking for the resignation of both Zeman and Klaus.

Havel stepped down in 2003 after ten years as Czech president, to be replaced by his old sparring partner, Václav Klaus. No Czech president is ever likely to enjoy the same moral stature, though by the end of his tenure even Havel's standing was not what it used to be. His marriage to the actress Dagmar Veškrnová, seventeen years his junior, in 1997, less than a year after his first wife, Olga, died of cancer, was frowned upon by many. And his very public fall-out with his sister-in-law, Olga Havlová, over the family inheritance of the multimillion-crown Lucerna complex in Prague, didn't do his reputation any favours either.

One of the biggest problems to emerge in the 1990s was the issue of **Czech racism towards the Romany minority** within the country. Matters came to a head in 1999 over the planned building of a wall to separate Romanies and non-Romanies in the north Bohemian city of **Ústí nad Labem**. The central government, under pressure from the EU, condemned the construction of the wall, and eventually the local council rehoused the white Czechs elsewhere. This is an issue that won't go away easily – only a concerted campaign of anti-racism, grass-roots social work and the implementation of equal opportunities policies will effectively counter the prejudices of the vast majority of Czechs.

The Czechs in the EU

In June 2003, just 55 percent of the population turned out to vote in the **EU referendum**, with 77 percent voting in favour of joining. On May 1, 2004, the Czech Republic formally joined the EU, along with nine other accession states. Despite their growing cynicism, Czechs genuinely celebrated their entry into the EU; for many, it was the culmination of everything that had been fought for in 1968 and 1989, a final exorcism of the enforced isolation of the Communist period.

EU accession has been fairly positive for the Czechs. Their **economy** has held up well, so there has been no great flight of labour from the country as there has been in Poland. Despite the global financial crisis, the conservative Czech financial system has remained relatively healthy. If anything, they have suffered from the crown being consistently overvalued, leading to a drop in the number of tourists in 2009 for the first time in twenty years.

The most persistent problem is the Czech political system itself, which continues to produce **weak coalition governments**, further alienating an already deeply cynical electorate. One of the sticking blocks is that the Communists continue to receive around 13 percent of the vote, but are shunned by all the other parties. The **2006 elections** were a case in point, with left and right gaining exactly 100 seats each. It took over six months before Mirek Topolánek of the ODS succeeded in winning a vote of confidence for his coalition government. Topolánek's coalition lasted just over two years before a vote of no confidence. The electorate's disenchantment with the traditional political parties was demonstrated in the **2010 elections** when support for the leading parties of the left and right almost halved.

Books

A great deal of Czech fiction and poetry has been translated into English and is easily available. The key moments in Czech twentieth-century history are also well covered in English. More recently, there have been a whole number of books published in English in Prague, and for these you may need to go to one of the city's English-language bookstores (listed on p.217). Books marked with ⚘ are particularly recommended.

History, politics and society

Chad Bryant *Prague in Black*. An intriguing scholarly investigation of the roots of Czech nationalism, first under Nazi occupation and then during the lead-up to the 1948 Communist coup.

Peter Demetz *Prague in Black and Gold: Scenes from the Life of a European City*. Demetz certainly knows his subject, both academically and at first hand, having been brought up in the city before World War II (when his account ends). His style can be a little dry, but he is determinedly un-partisan, and refreshingly anti-nationalist in his reading of history. In *Prague in Danger* Demetz intersperses his even-handed, objective account of resistance under the Nazi occupation with personal anecdotes of living as a *Mischling*, or "half Jew", in Prague through that period.

R.J.W. Evans *Rudolf II and his World*. First published in 1973, and still the best account of the alchemy-mad emperor, but not as salacious as one might hope.

Jan Kaplan and Krystyna Nosarzewska *Prague: The Turbulent Century*. This is the first real attempt to cover the twentieth-century history of Prague with all its warts. The text isn't as good as it should be, but the book is worth it just for the incredible range of photographs and images.

Karel Kaplan *The Short March: The Communist Takeover in Czechoslovakia, 1945–48*. An excellent account of

the electoral rise and rise of the Communists in Czechoslovakia after the war, which culminated in the bloodless coup of February 1948. *Report on the Murder of the General Secretary* is an incredibly detailed study of the country's brutal Stalinist show trials, and most famously that of Rudolf Slánský, number two in the Party until his arrest.

⚘ **Callum MacDonald** *The Assassination of Reinhard Heydrich*. Gripping account of the build-up to the most successful and controversial act of wartime resistance, which took place in May 1942, and prompted horrific reprisals by the Nazis on the Czechs.

Peter Marshall *The Theatre of the World: Alchemy, Astrology and Magic in Renaissance Prague*. Detailed account of Rudolf II's court and its famous luminaries: Tycho Brahe, Kepler, Arcimboldo and the magic makers.

Derek Sayer *The Coasts of Bohemia*. A very readable cultural history, concentrating on Bohemia and Prague, which aims to dispel the ignorance shown by the Shakespearean quote of the title, and particularly illuminating on the subject of twentieth-century artists.

Kieran Williams *The Prague Spring and its Aftermath: Czechoslovak Politics, 1968–70*. Drawing on declassified archives, this book analyses the attempted reforms under Dubček and takes a new look at the Prague Spring.

Elizabeth Wiskemann *Czechs and Germans*. Researched and written in the build-up towards Munich, this is the most fascinating and fair treatment of the Sudeten problem. Meticulous in her detail, vast in her scope, Wiskemann manages to suffuse the weighty text with enough anecdotes to keep you gripped. Unique.

Essays, memoirs and biographies

Margarete Buber-Neumann *Milena*. A moving biography of Milena Jesenská, one of interwar Prague's most beguiling characters, who befriended the author while they were both interned in Ravensbrück concentration camp.

Karel Čapek *Talks with T.G. Masaryk*. Čapek was a personal (and political) friend of Masaryk, and his diaries, journals, reminiscences and letters give great insights into the man who personified the First Republic.

Helen Epstein *Where She Came From: A Daughter's Search for her Mother's History*. Daughter of a Holocaust survivor, the author traces the effects of anti-Semitism through three generations of women.

Patrick Leigh Fermor *A Time of Gifts*. The first volume of Leigh Fermor's trilogy based on his epic walk along the Rhine and Danube rivers in 1933–34. In the last quarter of the book he reaches Czechoslovakia, indulging in a quick jaunt to Prague before crossing the border into Hungary. Written forty years later in dense, luscious and highly crafted prose, it's an evocative and poignant insight into the culture of *Mitteleuropa* between the wars.

Timothy Garton Ash *We The People: The Revolutions of 89*. A personal, anecdotal, eyewitness account of the Velvet Revolution (and the events in Poland, Berlin and Budapest). By far the most compelling of all the post-1989 books. Published as *The Magic Lantern* in the US.

Patricia Hampl *A Romantic Education*. This American author went to Prague in the 1980s in search of her Czech roots and the contrasting cultures of East and West; the book was reissued and updated in 1999 to mark the tenth anniversary of the Velvet Revolution.

Václav Havel The first essay in *Living in Truth* is "Power of the Powerless", Havel's lucid, damning indictment of the inactivity of the Czechoslovak masses in the face of "normalization". *Disturbing the Peace* is probably Havel's most accessible work: a series of autobiographical questions and answers in which he talks interestingly about his childhood, the events of 1968 when he was in Liberec and the path to Charter 77 and beyond (though not including his reactions to being thrust into the role of president).

Václav Havel et al. *Power of the Powerless*. A collection of essays by leading Chartists, kicking off with Havel's seminal title-piece. Other contributors range from the dissident Marxist Petr Uhl to devout Catholics like Václav Benda.

Miroslav Holub *The Dimension of the Present Moment and other essays*; *Shedding Life: Disease, Politics and Other Human Conditions*. Two books of short philosophical musings/essays on life and the universe by this unusual and clever scientist-poet.

John Keane *Václav Havel: A Political Tragedy in Six Acts*. The first book to tell both sides of the Havel story: Havel the dissident playwright and civil rights activist who played a key role in the 1989 Velvet Revolution, and Havel the ageing and increasingly ill president, who has, in many people's opinion, simply stayed on the stage too long.

Benjamin Kuras *Czechs and Balances* and *Is There Life After Marx?* Witty, light, typically Czech takes on national identity and central European politics. *As Golems Go* is a more mystical look at Rabbi Löw's philosophy and the Kabbalah.

Heda Margolius Kovaly *Prague Farewell*. An autobiography that starts in the concentration camps of World War II and ends with the author's flight from Czechoslovakia in 1968. Married to Rudolf Margolius, one of the Party officials executed in the 1952 Slánský trial, she tells her story simply and without bitterness. The best account there is of the fear and paranoia whipped up during the Stalinist terror. Published as *Under a Cruel Star* in the US.

Ivan Margolius *Reflections of Prague: Journeys Through the 20th Century*. A moving account of the lives of his parents, Heda and Rudolf Margolius (see above), and the story of his own return to Prague to find out the truth about his father.

Nicholas Murray *Kafka*. A superbly researched and very level-headed assessment of the German-Czech writer, who spent almost all of his short life in Prague.

Ota Pavel *How I Came to Know Fish*. Pavel's childhood innocence shines through particularly when his Jewish father and two brothers are sent to a concentration camp and he and his mother have to scrape a living.

Pressburger and Lappin *The Diary of Petr Ginz: 1941-1942*. Discovered in 2003, this is the diary of a fifteen-year-old boy who was taken first to Terezín and then to Auschwitz, where

he died. He was exceptionally gifted, writing a Czech-Esperanto dictionary among other things, and his writing offers parallels with Anne Frank.

Angelo Maria Ripellino *Magic Prague*. A wide-ranging look at the bizarre array of historical and literary characters who have lived in Prague, from the mad antics of the court of Rudolf II to the escapades of Jaroslav Hašek. Scholarly, rambling, richly and densely written – unique and recommended.

Josef Škvorecký *Talkin' Moscow Blues*. Without doubt the most user-friendly of Škvorecký's works, containing a collection of essays on his wartime childhood, Czech jazz, literature and contemporary politics, all told in his inimitable, irreverent and infuriating way. Published as *Headed for the Blues* in the US.

Ludvík Vaculík *A Cup of Coffee with My Interrogator*. A Party member until 1968, and signatory of Charter 77, Vaculík revived the *feuilleton* – a short political critique once much loved in central Europe. This collection dates from 1968 onwards.

Klaus Wagenbach *Kafka's Prague: A Travel Reader*. Hardback book that takes you through the streets in the footsteps of Kafka.

Zbyněk Zeman *The Masaryks: The Making of Czechoslovakia*. Written in the 1970s while Zeman was in exile, this is a very readable, none-too-sentimental biography of the country's founder Tomáš Garrigue Masaryk, and his son Jan Masaryk, the postwar Foreign Minister who died in mysterious circumstances shortly after the 1948 Communist coup.

Czech fiction

Josef Čapek *Stories about Doggie and Cat*. Josef Capek (Karel's older brother) was a Cubist artist of some renown, and also a children's

writer. These simple stories about a dog and a cat are wonderfully illustrated, and seriously postmodern.

Karel Čapek Karel Čapek was the literary and journalistic spokesperson for Masaryk's First Republic, but he's better known in the West for his plays, such as *The Insect Play* and *R.U.R.*, most of which are to be found in classic collections. Čapek's *Letters from England* had the distinction of being banned by the Nazis and the Communists for its naive admiration of England in the 1920s.

Daniela Fischerová *Fingers Pointing Somewhere Else*. Subtly nuanced, varied collection of short stories from dissident playwright Fischerová.

Ladislav Fuks *Mr Theodore Mundstock*. A very readable novel set in 1942 Prague, as the city's Jews wait to be transported to Terezín.

Jaroslav Hašek *The Good Soldier Švejk*. A rambling, picaresque tale by Bohemia's most bohemian writer of Czechoslovakia's famous fictional fifth columnist, *Švejk*, who wreaks havoc in the Austro-Hungarian army during World War I.

Václav Havel Havel's plays are not renowned for being easy to read (or watch). *The Memorandum*, one of his earliest works, is a classic absurdist drama that, in many ways, sets the tone for much of his later work, of which the *Three Vaněk Plays*, featuring Ferdinand Vaněk, Havel's alter ego, are perhaps the most successful. The 1980s collection includes *Largo Desolato, Temptation* and *Redevelopment*; freedom of thought, Faustian opportunism and town planning as metaphors of life under the Communists. *Leaving* is Havel's first play for twenty years and is a semi-autobiographical satire about a man giving up the top job.

Nancy Hawker (ed). *Povídky: Short Stories by Czech Women*. Varied collection of stories written by women across the generations, set variously against a background of pre- and post-Communist times.

Bohumil Hrabal Hrabal is a thoroughly mischievous writer. The slim but superb *Closely Observed Trains* is a postwar classic, set in the last days of the war and relentlessly unheroic; it was made into an equally brilliant film by Jiří Menzl. *I Served the King of England* follows the antihero Díte, who works at the Hotel Paříž, through the decade after 1938. *Too Loud a Solitude*, about a waste-paper disposer under the Communists, has also been made into a film, again by Menzl.

Alois Jirásek *Old Czech Legends*. A major figure in the nineteenth-century Czech *národní obrození*, Jirásek popularized Bohemia's legendary past. This collection includes all the classic texts, as well as the story of the founding of the city by the prophetess Libuše.

Franz Kafka A German-Jewish Praguer, Kafka has drawn the darker side of central Europe – its claustrophobia, paranoia and unfathomable bureaucracy – better than anyone else, both in a rural setting, as in *The Castle*, and in an urban one, in one of the great novels of the twentieth century, *The Trial*.

Ivan Klíma A survivor of Terezín, Klíma is another writer in the Kundera mould as far as sexual politics goes, but his stories are a lot lighter. *Judge on Trial*, written in the 1970s, is one of his best, concerning the moral dilemmas of a Communist judge. *Waiting for the Dark, Waiting for the Light* is a pessimistic novel set before, during and after the Velvet Revolution of 1989. *The Spirit of Prague* is a very readable collection of biographical and more general essays on subjects ranging from Klíma's childhood experiences in Terezín to the current situation in Prague. *No Saints or Angels* is a fairly bleak novel set in post-revolutionary Prague, and exploring three different generations' reactions to the fall of Communism. *Between*

Security and Insecurity takes a look at modern values in society, their causes and their possible futures.

Jan Kaplan *A Traveler's Companion to Prague*. A compilation of memoirs, letters and extracts from diaries and novels, from the medieval to modern, to accompany a stroll round Prague.

Pavel Kohout *Widow Killer* and *I am Snowing: The Confessions of a Woman of Prague*. The latter is set in the uneasy period just after the fall of Communism amid accusations of collaboration. The *Widow Killer* is a thriller about a naive Czech detective partnered with a Gestapo agent in the last months of World War II in German-occupied Prague.

Milan Kundera Milan Kundera is the country's most popular writer – at least with non-Czechs. His early books were very obviously "political", particularly *The Book of Laughter and Forgetting*, which led the Communists to revoke Kundera's citizenship. *The Joke*, written while he was still living in Czechoslovakia and in many ways his best work, is set in the very unfunny era of the 1950s. Its clear, humorous style is far removed from the carefully poised posturing of his most famous novel, *The Unbearable Lightness of Being*, set in and after 1968, and successfully turned into a film some twenty years later. *Identity* is a series of slightly detached musings on the human condition and is typical of his later works. *Testaments Betrayed*, on the other hand, is a fascinating series of essays about a range of subjects from the formation of historical reputation to the problems of translations. Kundera now writes in French.

Arnošt Lustig *Diamonds of the Night*; *Night and Hope*; *A Prayer for Kateřina Horovitová; Waiting for Leah*. A Prague Jew exiled since 1968, Lustig spent World War II in Terezín, Buchenwald and Auschwitz, and his novels and short stories are consistently set amid the horror of the Terezín camp.

Gustav Meyrink Meyrink was another of Prague's weird and wonderful characters. He started out as a bank manager but soon became involved in Kabbalah, alchemy and drug experimentation. *The Golem*, based on Rabbi Löw's monster, is one of the classic versions of the tale. *The Angel of the West Window* is a historical novel about John Dee, an English alchemist invited to Prague in the late sixteenth century by Rudolf II.

Jan Neruda *Prague Tales*. These are short, bittersweet snapshots of life in Malá Strana at the close of the last century. The author is not to be confused with the Chilean Pablo Neruda (who took his name from the Czech writer).

Karel Poláček *What Ownership's All About*. A darkly comic novel set in a Prague tenement block, dealing with Fascism and appeasement, by a Jewish-Czech Praguer who died in the camps in 1944.

Peter Sís *The Three Golden Keys*. Short, hauntingly illustrated children's book set in Prague, by Czech-born American Sís.

Josef Škvorecký A relentless anti-Communist, Škvorecký is typically Bohemian in his bawdy sense of humour and irreverence for all high moralizing. *The Cowards* (which briefly saw the light of day in 1958) is the tale of a group of irresponsible young men in the last days of the war, an antidote to the lofty prose from official authors at the time, but hampered by its dated Americanized translation. *The Miracle Game* enjoys a better translation and is set against the two "miracles" of 1948 and 1968. Less well known (and understandably so) are Škvorecký's detective stories featuring a podgy, depressive Czech cop, Lieutenant Boruvka, which he wrote in the 1960s at a time when his more serious work was banned.

Zdena Tomin *Stalin's Shoe*. The compelling and complex story of a girl coming to terms with her Stalinist childhood. *The Coast of Bohemia* is based on Tomin's experiences of the late 1970s dissident movement, when she was an active member of Charter 77. Although Czech-born, Tomin writes in English (the language of her exile since 1980) and has a style and fluency all her own.

Jáchym Topol *City, Sister, Silver*. Dissident writer and lyricist for Czech rock band Psí vojáci, Topol's first novel to be translated into English is an inventive take on the alienation and disappointment experienced by the younger generation after the Velvet Revolution.

Ludvík Vaculík *The Guinea Pigs*. This catalogues the slow dehumanization of Czech society in the aftermath of the Soviet invasion. *The Axe* centres on the cultural upheaval of the mid-1960s. Vaculík himself was expelled from the Party during the 1968 Prague Spring and went on to sign Charter 77.

Jiří Weil *Life With a Star; Mendelssohn is on the Roof*. Two novels written just after the war and based on Weil's experiences as a Czech Jew in hiding during the Nazi occupation of Prague.

Paul Wilson (ed.) *Prague: A Traveler's Literary Companion*. A great selection of short stories and snippets on Prague from, among others, Meyrink, Kisch and Čapek, plus contemporary writers like Jáchym Topol.

Poetry

Petr Borkovec *From the Interior – Poems 1995–2005*. Born in 1970, Borkovec writes poetry that is not political, but personal and lyrical. Translated by Justin Quinn in a dual text, it makes for very accessible reading.

Sylva Fischerová *The Tremor of Racehorses: Selected Poems*. Poet and novelist Fischerová in many ways continues in the Holub tradition. Her poems are by turns powerful, obtuse and personal, and were written in exile in Switzerland and Germany after she fled in 1968.

Josef Hanzlík *Selected Poems*. Refreshingly accessible collection of poems written over the last forty years by a poet of Havel's generation.

Miroslav Holub Holub is a scientist and scholar, and his poetry reflects this unique fusion of master poet and chief immunologist. Regularly banned in his own country, he was the Czech poet par excellence – classically trained, erudite, liberal and westward-leaning. The full range of his work, including some previously unpublished poems, are published in *Intensive Care: Selected and New Poems*.

Rainer Maria Rilke *Selected Poetry*. Rilke's upbringing was unexceptional, except that his mother brought him up as a girl until the age of six. In his adult life, he became one of Prague's leading authors of the interwar period and subsequently probably the best-known poet outside Czechoslovakia.

Marcela Rydlová-Herlich (ed) *Treasury of Czech Love Poems*. A good way to get a taste of a variety of Czech poetry from over 33 poets, most of whom are twentieth century.

Jaroslav Seifert *The Poetry of Jaroslav Seifert*. The only Czech writer to win the Nobel Prize for Literature, Seifert was a founder-member of the Communist Party and the avant-garde arts movement Devětsil, later falling from grace and signing the Charter in his old age. His longevity means that his work covers some of the most turbulent times in Czechoslovak history, but his irrepressible lasciviousness has been known to irritate.

Literature by foreign writers

David Brierley *On Leaving a Prague Window*. A very readable (if dated) thriller set in post-Communist Prague, which shows that past connection with dissidents can still lead to violence.

Bruce Chatwin *Utz*. Chatwin is from the "exotic" school of travel writers, hence this slim, intriguing and mostly true-to-life account of an avid porcelain collector from Prague's Jewish quarter.

Sue Gee *Letters from Prague*. The central character in this book falls in love with a Czech student in England in 1968, but she returns home when the Russians invade. Twenty years later, together with her 10-year-old daughter, she goes in search of him.

Sulamith Ish-Kishor *A Boy of Old Prague*. Deservedly back in print, this story, set in the Jewish ghetto in the sixteenth century, tells how a poor Christian boy discovers that Jews are not the monsters that he's been told. Aimed at children aged 8 to 11.

Kathy Kacer *Clara's War*. The story of a young girl and her family who are sent from Prague to Terezín in 1943. The horror is played down as the book is aimed at children of 10-plus, but nevertheless it is based on truth.

Anthony J. Rudel *Imagining Don Giovanni*. Mozart, Da Ponte and Casanova collaborate on the production of *Don Giovanni* with the Marquis de Sade thrown in. An imaginative evocation of the period which will delight music lovers.

Jill Paton Walsh *A Desert in Bohemia*. A gripping story set against the aftermath of World War II and the subsequent political upheaval in Czechoslovakia.

Prague's leading personalities – past and present

Beneš, Edvard (1884–1948). Hero to some, traitor to others, Beneš was president from 1935 until 1938 – when he resigned, having refused to lead the country into bloodshed over the Munich Crisis – and again from 1945 until 1948, when he acquiesced in the Communist coup.

Brahe, Tycho (1546–1601). Ground-breaking Danish astronomer, who was summoned to Prague by Rudolf II in 1597, only to die from over-drinking in 1601.

Braun, Matthias Bernard (1684–1738). Austrian sculptor who achieved his greatest fame in the Czech Lands, executing sculptures for the city's Baroque palaces, gardens and churches.

Brokoff, Ferdinand Maximilian (1688–1731). Along with Braun, Prague's most famous Baroque sculptor, several of whose works adorn the Charles Bridge.

Čapek, Josef (1887–1945). Cubist artist and writer and illustrator of children's books, Josef was older brother to the more famous Karel (see below); he died in Belsen concentration camp.

Čapek, Karel (1890–1938). Czech writer, journalist and unofficial spokesperson for the First Republic. His most famous works are *The Insect Play* and *R.U.R.*, which introduced the word *robot* into the English language.

Dientzenhofer, Kilian Ignác (1689–1751). One of the city's most prolific Baroque architects, whose most famous work is probably the church of sv Mikuláš in Malá Strana.

Dobrovský, Josef (1753–1829). Jesuit-taught pioneer in Czech philology. Wrote the seminal text *The History of Czech Language and Literature*.

Dubček, Alexander (1921–92). Slovak Communist who became First Secretary in January 1968, at the beginning of the Prague Spring. Expelled from the Party in 1969, but returned to become speaker in the federal parliament after 1989, before being killed in a car crash in 1992.

Dvořák, Antonín (1841–1904). Perhaps the most famous of all Czech composers. His best-known work is the *New World Symphony*, inspired by an extensive sojourn in the US.

Fučik, Julius (1903–43). Communist journalist murdered by the Nazis, whose prison writings, *Notes from the Gallows*, were obligatory reading in the 1950s. Hundreds of streets were named after him, but doubts about the authenticity of the work and general hostility towards the man have made him *persona non grata*.

Gottwald, Klement (1896–1953). One of the founders of the KSČ, general secretary from 1927, prime minister from 1946 to 1948, and president from 1948 to 1953, Gottwald is universally abhorred for his role in the show trials of the 1950s.

Hašek, Jaroslav (1883–1923). Anarchist, dog-breeder, lab assistant, bigamist, cabaret artist and People's Commissar in the Red Army, Hašek was one of prewar Prague's most colourful characters, who wrote the famous *The Good Soldier Švejk* and died from alcohol abuse in 1923.

Havel, Václav (1936–). Absurdist playwright of the 1960s, who became a leading spokesperson of Charter 77 and, following the Velvet Revolution, the country's first post-Communist president.

Havlíček-Borovský, Karel (1821–56). Satirical poet, journalist and nationalist, exiled to the Tyrol by the Austrian authorities after 1848.

Hrabal, Bohumil (1936–97). Writer and bohemian, whose novels were banned under the Communists, but revered worldwide.

Hus, Jan (1370–1415). Rector of Prague University and reformist preacher who was burnt at the stake as a heretic by the Council of Constance.

Husák, Gustáv (1913–91). Slovak Communist who was sentenced to life imprisonment in the show trials of the 1950s. Released in 1960, he eventually became General Secretary and president following the Soviet invasion. Resigned in favour of Havel in December 1989.

Jirásek, Alois (1851–1930). Writer who popularized Czech legends for both children and adults and became a key figure in the Czech national revival.

Jungmann, Josef (1773–1847). Prolific Czech translator and author of the seminal *History of Czech Literature* and the first Czech dictionary.

Kafka, Franz (1883–1924). German-Jewish Praguer who worked as an insurance clerk in Prague for most of his life, and also wrote some of the most influential novels of the twentieth century, most notably *The Trial*.

Kelly, Edward (1555–97). English occultist who was summoned to Prague by Rudolf II, but eventually incurred the wrath of the emperor and was imprisoned in Kokořín castle.

Kepler, Johannes (1571–1630). German Protestant forced to leave Linz for Denmark because of the Counter-Reformation. Succeeded Tycho de Brahe as Rudolf II's chief astronomer. His observations of the planets became the basis of the laws of planetary motion.

Kisch, Egon Erwin (1885–1948). German-Jewish Praguer who became one of the city's most famous investigative journalists.

Klaus, Václav (1941–). Known somewhat bitterly as "Santa Klaus". Prime minister (1992–97), president (since 2003), confirmed Thatcherite and driving force behind the country's present economic reforms.

Komenský, Jan Amos (1592–1670). Leader of the Protestant Czech Brethren. Forced to flee the country and settle in England during the Counter-Reformation. Better known to English-speakers as Comenius.

Mácha, Karel Hynek (1810–36). Romantic nationalist poet, great admirer of Byron and Keats and, like them, died young. His most famous poem is *Maj*, published just months before his death.

Masaryk, Jan Garrigue (1886–1958). Son of the founder of the republic (see opposite), foreign minister in the postwar government and the only non-Communist in Gottwald's cabinet when the Communists took over in February 1948. Died ten days after the coup in suspicious circumstances.

Masaryk, Tomáš Garrigue (1850–1937). Professor of philosophy at Prague University, president of the Republic from 1918 to 1935. His name is synonymous with the First Republic and was removed from all street signs after the 1948 coup. Now back with a vengeance.

Mucha, Alfons (1860–1939). Moravian graphic artist and designer whose Art Nouveau posters and artwork for Sarah Bernhardt brought him international fame. After the founding of Czechoslovakia, he returned to the country to design stamps, bank notes, and complete a cycle of giant canvases on Czech nationalist themes.

Němcová, Božena (1820–62). Highly popular writer who became involved with the nationalist movement and shocked many with her unorthodox behaviour. Her most famous book is *Grandmother*.

Neruda, Jan (1834–91). Poet and journalist for the *Národní listy*. Wrote some famous short stories describing Prague's Malá Strana.

Palacký, František (1798–1876). Nationalist historian, Czech MP in Vienna and leading figure in the events of 1848.

Purkyně, Jan Evangelista (1787–1869). Czech doctor, natural scientist and pioneer in experimental physiology who became professor of physiology at Prague and then at Wrocław University.

Rieger, Ladislav (1818–1903). Nineteenth-century Czech politician and one of the leading figures in the events of 1848 and the aftermath.

Rilke, Rainer Maria (1876–1926). Despite having been brought up as a girl for the first six years of his life, Rilke ended up as an officer in the Austrian army, and wrote some of the city's finest German *fin de siècle* poetry.

Santini, Jan Blažej (1677–1723). The most unusual architect of his day, Santini was innovative in his use of symbolism and his attempt to fuse Gothic and Baroque elements.

Smetana, Bedřich (1824–84). Popular Czech composer and fervent nationalist whose *Má vlast* (My Homeland) traditionally opens the Prague Spring Music Festival.

Svoboda, Ludvík (1895–1979). Victorious Czech general from World War II, who acquiesced in the 1948 Communist coup and was Communist president from 1968 to 1975.

Tyl, Josef Kajetán (1808–56). Czech playwright and composer of the Czech half of the national anthem, *Where is my Home?*

Werfel, Franz (1890–1945). One of the German Jewish literary circle that included Kafka, Kisch and Brod.

Žižka, Jan (died 1424). Brilliant, blind military leader of the Táborites, the radical faction of the Hussites.

Language

Language

Czech

T
he official language of the Czech Republic is **Czech** (český), a highly complex Western Slav tongue. Any attempt to speak Czech will be heartily appreciated, though don't be discouraged if people seem not to understand, as most will be unaccustomed to hearing foreigners stumble through their language. English is widely spoken in hotels and restaurants, slightly less universally in shops and museums. Among the older generation at least, German is still the most widely spoken second language.

Pronunciation

English-speakers often find Czech impossibly difficult to pronounce. In fact, it's not half as daunting as it might first appear from the "traffic jams of consonants", as Patrick Leigh Fermor put it, which crop up on the page. An illustration of this is the Czech tongue-twister, *strč prst skrz krk* (stick your finger down your neck). Apart from a few special letters, each letter and syllable is pronounced as it's written – the trick is always to **stress the first syllable** of a word, no matter what its length; otherwise you'll render it unintelligible. Note that there is no definite or indefinite article, and word endings change according to their function in the sentence.

Short and long vowels

Czech has both short and long vowels (the latter being denoted by a variety of accents). The trick here is to lengthen the vowel without affecting the principal stress of the word, which is invariably on the first syllable.

a like the u in c**u**p	í or ý as in s**ea**t
á as in f**a**ther	o as in n**o**t
e as in p**e**t	ó as in d**oo**r
é as in f**ai**r	u like the oo in b**oo**k
ě like the ye in **ye**s	ů or ú like the oo in f**oo**l
i or y as in p**i**t	

Vowel combinations and diphthongs

There are very few diphthongs in Czech, so any combinations of vowels other than those below should be pronounced as two separate syllables.

au like the ou in f**ou**l
ou like the oe in f**oe**

Consonants and accents

There are no silent consonants, but it's worth remembering that r and l can form a syllable if standing between two other consonants or at the end of a word, as in

Brno (Br–no) or Vltava (Vl–ta–va). The consonants listed below are those which differ substantially from the English. Accents look daunting, particularly the háček, which appears above c, d, l, n, r, s, t and z, but the only one which causes a lot of problems is ř, probably the most difficult letter to say in the entire language. Even Czech toddlers have to be taught how to say it.

c like the **ts** in boats	mě pronounced as mnye
č like the **ch** in chicken	ň like the **n** in nuance
ch like the **ch** in the Scottish loch	p softer than the English **p**
ď like the **d** in duped	r as in rip, but often rolled
g always as in goat, never as in general	ř like the sound of **r** and **ž** combined
h always as in have, but more energetic	š like the **sh** in shop
j like the **y** in yoke	ť like the **t** in tutor
kd pronounced as **gd**	ž like the **s** in pleasure; at the end of a word
ľ like the **lli** in colliery	like the **sh** in shop

Words and phrases

Basics

Yes	ano	Yesterday	včera
No	ne	Tomorrow	zítra
Please/excuse me	prosím vás	The day after tomorrow	pozítří
Don't mention it	není zač	Now	hnet
Sorry	pardon	Later	později
Thank you	děkuju	Leave me alone	dej mi pokoj
Bon appétit	dobrou chuť	Go away	jdi pryč
Bon voyage	šťastnou cestu	Help!	pomoc!
Hello/goodbye (informal)	ahoj	This one	tento
Goodbye (formal)	na shledanou	A little	trochu
Good day	dobrý den	Large/small	velký/malý
Good morning	dobré ráno	More/less	více/méně
Good evening	dobrý večer	Good/bad	dobrý/špatný
Good night (when leaving)	dobrou noc	Hot/cold	horký/studený
How are you?	jak se máte?	With/without	s/bez
Today	dnes		

Getting around

Over here	tady		On foot	pěšky
Over there	tam		By taxi	taxíkem
Left	nalevo		Ticket	jízdenka/lístek
Right	napravo		Return ticket	zpateční
Straight on	rovně		Railway station	nádraží
Where is ...?	kde je...?		Bus station	autobusové nádraží
How do I get to Prague?	jak se dostanu do Prahy?		Bus stop	autobusová zastávka
			When's the next train to Prague?	kdy jede další vlak do Prahy?
How do I get to the university?	jak se dostanu k univerzitě?		Is it going to Prague?	jede to do Prahy?
By bus	autobusem		Do I have to change?	musím přestupovat?
By train	vlakem		Do I need a reservation?	musím mit místenku?
By car	autem			

Questions and answers

Do you speak English?	mluvíte anglicky?		How much is it?	kolík to stojí?
I don't speak German	nemluvím německy		Are there any rooms available?	máte volné pokoje?
I don't understand	nerozumím		I would like a double room	chtěl bych dvou lůžkovy pokoj
I understand	rozumím			
Speak slowly	mluvíte pomalu		For one night	na jednu noc
How do you say that in Czech?	jak se tohle řekne česky?		With shower	se sprchou
			Is this seat free?	je tu volna?
Could you write it down for me?	mužete mí to napsat?		May we (sit down)?	můžeme (se sednout)?
			The bill please	zaplatím prosím
What	co		Do you have...?	máte...?
Where	kde		We don't have	nemáme
When	kdy		We do have	máme
Why	proč			

Some signs

Entrance	vchod		Women	ženy
Exit	východ		Ladies	dámy
Toilets	záchody/toalety		Gentlemen	pánové
Men	muži		Open	otevřeno

The alphabet

In the Czech alphabet, letters which feature a **háček** (as in the č of the word itself) are considered separate letters and appear in Czech indexes immediately after their more familiar cousins. More confusingly, the consonant combination ch is also considered as a separate letter and appears in Czech indexes after the letter h. In the index in this book, we use the English system, so words beginning with c, č and ch all appear under c.

Closed	zavřeno	No entry	vstup zakázán
Danger!	pozor!	Arrival	příjezd
Hospital	nemocnice	Departure	odjezd
No smoking	kouření zakázáno	Police	policie
No bathing	koupání zakázáno		

Days of the week

Monday	pondělí	Sunday	neděle
Tuesday	úterý	Day	den
Wednesday	středa	Week	týden
Thursday	čtvrtek	Month	měsíc
Friday	pátek	Year	rok
Saturday	sobota		

Months of the year

Many Slav languages have their own highly individual systems in which the words for the names of the months are descriptive nouns sometimes beautifully apt for the month in question.

January	leden	ice	July	červenec	redder
February	únor	hibernation	August	srpen	sickle
March	březen	birch	September	září	blazing
April	duben	oak	October	říjen	rutting
May	květen	blossom	November	listopad	leaves falling
June	červen	red	December	prosinec	slaughter of pigs

Numbers

1	jeden	18	osmnáct
2	dva	19	devatenáct
3	tří	20	dvacet
4	čtyři	21	dvacetjedna
5	pět	30	třicet
6	šest	40	čtyřicet
7	sedm	50	padesát
8	osm	60	šedesát
9	devět	70	sedmdesát
10	deset	80	osmdesát
11	jedenáct	90	devadesát
12	dvanáct	100	sto
13	třináct	101	sto jedna
14	čtrnáct	155	sto padesát pět
15	patnáct	200	dvě stě
16	šestnáct	300	tři sta
17	sedmnáct	400	čtyři sta

500	pět set	800	osm set
600	šest set	900	devět set
700	sedm set	1000	tisíc

Food and drink terms

Basics

chléb	bread	pečivo	pastry
chlebíček	(open) sandwich	pepř	pepper
cukr	sugar	polévka	soup
hořčice	mustard	předkrmy	starters
houska	round roll	přílohy	side dishes
knedlíky	dumplings	rohlík	finger roll
křen	horseradish	rybby	fish
lžíce	spoon	rýže	rice
máslo	butter	sklenice	glass
maso	meat	snídaně	breakfast
med	honey	sůl	salt
mléko	milk	šálek	cup
moučník	dessert	talíř	plate
nápoje	drinks	tartarská omáčka	tartare sauce
nůž	knife	večeře	supper/dinner
oběd	lunch	vejce	eggs
obloha	garnish	vidlička	fork
ocet	vinegar	volské oko	fried egg
ovoce	fruit	zeleniny	vegetables

Soups

boršč	beetroot soup	kapustnica	sauerkraut, mushroom and meat soup
bramborová	potato soup		
čočková	lentil soup	kuřecí	thin chicken soup
fazolová	bean soup	rajská	tomato soup
hovězí vývar	beef broth	zeleninová	vegetable soup
hrachová	pea soup		

Fish

kapr	carp	rybí filé	fillet of fish
losos	salmon	sardinka	sardine
makrela	mackerel	štika	pike
platys	flounder	treska	cod
pstruh	trout	zavináč	herring/rollmop

269

Meat dishes

bažant	pheasant	ledvinky	kidneys
biftek	beef steak	řízek	steak
čevapčiči	spicy meat balls	roštěná	sirloin
dršťky	tripe	salám	salami
drůbež	poultry	sekaná	meat loaf
guláš	goulash	skopové maso	mutton
hovězí	beef	slanina	bacon
husa	goose	svíčková	fillet of beef
játra	liver	šunka	ham
jazyk	tongue	telecí	veal
kachna	duck	vepřový	pork
klobásy	sausages	vepřové řízek	breaded pork cutlet or schnitzel
kotleta	cutlet		
kuře	chicken	zajíc	hare
kýta	leg	žebírko	ribs

Vegetables

brambory	potatoes	kyselá okurka	pickled gherkin
brokolice	broccoli	kyselé zelí	sauerkraut
celer	celery	lečo	ratatouille
cibule	onion	lilek	aubergine
česnek	garlic	okurka	cucumber
chřest	asparagus	pórek	leek
čočka	lentils	rajče	tomato
fazole	beans	ředkev	radish
houby	mushrooms	řepná bulva	beetroot
hranolky	chips, French fries	špenát	spinach
hrášek	peas	zelí	cabbage
karot	carrot	žampiony	mushrooms
květák	cauliflower		

Fruit, cheese and nuts

banán	banana	jahody	strawberries
borůvky	blueberries	kompot	stewed fruit
broskev	peach	maliny	raspberries
brusinky	cranberries	mandle	almonds
bryndza	goat's cheese in brine	meruňka	apricot
citrón	lemon	niva	semi-soft, crumbly, blue cheese
grejp	grapefruit		
hermelín	Czech brie	oříšky	peanuts
hrozny	grapes	ostružiny	blackberries
hruška	pear	oštěpek	heavily smokedcurd cheese
jablko	apple		

parenica	rolled strips of lightly smoked, curd cheese	třešně	cherries
pivní sýr	cheese flavoured with beer	tvaroh	fresh curd cheese
		urda	soft, freshwhey cheese
pomeranč	orange	uzený sýr	smoked cheese
rozinky	raisins	vlašské ořechy	walnuts
švestky	plums		

Common terms

čerstvý	fresh	s.m. (s máslem)	with butter
domácí	home-made	sladký	sweet
dušený	stew/casserole	slaný	salted
grilovaný	roast on the spit	smažený	fried in breadcrumbs
kyselý	sour	studený	cold
na kmíně	with caraway seeds	syrový	raw
na roštu	grilled	sýrový	cheesy
na zdraví	cheers!	teplý	hot
nadívaný	stuffed	uzený	smoked
nakládaný	pickled	vařený	boiled
(za)pečený	baked/roast	znojmský	with gherkins
plněný	stuffed		

Drinks

čaj	tea	s ledem	with ice
destiláty	spirits	soda	soda
káva	coffee	suché víno	dry wine
koňak	brandy	šumivý	fizzy
láhev	bottle	svařené víno/svařák	mulled wine
minerální (voda)	mineral (water)	tonic	tonic
mléko	milk	vinný střik	white wine with soda
pivo	beer	víno	wine
presso	espresso		

A glossary of Czech words and terms

brána gate

český Bohemian

chata chalet-type bungalow, country cottage or mountain hut

chrám large church

divadlo theatre

dóm cathedral

dům house

dům kultury generic term for local arts and social centre; literally "House of Culture"

hora mountain

hospoda pub

hostinec pub

hrad castle

hřbitov cemetery

kaple chapel

katedrála cathedral

kavárna coffee house

klášter monastery/convent

kostel church

koupaliště swimming pool

Labe River Elbe

lanovka funicular or cable car

les forest

město town

most bridge

muzeum museum

nábřeží embankment

nádraží train station

náměstí square

ostrov island

palác palace

památník memorial or monument

pasáž indoor shopping mall

pivnice pub

radnice town hall

restaurace restaurant

sad park

sál room or hall (in a chateau or castle)

schody steps

svatý/svatá saint; often abbreviated to sv

třída avenue

ulice street

věž tower

vinárna wine bar or cellar

Vltava River Moldau

vrchy hills

výstava exhibition

zahrada garden

zámek chateau

An architectural glossary

Ambulatory Passage round the back of the altar, in continuation of the aisles.

Art Nouveau French term for the sinuous and stylized form of architecture dating from 1900 to 1910; known as the Secession in the Czech Republic and as *Jugendstil* in Germany.

Baroque Expansive, exuberant architectural style of the seventeenth and mid-eighteenth centuries, characterized by ornate decoration, complex spatial arrangement and grand vistas.

Chancel The part of the church where the altar is placed, usually at the east end.

Empire Highly decorative Neoclassical style of architecture and decorative arts, practised in the early 1800s.

Fresco Mural painting applied to wet plaster, so that the colours immediately soak into the wall.

Functionalism Plain, boxy, modernist architectural style, prevalent in the late 1920s and 1930s in Czechoslovakia, often using plate-glass curtain walls and open-plan interiors.

Gothic Architectural style prevalent from the fourteenth to the sixteenth century, characterized by pointed arches and ribbed vaulting.

Loggia Covered area on the side of a building, often arcaded.

Nave Main body of a church, usually the western end.

Neoclassical Late eighteenth- and early nineteenth-century style of architecture and design returning to classical Greek and Roman models as a reaction against Baroque and Rococo excesses.

Oriel A bay window, usually projecting from an upper floor.

Rococo Highly florid, fiddly, though (occasionally) graceful, style of architecture and interior design, forming the last phase of Baroque.

Romanesque Solid architectural style of the late tenth to thirteenth century, characterized by round-headed arches and geometrical precision.

Secession Linear and stylized form of architecture and decorative arts imported from Vienna as a reaction against the academic establishment.

Sgraffito Monochrome plaster decoration effected by means of scraping back the first white layer to reveal the black underneath.

Stucco Plaster used for decorative effects.

Trompe l'oeil Painting designed to fool the onlooker into believing that it is actually three-dimensional.

Small print and

Index

A Rough Guide to Rough Guides

Published in 1982, the first Rough Guide – to Greece – was a student scheme that became a publishing phenomenon. Mark Ellingham, a recent graduate in English from Bristol University, had been travelling in Greece the previous summer and couldn't find the right guidebook. With a small group of friends he wrote his own guide, combining a highly contemporary, journalistic style with a thoroughly practical approach to travellers' needs.

The immediate success of the book spawned a series that rapidly covered dozens of destinations. And, in addition to impecunious backpackers, Rough Guides soon acquired a much broader and older readership that relished the guides' wit and inquisitiveness as much as their enthusiastic, critical approach and value-for-money ethos.

These days, Rough Guides include recommendations from shoestring to luxury and cover more than 200 destinations around the globe, including almost every country in the Americas and Europe, more than half of Africa and most of Asia and Australasia. Our ever-growing team of authors and photographers is spread all over the world, particularly in Europe, the US and Australia.

In the early 1990s, Rough Guides branched out of travel, with the publication of Rough Guides to World Music, Classical Music and the Internet. All three have become benchmark titles in their fields, spearheading the publication of a wide range of books under the Rough Guide name.

Including the travel series, Rough Guides now number more than 350 titles, covering: phrasebooks, waterproof maps, music guides from Opera to Heavy Metal, reference works as diverse as Conspiracy Theories and Shakespeare, and popular culture books from iPods to Poker. Rough Guides also produce a series of more than 120 World Music CDs in partnership with World Music Network.

Visit www.roughguides.com to see our latest publications.

Rough Guide credits

Text editor: Alice Park
Layout: Ajay Verma
Cartography: Rajesh Mishra
Picture editor: Mark Thomas
Production: Erika Pepe
Proofreader: Jennifer Speake
Cover design: Daniel May and Nicole Newman
Photographers: John Cunningham and Natascha Sturny
Editorial: **London** Andy Turner, Keith Drew, Edward Aves, Lucy White, Jo Kirby, James Smart, Natasha Foges, Róisín Cameron, James Rice, Emma Beatson, Emma Gibbs, Kathryn Lane, Monica Woods, Mani Ramaswamy, Harry Wilson, Lucy Cowie, Alison Roberts, Lara Kavanagh, Eleanor Aldridge, Ian Blenkinsop, Joe Staines, Matthew Milton, Tracy Hopkins; **Delhi** Madhavi Singh, Jalpreen Kaur Chhatwal
Design & Pictures: **London** Scott Stickland, Dan May, Diana Jarvis, Nicole Newman, Sarah Cummins, Emily Taylor; **Delhi** Umesh Aggarwal, Jessica Subramanian, Ankur Guha, Pradeep Thapliyal, Sachin Tanwar, Anita Singh, Nikhil Agarwal, Sachin Gupta

Production: Rebecca Short, Liz Cherry, Louise Daly
Cartography: **London** Ed Wright, Katie Lloyd-Jones; **Delhi** Rajesh Chhibber, Ashutosh Bharti, Animesh Pathak, Jasbir Sandhu, Swati Handoo, Deshpal Dabas, Lokamata Sahu
Online: **London** Faye Hellon, Jeanette Angell, Fergus Day, Justine Bright, Clare Bryson, Aine Fearon, Adrian Low, Ezgi Celebi; **Delhi** Amit Verma, Rahul Kumar, Narender Kumar, Ravi Yadav, Debojit Borah, Rakesh Kumar, Ganesh Sharma, Shisir Basumatari
Marketing & Publicity: **London** Liz Statham, Jess Carter, Vivienne Watton, Anna Paynton, Rachel Sprackett, Laura Vipond; **New York** Katy Ball; **Delhi** Aman Arora
Digital Travel Publisher: Peter Buckley
Reference Director: Andrew Lockett
Operations Assistant: Becky Doyle
Operations Manager: Helen Atkinson
Publishing Director (Travel): Clare Currie
Commercial Manager: Gino Magnotta
Managing Director: John Duhigg

Publishing information

This eighth edition published March 2011 by
Rough Guides Ltd,
80 Strand, London WC2R 0RL
11, Community Centre, Panchsheel Park, New Delhi 110017, India

Distributed by the Penguin Group

Penguin Books Ltd,
80 Strand, London WC2R 0RL

Penguin Group (USA)
375 Hudson Street, NY 10014, USA

Penguin Group (Australia)
250 Camberwell Road, Camberwell, Victoria 3124, Australia

Penguin Group (NZ)
67 Apollo Drive, Mairangi Bay, Auckland 1310, New Zealand

Rough Guides is represented in Canada by Tourmaline Editions Inc. 662 King Street West, Suite 304, Toronto, Ontario M5V 1M7

Cover concept by Peter Dyer.

Typeset in Bembo and Helvetica to an original design by Henry Iles.

Printed in Singapore
© Rob Humphreys, 2011
Maps © Rough Guides

288pp includes index
A catalogue record for this book is available from the British Library
ISBN: 978-1-84836-624-4

Help us update

We've gone to a lot of effort to ensure that the eighth edition of **The Rough Guide to Prague** is accurate and up-to-date. However, things change – places get "discovered", opening hours are notoriously fickle, restaurants and rooms raise prices or lower standards. If you feel we've got it wrong or left something out, we'd like to know, and if you can remember the address, the price, the hours, the phone number, so much the better.

Please send your comments with the subject line "**Rough Guide Prague Update**" to ⓔmail @uk.roughguides.com. We'll credit all contributions and send a copy of the next edition (or any other Rough Guide if you prefer) for the very best emails.

Find more travel information, connect with fellow travellers and book your trip on ⓦwww .roughguides.com

Acknowledgements

Rob Humphreys would like to thank Kate for helping shepherd the numbs, and Josh and Rosie for investigating absinthe, and thanks to Alice for being brilliantly level-headed.

Readers' letters

Thanks to all the readers who have taken the time to write in with comments and suggestions (and apologies if we've inadvertently omitted or misspelt anyone's name):

David Dutta; Michael Heppner; Judy Lynn; Peter Mair, Paul and Elsie Smith; Frederik Schutyser; Carrie Schwender; Joanne Taylor; Louise and Simon Wagman; Rachael Westwood

Index

Map entries are in colour.

INDEX

So now we've told you about the things not to miss, the best places to stay, the top restaurants, the liveliest bars and the most spectacular sights, it only seems fair to tell you about the best travel insurance around

WorldNomads.com
keep travelling safely

Recommended by Rough Guides

Map symbols

maps are listed in the full index using coloured text

– – –	Chapter division boundary	⊙	Statue
═══	Road	ⓘ	Information office
▰▰▰	Passageway	⊠	Post office
▥▥▥	Steps	Ⓜ	Metro station
⁚⁚⁚⁚	Tunnel	✈	Airport
– – – –	Path	◉	Hotel
—㉔—	Tram line	✡	Synagogue
══	Railway	▮	Building
— —	Ferry route	◯	Stadium
——	Waterway	➕	Church
▬▬	Wall	⊤	Christian cemetery
··········	Funicular	▢	Jewish cemetery
▲	Mountain peak	▨	Park

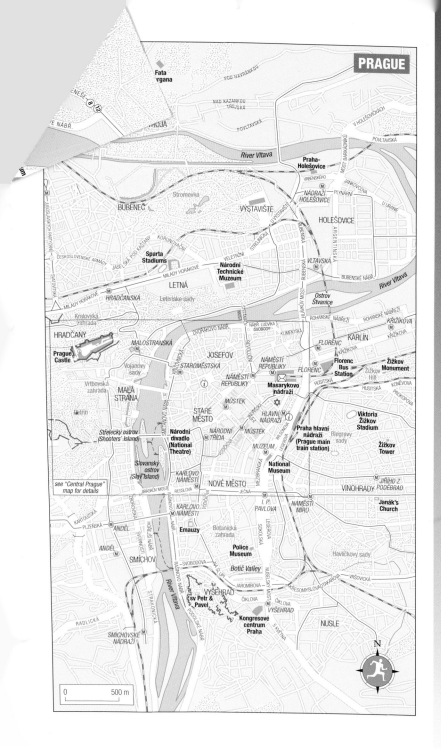

PRAGUE

Fata Morgana

POD HAVRÁNKOU

NAD KAZANKOU
TROJSKÁ

POVLTAVSKÁ

TROJA

River Vltava

Praha-Holešovice

VRBENSKÉHO

JANKOVCOVA

NÁDRAŽÍ HOLEŠOVICE

PLYNÁRNÍ

U URANIE

POVLTAVSKÁ

MOST BARKLÁNDKU

Stromovka

BUBENEČ

VÝSTAVIŠTĚ

HOLEŠOVICE

ARGENTINSKÁ

KORUNOVAČNÍ

ČESKOSLOVENSKÉ ARMÁDY

JASELSKÁ POD KAŠTANY

Sparta Stadiums

VELETRŽNÍ

STRNICKÁ

U VÝSTAVIŠTĚ

BUBENSKÁ

VLTAVSKÁ

BUBENSKÉ NÁBŘ.

River Vltava

MILADY HORÁKOVÉ

Národní Technické Muzeum

LETNÁ

HRADČANSKÁ

Letenské sady

MILADY HORÁKOVÉ

ŠTEFÁNIKŮV MOST

Ostrov Štvanice

HLÁVKŮV MOST

ROHANSKÉ NÁBŘEŽÍ

ROHANSKÉ NÁBŘEŽÍ

KŘIŽÍKOVA

Kralovská zahrada

DVOŘÁKOVO NÁBŘ.

NÁBŘ. LUDVÍKA SVOBODY

KLIMENTSKÁ

FLORENC

KARLÍN

KŘIŽÍKOVA

HRADČANY

MALOSTRANSKÁ

CHOTKOVA

JOSEFOV

REVOLUČNÍ

NÁMĚSTÍ REPUBLIKY

FLORENC

KŘIŽÍKOVA

Florenc Bus Station

Žižkov Monument

Prague Castle

STAROMĚSTSKÁ

NÁMĚSTÍ REPUBLIKY

Masarykovo nádraží

HUSITSKÁ

Žižkov Hill

KONĚVOVA

Vojanovy sady

Vrtbovská zahrada

MALÁ STRANA

SMETANOVO NÁBŘ.

MŮSTEK

HLAVNÍ NÁDRAŽÍ

HUSITSKÁ

PROKOPOVA

Viktoria Žižkov Stadium

Petřín

STARÉ MĚSTO

MŮSTEK

Praha hlavní nádraží (Prague main train station)

Žižkov Tower

Střelecký ostrov (Shooters' Island)

Národní divadlo (National Theatre)

Národní TŘÍDA

MŮSTEK

MUZEUM

LEGEROVA

Rieger y sady

Slovanský ostrov (Slav Island)

KARLOVO NÁMĚSTÍ

NOVÉ MĚSTO

National Museum

JIŘÍHO Z PODĚBRAD

see "Central Prague" map for details

JIRÁSKŮV MOST

RAŠÍNOVO NÁBŘ.

RESSLOVA

JEČNÁ

MEZIBRANSKÁ

VINOHRADY

KARLOVO NÁMĚSTÍ

I. P. PAVLOVA

NÁMĚSTÍ MÍRU

Janák's Church

PLZEŇSKÁ

ANDĚL

HOŘEJŠÍ NÁBŘ.

SVORNOSTI

Emauzy

Botanická zahrada

SOKOLSKÁ

LEGEROVA

ANDĚL

SMÍCHOV

SVOBODOVA

VA ST LPI

Police Museum

Havlíčkovy sady

RADLICKÁ

KARTOUZSKÁ

ZBOROVSKÁ

River Vltava

STRAKONICKÁ

PODOLSKÉ NÁBŘ.

Botič Valley

VYŠEHRAD

sv Petr & Pavel

JAROMÍROVA

ČIKLOVA

NUSELSKÝ MOST

ČÍKLOVA

VYŠEHRAD

TĚSNOMYSLOVA

VRATISLAVOVA

TÁBORSKÁ

VRŠOVICKÁ

SVATNÍ

NUSLE

SMÍCHOVSKÉ NÁDRAŽÍ

Kongresové centrum Praha

N

0   500 m

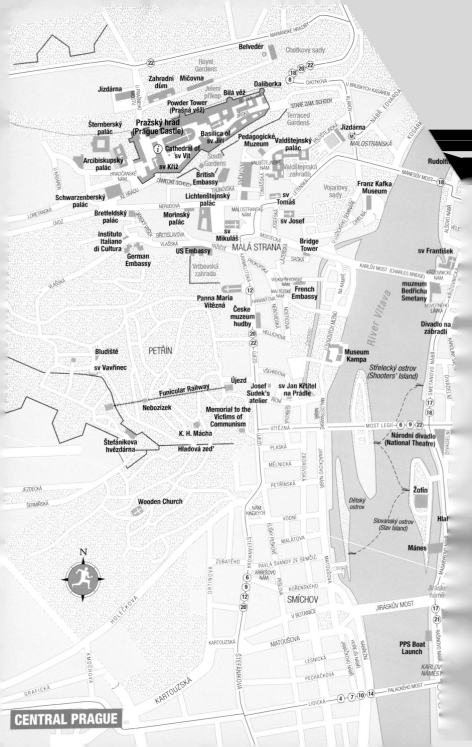

CENTRAL PRAGUE

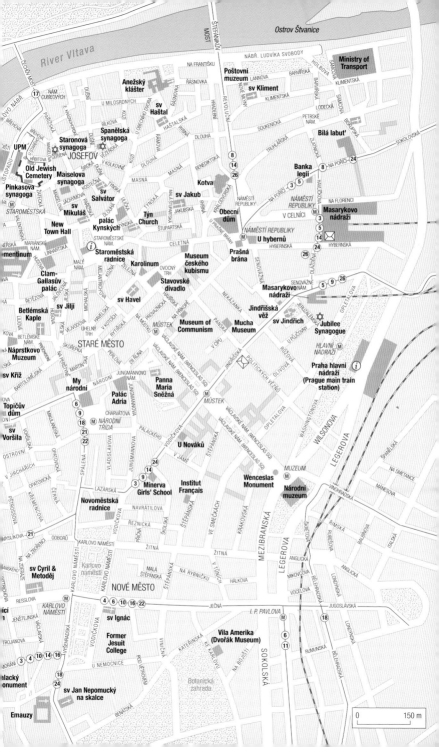

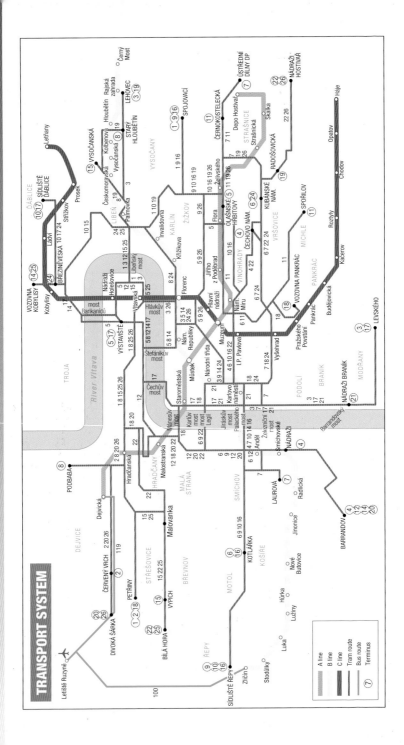

TRANSPORT SYSTEM